A Student's Guide to 50 British Novels has been edited by Abraham H. Lass, a well-known teacher, school administrator, and writer. Mr. Lass is Principal of Abraham Lincoln High School in Brooklyn, New York, and the author of **How to Prepare for College, The College Student's Handbook, The Way to Write,** and many other works.

Equally well-known in the field of college counseling, Mr. Lass has for a number of years written a popular weekly column, "College and You," which has appeared in the *New York Herald Tribune, New York Post, Boston Traveler, The Detroit Free Press, The Philadelphia Inquirer,* and other newspapers.

The plot summaries, critical essays, and character analyses collected in this volume and its companion works, **A Student's Guide to 50 American Novels** and **A Student's Guide to 50 European Novels,** are designed to enrich the reader's understanding and appreciation of the great and famous books that are a vital part of our literary heritage. A special section, "How to Read a Novel," provides the reader with the basic skills and insights that will give his reading new and more meaningful dimensions.

A Student's Guide to
50 British Novels
edited by Abraham H. Lass
Principal, Abraham Lincoln High School, Brooklyn, New York

WASHINGTON SQUARE PRESS
POCKET BOOKS • NEW YORK

A STUDENT'S GUIDE TO 50 BRITISH NOVELS

WASHINGTON SQUARE PRESS edition published April 1966

7th printing........................February, 1974

Published by
POCKET BOOKS, a division of Simon & Schuster, Inc.,
630 Fifth Avenue, New York, N.Y.

WASHINGTON SQUARE PRESS editions are distributed
in the U.S. by Simon & Schuster, Inc., 630 Fifth Avenue,
New York, N.Y. 10020, and in Canada by Simon & Schuster of Canada, Ltd., Richmond Hill, Ontario, Canada.

TO
BETTY AND JANET

Preface

"Of making many books there is no end," goes the complaint in Ecclesiastes; and the modern reader is tempted to add, "and much study of books-about-books is a weariness of the flesh."

What purposes, then, are to be served by this book?

We hope to reach two kinds of readers. First, the reader who is not yet the reader he wishes to be—who knows there is much in store for him, who has not tasted more than a portion of the feast, and who is grateful for a bill of fare. To him we offer an overview so that he may fall to with a whetted appetite. He will *know about* these novels (characters, plots, themes, styles) before he goes on to *know* them. Second, the reader who has sampled many of these novels and needs little more than a review of what he has already enjoyed . . . or a reference guide as an ever-ready help for study.

For each novel we present the following:

(1) an annotated list of the main characters
(2) a full, clear, comprehensible summary of the significant incidents and themes
(3) a digest of present-day critical opinion of the novel, placing it in its proper context in the development of the novel and indicating how contemporary readers and critics evaluate it
(4) a biographical sketch of the author

While no selection of titles could please everyone, we believe that the novels chosen for this book will challenge the intelligent person to make his own rich and varied reading program. Here are the masterpieces and the milestones, the "classics and commercials," the great books and the near-great. Here are the seed books, the novels from which have sprung new novels and new ideas. All of them are still widely read and discussed. They are part of every reader's heritage.

If these novels have one thing in common despite differences in age and manners, it is that they have all (in Wordsworth's phrase) "kept watch o'er man's mortality"; they have something everlasting to report to us about ourselves, and they report it in the syllables of art.

To read or to reread these novels—and this book will have achieved its purpose if it sends you back to the originals—is to take part in a magnificent adventure of the spirit: to understand what made D. H. Lawrence say, with an artist's pardonable license, "Being a novelist, I consider myself superior to the saint, the scientist, the philosopher, and the poet. The novel is the one bright book of life."

February, 1966   A. H. L.

Contents

How To Read a Novel

Why do we pick up a novel? For the moment, the world we know is too much for us—or it is not enough. We seek surcease or discovery. And so we turn a page and step into another man's world.

In one novel we may find what Graham Greene calls "an entertainment," a tale unfolded for our enjoyment; we shall not even mind a few tears in the telling of it. In another novel, perhaps we find a few of the answers. What we have only half-suspected of human experience is blindingly clear in the author's searchlight; a facet of man has been illuminated.

Often a novel offers us both adventure and insight. Joseph Conrad in *Lord Jim* takes us on an exciting voyage to such seaports as Bombay, Calcutta, Rangoon, Penang, Batavia; to the deck of the steamer *Patna* in the Arabian Sea, and to the Malaysian jungle of Patusan. Yet it is a means to exploring ourselves. When we are home again, we are richer for understanding certain profound "psycho-moral" ambiguities in Jim's, in all men's, experience.

Whatever the novel, it is well to look sharp in the writer's world. For each novel is the individual vision of an artist, his direct impression of reality. To share his discoveries we must look at the view he sees from his personal porthole. If every prospect immediately displeases and every man seems vile, we may be allowing our prejudices to come between us and the writer's sights. (Tess and Jude once scandalized Thomas Hardy's public so much that after the hostile reception of *Jude the Obscure* he stopped writing novels entirely; the Rector of Broxton in *Adam Bede* was "little more than a pagan" to George Eliot's readers; Heathcliff apparently struck the first readers of *Wuthering Heights* with such unpleasant force that Charlotte Brontë felt it necessary to come to her sister's defense in the famous statement which begins, "Whether it is right or advisable to create beings like Heathcliff, I do not know: I scarcely think it is.") Before we complain to the novelist that we find his country uninhabitable, we should be humble, and permit him to show us its "manners, climates, councils, governments."

The Novelist's View of Reality

Very well, says the reader with humility to the novelist, show me a slice of life.

Novelist A may choose to cut his slice horizontally; Novelist B, vertically. The method calls for close attention.

A, following a straight chronological line, begins at the beginning of his hero's story, goes on through the middle until he comes to the end, and then stops. Peter Prentice is born, goes to school, meets Lucy Lovelace, weeps his pints, is off to the wars, and (after a suitable number of interesting complications linked by character and motive) marries or dies.

B, on the other hand, is going to ignore chronology and cut Peter down the middle for our examination; like Macbeth, he'll "unseam" him from the nave to the chaps. He will disclose his memories, agonies, ecstasies, reveries—with no respect to time. There will be a flashback to Lady Grasmere's garden party, when Lucy first met that bounder Cyril Hyssop, and Peter had the strange talk with the Swami Vitrananda. If Novelist B is quite modern, he will not end his novel at all, but will leave his hero (who is not a hero at all) in the middle of a moment of consciousness which can be traced backward or forward in time, as the reader wishes.

The meaning of the real, the nature of reality, has been a point of dispute among novelists, as between philosophers and physicists, for more than half a century. One of the most illuminating quarrels was carried on between Virginia Woolf and a group of novelists—Arnold Bennett, H. G. Wells, John Galsworthy—whose "materialism" seemed to Mrs. Woolf to be the negation of life. In "Mr. Bennett and Mrs. Brown," she pointed out how these novelists had crowded out reality with the furniture of their novels; they had laid so much dull stress on environment, social setting, the fabric instead of the substance, that the essence of being had escaped them.

In a famous statement in her essay "Modern Fiction" in *The Common Reader*, Mrs. Woolf put the case for all the novelists of sensibility, the "stream of consciousness" stylists who were to follow. "Life is not a series of gig-lamps symmetrically arranged," said Mrs. Woolf (demolishing Novelist A); life is *"a luminous halo, a semi-transparent envelope"* (italics mine) which surrounds man from the beginning of consciousness to the end.

Mrs. Woolf developed her own luminous style—a delicate and subtle handling of those subcurrents of consciousness where she believed the truth of "reality" lay—in her novels *Mrs. Dalloway, To the Lighthouse,* and *The Waves.* The "stream of consciousness" became, in her work and in Joyce's, and in the work of many of our contemporaries, an almost lyrical flow.

For one of Mrs. Woolf's characters, Mrs. Ramsay in *To the Lighthouse,* when life sinks down for a moment and there is no need to act, the range of implicit experience seems almost limitless. In the depth of being herself, "a wedge-shaped core of darkness," she triumphs over life; things come together in "this peace, this rest, this eternity. . . ."

This is a very different kind of reality, of course, from that in many novels, or for that matter in many people's experience. Meeting it in prose fiction today, the reader does well to approach it as he approaches the reality of a poem: with a response to its rhythms, its imagery, its timeless flow of memories and impressions.

Character in the Novel

Mr. Bennett and Mrs. Woolf were agreed on one point at least: The essential concern of the novelist is with "character in itself"; only if the characters are real has the novel any chance of surviving.

The reason for this, perhaps, is that the characters above all in a novel, in E. M. Forster's word, can *solace* us. We who can hardly understand ourselves, much less one another, in our imperfect world, meet in the novelist's world "a more comprehensible and thus a more manageable human race" and we have the enormously comforting illusion of understanding, at last, the secret, invisible truth of people.

When the reader puts together all the clues to character that the novelist has included in his book, when he perceives the truth of Heathcliff or Philip Carey or Pecksniff or Becky Sharp, even though none of these may know it of himself, he is almost like the Creator in all-knowing wisdom.

Yet, according to Elizabeth Bowen, a subtle novelist and, in her "Notes on Writing a Novel," a most illuminating critic, characters are not *created* by the novelist at all. They are *found;* they pre-exist in his consciousness and reveal themselves slowly to his perception as he is writing, as might "fellow-trayellers seated opposite one in a dimly lit railway carriage."

What the novelist is inviting the reader to do, then, is to *recognize* the people of the novel as they play their roles in the story.

We use the word *play* advisedly. The people of the novelist's world are very busy every moment. They are making choices of alternative behavior; they are speaking or not speaking in a certain way; when they are not around, they are being discussed by other characters.

To recognize Eustacia Vye, the reader of Hardy's pages might well imagine that he is watching her in a drama literally played upon a stage. He may ask himself the same questions about the people in a novel that he subconsciously asks about the figures in grease paint who move before footlights:

What is the effect on these people of the *setting* they are in?

What do I know of the *antecedent action?*

What signs of *motive* do I perceive?

Where are the evidences of *conflict* (within and without)?

How does this person see himself? How does he wish others to see him? How is he seen by others?

How does he give himself away—in gesture, inflection, choice of words?

Where is the *climax* of this person's conflict? Is it inevitable in terms of what has gone before?

And so on. It is a game only a little different from the one the reader plays every day. Listening to his neighbor protest, "I am the last person in the world to gossip," he knows her for a talebearer; trying to solve the riddle of the face opposite him in the subway (eyes full of pain, slack mouth, shaving-cut on chin), he wonders what the combination of all these features means. In novels, however, the characters are explicable; the writer has willed it so. If the reader is perceptive enough, he can pluck out the heart of each man's mystery.

Sometimes the clues are tiny. Every reader understands the significant event, the major decision. But it is also a revealing incident, says Henry James, when a woman stands up with her hand resting on a table and looks at you in a certain way. A chance word or sigh, Forster reminds us, is just as much evidence as a speech or a murder.

The playwright, of course, has always understood this, and that is why we urge the novel reader to behave as if he were watching a play.

Chekhov, in whose dramas there is no melodrama, only the reverberation of the thousand small shocks that make life palpable, said in one of his letters that the things that happen onstage should be as complex and yet as simple as they are in daily reality. "For instance, people are having a meal at a table, just having a meal, but at the same time their happiness is being created, or their lives are being smashed up."

How many meals are eaten in novels! And every one of them is "evidence." The ineffable Mr. Collins, enjoying a repast with his noble patroness, the Lady Catherine de Bourgh, is condemned by Jane Austen with words from his own mouth as a small-souled snob. The children of Plumstead, eating hot buns at tea in *Barchester Towers*—had they not set all Barchester by the ears on the subject of Sabbath-day schools? Little Pip, at Mrs. Joe Gargery's Christmas party in *Great Expectations*, is being "naterally wicious," the company agrees, but we can see that he is eating his heart out along with his Christmas dinner.

(Dickens' characters, by the way, are often not characters at all, but caricatures: They are the same each time they appear, they never surprise us, they are readily identifiable by tag lines and stock reactions. Mr. Micawber is predictably optimistic; Uriah Heep consistently 'umble. Such static characters are "flat," to use Forster's terminology, in contrast to characters who are "round," who are dynamic, who develop and behave unpredictably, although always inevitably. Elizabeth Bowen believes that ideal novels should contain only "round" characters—yet what a pity to lose Dickens' people on a literary technicality! Genius, having invented and populated a world, can also animate it with "flats.")

Living characters in novels, once fully perceived, are life-stretchers for us all. We love, suffer, hate, comprehend with them vicariously. They satisfy our hunger to share the news about the human condition. Real people have a way of keeping themselves to themselves; characters in books open their hearts. We know what Robinson Crusoe felt and thought on that lonely island. We hear from Moll Flanders about all the husbands she married.

Sharing is a two-way journey. What is the reader's part? Empathy, imaginative sympathy, understanding of human values. As the characters grow larger in our imagination and sympathy, they take on meanings larger than themselves, possibly larger than life. Sydney Carton is no longer an eighteenth-century lawyer; he is a symbol of all charming wastrels and self-sacrificing romanticists.

At the very least, the reader of novels will have, as Thoreau did at Walden, a great deal of company in his house, especially in the morning, when nobody calls.

The Novelist at Work

"Why should a story not be told in the most irregular fashion that an author's idiosyncrasy may prompt," asked George Eliot, "provided that he gives us what we can enjoy? . . . The dear public would do well to reflect that they are often bored from the want of flexibility in their own minds. They are like the topers of 'one liquor.' "

No two novelists are alike; there are as many kinds of novel today—there have always been as many kinds of novel—as there are readers to discover them. Without too much literary analysis, it is possible to satisfy one's curiosity about the way in which a novelist has set about making us enjoy his book.

Here is a brief list of checkpoints. Each novelist will have approached a checkpoint in his own way.

Description of the Characters

The storyteller is no painter, but he must leave images in the reader's mind.

In *Pride and Prejudice*, Mr. and Mrs. Bennet are sketched with rapid brilliance:

Mr. Bennet was so odd a mixture of quick parts, sarcastic humour, reserve, and caprice, that the experience of three and twenty years had been insufficient to make his wife understand his character. *Her* mind was less difficult to develop. She was a woman of mean understanding, little information, and uncertain temper. When she was discontented she fancied herself nervous. The business of her life was to get her daughters married; its solace was visiting and news.

Doesn't the fun of the passage increase if you collaborate with Miss Austen? Here is another of her descriptions: Emma's first view of Mrs. Elton, in *Emma:*

She did not really like her. She would not be in a hurry to find fault, but she suspected that there was no elegance;—ease, but no elegance—she was almost sure that for a young woman, a stranger, a bride, there was not much ease. Her person was rather good; her face was not unpretty; but neither feature, nor air, nor voice, nor manner, were elegant. Emma thought at least it would turn out so.

This tells us as much about Emma Woodhouse's world of Hartfield—as much about Jane Austen's world—as about poor Mrs. Elton.

In *Great Expectations,* Dickens re-creates people with such a wealth of sensuous and vivid detail that the whole world seems to be his own invention. For example, here is his description of Pip's visit to Mr. Trabb to be measured for a new suit:

Mr. Trabb had sliced his hot roll into three feather beds, and was slipping butter in between the blankets, and covering it up . . . When I had entered, [Mr. Trabb's boy] was sweeping the shop, and he had sweetened his labors by sweeping over me. . . Mr. Trabb, taking down a roll of cloth, and tiding it out in a flowing manner over the counter, preparatory to getting his hand under it to show the gloss. . . .

And so forth—to be enjoyed by the reader with the novelist's own gusto in the simplest acts of living.

Point of View

"The whole intricate question of method, in the craft of fiction," writes Percy Lubbock, "I take to be governed by the question of the *point of view*—the question of the relation in which the narrator stands to the story."

In *The Craft of Fiction*, Mr. Lubbock tells us that the novelist can describe his characters from the outside, as an impartial or a partial observer; or from the inside, as a presumably omniscient force. He can also take the viewpoint of one character who does not know the motives of the others.

Although Henry James felt that the novelist should stick to one point of view in a story and not shift arbitrarily, Forster has been able to cite a number of instances where a novelist has been able to manage more than one shift rather well— genius, as always, making its own rules. For our part it matters very little how the novelist manages his camera-eye just so he puts in focus for us a world that is both plausible and lasting. What he shows us will depend on his *moral* lens.

Stendhal, writing to Balzac: "I see but one rule, *to be clear*. If I am not clear, all my world crumbles to nothing."

Plot, Story, Theme

These are words to play with. When they are well handled by a writer, the reader does not have to notice them at all. But if you lift an eyebrow at cavalier treatment of textbook terms, here are some definitions:

> The *story* is the answer to "And then what happened?"
> The *plot* tells why it happened just that way.
> The *theme* explains the writer's need to tell this particular story.

Or, in Forster's delightful simplification: "The King died and then the Queen died" is a story. "The King died and then the Queen died of grief" is a plot. (We do not have a theme for this yet.)

Causality is everything. Well, nearly everything. In his introduction to Henry James's *The Princess Casamassima*, Lionel Trilling outlines a story which has run through a number of nineteenth-century novels in several countries, the story of The Young Man from the Provinces, of humble and even mysterious origin, who will move into society. In one way or another, this is the skeleton of *Great Expectations, The Red and the Black, The Great Gatsby*. Yet plot, story, theme are nothing without the essence of all, which is the novelist's personal idiom, his statement outside logic or causality; a statement poetic in that it is always its own excuse for being.

And that brings us to the question of style.

Style

In Leo Tolstoi's *Talks with Tolstoi*, we have the following description of a writer's approach to his art:

> Sophie Andreevna said: "It was the last time Turgenev stayed at Yasnaya, not long before his death. I asked him: 'Ivan Sergeevich, why don't you write now?' He answered: 'In order to write I had always to be a little in love. Now I am old I can't fall in love any more, and that is why I have stopped writing.'

And Tolstoi himself, speaking in exasperation:

> One ought only to write when one leaves a piece of one's flesh in the ink-pot each time one dips one's pen.

Lest you think, "Ah well, the Russians—!" here is another novelist's statement of what it means to write. Arnold Bennett, in his *Journals*:

> The novelist should cherish and burnish this faculty of seeing crudely, simply, artlessly, ignorantly; of seeing like a baby or a lunatic, who lives each moment by itself and tarnishes by the present no remembrance of the past.

There we have it: On every page the novelist has left his signature for us to read. The oldest quotation of all, Buffon's "The style is the man," is still the most accurate.

And now we return to the question of how to read a novel. Why, by sitting down in an armchair, seeing that there is a good light over our left shoulder, and turning the page.

Here we are in another man's world.

February, 1966

                                                    A. H. L.

The Seventeenth Century

The Pilgrim's Progress

by

JOHN BUNYAN (1628–1688)

Main Characters

Christian—A simple, earnest man making a pilgrimage from the City of Destruction to the Celestial City.

Evangelist—Christian's faithful guide through his travail.

Faithful—A fellow pilgrim who receives his heavenly reward when he is martyred in Vanity Fair.

Hopeful—Christian's companion during the latter part of his journey, who keeps up his courage even in Doubting Castle and the River of Death.

Mr. Worldly Wiseman—A man of the world who tries to lead Christian astray with tales of town life.

Apollyon—A giant fiend who nearly kills Christian.

Giant Despair—The bloodthirsty master of Doubting Castle who keeps Christian and Hopeful prisoner.

1

The Story

Wandering through the wilderness of this world, John Bunyan falls asleep in a cave and has a dream. In it he sees Christian who is dressed in rags and carries a Bible in his hand and a great burden on his back. Christian cries out that he has left his city because he has read in the Good Book that the wrath of God is about to descend on it. His family has refused to escape with him from the City of Destruction, and he doesn't know which road to take in order to reach the Celestial City.

When Evangelist, the Preacher of Christianity, shows him a vision of the destruction to come, Christian tries to warn his family and neighbors, but they all think him mad. Evangelist tells him to knock at a wicket gate where he will find Eternal Life, but Christian does not know the way to the gate.

He is joined in his search by two neighbors, Pliable and Obstinate, who ask him where he is going. When he tells them, Obstinate turns home in disgust but Pliable promises to go with Christian. Not noticing the road they are taking, Christian and Pliable fall into a treacherous mire, the Slough of Despond. Weighed down by the great burden of sins on his back, Christian is in danger of sinking into the mud over his head, but Help soon comes and rescues him. When Pliable, by a great effort, emerges from the Slough, he leaves Christian in dismay at the difficulty of the journey, and makes his way home.

Resuming his pilgrimage, Christian next encounters Mr. Worldly Wiseman, a suave, sophisticated man who tries to convince the pilgrim that his journey is folly. He tells Christian that Christian would be happy if only he allowed Mr. Legality and Mr. Civility, dwellers in the village of Morality, to remove his burden from him. Christian nearly falls into Mr. Worldly Wiseman's persuasive trap (it would be so much more pleasant to live in the easy-going town than to continue the hard journey in search of salvation) but Evangelist intervenes. He warns Christian that Mr. Legality is a fraud and Mr. Civility a hypocrite, and sets Christian on the right path again.

Christian finally arrives at the wicket gate, on which is written, "Knock, and it shall be opened unto you," and is met by Good-Will. An Interpreter invites him into the gatekeeper's house and explains the Christian mysteries to him. Shown a vision of the Day of Judgment, Christian is filled with fear of Hell and hope of Heaven.

Continuing on his journey, he comes to the Holy Cross and the Sepulchre of Christ, where miraculously his burden of sins falls from his back. He is beside himself with joy. Passing Sloth, Presumption, Simple, Formalism, and Hypocrisy, and escaping two terrifying lions who block his path, Christian makes his way to the House Beautiful where he is given hospitality and a good sword by four fair maidens, Charity, Discretion, Prudence, and Piety.

Armed with the sword and shield of Christian faith, the pilgrim next finds himself in the Valley of Humiliation, where the foul fiend Apollyon, who takes pride in his shiny scales, blocks Christian's way and warns him, "Prepare to die." Christian joins battle with Apollyon and finally, after a desperate struggle in which he is wounded by flaming darts, drives the beast away. Christian heals his wounds with leaves from the nearby Tree of Life and is able to resume his journey.

Even more terrifying than the Valley of Humiliation is the next place Christian comes upon: the Valley of the Shadow of Death. There, on one side of a narrow path, he sees a deep ditch into which the blind have led the blind to eternal death. On the other side is a bottomless quagmire. Christian must travel the straight and narrow path between these two dangers, past one of the mouths of Hell from which devils taunt him. Christian drives them off by declaring, "I will walk in the strength of the Lord God!" When day breaks, Christian resumes his journey past the caves of the giants Pope and Pagan, and is joined by Faithful, a neighbor from the City of Destruction.

Warned by Evangelist of its dangerous lures, Christian and Faithful come to the town of Vanity, which holds a year-long Fair created by Beelzebub and the fiends of Hell where all the people are consumed with the vanity that entices men away from the true road to salvation. The cruel townspeople taunt Christian and Faithful, arrest them on false charges of disturbing the peace, and beat them. (The pilgrims' "crime" is their refusal to buy the town's goods.) Christian is thrown into prison and Faithful is burned alive. As Faithful gives up the ghost at the stake, a great chariot descends from Heaven and carries him off to the Celestial City. Christian is rescued from jail by a young man named Hopeful who has been impressed by Faithful's heavenly reward.

Christian and Hopeful come upon a lovely plain named Ease which has in it a silver mine called Lucre. The mine is open to all, but those who dig in it are smothered. Christian and Hopeful leave the plain and come upon Lot's wife, who was turned into a pillar of salt when she disobeyed God's command and looked back upon Sodom and Gomorrah. They come to the River of Life where they refresh themselves.

The road now becomes stony and hard. It leads to Doubting Castle, which Christian and Hopeful reach in dark, stormy weather. There Giant Despair captures them and throws them into a dreadful dungeon, where he flogs them. Because they survive the floggings, the giant tries to persuade them to commit suicide, but Christian and Hopeful pray fervently and retain their faith. Christian remembers that he has a key called Promise with him, and they use this to escape from the prison. Giant Despair pursues them but is blinded by radiant sunlight.

Continuing on the stony path around Doubting Castle, Christian and Hopeful meet four shepherds named Knowledge, Experience, Watchful, and Sincere, who lead them to the peak of the Delectable Mountains, from which they can see, in the distance, the Celestial City. But the shepherds warn them that they can still mistake the road and take the path to Hell. On the narrow path down the mountain, they meet Flatterer, a dark man in shining costume, who says he will guide them. Instead, however, he entangles them in a net from which they finally extricate themselves with great difficulty.

Eventually the pilgrims pass through the Enchanted Land into the lovely land of Beulah, where the air is so clear that they can see the Celestial City before them, glistening with pearls and precious stones and paved with gold. Although their strength is now failing, Christian and Hopeful are determined to go on. Before the gates of the city, however, is the River of Death, deep and treacherous, with no bridge spanning it. The pilgrims plunge into the river. As the billows swirl around him, Christian fears the river is bottomless, but Hopeful shouts to him to be of good cheer. Christian touches bottom. A great darkness comes over him, but he recovers and finds he has made it to the opposite shore where Hopeful gives him a hand. Having left their mortal garments behind, the two pilgrims ascend the steep hill to the Celestial City where the gate is opened wide for them. They are greeted joyously by a company of the Heavenly Host, are given shining raiments and harps, and join the angelic choir in praise of God. With this glorious vision John Bunyan awakens from his dream.

Critical Opinion

In the years since its first publication, *The Pilgrim's Progress* has taken an honored place next to the Bible and Milton's *Paradise Lost* in the hearts of devout Englishmen. That its appeal is not restricted to England, however, is demonstrated by the fact that it has been translated into 108 different languages and dialects.

In form *The Pilgrim's Progress* is an allegory, a narrative in which such abstractions as virtue, sin, love, and evil are personified by individual characters through whom the moral of the story is made dramatically effective. Thus Christian is not only a Bedfordshire peasant of the seventeenth century but also a symbol of every man in search of salvation. We become simultaneously involved with his physical and his spiritual travail; and because of the simple but compelling suspense of the individual episodes in the story, we are inexorably caught up in Bunyan's moral vision.

Although allegory was a traditional device of the lay preachers of Bunyan's day, it is an extremely difficult form to handle successfully. No one has handled it more vividly or interestingly than Bunyan.

The Pilgrim's Progress is not a ponderous religious tract. It is rich in clever satire of the eternal human foibles. Bunyan is very hard on the glib, the hypocritical, and the superficial; his Vanity Fair is a brilliantly terse commentary on the materialistic life. The nonreligious Thackeray found it a useful title for his great satiric novel about society.

Although allegory is rare in English fiction, *The Pilgrim's Progress*, for all the crudeness of its fictional technique, exercised a great influence on the English novel, particularly in the eighteenth century. Its vivid handling of scenes from common English life—the roads, the scenery, the simple peasant homes that Christian comes upon—was not lost upon the more sophisticated novelists such as Fielding, Smollett, and, later, Dickens.

Because an unauthorized sequel to *The Pilgrim's Progress* by one Thomas Sherman appeared in 1684, Bunyan decided to write a sequel himself, narrating the path to salvation taken by Christian's wife, Christiana, and her children. As so often happens with sequels, the second part of *The Pilgrim's Progress* is not as successful as the first, largely because Bunyan did not think the road to conversion was fraught with as many dangers for women and children as for men. Thus the second part, though full of charming, homely detail, lacks the high suspense of the first part.

The Author

The man who gave to the English language the concepts of "Vanity Fair" and "Slough of Despond" came, as he said, "of a low and inconsiderable generation." *John Bunyan*, the son of a tinker, was born in Bedfordshire in 1628. He learned to read and write at the village school, but was soon apprenticed to his father's trade.

When he was sixteen, Bunyan served in the Parliamentary Army for two years. During his youth, he had a reputation as a roisterer who indulged "in all manner of vice and ungodliness." The "vices" of which he later accused himself were cursing, swearing, dancing, and unwarranted ringing of the church bell. In 1648 or 1649 he married a poor, devout woman who brought with her a few religious books which deeply influenced Bunyan.

When his wife died in 1656, leaving him to care for four children, Bunyan immersed himself in the study of the Bible. He had done some itinerant preaching, and had, in 1653, joined a Nonconformist church in Bedford. But after his wife's death he "was never out of the Bible either by reading or meditation."

Bunyan remarried in 1659, and the following year was arrested for preaching without a license. The next twelve years Bunyan spent in prison, where he wrote many of his early religious tracts and books. The most important of these is *Grace Abounding* (1666), the autobiographical account of his conversion and early career as a preacher. Released in 1672 by Charles II's Declaration of Indulgence, Bunyan was appointed pastor of the Bedford church, but was again imprisoned for preaching in 1675. During this six-month sentence he composed *The Pilgrim's Progress from this World to that which is to come*, published in 1678.

At two-year intervals thereafter, Bunyan published his two other major works, *The Life and Death of Mr. Badman*, a demonstration "that wickedness like a flood is like to drown our English world," and *The Holy War*, a complex political and spiritual allegory based in part on Bunyan's early military experiences.

Bunyan's last years were spent preaching in many places, including London, but he never ran into trouble with the law again. He died in 1688 and was buried in Bunhill Fields, London.

The Eighteenth Century

Robinson Crusoe

by

DANIEL DEFOE (1660–1731)

Main Characters

Robinson Crusoe—An ingenious and self-reliant sailor who carves out an existence for himself while a castaway on a desert island.
Friday—The cannibal who, civilized by Crusoe, becomes his loyal servant and friend.

The Story

Although his father wants him to become a lawyer, young Robinson Crusoe is determined to go to sea. On September 1, 1651, in the seaport town of Hull, the nineteen-year-old boy decides to ship aboard a vessel bound for London. Just out of port, they strike a great storm, and young Crusoe vows that if he ever reaches shore alive he will obey his parents and never go to sea again. But when the sea becomes calm, he forgets his resolution. Impressed by the courage and good fellowship of his shipmates, he takes up a life of adventure.

Aboard an African trading vessel, when it is boarded by Turkish buccaneers, Crusoe is sold into slavery. He manages a desperate escape in a boat no larger than a dory and is picked up by a Portuguese freighter bound for Brazil. There he sets up as a successful sugar planter; but, finding that he needs slaves for his plantation, he is persuaded by another English planter to sail to the slave coast of Africa. The ship is wrecked off an unknown island near the northeast coast of South America. Crusoe is the only survivor.

He is washed ashore on a deserted island with only his knife, a pipe, and some tobacco. Fortunately the ship has not actually sunk, but has foundered on some rocks. The next day, in clear weather, Crusoe is able to swim out to the wrecked ship which he finds loaded with useful supplies in good condition. Back on the island he constructs a crude raft which he plies back and forth between ship and shore for two weeks, bringing back with him firearms, powder, saws, an ax, and a hammer. He also finds £36 aboard the ship. He takes the money with him although he realizes that all the gold in the world is of no use to a castaway. Crusoe thanks Providence that his life has been spared and that he now has a chance for survival on the island. He begins to keep a daily diary of his activities and reflections.

After he recovers from a fever, Crusoe slowly starts building a permanent dwelling. For food and clothing he hunts wild goats and tans their hides. He plants some barley and corn—half of his precious stock from the ship—but finds to his horror that he has planted them at the wrong season and they are wasted. His every effort, from making pottery in which to store fresh water to felling and planting trees for his shelter, is enormously difficult and often meets with failure. Most frustrating of all is his attempt to build a canoe that will carry him away from the island. For five months he works on a great cedar tree, hewing and shaping it until it is seaworthy, only to find that it is so heavy he cannot get it from the construction site to the shore.

Eventually Crusoe learns to plant crops, domesticate goats

for milk, and even train a parrot for a pet. Although he has never seen another living soul on the island, he makes himself a safe hiding place. It is well that he has done so, for after twelve years of utter isolation on the island, Crusoe one day makes a startling discovery: On the beach far from his shelter he finds a human footprint in the sand. Determined to find out who the intruder is, Crusoe constructs a hiding place in a cave near the footprint and spends years searching that part of the island.

When he has been on the island about twenty-two years, Crusoe makes another shocking discovery. On the beach where he first saw the footprint are human bones and mutilated flesh. Apparently cannibals from the mainland have paddled over with their prisoners of war whom they murdered and ate.

Crusoe's first reaction is one of terror, but soon he becomes so indignant that he determines to ambush the savages the next time they arrive and kill as many as he can. He sets up a small fortress in a cave. One day, from his lookout post, he sees about thirty savages dancing obscenely before a fire. They have already cooked one prisoner and are getting ready to murder two more when Crusoe attacks them with his two loaded muskets and a sword. He shoots several of the cannibals. The others run off in panic, leaving one of their prisoners behind. After twenty-four years of solitude, Crusoe at last has a companion.

The man he rescues is also a cannibal, but Crusoe soon teaches him to loathe his former habits. He names him Friday, for the day of his rescue. Crusoe brings Friday back to his shelter and gradually teaches him enough English so they can communicate with one another. The grateful Friday, who is basically intelligent and comes from a superior tribe, becomes Crusoe's loyal and trustworthy servant and friend.

Friday informs Crusoe that on his native island seventeen white men are unharmed but being held captive. Crusoe decides to get to them and perhaps with their help return to civilization. Aided by Friday, Crusoe builds another seaworthy boat—this time right at the shore.

They are just about to set sail when three canoes full of savages land on the island with three prisoners—one a white captive. Crusoe and Friday attack with all the firepower at their command, kill all but four of the twenty-one savages, and save two of the captives. One of them turns out to be Friday's father. Father and son greet each other joyfully.

The white man they save is an old Spaniard who had been aboard a ship that Crusoe had seen wrecked some years before. Crusoe sends the Spaniard back with Friday's father to the island in his newly made boat to rescue the other white prisoners. Meanwhile, he sights an English ship anchored off shore. The captain and two loyal crew members are sent ashore by a rebellious crew. Crusoe and Friday help them recapture the ship, and they depart with the captain for England. The crew say they would rather remain on the well-stocked island than face trial and inevitable hanging in England. They are left behind.

Learning later that the Spaniard and Friday's father have succeeded in rescuing the captive seamen on Friday's island, Crusoe determines to visit them someday.

But first he returns to England with Friday, after an absence of thirty-two years. Crusoe is now a rich man. Besides the money from the sunken Spanish ship, he has an estate in Brazil, kept intact all the time he was away by an honest Portuguese captain, and £10,000 waiting for him in Portugal. He learns that both his parents are dead. After a visit to Portugal to settle his estate, Crusoe returns to England, marries, and has children. When his wife dies, Crusoe sets sail once again to see what has happened on his island.

In Defoe's sequel, *The Farther Adventures of Robinson Crusoe*, the shipwrecked Spaniards and the mutinous English sailors have joined forces, married native women from another island, and established a thriving colony.

After several more adventures, in one of which the faithful Friday is killed, Robinson Crusoe returns for the last time to England, where he lives out the rest of his years in peace and contentment.

Critical Opinion

In 1711 Alexander Selkirk caused a sensation in England. Having run away to sea, he returned after spending five years as a solitary castaway on Juan Fernandez Island off the coast of Chile. Selkirk, after a quarrel with his captain, had been put ashore the island at his own request, and was ultimately rescued by one Captain Woodes Rogers.

The ways in which the castaway had survived on his island fascinated people, and several accounts of his story were published on his return. Never one to let a literary opportunity pass, Defoe wrote his most famous book, *Robinson Crusoe*, a fictional elaboration of Selkirk's adventures, couched in so plain and unadorned a narrative style that it appeared to be true.

Robinson Crusoe has influenced many authors, including Swift (*Gulliver's Travels*), Stevenson (*Treasure Island*) and, of course, Wyss (*The Swiss Family Robinson*).

Despite its plain, crude style, *Robinson Crusoe* has epic qualities often reminiscent of the *Odyssey*. Frightfully lonely, sometimes sick, and often afraid, Crusoe manages not only to stay sane during his long years of isolation, but to build a little civilization of his own on his island. Defoe seems to be saying that no matter how morally weak the average man may be, he has unknown and untapped sources of courage, stamina, and ingenuity.

While a modern writer would have been much more concerned with Crusoe's psychology, Defoe concentrates on his physical activities. Crusoe suffers, to be sure, from moments of terrible loneliness and pangs of religious guilt for having disobeyed his parents. But early in his stay on the island, he makes his peace with God, who, he feels, has mercifully spared his life and provided him with the wherewithal for existence. From that point on, he spends his time in making a little England of his island. The resourcefulness and single-mindedness with which he goes about this task is the most appealing aspect of the book.

When Friday appears on the scene, Crusoe, a slaveholder in Brazil, naturally makes him a servant and forms a two-man colonial system. But Friday is also a valued friend who shows his loyalty and gratitude to his master in countless ways.

The people of Defoe's time had limitless faith in man's ability to carve a life for himself out of the wilderness. This faith, which made possible the exploration and taming of the American continent, is implicit in almost every page of *Robinson Crusoe*.

The Author

Daniel Defoe was born in London, probably in 1660, the son of a butcher. Not much is known of his early life except that he married Mary Tuffley when he was about twenty-three years old, became a hosiery merchant, traveled extensively in Europe, and joined William III's army in 1688.

In 1702 Defoe published an ill-fated pamphlet called "The Shortest Way with Dissenters," in which he ironically advised brutal suppression of the religious sect to which he belonged. Intending it as a satire against intolerance, Defoe was completely misunderstood and fined, pilloried, convicted of slander, and thrown into jail.

His jail sentence seems to have affected his character, for Defoe became suspicious and very careful with money. He wrote extensively, publishing in his lifetime more than 250 separate works, many of them political tracts.

The five years after the publication of *Robinson Crusoe* in 1719 were the years of Defoe's great fiction. They saw the appearance of *Moll Flanders* and *Roxana*, two classic studies of women of easy virtue, and the *Journal of the Plague Year*. In the *Journal*, Defoe's powers as a realistic writer were employed to their utmost. He recounted the Great Plague that swept London in 1665 as if he had been an eyewitness to it, when in actual fact he was only five years old at the time. His novels were immensely important in establishing fiction as a genre in English literature. Their realism and their concern with everyday life rather than with idealized fantasy inspired the most enduring strain in English fiction.

Defoe was also a prolific and facile journalist. He wrote nine volumes of a newspaper called *The Review*, and contributed regularly to other papers.

By contemporary accounts Defoe appears to have been a rather shifty, shrewd man, and a political opportunist. His contemporary, the great essayist Joseph Addison, once described him as "a false, shuffling, prevaricating rascal . . . unqualified to give his testimony in a Court of Justice."

As a religious dissenter and a political hack writer of extraordinarily persuasive force, Defoe was always in danger of imprisonment or worse, but he generally managed to keep a few steps ahead of his enemies. He died on April 26, 1731, in his London lodgings.

By the Same Author

Moll Flanders: Even more than *Robinson Crusoe, Moll Flanders,* written three years later, is of paramount importance in the early history of the English novel. Based on the theme that "poverty is the worst of all snares," it tells about the exciting life of Moll Flanders. Born in Newgate Prison, desired and won by many men, often married, and the mother of twelve children, Moll Flanders is sent to Newgate for pick-pocketing. She successfully convinces her captors that she is remorseful; and, instead of being hanged, she is allowed to go to Virginia with her new consort, a highwayman she met in Newgate. In Virginia she ends her days as a respectable matriarch and plantation owner. In the course of her adventures, a vast panorama of life in early eighteenth-century England unfolds. Moll leads a lusty and dangerous life, but with an unconquerable spirit akin to Robinson Crusoe's, she always manages to survive for still another adventure. Although she is often no more than a prostitute, Moll has Defoe's own middle-class outlook, which patiently survives all disgrace and sordidness, determined to make its way in the world. She is one of the timeless heroines of English fiction.

Gulliver's Travels

by

JONATHAN SWIFT (1667–1745)

Main Characters

Lemuel Gulliver—A simple, naïve, English surgeon and seaman whose love of adventure sends him journeying to
distant and exotic lands.

The Emperor of Lilliput—A monarch a little over six inches
high, referred to by his loyal subjects as the "delight and
terror of the universe."

Flimnap—The wily, jealous Treasurer of Lilliput, he becomes
Gulliver's mortal enemy at court.

Reldresal—The Lilliputian Secretary for Private Affairs, Gulliver's friend.

Glumdalclitch—A Brobdingnagian farmer's daughter who befriends Gulliver and treats him as gently as a little doll.

The King of Brobdingnag—A peace-loving giant who nevertheless maintains a standing army.

Lord Munodi—An efficient Laputian out of favor at court
because his house stays up and his fields yield crops.

The Struldbrugs—A race of unhappy immortals whose only
wish is that they may be allowed to die.

The Yahoos—A filthy race of ape-like creatures who claim
Gulliver for one of their own.

The Houyhnhnms (pronounced Whinnims)—A race of rational, gentle horses who rule over the Yahoos.

Pedro de Mendez—The kindly Portuguese sea captain who
tries to convert Gulliver from his hatred of mankind.

The Story

When Lemuel Gulliver's medical practice in London fails because he is too ethical, he books passage as a ship's doctor aboard the *Antelope*. The ship leaves Bristol for the South Seas on May 4, 1699. Northwest of Van Diemen's Land it is wrecked in a sudden storm, but Gulliver manages to swim ashore where he falls asleep on the beach. When he awakes, he finds himself tied to the ground by thousands of delicate threads. He is the prisoner of the natives of Lilliput, a hitherto unexplored island inhabited by people six inches high who swarm all over him and threaten him with poisoned arrows.

Gulliver is a source of wonder to the Lilliputians, who have never seen anyone his size. He is brought to the capital city of Mildendo where he is instructed in the language and inspected by the Emperor. His comb, pistol, and watch cause great wonder among the Lilliputians who refer to him as Quinbus Flestrin, or Great Man-Mountain.

For a time Gulliver charms the Lilliputians by his simple, friendly manner and his desire to learn their language and customs, which are very curious. Lilliput is at war with Blefuscu, another country exactly like it, and is torn by internal conflict as well. There are two political parties, the High-Heels and the Low-Heels, and two opposing religious sects, the Big Endians and the Little Endians, who fight bitterly about which end of an egg it is better to break. Political favor at court is won by doing a complicated and degrading rope dance.

The Lilliputians, Gulliver learns, seem physically beautiful to him because they are so small that he cannot see their blemishes. Their tiny size makes them ingenious at mechanical work but petty and small minded as well.

Gradually, Gulliver becomes involved in court intrigues. He is given the honorary title of Nardac, and becomes an arch-enemy of Flimnap, the Treasurer. (Flimnap wants him killed because he costs too much to feed [1,728 Lilliputian portions of everything], and because he suspects Gulliver of carrying on an affair with his wife.) Gulliver's new friend, Reldresal, warns him of the indictments being prepared against him at court. When Gulliver tries to ingratiate himself by putting out a fire in the Queen's Palace, he is only further condemned for the unorthodox way in which he does it.

Gulliver is informed that there is one great service he can do for the Lilliputians. The enemy island of Blefuscu is preparing an invasion. With his superior size he can easily destroy their fleet. Gulliver obligingly wades the 800 yards between the islands, and, under the fire of Blefuscudian arrows, succeeds in hauling the Blefuscu fleet back to Lilliput.

This action momentarily regains for Gulliver the favor of the court; but a new dispute arises when Gulliver refuses to crush the Blefuscudians completely and make them the slaves of Lilliput. Championing Blefuscudian freedom makes Gulliver a marked man in Lilliput. When he learns that he is to be killed, Gulliver seeks shelter in Blefuscu where he is well treated.

One day a large boat is washed ashore and Gulliver, homesick for England, outfits it for the voyage. At sea he is picked up by a passing ship and returns home, bringing with him samples of the minute Lilliputian cattle to prove his story.

Back in England with his wife and children, Gulliver becomes restless again and sets sail for India aboard the *Adventure*. The ship veers from its course. The sailors make for an unknown land to look for supplies. Gulliver loses the rest of the landing party and finds himself in a field of grain forty feet high where giant farmers are threshing the grain. One of them discovers Gulliver and brings him home in his pocket to entertain his nine-year-old daughter, Glumdalclitch. Gulliver learns that he is in Brobdingnag, a land 6,000 miles long and 5,000 miles wide. The people there are giants as gross and coarse-featured as the Lilliputians were delicate.

In Brobdingnag, Glumdalclitch treats Gulliver like a pet. Her father, hoping to make a fortune, goes about the country displaying Gulliver in a box as a freak. When Gulliver gets sick as a result of this rough handling, the farmer increases the number of shows in order to make as much money as possible before Gulliver dies. Fortunately for Gulliver, the farmer eventually sells him to the Queen who adopts him as a pet.

At the court the philosophers and wise men laugh at Gulliver. How can there be a whole race of men so tiny? The King asks him many searching questions about life in England, and Gulliver, filled with pride and homesickness, tells him of the great glories of English military might. Gulliver is startled, however, to find the King appalled at the effrontery of such small creatures carrying on war.

Life in Brobdingnag is a daily source of terror to Gulliver. His size makes him vulnerable to all sorts of disasters. He must fight off immense, ferocious rats and is menaced by hailstones as large as tennis balls. Even in the palace he is in constant danger. One day the thirty-foot court dwarf becomes jealous of him and tosses him into the cream pitcher. He barely escapes drowning. When Gulliver looks into a mirror, he seems, even to himself, puny and insignificant. The court ladies behave coarsely before him, unable to take his manhood seriously.

After two years of constant peril, Gulliver escapes one day when a giant bird lifts the box in which he lives and carries it in its beak over the water. The bird drops the box into the sea. Gulliver is spotted by a vessel heading for England and is hauled aboard.

When he has recovered from his adventures in Brobdingnag, Gulliver is once again attacked by wanderlust and sets out to sea a third time. On this voyage, his ship is attacked by pirates, and he is set adrift in a small boat. He lands on the island of Balnibarbi, just east of Japan. Balnibarbi is a colony ruled from above by a floating island called Laputa. The Laputians are normal in size, but they have only two interests in life: music and mathematics. They are keen theoreticians, always rapt in abstract thought from which they must be roused by servants rattling bladders in their faces. For all their intellectual prowess, however, the Laputians are totally unable to do anything practical. Their clothes do not fit, and their houses are lopsided shambles. Only one of them, Lord Munodi, has been able to build a real house and farm his land profitably. For these accomplishments he is scorned by the other Laputians.

The King of Laputa keeps the colony of Balnibarbi under control by dropping huge rocks on it from above to prevent the natives from revolting.

The pride of Laputa, Gulliver discovers, is the Academy of Projectors in the capital city of Lagado. Here Laputian scientists labor for years on such foolish projects as extracting sunbeams from cucumbers and reducing human excrement to its original food. In the Academy the blind select colors by touch. Houses are built from the top down.

From Lagado Gulliver travels to Glubbdubdrib, an island of sorcerers. There the Governor summons for Gulliver such famous figures of history as Alexander the Great, Hannibal, Caesar, and Pompey. One after another they appear and answer Gulliver's questions about their great deeds. Each has a disillusioning story to tell, showing that the official accounts of history are a pack of lies.

A further disillusionment awaits Gulliver on the island of Luggnagg, where he meets the Struldbrugs, a race of immortals. Gulliver assumes that these must be the happiest and wisest of men because they have had so much time to learn the secrets of the universe. He finds, however, they are merely senile and embittered. Although they do not die, they keep growing progressively older and weaker, losing all zest for life and yearning for the blessed release of death.

Gulliver then returns to England by way of Japan. Once again, in August 1710, after staying with his family for a short time, he sets sail for foreign parts, this time as captain of the ship. In the South Seas, Gulliver's crew seizes the ship and confines Gulliver to his quarters. Eventually they set him adrift in a longboat. He lands on a strange shore where he encounters a filthy, disgusting race of ape-like men known as Yahoos. After befouling Gulliver, the Yahoos flee in terror at the approach of some horses called Houyhnhnms (after the whinnying sound they make). They are the masters of the island.

The Houyhnhnms assume that Gulliver is a Yahoo—albeit a more delicate and rational one—because he looks more like a Yahoo than like a horse. Just as the Yahoos are savage and irrational, the horses are gentle, civilized, and highly reasonable creatures. They marry according to genetic laws, and they accept death calmly. Gulliver is housed in the stable of a family of Houyhnhnms where he even learns to enjoy their diet of milk, herbs, and oatcakes. Ever resourceful, he makes his own clothes when necessary, but the Houyhnhnms are amazed that he does not go naked. They attribute this eccentricity to his inferior physique.

Gulliver describes life in England to the Houyhnhnms who (like the King of Brobdingnag) are appalled that such a cantankerous, evil race as men should think themselves lords of creation when in fact they are only slightly more refined Yahoos. The horses cannot understand the concept of lying, for they consider words to be meant for communication, not for concealment. They are insulted that horses should be used as beasts of burden in England. When Gulliver describes the horrors of war, he is more cautious and less patriotic than he was during his stay in Brobdingnag. He agrees with the Houyhnhnms that man is vile, and finds himself living happily with the horses in a totally rational society.

His happiness and peace, however, are short lived. The Houyhnhnm Grand Assembly, a sort of parliament, decides that Gulliver must really be a Yahoo although he may seem more civilized than the vile local breed of apes. He is even sexually attractive to the female Yahoos. As an intelligent Yahoo, the horses reason, he poses a threat to their ideal civilization. So, much against his will, Gulliver is ordered to leave. He builds a canoe and sails away, being picked up eventually by a Portuguese ship under the command of a kindly, understanding captain, Pedro de Mendez.

Gulliver has now become a complete misanthrope. He sulks in his cabin on the return trip to Europe. But Mendez tries to bring him back to his own kind by showing, in his own actions, that not all men are as detestable as Yahoos. Nevertheless, when Gulliver finally returns home from his last voyage, he is unable to endure his family, and for a long time is able to bear only the company of horses.

Critical Opinion

A satirical fantasy in the form of a travel book, *Gulliver's Travels* is known both as a delightful children's book (in expurgated editions) and as the most bitter attack on human depravity in the English language. Some of the objects of Swift's scathing satire are politics, court intrigue, bigotry, and human selfishness and cruelty in all their forms. In his four travels to distant parts of the earth, Gulliver discovers that for all their physical and cultural differences, men everywhere are basically the same. Starting out as an easy-going optimist, Gulliver eventually comes to the conclusion that, in the words of the King of Brobdingnag, human beings are "the most pernicious race of little odious vermin that nature ever suffered to crawl upon the surface of the earth." Only a few decent individuals escape Swift's withering condemnation of the human race.

Gulliver's Travels is representative of Swift's satiric genius at its best. His obsession with language finds an outlet in the invention of languages for all the strange lands Gulliver visits. His involvement with politics is reflected in the satire on English government intrigues in the court of Lilliput. His distrust of theoretical science emerges from the satire on the Grand Academy of Lagado, a parody of the English Royal Society.

Each country Gulliver visits thinks itself the greatest on earth, inhabited by the lords of creation. But everyone, large or small, apes or horses, suffers from gross human defects. Gulliver, as his name suggests, is gullible, naïve, and innocent. But in the course of his travels he is exposed to the petty, scheming Lilliputians, the gross, selfish Brobdingnagians, the abstracted, inhuman Laputians, and the foul, subhuman Yahoos. Even the Houyhnhnms, the most sympathetic creatures in the book, are too rational, as their expulsion of Gulliver demonstrates. By the end of his travels, Gulliver has become a sadder, wiser man.

Swift believed that man's inhumanity to man is made even more detestable because he is capable of reason but either misuses it or doesn't use it at all, and because he takes inordinate pride in himself—a pride hardly justified by his love for war, cruelty, and bloodshed.

The Author

Jonathan Swift, the greatest English satirist, was born in Dublin of English parents in 1667. A cousin of the poet John Dryden, he was educated at Trinity College, Dublin, where he got into trouble for offenses against discipline. He became secretary to Sir William Temple, in whose service he wrote his first major satires, *The Battle of the Books* and *A Tale of a Tub*, published together in 1704. At this time, too, he fell in love with Esther (Stella) Johnson whom he may later have secretly married.

When Temple died in 1699, Swift became a clergyman and was given a living in Ireland. On his frequent trips to

England, he became deeply involved in politics and literature. Although he started out as a Whig, he went over to the Tories in 1710 and became Dean of St. Patrick's three years later.

Although Swift is known for his caustic view of human nature, he seems to have been an amiable man capable of great friendships with the leading literary lights of his day, Pope, Arbuthnot, and Gay, with whom he formed the Scriblerus Club. He also became a hero to the Irish whom he defended against English rule in a series of savage satires of which "A Modest Proposal" (1729) is the most famous.

In Swift's last years he suffered from a progressive mental disease. Nothing sums up Swift's character as well as the epitaph he wrote for himself: "Here lies one . . . whose heart was lacerated with savage indignation."

Tom Jones

by

HENRY FIELDING (1707–1754)

Main Characters

Squire Allworthy—Rich, generous, and good-natured, the
model of an English country squire.
Bridget—Squire Allworthy's plain, kindly sister.
Blifil—Bridget's scheming son.
Tom Jones—Open-hearted and outgoing, a foundling whose
indiscretions always get him into trouble.
Mr. Partridge—A poor, naïve schoolmaster.
Squire Western—Red-faced and hot-tempered, chiefly ad-
dicted to eating, drinking, and hunting.
Sophia—Squire Western's beautiful, headstrong daughter.
Thwackum and Square—Two hypocritical pedagogues.
Black George—Squire Allworthy's drunken, good-for-nothing
gamekeeper.
Mrs. Fitzpatrick—Sophia's cousin, running away from her
insanely jealous husband.
Lady Bellaston—A sophisticated London friend of Mrs. Fitz-
patrick's.

The Story

Of all the landed gentry in Somersetshire, Squire Allworthy
is the most highly regarded for his benevolence, good nature,

and wealth. He lives in peaceful retirement with his maiden sister, Bridget. Returning one night from a several months' stay in London, he is shocked to find a baby boy lying in his bed. He takes to the foundling and insists on bringing it up himself rather than leave it on the churchwarden's doorstep.

The foundling's parentage is a great mystery. The Squire and his sister act on the assumption that the mother must be Jenny Jones, a servant of the local schoolmaster, Partridge; Jenny Jones had spent some time nursing Bridget during an illness. Fearing local gossip, Squire Allworthy sends Jenny away. The schoolmaster leaves the county, too. The foundling is named Tom Jones.

Soon after, Bridget marries the fortune-hunting half-pay officer, Captain Blifil, by whom she has a son. The two boys are brought up together. Captain Blifil, who had hoped to inherit Squire Allworthy's money, dies of an apoplectic fit while his son is still a boy.

Tom and young Blifil don't get along together, for Tom is good-natured, easy-going, and highly mischievous, while Blifil is a spiritless prig, always concerned with the impression he is making on his elders. Allworthy hires Thwackum and Square to educate Tom. This they try to do with frequent beatings. But when Tom catches the pompous Square in bed with the local slut, Molly Seagrim, his education ends. Tom's one friend is Allworthy's lazy, shiftless gamekeeper, Black George, and together they go poaching about the countryside and getting into scrapes which sadden the affectionate Squire.

On an estate nearby lives Squire Western with his lovely daughter, Sophia. The Squire is a hard-drinking, hard-riding, choleric man. Tom spends a good deal of time with the Westerns because the Squire admires his rough and ready manners and his horsemanship while Sophia is impressed with his goodness of heart. One day while out hunting, Tom breaks his arm catching Sophia's runaway horse. He stays with the Westerns while recovering. He and Sophia fall in love.

When Tom learns that Squire Allworthy is ill and not likely to recover, he rushes to his benefactor's bedside, where he finds Blifil in obsequious attendance. But Allworthy makes a miraculous recovery, and Tom is so delighted that he gets roaring drunk. Blifil, whose mother has recently died, takes offense at Tom's behavior. Tom offers to apologize, but Blifil insultingly refers to his illegitimate birth and the two lads fight.

Meanwhile, Sophia becomes interested in Blifil, a favorite with the ladies, in order to conceal her real love for the penniless, imprudent Tom. When her aunt arrives from London, she assumes that Sophia and Blifil will marry, and tells Squire Western to prepare for the wedding. When Sophia's aunt learns the truth, both she and Western are outraged. Much as the fox-hunting squire likes Tom, he refuses to consider a foundling as a son-in-law.

Now that Squire Allworthy is fully recovered, Blifil tells him about Tom's drunken behavior the night he was so sick, implying that Tom didn't care what happened to him and couldn't wait for the reading of the will. Enraged and disillusioned with Tom, whom he liked more than his legitimate nephew, Allworthy reproaches Tom—who is too dismayed to defend himself—and banishes him from the house. He gives Tom £500 to help him make his way in the world. Tom carelessly loses the money.

Sophia, too, is in disgrace. Refusing to marry Blifil under any circumstances, she is locked up in her room by her father. But with the connivance of her maid Honour, she manages to slip out at night and heads for her aunt's house in London.

On the road, Tom falls in with a band of rowdy soldiers and gets into a fight with them at an inn. His wounds are treated by the local barber, who turns out to be the banished Partridge. Partridge becomes Tom's companion on his adventures. They meet a beautiful, middle-aged woman named Mrs. Waters, who is fighting off the advances of a soldier in a forest. Tom rescues her and takes her to the inn at Upton, where she lures him into her bed.

Also arriving at the Upton inn on their way to London are Sophia and her maid. Before long the inn is in an uproar when an enraged husband looking for his runaway wife shows up and is led to Tom's room, where he discovers Tom with Mrs. Waters, who starts to scream. The man is a Mr. Fitzpatrick, not Mrs. Waters' husband at all; but by the time everything is straightened out, Partridge has inadvertently revealed to Sophia her lover's infidelity. Sophia departs in a fury, leaving her muff behind for Tom to discover in the morning.

Soon after she leaves the inn, Sophia meets Mrs. Fitzpatrick, her cousin, who fled the inn when her jealous husband caused the row with Tom. Together they travel to London. Here Sophia is introduced to the sophisticated Mrs. Bellaston, who promises to show the unspoiled country girl the pleasures of the town.

Tom and Partridge follow Sophia to London, where they find congenial lodgings at the home of Mrs. Miller. Soon Tom is admitted to the social circle and to the beds of Lady Bellaston and Mrs. Fitzpatrick. One night, seeing Sophia at a play, he assures her of his eternal devotion and promises to reform. The quarrel is patched up. Partridge finds love, too, in London with Nancy Nightingale, whose father objects to him as a suitor. However, Tom good-naturedly persuades Nightingale to allow the match, to the delight not only of Partridge but of Nancy's friend Mrs. Miller, as well.

When he learns of Sophia's escape from his house, Squire Western abandons fox-hunting long enough to pursue his daughter to London. He finds her at Lady Bellaston's lodgings and removes her to his own. Tom is broken-hearted because he knows the squire will never approve of his marriage to Sophia. To add to his misery, Partridge brings the news that Squire Allworthy has also arrived in London with Blifil who is now going to marry Sophia. Tom goes to Mrs. Fitzpatrick for advice, but with typical bad luck he is discovered there by her jealous husband, who challenges him to a duel. Tom wounds him and is immediately hustled off to jail.

In his cell Tom is visited by the Mrs. Waters with whom he spent the night at Upton. Partridge later identifies her as the former Jenny Jones, reputedly Tom's mother. The lad is so shocked by this coincidental incest that he determines to reform his casual, promiscuous ways. Mrs. Miller defends Tom, telling Squire Allworthy that Tom was not at fault in the duel with Mr. Fitzpatrick, a fact that Mr. Fitzpatrick, on recovering from his wound, graciously acknowledges.

Indeed, Squire Allworthy is about to forgive Tom when he learns of Tom's behavior with Mrs. Waters. Once again the good man is furious with Tom, but Mrs. Waters assures him that she is not, indeed, Tom's mother. The real mother, she tells the Squire, was his own sister, Bridget. On her deathbed, Bridget left a message with Blifil concerning Tom's true parentage. Blifil had treacherously destroyed the message.

Blifil had also tried to bribe witnesses to get Tom hanged for the duel with Mr. Fitzpatrick, even though that gentleman had not died of his wounds.

Now that Tom is exonerated, he is released from prison and his fortune improves. Squire Allworthy's affection for him returns. He apologizes to Sophia for trying to force Blifil on her and tells Squire Western that Tom is his heir, for the young man is indeed his nephew. This convinces Squire Western that Tom, after all, is worthy to marry Sophia, and the match takes place. Everyone rejoices except the odious Blifil who is sent away with a yearly stipend. Tom and Sophia live happily on Squire Allworthy's estate.

Critical Opinion

As in *Joseph Andrews*, Fielding was concerned in *Tom Jones* with writing what he called the comic epic in prose—a work in which "the plain and simple workings of honest nature" would be explored on a large scale, but without fanciful diction, absurd events, or lofty moralizing. Drawing on his long experience as a dramatist, Fielding plotted *Tom Jones* with consummate skill. Writing while the English novel was in its infancy, he set for it standards of structure, characterization, and tone that have endured to this day.

Tom Jones is neatly and evenly divided into three parts: the first in the country, at the Allworthy and Western estates; the second on the road, culminating in the farcical scene at the inn at Upton; and the third in London. Thus Fielding managed, without distorting his plot, to delineate the whole of English life of his day. His section on the highways and country inns of eighteenth-century England particularly influenced Dickens. The panoramic sweep of *Tom Jones* has inspired many English novelists since.

Each book of *Tom Jones* is prefaced by a delightfully witty essay analyzing the action up to that point and making shrewd observations about the characters and about human nature. These asides to the reader also had their influence—not always beneficial—on Dickens, Thackeray, and Trollope. In these asides Fielding's tone is invariably that of the wise and humane man of the world addressing his peers.

The theme of *Tom Jones* lies deeply rooted in eighteenth-century enlightened optimism. In pitting Tom against Blifil, Fielding is saying that, in general, human nature is careless, imprudent, and pleasure loving, but essentially good, and is best left alone to develop a moral sense in its own time. While Tom blunders thoughtlessly into one scrape after another, he finally emerges a genuinely righteous man.

Blifil, on the other hand, observes all the proprieties, is exceedingly polite and, on the surface, thoughtful. But he is a complete hypocrite and villain, resorting to every possible treachery to obtain Squire Allworthy's fortune. Ultimately his scheming brings about his downfall. Fielding's world is moral, but not puritanical.

The Author

Although *Henry Fielding* was a gentleman, the great-grandson of the Earl of Desmond, he had to struggle for a living most of his life. Born on April 12, 1707, at Sharpham Park, near Glastonbury in Somersetshire, he attended Eton and studied law at the University of Leyden. When he returned to England, he supported himself by writing farces and musicals for the popular stage. Between 1728 and 1737, he produced a number of potboilers, the most notable being a burlesque of serious stage conventions, *Tom Thumb* (1730).

In 1734 Fielding married Charlotte Cradock, supposedly the model for Sophia in *Tom Jones* and for Fielding's last heroine, Amelia. Fielding returned to the law and was admitted to the bar in 1740. To eke out a living, however, he managed a small London theater and practiced journalism, editing the *Champion* between 1739 and 1741. His wife died in 1744, and three years later Fielding married her maid, Mary Daniel.

Fielding first tried his hand at fiction with *Joseph Andrews* (1742) and the savagely ironical *Jonathan Wild* (1743); but it was the experience with all segments of society that he had gained during his appointment as justice of the peace for Middlesex and Westminster in 1748 that provided the broad scope of his last two novels, *Tom Jones* (1749) and *Amelia* (1751).

In 1740 Samuel Richardson published what is generally considered the first true English novel, the heavily moralizing

Pamela. Offended at what he considered the false, hypocritical morality of this immensely popular book, Fielding first wrote a brief parody of it called "Shamela," and then set to work on a more detailed ironic treatment in *Joseph Andrews.* But what started as mere burlesque became a typically robust, good-humored Fielding novel, rich in character and incident.

Fielding was an intensely vital and humane man whose experiences as a Grub Street hack and as a man of the law made him deeply aware of social injustice. Much less sheltered than Richardson, Fielding developed a common-sense view of life which pervades his great novel, *Tom Jones.* Nothing human was alien to him except injustice, against which he argued both from the bench and in a multitude of pamphlets and essays in *The Covent Garden Journal,* which he founded in 1752.

In 1754 his health broke down and he traveled to Portugal, leaving a very moving account of his journey in search of health in the posthumously published *Journal of a Voyage to Lisbon.* He died in that city on October 8, 1754.

By the Same Author

Joseph Andrews: Amused by the sentimental puritanism of Richardson's *Pamela,* Fielding set out in *Joseph Andrews* to chronicle the adventures of Pamela's brother, footman to the lascivious Lady Booby, who tries to seduce this hypervirtuous young man. Failing, she dismisses both Joseph and his true love, Fanny Goodwill, from her service. Fanny is saved from the wicked world, however, not by Joseph but by Parson Adams, a man of great simplicity and charm, who dominates the book and who probably served as a model for Dr. Primrose, the Vicar of Wakefield. Writing, as he admitted, "in imitation of Cervantes," Fielding created in *Joseph Andrews* a novel that starts out as burlesque and ends up as a vision of English life in the eighteenth century.

Amelia: Written at the end of Fielding's life, *Amelia* lacks the high spirits of his earlier novels. It is, in fact, a completely serious treatment of the injustice of eighteenth-century law courts and jails. A weak-willed, innocent man, William Booth, confined to debtors' prison, tells a fellow prisoner of his love and courtship of the long-suffering Amelia. The listener, a murderess named Miss Matthews, seduces William. Meanwhile Amelia is having difficulties outside the jail. Eventually, through a last-minute inheritance, William and Amelia are able to achieve peace as husband and wife outside the confines of the debtors' prison.

The Vicar of Wakefield

by

OLIVER GOLDSMITH (1728–1774)

Main Characters

Charles Primrose—The kindly, unworldly vicar of Wakefield, whose innocence and simplicity often lead him into trouble, but who bears good fortune with humility and ill fortune with fortitude.

Deborah Primrose—The vicar's wife, a good woman, although sometimes inclined to be a social climber, who must be brought back to reality by her husband.

George—The Primroses' eldest son, who joins the army after trying his hand unsuccessfully at many careers.

Moses—The Primroses' younger son, educated at home and intended for business, who is even more naïve than his father.

Olivia—The Primroses' older daughter, gay, vivacious, and flirtatious, the family beauty who becomes the family heartache.

Sophia—Olivia's younger sister, soft, modest, and gentle, a more serious, less coquettish girl than Olivia.

Squire Thornhill—Mr. Primrose's landlord, a handsome, unscrupulous ladies' man.

Mr. Burchell—Actually Squire Thornhill's uncle, Sir William Thornhill, in disguise, whose honesty antagonizes the Primroses until they discover his merits.

Arabella Wilmot—George Primrose's fiancée.

Ephraim Jenkinson—A rogue in many disguises, whose surface knowledge of philosophy and ancient languages impresses his victims.

The Story

Mr. Charles Primrose, the vicar of Wakefield, is one of the most contented men in England. Married to a good wife and father of six healthy, beautiful children, he takes pleasure in the simple things of life. As the novel opens, his oldest son, George, just down from Oxford, has fallen in love with Arabella Wilmot, a neighbor's daughter, and both families are joyfully preparing for the wedding.

One day, however, Mr. Primrose quarrels with Arabella's father about whether a man should remarry after his wife's death. (Mr. Primrose is a strict monogamist. Mr. Wilmot is about to wed for the fourth time.) Suddenly Mr. Primrose learns that his comfortable fortune has been lost by a broker and that he is now dependent solely on his meager living as a vicar. Because of this sudden change in fortune and the quarrel with Mr. Wilmot, the engagement between George and Arabella is broken off.

George is sent off to London to make his way, and the Primrose family move to another, even less lucrative living. On the way to their new home, they meet Mr. Burchell, a handsome man who endears himself to them by his impulsive act of charity to another traveler. Riding with the Primroses a way, Mr. Burchell tells them about their new landlord, Squire Thornhill. He is the wealthy, woman-chasing nephew of Sir William Thornhill, a great and magnanimous man. Mr. Burchell further endears himself to the Primroses when he rescues Sophia who is thrown from her horse. He is assured of a warm welcome any time he cares to visit the Primroses in their new home.

One autumn afternoon shortly after the Primroses are established in the vicarage, they meet their landlord, Squire Thornhill, while he is out riding. Olivia falls in love with the gallant squire, but her father is troubled by Thornhill's reputation for seducing all the pretty girls in the neighborhood. Mrs. Primrose, however, impressed by his wealth and social position, encourages his attentions to her older daughter, certain that he will marry her. She finds him more eligible than the far less wealthy Mr. Burchell, now a frequent visitor. Mr. Burchell is interested in serious, quiet Sophia, and makes a point of bringing gingerbread cookies for the Primroses' youngest boys, Dick and Bill. Mr. Primrose is worried because Mr. Burchell does not seem particularly prudent with the little money he has.

The women of the household are all agog one evening when Squire Thornhill brings two finely dressed ladies to visit. Lady Blarney and Miss Carolina Wilelmina Amelia Skeggs make a grand entrance, taking the Primroses by surprise while they are playing homely fireside games with their rough, honest, farmer neighbor, Mr. Flamborough. Sophia and Olivia are impressed with the sophisticated conversation of the ladies, and are overwhelmed with pleasure when the ladies suggest that they join them in London as companions. Mrs. Primrose welcomes the suggestion, feeling that some time spent in London will polish her daughters' manners and make them more suitable for fine social matches. But Mr. Primrose and Mr. Burchell object to London as a place not fit for innocent, well-bred young ladies.

Mrs. Primrose begins to get grand ideas, and insists that the family sell its clumsy horse and buy a finer one to take them stylishly to church on Sundays. So Moses, the Primroses' second son, who is supposedly training for a business career, is sent to town to make the trade. He manages to sell the horse for a fair price but then is cheated by a smooth-talking confidence man into buying a gross of green spectacles. He proudly brings his purchase home, only to discover that it is worthless; the "silver" rims are only copper.

Despite Mr. Burchell's strong objections to the project, all is set for the girls to go to London. But the trip is abruptly canceled because Mrs. Primrose learns that the London ladies have received slanderous reports about the character of her two daughters. When the Primroses learn that the slanderer is Mr. Burchell, the vicar tells him to leave the house. Unrepentant, Mr. Burchell leaves.

Squire Thornhill now calls even more frequently at the vicarage, but Mrs. Primrose begins to suspect that marriage is not uppermost in his mind. She and Olivia decide to spur Squire Thornhill's interest in marriage by concocting a plot to convince him that Olivia is shortly to marry Mr. Williams, a local farmer. Mr. Primrose disapproves of the plot, although he thinks Olivia actually ought to consider marrying the good but somewhat plodding Mr. Williams if Squire Thornhill still fails to ask for her hand. All thought of this marriage disappears, however, when, four days before the wedding is supposed to take place, Dick Primrose sees Olivia going off with two men in a carriage.

At first the Primroses assume the abductor is Squire Thornhill, but he protests his innocence. The finger of blame points to Mr. Burchell. Mr. Primrose sadly determines to go in search of his errant daughter. During the search he falls ill and is bedridden at an inn for three weeks. On recovering, he sets out on his journey once again and meets Arabella Wilmot who asks him about George. Mr. Primrose replies that he has not heard from his son since George went to London to seek his fortune. Arabella is now being courted by Squire Thornhill who rubs salt into the vicar's wounds by asking Olivia's whereabouts.

The missing George turns up with a troupe of actors at a country house where Mr. Primrose meets them. George has been wandering through Europe, tutoring and playing music, but he has less money now than when he first left for London. Squire Thornhill, wanting George out of the way, buys him a commission in the army.

The vicar finds Olivia, abandoned and wretched, at a country inn, where she confesses the story of her abduction. It was Squire Thornhill after all, and not Mr. Burchell, who had run off with her. After a fake wedding ceremony performed by a bogus priest, the squire had seduced her. Soon tiring of her, he abandoned her in London, leaving her to make her way home alone. The two fine London ladies whom he had introduced to the vicarage were in fact prostitutes. The vicar forgives his penitent daughter, and together they set out for the homeward journey.

Just as they arrive home that night, the vicar sees his house going up in flames and his wife Deborah crying that the two little boys, Dick and Bill, are lost in the fire. Mr. Primrose rushes into the burning house and rescues his sons, but he is badly burned. Now the Primroses must settle in an outbuilding on the estate, for all their possessions have been destroyed. Kind neighbors help them move into the wretched little shack.

Olivia's misery is increased by the news that Squire Thornhill, whom she still loves, is about to marry Arabella Wilmot. This news infuriates Mr. Primrose, who treats the squire to a stern lecture when the squire has the effrontery to ask the vicar's blessing on the impending marriage and to suggest that Olivia be married off to a local man in order to be always at the squire's disposal. The squire reacts to being thrown out of the Primrose shack by demanding his quarterly rent which the vicar cannot pay. On the following day despite the angry protests of his parishioners, the vicar is led to debtors' prison. His family finds wretched accommodations in town to be near him, and the two youngest boys stay with their father in his prison cell.

While in jail, Mr. Primrose meets Ephraim Jenkinson, the confidence man who had fobbed off the worthless green spectacles on Moses, and had even cheated the vicar. Sick of his life of crime, he is trying to reform. Mr. Primrose preaches to him and to the other wretched convicts, taking his mind off his own misfortunes and giving them the strength to endure theirs. These misfortunes turn into tragedy when Jenkinson tells the vicar that Olivia, who has been pining away with remorse ever since her abduction, is dead. Deborah Primrose adds to the gloom of the occasion with the awful news that Sophia has been carried off by a gang of kidnappers.

Mr. Primrose is cast further into the depths of despair when his son George, battered and bruised, is led into the jail. When informed of Squire Thornhill's ill-treatment of Olivia, George had sped to Thornhill Castle to seek vengeance on the squire. There he was attacked by some servants, one of whom he injured in the scuffle. George is now to be hanged. Wretched and ill, Mr. Primrose writes to Sir William Thornhill, detailing his nephew's treachery and cruelty.

At this lowest ebb in the fortunes of the Primroses, things begin to look up. First Mr. Burchell arrives with Sophia, whom he has rescued from the ruffians who had abducted her. Overwhelmed with joy, the vicar promises Mr. Burchell Sophia's hand in marriage. It is then revealed that Mr. Burchell is actually the wealthy and magnanimous Sir William Thornhill, the squire's uncle, in disguise. (He had not revealed his identity to make sure that Sophia loved him for his own merits and not for his money.) The slanderous letter to the ladies in London had been written because he knew they would corrupt the Primrose girls if the girls ever fell into their clutches. Sophia's abductors were in the pay of Squire Thornhill, who, seeing that he could not have the one daughter, was determined to get the other. Sir William has pieced the story together with the aid of Mr. Primrose, and is thoroughly disillusioned with his nephew.

Then Ephraim Jenkinson informs everyone that Olivia and Squire Thornhill had been legitimately married all along. Jenkinson had been ordered by the squire to procure a fake priest for the wedding; but thinking he would be able to blackmail his master later if the squire were really wed, Jenkinson had obtained an ordained priest to perform the marriage.

Best of all, Mr. Primrose learns that Olivia is still alive. Jenkinson had spread the false tale of her death to persuade Mr. Primrose to give his blessing to the wedding of Squire Thornhill and Arabella Wilmot, thinking this would be the only way to stop the squire's persecution of Jenkinson's new friend. Since the marriage between the squire and Olivia is a real one, the squire cannot, of course, marry Arabella Wilmot. To cap the climax, the broker who absconded with Mr. Primrose's fortune is caught at Antwerp; the money is refunded to its rightful owner. There is nothing more for the sorely tried vicar to wish for in this life but that his "gratitude in good fortune should exceed [his] submission in adversity."

Critical Opinion

The Vicar of Wakefield has always been one of the best-loved novels of the eighteenth century. The reasons for its enduring appeal are clear. First, the various reversals in the fortunes of the Primrose family are sufficiently dramatic (the prison scenes particularly remind us that Goldsmith was a skilled playwright) to intrigue most readers, although the most sophisticated are likely to be put off by Goldsmith's sentimentality and his heavy reliance on coincidence. Second, we all like to read about a good man whose fortunes keep getting worse and worse until at the end all goes well for him again. Mr. Primrose is one of the most successful in a long line of innocent English country clergymen, starting with Fielding's Parson Adams in *Joseph Andrews*. Finally, Goldsmith possessed one of the finest styles of his time: easy and fluent, mildly satiric, elegant without being pretentious. The prose of *The Vicar of Wakefield* is classic in its simplicity.

For the more mature reader, Goldsmith's novel is a matchless description of humble country life in eighteenth-century England. As in his poem, "The Deserted Village," Goldsmith is expert at genre painting. He shows us vividly the inns, roads, and prisons, the country estates, and best of all, the vicar's family gathered around the fireside to enjoy the pleasures of a less complex, less harrowing age than our own.

In a sense, *The Vicar of Wakefield* is a Christian version of the Greek tale of Prometheus or the Hebrew story of Job. Unlike Prometheus and Job, however, Mr. Primrose never curses or even questions the God who seems to have turned against him. Instead, he bears up with cheerful fortitude, convinced that all will turn out for the best in the end, as indeed it does.

For all its unpretentious charm, *The Vicar of Wakefield* is essentially a serious treatment of the theme of stoic fortitude. And for all its naïve plotting and reliance on coincidence, it has had an immense influence on the English novel. Dickens loved it and learned much from it. In fact, his early pen name, "Boz," comes from the way he pronounced, as a child, the name of Mr. Primrose's second son, Moses. Goldsmith's charming pictures of rural life influenced Jane Austen and George Eliot. Although the cynical may ridicule it, *The Vicar of Wakefield* has a unique place in the history of English fiction.

The Author

The vagabond life of George Primrose in search of a living, as narrated in Chapter XX of *The Vicar of Wakefield*, is essentially autobiographical. For *Oliver Goldsmith*, born November 10, 1728, the son of an Irish clergyman, enjoyed far more wit and talent than money during his lifetime. He was educated at Trinity College, Dublin, and, after running away from school at least once, finally received his BA in 1749. He tried to take holy orders, but was rejected. He then studied medicine at Edinburgh and Leyden, probably receiving his medical degree on the continent during his year of wandering about France, Switzerland, and Italy.

Arriving in London in 1756, he tried desperately to make a living in medicine and teaching, but failure in these fields drove him to doing hack work for various periodicals. In 1761 he made one of the most important friendships of his life, with Samuel Johnson, the great dictator of the English literary scene. Goldsmith became a member of the informal but famous "Club" which included such luminaries as James Boswell, Johnson's biographer; David Garrick, the great actor; and Sir Joshua Reynolds, whose portrait of Goldsmith is the best we have.

One day Johnson received a panicky summons from Goldsmith to keep Goldsmith out of debtors' prison. Seeing the manuscript of *The Vicar of Wakefield* in Goldsmith's poverty-stricken room, Johnson took it to a publisher, from whom he got £60, enough to pay Goldsmith's debt.

Johnson had a high opinion of Goldsmith's literary abilities although most other members of the "Club" saw him as a poor, fumbling buffoon, inarticulate in the presence of the great. (Garrick made affectionate fun of Goldsmith's stutter in the epitaph: "He wrote like an angel, and talked like poor Poll.")

Goldsmith was proficient in all genres, from poetry and plays to political journalism and history. His works are filled with gaiety, charm, and common sense. Besides *The Vicar of Wakefield*, Goldsmith's best-known writings are: "The Deserted Village," (1770); two delightful plays, *The Good-natur'd Man* (1768) and *She Stoops to Conquer* (1773); and the fine series of satiric "letters," *The Citizen of the World*, (1762).

Despite the popularity of some of the poems and plays during his lifetime, Goldsmith was never free of worry and debt. He died, ironically enough, of his own medical treatment, on April 4, 1774. Johnson's "Club" erected a monument to Goldsmith in Westminster Abbey.

Tristram Shandy

by

LAURENCE STERNE (1713–1768)

Main Characters

Tristram Shandy—The narrator and "hero" is an ill-starred nonentity who is not even born until halfway through the novel.

Walter Shandy—Tristram's father, fond of far-ranging philosophical speculations on the subtlest points, but somewhat divorced from reality.

Toby Shandy—Tristram's Uncle Toby, an old soldier and a kindly gentleman who delights in recalling his past campaigns.

Corporal Trim—Uncle Toby's loyal and innocent servant.

Mr. Yorick—An absurdly fanciful clergyman.

Dr. Slop—An ill-humored, inept quack doctor.

Widow Wadman—An amorous widow who lives near Shandy Hall and hopes to entice Uncle Toby into marriage.

The Story

Tristram Shandy can always attribute the peculiarity of his nature and the strange events of his life to the fact that, when he was on the point of being conceived, his mother asked his father, the eccentric, henpecked Walter Shandy, whether he had not forgotten to wind the clock.

Immediately after Tristram's conception, which occurred sometime between the first Sunday and the first Monday of March, 1718, Tristram's father journeyed from Shandy Hall, the ancestral estate, to London, a trip his sciatica had hitherto prevented him from making. Both noteworthy occurrences can be verified in Mr. Shandy's meticulously kept diary.

The reason that Tristram was born in Shandy Hall, instead of in London, and delivered by a mere midwife, instead of a real doctor, is ascribed to the peculiar marriage settlement between the elder Shandys. According to its terms, Mrs. Shandy would be allowed to bear her child in London, but if she ever falsely persuaded her husband to take her to the capital, she surrendered this right and would have to settle for a home delivery. Since she has done this once, Mr. Shandy feels justified in sparing himself the expense of taking his wife on a second trip to London, although he enjoys going there by himself.

On the night Tristram is born, his father and his Uncle Toby are comfortably debating some complicated and endless issue before a cheerful fire. When Susannah, the maid, informs them of the impending birth, they send for a midwife and for Dr. Slop, a local quack practitioner who had once written a cheap pamphlet on the history of childbirth. Dr. Slop's chief function at local births is to allow the midwife to do the delivering while he charges a handsome fee for drinking the father's best wine.

Before either doctor or midwife can arrive, Walter Shandy and his brother have some fine conversations about their past life. Uncle Toby was an honorable soldier in his day, but during the Siege of Namur in 1695 he received a wound in an embarrassing place and left the army to retire to the country. His loyal servant, Corporal Trim, joined him and suggested an ideal occupation for the retired military man. Near Shandy Hall is a patch of lawn where Trim constructed a miniature battlefield. There Uncle Toby reconstructs his campaigns by means of toy fortifications, trenches, and soldiers.

His delight in this pastime is not, however, shared by his more philosophical brother, who constantly interrupts his long-winded tales of vanished military glory with equally long-winded philosophical speculations. Walter Shandy has theories about everything, and they are often highly ingenious, but they are never even remotely applicable to the problem at hand, and usually get bogged down in oceans of arcane facts and meaningless, if charming, lore. One such philosophical divertissement, begun while the brothers await the arrival of the midwife and Dr. Slop, concerns itself with the reasons for Mrs. Shandy's preference for a female rather than a male attendant at her delivery. Uncle Toby suggests it might just be female modesty, but this idea is too simple to suit Walter Shandy who goes into a long and incomprehensible philosophical harangue about the complex nature of women.

The talk is interrupted by the arrival of Dr. Slop. While Corporal Trim diverts the Shandy brothers with the reading of a long sermon, Dr. Slop goes about his work with typical ineptitude. Mistaking the infant's hip for his head, the doctor flattens Tristram's nose with his forceps. Another portion of Tristram's anatomy will receive an insult on a later occasion when, as a boy, Tristram relieves himself out of a window only to have the window come crashing down on him. These episodes, Tristram feels, with some justice, have blighted his life.

Finally, the lad is born, while Mr. Shandy reads the company his translation from a Latin treatise on noses by a German scholar named Hafen Slawkenbergius. (Both author and work are Sterne's inventions.) When Mr. Shandy hears of the nearly disastrous episode with the forceps, he fears for his child's safety. Learning that the baby is unusually sickly, he sends immediately for the local parson, Mr. Yorick, to baptize the infant before any further mishaps occur.

Hastening to dress for the event, Mr. Shandy sends Susannah on ahead to tell Yorick that he wants his son baptized "Trismegistus" in honor of his favorite philosopher. But Susannah finds the odd name difficult to remember, and by the time she conveys the request to Mr. Yorick, she has transformed the name into Tristram, which also happens to be the clergyman's first name. This coincidence thrills Mr. Yorick. The child is baptized accordingly, and by the time Mr. Shandy arrives, fully clothed at last, he is too late to change matters, although he thinks Tristram is the worst name in the world and can only bring bad luck. The only hope for this disaster-hounded child now is a proper education.

Tristram's boyhood is marred by one sad event—the death at Westminster School of his older brother, Bobby. Different members of the family react differently to the untimely tragedy: Mr. Shandy philosophizes about the nature of death; in her grief, Susannah finds joy in the thought that she will inherit all her mistress' dresses when Mrs. Shandy goes into mourning; and Corporal Trim symbolically drops his hat as if he himself had died and delivers a magnificent funeral oration on the spot.

The Shandy family's next problems concern the sort of tutor, if any, to get for Tristram and the age at which the boy will be ready to wear long trousers. But these practical considerations take second place to the tale of Uncle Toby's pursuit by the Widow Wadman, a buxom lady who lives near Shandy Hall. The gentle Uncle Toby bears up well under the widow's efforts to win his heart.

One day, however, the Widow Wadman, more anxious than ever to be married, asks Uncle Toby an embarrassing question: precisely where was he wounded? He assures her he will allow her to touch the actual place where he received his famous wound; he then produces a map of Namur and puts her trembling finger on the appropriate portion of the battlefield.

Corporal Trim, less naïve if just as good-hearted as Uncle Toby, has to point out to him that it is the spot on his person, not on the battlefield, that the Widow Wadman has in mind. When he is finally made to realize the awful truth, Uncle Toby beats a hasty retreat from any idea of marriage.

At the end of the novel, Tristram's mother asks, reasonably enough, "Lord, what is all this story about?"

"A Cock and a Bull," replies Yorick, "and one of the best of its kind I ever heard."

Critical Opinion

It is one of the glories of the English novel that at its very inception in the mid-eighteenth century a work should have appeared which mocked all its newborn conventions; which told its minuscule story backwards and at great length with absurd digressions; and which was, in fact, that very modern phenomenon, an anti-novel with an anti-hero, with impotence as one of its major themes.

It is no accident, then, that *Tristram Shandy* should have

exerted a profound influence on the fiction of James Joyce, for both Sterne and Joyce are irrepressible jokers who delight in exploding the possibilities of prose fiction into something very different from the ordinary novel—perhaps best called the comic epic in prose. By means of caricature, digressions, absurdly inflated language to describe the most mundane things, puns, and a panoply of wildly eccentric characters, Sterne makes glorious fun in *Tristram Shandy* of such a sober predecessor as Samuel Richardson, and even of the more worldly Fielding.

Beneath the practical jokes played on his fellow novelists and on his readers, however, Sterne has laid a very solid substratum which gives *Tristram Shandy*, for all its seeming chaos, a strength of form and theme that has made it endure long after most practical jokes are forgotten. This substratum consists of the very human story, told in loving, even sentimental detail, of the two immortal Shandy brothers—Walter and Toby—and their occasionally philosophical, occasionally ridiculous responses to the world around them. Both men are henpecked; Walter Shandy by his wife, Uncle Toby by the voracious Widow Wadman. Both men see the world conspiring against their pleasure and ease. And both refuse to submit to the pressures of the world.

Uncle Toby's "hobbyhorse," by means of which he escapes from a drab world, is his military past, which he and Corporal Trim never tire of discussing. It is one of the infinite number of paradoxes in the book that so gentle and considerate a man as Uncle Toby should have been a menace on the battlefield.

Totally unsympathetic to the military, and riding a "hobbyhorse" of his own, is Walter Shandy who escapes from the burdens of existence through a super-subtle and highly abstract philosophy that nobody else can understand. Occasionally, like lunatics in an asylum, the two brothers cooperate in each other's manias, and the resulting fun is both hilarious and heart-warming.

Underlying the extraordinary technical virtuosity of the novel are a complex and very modern philosophy of time (it takes the hero four books in which to be born) and a sentimentality about the sacredness of life and individuality that give emotional coherence to an otherwise seemingly slapdash effort of the imagination.

The Author

Laurence Sterne's early years were spent in the military environment that he was later to describe with such affectionate amusement in the career of Uncle Toby in *Tristram Shandy*. He was born in 1713, son of an ensign in an infantry regiment, at Clonmel in Ireland. Until his father's death, when Sterne was eighteen, the family moved constantly from garrison to garrison, taking time out, when the boy was ten, for him to go to grammar school at Halifax.

When his father died, Sterne was left penniless. Through the good offices of a cousin he was enabled to go to Cambridge where he made friends with one John Hall (later Hall-Stevenson), who often played host to Sterne in his bizarre home known as Crazy Castle.

In 1736 Sterne took his BA and was ordained a clergyman. Two years later he became vicar of Sutton-in-the-Forest, where he met and married Miss Elizabeth Lumley in 1741. Sterne's philandering with other women became notorious, however. In 1758 his wife became insane. In addition to his amorous escapades in the years preceding the writing of *Tristram Shandy*, Sterne was also involved in the rather weird goings-on at Crazy Castle. Sterne and others formed a group calling themselves the Demoniacks, which indulged in practical jokes and experiments in mock diabolism, all considered terribly shocking for a clergyman.

It is therefore not surprising that in 1759 Sterne left his vicarage and began the writing of *Tristram Shandy*. The first two volumes, published in 1760, made an immediate sensation in London literary society. Never had a book so eccentric and idiosyncratic as this been presented in the form of a novel, although there were obvious precursors in Burton's *Anatomy of Melancholy* and Rabelais' *Gargantua and Pantagruel*.

Sterne went to London to capitalize on this success, and by 1761 four more volumes of *Tristram Shandy* had appeared. Its success was somewhat dampened by the denunciations from several pulpits of its alleged "immorality." Dr. Johnson and Goldsmith, among others, found the novel repugnant on both moral and literary grounds.

In 1760 Sterne became curate at Coxwold. Two years

later he voyaged to France because of ill health. His amorous experiences there led to the writing of *A Sentimental Journey Through France and Italy* (1768). In 1767 Sterne parted permanently from his wife. It was the year of the appearance of the ninth and final volume of *Tristram Shandy* and of the third and fourth volumes of Sterne's *Sermons*. In 1768, heartbroken at having to part also from his daughter, Sterne died of pleurisy in his London lodgings, insolvent and disillusioned.

*

By the Same Author

A Sentimental Journey Through France and Italy: Written in 1768 as Sterne was facing death, this charming travel story is a sort of epilogue to the unfinished *Tristram Shandy*. The narrator this time is the Reverend Mr. Yorick who is a barely disguised portrait of Sterne himself. Written partly as an answer to Smollett's highly unsentimental *Travels in France and Italy* (1766), Sterne's slim book recounts various adventures, usually with complaisant chambermaids and other damsels, in a series of self-contained episodes. Less eccentric and more elegant in style than *Tristram Shandy, A Sentimental Journey* was designed, in Sterne's words, "to teach us to love the world and our fellow creatures better than we do."

Humphry Clinker

by

TOBIAS SMOLLETT (1721–1771)

Main Characters

Matthew Bramble—A middle-aged hypochondriac, basically amiable except when his delicate sensibilities are offended.

Tabitha Bramble—His man-hunting sister, a unique combination of stupidity, primitive shrewdness, and religious hypocrisy.

Lydia Melford—Bramble's niece, a romantic girl just out of boarding school.

Jerry Melford—Bramble's nephew and ward, a recent Oxford graduate.

Winifred Jenkins—Tabitha's muddle-minded handmaid whose misspellings and malapropisms are often hilarious.

Humphry Clinker—A simple-minded but loyal servant.

Lieutenant Obadiah Lismahago—An ungainly middle-aged Scotch lieutenant who had once been scalped by Indians.

Mr. Dennison—A country gentleman and college friend of Bramble's.

George Dennison—His son who, disguised as an actor named George Wilson, is in loving pursuit of Lydia Melford.

47

The Story

Squire Matthew Bramble is a basically kind, if disillusioned, man, whose temper is sorely tried by persistent attacks of gout. Although he has little faith in the honesty or intelligence of doctors, he decides to take their advice and visit Bath, where the waters are reputed to have healing qualities. Accordingly, he sets forth for that elegant city accompanied by his starchy maiden sister, Miss Tabitha Bramble (who hopes to catch a fine husband at the resort), and by Winifred Jenkins, Tabitha's maid-servant.

Also accompanying the Brambles on their expedition are Mr. Bramble's niece and nephew, Lydia and Jerry Melford, pleasant young people and wards of the old gentleman. Mr. Bramble hopes that the journey will make Lydia forget the strolling actor whom she fell in love with at boarding school. Jerry Melford hopes someday to find and fight a duel with the actor who has wronged him. But so far the opportunity has not presented itself.

On the way to Bath, the actor, who goes under the name of George Wilson, presents himself, in the disguise of a Jewish eyeglass peddler, to Mr. Bramble. He manages to disclose his true identity briefly to the love-smitten Lydia, but they are interrupted and Lydia asks Winifred Jenkins to follow her swain and find out his true identity. Winifred does so, but she is so muddle-headed that she forgets his real name before she has a chance to divulge it to Lydia. All she remembers is that the actor told her that he was a true gentleman who hoped someday to court Lydia in a more appropriate style.

When the group finally arrives at Bath, Tabitha sets out to find a husband, while her brother Matthew samples the supposedly miraculous waters and finds them merely filthy and ill-smelling.

Bramble's disillusionment with the waters and Lydia's patent unhappiness over her lost actor cause the party to leave Bath for London. En route to London, however, their coach is upset, and there is a fracas between Tabitha Bramble and the squire's servant over Tabitha's lapdog, which has bitten the servant's hand. At his sister's imperious command,

Bramble must dismiss not only his servant but the coachman as well who, Tabitha feels, was responsible for upsetting the carriage.

To replace the clumsy postillion, Matthew Bramble hires a homely, ragged, shirtless youth named Humphry Clinker. Since Clinker's condition shocks Miss Bramble, Squire Bramble gives him a guinea to buy some respectable clothes before he can assume his new duties.

In London, Squire Bramble discovers that Clinker is preaching Methodist sermons. This he regards as unseemly behavior in a servant. Tabitha and her maid, however, are entranced by the lad's religiosity, and they beg Matthew Bramble to permit him to continue his sermonizing.

When Clinker is arrested and jailed on a false charge of being a brigand (the charge is made by a professional informer, himself a former convict), his preaching impresses even the jailer, and he makes converts of some of his fellow prisoners. Squire Bramble manages to find the man who had been robbed and whose evidence clears Clinker of any guilt. Clinker is released and continues his highly successful preaching.

After visiting the famous Vauxhall Gardens, the family leaves London to journey north to Scotland. At Scarborough, Bramble hires a bathing machine—a small cart rolled down the beach to the water in which he can change his clothes in privacy. The squire plunges nude into the surf which turns out to be so cold that he cries out in shock. Hearing his master's cries, Humphry assumes he is drowning and plunges into the ocean to rescue him. He drags the nude squire to the shore where Bramble is profoundly embarrassed by the crowd of spectators that has gathered.

In Durham, the party meets a gaunt, middle-aged Scots lieutenant named Obadiah Lismahago. A sad-faced, lantern-jawed man, he entertains the Brambles with tales of his exploits among the North American Indians. The ex-army officer captivates Tabitha Bramble, and even her normally misanthropic brother enjoys the company of the tough, proud Lieutenant Lismahago. Meanwhile, Tabitha's simple-minded maid, Winifred Jenkins, finds herself falling in love with the loyal, mild-mannered Humphry Clinker.

Eventually the party reaches Edinburgh, where they are

royally entertained everywhere. But the squire realizes that his niece has still not forgotten her actor suitor, George Wilson, when she faints in the street at the sight of someone who looks like the missing man. Setting back toward England again, the party is rejoined by Lieutenant Lismahago, who once more becomes the object of Tabitha's amorous attentions. He helps Jerry Melford rescue the women when the coach is upset in a river, but the squire is trapped in the coach and is in danger of drowning until Humphry, by heroic effort, manages to free him and bring him to safety.

While resting at the local inn until the coach can be repaired, Bramble meets an old college acquaintance named Dennison, now a prosperous local gentleman farmer. Dennison addresses Bramble as Lloyd, a name that the squire once adopted for legal reasons for a short time. When Humphry Clinker hears the name, he becomes very excited and shows the squire certain papers he has always carried with him proving that he is Bramble's illegitimate offspring. Bramble welcomes him as his son and clarifies the matter before the whole group. Poor Winifred is afraid that Humphry will put on airs and refuse to have anything to do with her, now that he has been established as the squire's son. But Humphry remains simple and unspoiled.

Squire Bramble is again surprised when he learns that the mysterious actor who has been pursuing his niece, Lydia, is in reality his old friend Dennison's son. The young man had run away from home to become a strolling player only because his father wanted to force him into a marriage he detested. Because he knew Squire Bramble only as Lloyd, Dennison had not realized that the Lydia his son had spoken of so glowingly was the niece of his old friend.

Now, with all complications cleared up, Lydia and George are at last united. A triple wedding follows, for Tabitha manages to get Lieutenant Lismahago to propose to her, and Humphry Clinker proposes to Winifred Jenkins.

With all his friends and relatives married off, there is nothing further for Squire Bramble to do but to return to the comfort of his own home, Brambleton Hall, to argue with his doctor and reflect on his past adventures.

Critical Opinion

Humphry Clinker, Smollett's last and greatest novel, combines two fictional traditions with grace and mastery. The first is that of the epistolary novel—a novel told in the form of letters to and from the various characters involved. This was the form of what some critics consider the first English novel, Samuel Richardson's *Pamela* (1741), and the form also of Richardson's masterpiece, *Clarissa* (1748).

The use of letters as a narrative device occasionally proves awkward, but it can, nevertheless, be invaluable as a means of characterization. We learn, for instance, much about the character of the relatively minor figure Winifred Jenkins from the hilarious malapropisms strewn throughout her letters written during the Brambles' journeys. Even more important, however, is the ease with which different and sometimes opposite points of view can be explored through letters. Thus Matthew Bramble's clear-sighted, level-headed view of the snobbery and affectation of Bath society is cleverly juxtaposed against his sister Tabitha's all-accepting, unthinking attitude toward the same society. The middle-aged responses of Matthew Bramble stand in sharp contrast to the fresh, naïve responses of his niece Lydia. Thus the theme of youth versus middle age is subtly explored.

The other tradition employed in *Humphry Clinker*, dating back to Cervantes' *Don Quixote* and to Le Sage's *Gil Blas*, is that of the picaresque novel. This genre, which Smollett employed in *Roderick Random* and *Peregrine Pickle* as well, consists of a loosely strung-together series of adventures, usually taking place on the road and in local inns. The hero may be a *picaro*, or rogue, as in *Roderick Random*, but not necessarily so. During the course of his travels the central character meets a variety of characters representing all levels of society, some of whom enrich the story with their own life histories. The meeting with the Quixote-like Lieutenant Lismahago, who tells the group of his adventures fighting Indians in North America, is a typical picaresque episode.

Humphry Clinker presents a refinement of the picaresque adventure tale, for although the group travel all over England and Scotland, their adventures are credible and are not as

loosely strung together as usual. Thus Lieutenant Lismahago does not appear only to disappear and be forgotten. He
becomes an intrinsic part of the plot and marries Tabitha. The
adventures are woven into a more coherent and tightly knit
plot than in Smollett's earlier novels, and offer us a splendid
view of life in eighteenth-century England.

The Author

Although with typical hard-headed irony *Tobias Smollett*
referred to himself as "a lousy Scot," he was born into a very
good family in Dumbartonshire, in 1721. He attended Glas-
gow University, where he studied medicine, and soon drifted
to London in search of fame and fortune. Like his hero,
Roderick Random, Smollett soon found himself working as a
ship's surgeon aboard the *Chichester*, a vessel that took part
in the 1741 attack on Cartagena in the West Indies, a cam-
paign challenging Spain's dominance in South America.

Smollett's stay in the navy provided him with invaluable
material for the novels he was later to write. The rough and
ready life on board ship supplied much of the material for
satirical treatment both in *Roderick Random* (1748) and
Peregrine Pickle (1751).

For a while Smollett settled in Jamaica, where he married.
In 1744 he returned to London with his wife to settle down
as a surgeon. In Chelsea he engaged in a great deal of hack
journalism and translating, writing an English version of *Don
Quixote* in 1755 and editing the *Critical Review* the next year.
An article in the *Critical Review* brought a libel suit against
Smollett for which he was briefly imprisoned in 1759.

Smollett's fresh attempt at periodical journalism, *The
Briton*, met with little success. Broken in health, he traveled
abroad to France and Italy in 1763, spending most of his
time at Nice. An inveterate traveler, he returned to England
two years later; and in 1766 he incorporated his continental
experiences into a typically humorous but ill-tempered travel
book, *Travels in France and Italy*, a work that so enraged
Laurence Sterne that he called its author "Smelfungus" and
tried to set the record straight with his own *A Sentimental
Journey Through France and Italy*.

Back in England, Smollett lived generally at the fashionable resort of Bath, scene of some of the finest escapades in what was to prove his last and greatest novel, *Humphry Clinker*. He left England on his last trip in 1768, living in Leghorn in northern Italy. Here he wrote *Humphry Clinker* which was published three months before his death in 1771.

Like Matthew Bramble, who is generally recognized as a somewhat idealized self-portrait, Smollett had few illusions about life. He was often quick-tempered but basically kind and of a philosophical cast of mind. His medical training made him hypersensitive to the wretched sanitary conditions of the England of his time. Much of his corrosive satire is directed at the physical rottenness and decay underlying the elegant pretensions of eighteenth-century society. Nevertheless, such is the vigor of Smollett's satire and the vividness with which he portrays the world around him that his books still hold and interest readers.

By the Same Author

Roderick Random: Smollett's first novel is a semi-autobiographical account of a young rogue determined to make his way in the world by fair means or foul. A vivid evocation of low life in the eighteenth century, *Roderick Random* traces its hero's course from a childhood marked by cruel treatment at school, through his apprenticeship to an apothecary, his nightmarish adventures as a sailor and later as a surgeon's mate, and his love affair with the beautiful Narcissa. Accompanied on many adventures by his faithful friend, Hugh Strap, he is finally able, after a stroke of good fortune, to marry Narcissa and settle on his ancestral estate in Scotland. Loosely strung together, the individual episodes of *Roderick Random* have a dash and vigor that were to become typical of Smollett. The work is most noteworthy for its scenes aboard various men-of-war, the first serious naval scenes in English fiction.

Peregrine Pickle: For his second novel Smollett chose an English rather than a Scottish hero, but in all essentials the formula is much as before. Pickle could be a blood-brother of Roderick Random. Secondary characters, however, are more richly realized than in the earlier book, the most memorable being a grand old eccentric, Commodore Hawser Trunnion, a man so in love with the sea that he has outfitted his country house to look like a battleship. Commodore Trunnion's riding gallantly off to his wedding to Pickle's Aunt Grizzle is one of the most richly comic scenes in eighteenth-century fiction.

Pride and Prejudice

by

JANE AUSTEN (1775–1817)

Main Characters

Mr. Bennet—The drily humorous father of five daughters, a gentleman with a modest estate in Hertfordshire.

Mrs. Bennet—His silly wife, a confirmed gossip and matchmaker.

Elizabeth Bennet—The Bennets' second daughter, witty and vivacious, and a keen observer of society.

Jane Bennet—Elizabeth's beautiful older sister, docile and gentle.

Charles Bingley—An amiable, wealthy young gentleman who rents Netherfield, an estate near the Bennets'.

Fitzwilliam Darcy—Bingley's immensely wealthy, proud friend.

George Wickham—A dashing, dissolute young officer.

Caroline Bingley—Bingley's younger sister, who wants to marry Darcy.

The Reverend William Collins—A remarkable combination of conceit and fatuity, whose patroness is the Lady Catherine de Bourgh.

Charlotte Lucas—A plain young woman, Elizabeth's friend.

Lady Catherine de Bourgh—Darcy's arrogant aunt, who exacts complete, unswerving subservience from everyone.

The Story

When Mr. Bingley, a rich young bachelor, rents Netherfield Park, one of the neighboring estates, excitement stirs in the Bennet family, which includes five marriageable daughters. The flighty Mrs. Bennet immediately begins plotting which daughter to marry off to the unsuspecting Bingley, but her long-suffering husband suggests that Mr. Bingley might want some choice in the matter. Before long Mr. Bennet is persuaded by his wife to pay a formal call at Netherfield Park.

The Bennet daughters meet Mr. Bingley at the Meryton Ball. Also in attendance is Mr. Bingley's aristocratic friend, Fitzwilliam Darcy, who turns up his nose at the vulgarity of Mrs. Bennet and snubs her daughters. Elizabeth Bennet, the liveliest and most intelligent of the Bennet girls, overhears the newcomer making condescending remarks about the local provincial society. When he refuses to be introduced to her, Elizabeth Bennet becomes instantly prejudiced against him, despite his good looks and great wealth.

More successful at the ball are the amiable Mr. Bingley and Elizabeth's lovely, good-natured older sister, Jane, to whom Elizabeth is closely attached. Soon after, Bingley and his sisters become friends with Jane Bennet, and the romance between Bingley and Jane seems to flourish. Eventually Darcy unbends a bit toward Elizabeth, and the two engage in ironic banter.

One day while visiting the Bingleys in the rain, Jane comes down with a bad cold and is compelled to stay at Netherfield Park. Elizabeth walks three miles through the mud to visit and nurse her sister. Her disheveled appearance when she arrives is meat for Caroline's gossip, but Mrs. Bennet sees the episode as a great opportunity to cement relations between Jane and Bingley. While Elizabeth is nursing her sister, Darcy pays her more attention, and Caroline's jealousy rages.

Bingley's sister Caroline is interested in Darcy herself. She tries unsuccessfully to poison his mind against Elizabeth. A more serious obstacle to the romance is Darcy's distaste for Elizabeth's vulgar, scheming mother and for the younger Bennet girls: flighty, officer-crazy Lydia and Kitty, and dull, plain Mary.

Meanwhile the Reverend William Collins, a cousin of the Bennets, who is in line to inherit Mr. Bennet's estate, comes to visit. The supremely conceited Mr. Collins talks constantly about his patroness, the rich and arrogant Lady Catherine de Bourgh, an aunt of Darcy's. Since she has urged him to marry (and her word is his command), he proposes to Elizabeth in a ludicrously pompous manner. She rejects him immediately, displeasing her mother but immensely satisfying her father who is fonder of her than of his other daughters.

Unabashed by his rejection, Mr. Collins proposes again, but finally concedes defeat. Immediately after, he becomes engaged to a friend of Elizabeth's, the placid, unimaginative Charlotte Lucas.

One of Darcy's acquaintances is a dashing young officer, George Wickham, who poisons Elizabeth's mind against Darcy by telling her that Darcy is a wicked, cold-hearted man who has refused to carry out the wishes of his father's will, cheating Wickham out of a legacy. Fearing to meet Darcy face to face, Wickham stays away from a ball which he knows Darcy will attend. Misinterpreting Wickham's motives, Elizabeth becomes increasingly suspicious of Darcy.

Shortly after the ball, Bingley and his sisters suddenly leave Netherfield for London. Elizabeth is convinced that Bingley's sisters are trying to keep him from marrying Jane whom they consider beneath him. Jane accepts the break with outward composure, but soon visits her aunt, Mrs. Gardiner, in London, hoping to see Bingley there by chance. When Elizabeth joins Jane in London, she learns that Bingley has never called on Jane. Elizabeth believes that Darcy has deliberately kept Jane's presence in the city from Bingley.

In March, Elizabeth visits her friend Charlotte Lucas, now married to Mr. Collins, in Kent. She realizes with a sudden wave of sympathy that Charlotte, a rather homely girl of advancing years, married Mr. Collins out of necessity, fearing a lonely and poverty-stricken life as an old maid.

While in Kent, Elizabeth again meets Darcy who is visiting his aunt, Lady Catherine de Bourgh. Again, Darcy is attracted to Elizabeth. He proposes to her in so haughty a manner that she rejects him and upbraids him for what she considers his mistreatment of her sister and of the unfortunate Wickham. Darcy listens to her accusations in silence. The next day he writes her a letter admitting that he has tried to keep

Bingley from Jane because he considers the Bennet family beneath his friend's attentions. He strongly denies having wronged Wickham, however, and demolishes the officer's claim that he has been cheated out of an inheritance. Furthermore, he informs Elizabeth, Wickham had been carrying on an intrigue with Darcy's sister Georgiana.

Despite its condescension toward the Bennet family, the letter begins to allay Elizabeth's prejudice against Darcy. Under no illusions about her mother and younger sisters, Elizabeth begins to see Darcy's inherently honest character. Her new impression of him is strengthened by the evidence of an old Darcy family retainer who has nothing but good to say of Darcy. Elizabeth again meets Darcy while she is traveling with her intelligent and fashionable uncle and aunt.

Earlier Lydia has insisted, over Elizabeth's objections, on going to Brighton, where Wickham's regiment is now stationed. Before long, Elizabeth is shocked by a letter from Jane informing her that Lydia has run off with Wickham. Elizabeth tells Darcy what has happened and returns home, full of anxiety for her irresponsible younger sister.

To add to Elizabeth's woes, she now feels that Darcy, whom she has begun to love, will have nothing to do with her, for Lydia's behavior confirms all he has ever said about the commonness of the Bennet family. To Elizabeth's surprise, however, Darcy, who is now deeply in love with her, has gone off secretly to London, where he finds Lydia and Wickham, pays Wickham's many debts, and gives him £1,000 with which to marry Lydia.

Mr. Bennet had also gone in search of the couple but has returned from London without success. When Lydia returns home, she tells Elizabeth that Darcy had attended her wedding. Elizabeth's suspicions of Darcy's part in the affair are confirmed by a letter from her aunt, Mrs. Gardiner, whom Darcy had sworn to secrecy.

After Lydia and Wickham leave, Mr. Bingley returns to Netherfield Park, accompanied by Darcy. Bingley soon becomes engaged to Jane, much to the Bennets' satisfaction.

The arrogant Lady Catherine de Bourgh descends on Longbourn, furious because of a rumor that Elizabeth and Darcy have become engaged. (Lady Catherine wished Darcy to marry her own daughter, a pathetically listless and unattractive girl.) Haughtily she demands that Elizabeth give up Darcy. Elizabeth, however, is more than adequate to the challenge. Without losing her temper, she coolly tells Lady Catherine to mind her own business. When Lady Catherine tells Darcy that Elizabeth refuses to give him up, Darcy begins to hope that Elizabeth returns his love.

Thus encouraged, Darcy again proposes to Elizabeth, this time with proper humility, and is happily accepted. Mrs. Bennet, having married off three of her daughters, is filled with joy. Mr. Bennet philosophically awaits any further suitors who may come along.

Critical Opinion

"I write about Love and Money; what else is there to write about?" Jane Austen once remarked. *Pride and Prejudice* is a perfect example of a social comedy based on the interaction of love and money: the class differences between Darcy, the Bingleys, and the Bennets shaping the love affairs between Bingley and Jane, Darcy and Elizabeth. Influencing these differences is the emergence of the middle class as a social force in England; hitherto a match between a man like Darcy and the bourgeois Elizabeth would have been a rarity. Even at the time in which the story takes place, many barriers must be hurdled before the couple are happily matched.

The conflict that gives the novel its title centers around Darcy's coldly aristocratic pride and Elizabeth's instinctive feminine prejudice against a man who has snubbed her at a dance. Before it is resolved, this conflict is the basis for the exquisite play of wit between hero and heroine, reminiscent of the ironic banter between Beatrice and Benedick in Shakespeare's *Much Ado About Nothing*.

Despite its surface wit and lightness, *Pride and Prejudice* is not without its underlying pathos. It stems largely from Jane's acceptance of Bingley's supposed indifference, and from the plight of Elizabeth's friend, Charlotte Lucas, a symbol of any girl on the brink of spinsterhood who makes the best of a bad bargain in choosing a spouse. Although Elizabeth deftly escapes from the attentions of Mr. Collins, we are haunted, after putting down the book, by the thought of the life to which the less fortunate Charlotte has consigned herself. The pathos of her condition is all the more moving for the tact with which Jane Austen treats it.

The uniqueness of Jane Austen's art lies in the way she plumbs such emotional depths within the extremely circumscribed life she knows. Her world consists of visits to country houses, teas, dances, and other minor social functions. She never describes any aspect of life she has not personally witnessed, and for that reason there is never a scene in any of her novels in which two men are together without a woman. Within these limitations, however, Jane Austen is matchless in her analysis of the pressures of society, especially on young people in love. Sympathizing equally with the needs of the individual and the often conflicting demands of social decorum, she finds comedy in the resulting stresses.

The Author

Jane Austen was born on December 16, 1775, in the small rural rectory of Steventon, in Hampshire, where her father was a clergyman. The family was large, consisting of six boys and another girl, Jane's beloved sister Cassandra. Although the Austens were an educated family, they were never particularly well off. Like most girls of her time, Jane was educated at home. Her matchless ear for dialogue first revealed itself when, at fourteen, she began writing little plays for home theatricals. As a girl, she also wrote satirical burlesques and nonsense stories intended solely to give her family pleasure. These were filled with references to friends and neighbors which only the Austens could understand.

The family seems to have been a happy one; and, more important for the future novelist, the Austens were, in Jane's words, "great novel-readers and not ashamed of being so."

When her father retired in 1801, the Austens moved to the then fashionable seaside resort of Bath where Jane's social perspective broadened. Five years before the move, however, Jane had written the first draft of *Pride and Prejudice,* then entitled *First Impressions.* Undiscouraged by her failure to get it published, she continued with her writing, producing in 1797 first drafts of what were later to be *Sense and Sensibility* and *Northanger Abbey.*

The years spent in Bath were more productive of observations of society to be used in later books than of novels themselves. When Mr. Austen died, the family moved to Southampton where they stayed from 1806 to 1809, but Jane seems to have found the town uncongenial. It was only when the Austens moved to Chawton, a town as small as Steventon, that Jane felt ready to continue with her writing. She began *Mansfield Park,* her most ambitious novel, in 1811; *Emma* in 1814, and what was to prove her last novel, the unusually romantic *Persuasion,* in 1815.

Thus, Jane Austen's six major novels fall into two groups separated by about a decade of silence. Discouraged by the neglect of publishers and public, Jane Austen gave her last novels a graver and more serious tone than the first three. Indeed, *Mansfield Park* and *Persuasion* have little of the ebullience and high spirits of her earlier books.

Jane Austen's outward life was singularly free of conflict. Even the Napoleonic Wars, which raged through Europe during her lifetime, seem to have had little effect on her although two of her brothers were in the Royal Navy. She died on July 18, 1817, generally unrecognized for the perceptive novelist she was.

By the Same Author

Sense and Sensibility: This early novel announces most of the major themes with which Jane Austen was to be concerned during her writing life. It describes in loving detail two sisters of opposite character: Elinor, the paragon of good common sense, and Marianne, a girl filled with romantic "sensibility," or hypersensitivity. Both experience unhappy love affairs: Elinor with Edward Ferrars, who is in the clutches of Lucy Steele and is disinherited by his mother; and Marianne with a dashing scoundrel, John Willoughby. Ferrars ultimately comes back to Elinor, while Marianne, like Lydia in *Pride and Prejudice,* nearly ruins her reputation by following her caddish lover to London. She ultimately abandons her romantic notions and marries an upright, if less dashing, middle-aged man.

Emma: Emma is a richly comic exploration of class distinctions and courtship customs in a small English village. Emma Woodhouse, a vigorous, restless girl, takes under her wing the rather commonplace Harriet Smith, hoping to educate her in the ways of the world and enable her to attract the local rector as a mate. Emma's well-intentioned interference in her friends' affairs, however, nearly goes awry. But when Harriet mistakenly imagines that John Knightly is in love with her, Emma, who had always regarded Mr. Knightly as a friend, realizes that she is in love with him herself. The comedy of errors comes to a close when Knightly proposes to Emma and Harriet marries a farmer. *Emma* is a richer and more complex novel than *Pride and Prejudice,* but has less of the earlier novel's vivacity.

The Nineteenth Century

Ivanhoe

by

SIR WALTER SCOTT (1771–1832)

Main Characters

Cedric the Saxon—Lord of Rotherwood Grange, bitterly opposed to the Normans.
Rowena—Cedric's lovely niece and ward.
Athelstane of Coningsburgh—Rowena's nobly born Saxon fiancé.
Wilfred of Ivanhoe—Cedric's son, disinherited for following the Norman King, Richard the Lion Hearted, on the Crusades.
Sir Brian de Bois-Guilbert—The haughty commander of the Norman Order of Knights Templar.
Reginald Front de Boeuf—A tyrannical Norman knight.
Lucas de Beaumanoir—Grand master of the Knights Templar.
Isaac of York—A persecuted Jewish moneylender.

Rebecca—Isaac's beautiful, strong-willed daughter.

King Richard I—Called Richard the Lion Hearted for his valor during the Crusades, absent from England for many years.

Prince John—Richard's evil, ambitious brother, Regent of England in Richard's absence.

Gurth—An honest Saxon swineherd.

Wamba—Gurth's companion, a court jester.

The Story

Gurth, the swineherd, and Wamba, the court jester, are talking late one evening in the forest when Prior Aymer of Jorvaux and the arrogant Sir Brian de Bois-Guilbert, commander of the Order of Knights Templar, who are on their way with their retinue to the royal tournament at Ashby de la Zouche, ask for directions to Rotherwood, the home of Cedric the Saxon, where they hope to get shelter for the night. The Saxon serfs deliberately mislead the hated Normans, but a pilgrim returning from the Crusades, also headed for Rotherwood, guides them there. Cedric and his retainers are already seated at the great wooden table when the Normans arrive.

Although Cedric has not yet reconciled himself to the Norman conquest of England, he obeys the laws of hospitality and offers food and shelter to the visitors. When Cedric's lovely niece and ward, the lady Rowena, enters, Brian de Bois-Guilbert stares lustfully at her. Rowena, descended from the Saxon royal family and engaged to be married to Athelstane of Coningsburgh, a descendant of King Alfred, veils her face.

A dispute arises at the table over who served the Crusade most worthily—Norman or Saxon. When Bois-Guilbert boasts of his exploits, he is challenged by the pilgrim, who is actually Ivanhoe, son of Cedric, disinherited for following the Norman King Richard. Even his father is unaware that Ivanhoe has secretly returned to England and is sitting at his table. Bois-Guilbert admits that Ivanhoe is a valorous fighter but boasts that he would not fear meeting him again in hand-to-hand combat.

Also seeking shelter that night at Rotherwood is Isaac of York, an old Jewish moneylender. Isaac is warned by Ivanhoe, who has overheard a whispered conversation between Bois-Guilbert and his retainers, that the Knight Templar is after his moneybag. Early the next morning, Ivanhoe helps the Jew slip out of the house. In gratitude, Isaac equips Ivanhoe with horse and armor for the coming tournament at Ashby de la Zouche.

The tournament is attended by Prince John, Richard the Lion Hearted's evil brother, who is trying to usurp the throne while Richard is away at the Crusades. Prince John announces to the colorful throng that the winner of the joust will be allowed to name the Queen of Love and Beauty, and the passage of arms begins.

First, five Normans led by Bois-Guilbert take on all challengers, and are successful. Then a new champion enters, whose armor displays the motto, "Desdichado," or disinherited. It is, of course, Ivanhoe in still another disguise, and he challenges and defeats Bois-Guilbert and the other Norman knights. This wins him the privilege of naming the Queen of Love and Beauty who will preside over the next day's tourneys. He names Rowena, and then rides off before he can be properly acclaimed by the crowd.

The next day's combat is a free-for-all between two groups of fifty knights each, one led by Ivanhoe, the disinherited knight, and the other by Bois-Guilbert. Ivanhoe, set upon by three combatants, is hard pressed until a knight in black armor, called the Black Sluggard by the crowd because he had previously refrained from combat, comes to Ivanhoe's aid. Together they rout their opponents, even Bois-Guilbert, whose horse has been wounded.

When Ivanhoe removes his helmet to receive the prize from Rowena, she cries out in recognition. As he kisses Rowena's hand, he faints from the wounds he has received in combat. Rebecca, Isaac of York's beautiful black-haired daughter, suggests that they bring Ivanhoe home to nurse him back to health. The Black Knight rides away secretly, but Isaac, Rebecca, and Ivanhoe are joined by Athelstane and Cedric the Saxon, still unaware of his son's identity.

The party is soon waylaid, however, by Bois-Guilbert and his fellow knights, Maurice de Bracy and Reginald Front de Boeuf, and are carried off to Front de Boeuf's castle, Torquilstone. De Bracy covets Rowena because, even though she is a Saxon, she is of royal blood. Bois-Guilbert wants the lovely Rebecca, and Front de Boeuf hopes to ransom the party to get money from Isaac and his moneylender friends. Separating father from daughter, Bois-Guilbert tries to persuade Rebecca to become a Christian so they can marry. She scornfully rejects him.

Unknown to the Norman captors, Gurth, the swineherd, has rallied a group of Saxon yeomen and outlaws, including Robin Hood and his band. Led by the Black Knight, who is really Richard the Lion Hearted in disguise, the Saxons storm Torquilstone and set it on fire. The Black Knight succeeds in rescuing Ivanhoe and Rowena, but Bois-Guilbert abducts Rebecca, and Isaac prepares to ransom his daughter. In fighting, Athelstane tries to kill Bois-Guilbert with a mace, but is himself felled by a sword blow and appears to be dead. De Bracy, who escapes the flames, hastens to tell Prince John that the Black Knight is his brother, Richard Plantagenet, who knows of John's usurpation of the throne and has returned secretly to England to wrest it back from him. John determines to put Richard in prison.

Isaac goes to Lucas de Beaumanoir, the grand master of the Knights Templar, to beg that Rebecca be returned to him. Bois-Guilbert, to save his pride, claims that Rebecca is a witch who put a spell on him which he could not resist. Lucas condemns the girl to be burned at the stake, but when Rebecca demands a champion to defend her, as is the custom, de Beaumanoir agrees.

Tied to the stake, Rebecca awaits her champion. After the heralds summon him three times, Ivanhoe rides in, announcing himself as Rebecca's defender. Bois-Guilbert, champion for the Knights of Templar, at first declines to fight with the wounded Ivanhoe, but Ivanhoe insists, and the two lock in mortal combat. Following a desperate struggle, during which Ivanhoe is unhorsed, Bois-Guilbert falls dead of a stroke. Rebecca is released. She and her father will journey to Spain, hoping there to find refuge from persecution.

Meanwhile, grateful for his rescue from the burning Torquilstone, Cedric has invited the Black Knight to Rotherwood. Richard replies that he will accept but "will ask such a boon as will put even thy generosity to the test." Then, at a funeral banquet for the fallen Athelstane, the Black Knight reveals himself to Cedric as King Richard and asks his boon: that Cedric forgive Ivanhoe. Ivanhoe kneels to his father, and the old man relents. He knows that Ivanhoe hopes to marry Rowena but decrees that a two-year period of mourning for her fiancé, Athelstane, must elapse before he can claim her hand.

Just then, to everyone's surprise, Athelstane himself enters, pale and ghostly. He tells them that he was only stunned by the flat of Bois-Guilbert's sword, and recovered his senses when he was lying in an open coffin in a chapel. Admitting that Rowena loves Ivanhoe more than him, he offers her to the knight.

The Black Knight comes to the Knights Templar and accuses them of plotting against the lawful sovereign of England. He proclaims himself king again, and the royal flag flies once more over the Temple. Robin Hood and his outlaws affirm their loyalty to Richard who attends the wedding of Ivanhoe and Rowena.

Both Norman and Saxon nobles attend the ceremony. Now that Richard has been restored to his throne and his friend Ivanhoe to his rightful heritage, there is hope that peace will once again reign in divided England.

Critical Opinion

Ivanhoe was written during a brief respite from the ill health that plagued Scott in 1819. He decided to change the background if not the formula of his fiction and venture for the first time away from purely Scottish material. The result, although the most popular of Scott's novels, is not among his best.

For his departure from Scotland as a locale, Scott picked two favorites of English history and legend: King Richard the Lion Hearted and Robin Hood, weaving them into a complicated tale of chivalric honor and rivalry. Even bitter enemies like Ivanhoe and Brian de Bois-Guilbert address one another in high-flown chivalric rhetoric and fight strictly according to the laws of feudal combat. Athelstane the Saxon nobly gives Rowena over to his rival, Ivanhoe, when he sees she is really in love with him. Cedric the Saxon, for all his hatred of Normans, extends a courteous welcome to Bois-Guilbert in his home. All actions in *Ivanhoe* spring from a feudal code of honor which was to Scott the most important thing in life and which he punctiliously obeyed centuries after the death of feudalism.

The faults of *Ivanhoe* are legion. The plot is overcomplicated, depending too heavily on coincidence to please sophisticated modern tastes. The characters are without exception one dimensional, and they speak in a stilted, lofty, unnatural rhetoric that often makes for tedious reading. Too, Scott cannot resist frequent pedantic asides on twelfth-century English customs.

How then has the book retained its popularity? The answer is that Scott is a master of the conventions of adventure fiction and employs all its devices to great effect in *Ivanhoe*. Suspense is sustained by not one but *two* heroes in disguise (Ivanhoe and Richard I). The many scenes of high action and adventure (the prolonged tournament at Ashby, the storming of Torquilstone, and the rescuing of Rebecca from the stake) go far to redeem the novel from its pretentious style.

Above all, Scott had sufficient humanity to make even characters outside the aristocracy—Isaac and Rebecca, Gurth and Wamba—vivid and alive.

The Author

Sir Walter Scott was born in Edinburgh on August 15, 1771. He attended Edinburgh High School and University, and was called to the bar in 1792. His first great love, however, was folklore and ballads. In 1802–1803 he published a three-volume collection of *Minstrelsy of the Scottish Border*. Scott made his debut with romantic poetry strongly colored by legend and folk strains. The first of these poems, *The Lay of the Last Minstrel* (1805), was an immediate success, which Scott followed with *Marmion* (1808) and *The Lady of the Lake* (1810).

After the appearance of Byron's *Childe Harold* in 1812, which was a serious new rival in romantic narrative verse, Scott turned his attention to the novel, beginning his prolific career with *Waverley* in 1814. Because the fiction of the time was held in such low esteem, Scott allowed his novels to appear anonymously. He did not acknowledge their authorship until 1827, seven years after he was made a baronet.

Scott's passion for Scottish folklore formed the basis for his first novels, all of which deal with historic events from the Scottish past about which Scott made himself an authority. *Waverley* was followed by *Guy Mannering* (1815), *Old Mortality* (1816), and *The Heart of Midlothian* (1818), considered by most critics the finest of the Waverley novels.

It was not until *Ivanhoe*, in 1819, that Scott turned to other than Scottish material for his fiction; but despite the popular success of that novel, and of *Quentin Durward* (1823), which has a French historical background, it is the Waverley or Scottish novels that are considered his finest artistic accomplishments.

In 1812, Scott's love of the antique and his aristocratic pride inspired him to buy some farmland on the Tweed River and build Abbotsford, a great gothic castle. An ill-advised publishing venture and the general economic depression in England plunged Scott into financial disaster. In 1826, he found himself £130,000 in debt.

A less honorable man might have evaded his creditors, but Scott met with them and worked out a plan for repayment that ultimately hastened his death. He had always been a facile writer, but writing now at a superhuman pace (in two years he was able to pay back £40,000), Scott exhausted himself. The pace told not only on his constitution but on the quality of his work, for the later novels are slapdash and lack the credibility and high romantic spirit of the earlier ones. Nevertheless they remained popular with readers, and Scott managed to pay all his creditors. Traveling to Italy to regain his health, Scott was soon brought back to Abbotsford where he died September 21, 1832.

By the Same Author

Quentin Durward: Like *Ivanhoe*, *Quentin Durward* is not one of the Waverley novels, although its hero is a young Scot come to France in the era of Louis XI to make his fortune. He gets embroiled in treacherous court politics and succeeds in rescuing the beautiful Countess Isabelle de Croye from an attempted kidnapping by the villainous William de la Marck. After a series of harrowing adventures involving plots and counterplots, Quentin and Isabelle finally marry.

The Heart of Midlothian: Generally considered the finest of the Waverley novels, *The Heart of Midlothian,* based on a real event, is set in the city jail of Edinburgh where Effie Deans is imprisoned on charges of murdering her illegitimate infant. Although her half sister, Jeanie, is too honorable to tell the white lie that will rescue Effie, she goes to no end of trouble to win an acquittal for her. Free from the over-plotting and confusing number of characters that slow down most of Scott's novels, *The Heart of Midlothian* is unique in its psychological study of Jeanie Deans. A woman torn between love for her sister and a rigid sense of honor, she is probably the finest single character in Scott's fiction.

The Last Days of Pompeii

by

EDWARD BULWER-LYTTON (1805–1873)

Main Characters

Glaucus—A rich young Athenian living in Pompeii.
Clodius—Foppish and selfish. A Roman friend of Glaucus, he lives for pleasure and gambling.
Arbaces—A mysterious, evil Egyptian of great wealth, famous in Pompeii for his occult powers.
Ione—Arbaces' beautiful Neapolitan ward.
Apaecides—Ione's troubled brother, brought up in the Egyptian priesthood, but a skeptic about the cult of Isis.
Olinthus—A zealous convert to the new religion of Christianity.
Nydia—A blind young slave girl who sings and sells flowers for a living.
Diomed—One of the vulgar rich of Pompeii, who gives lavish banquets to achieve status with the aristocrats.
Julia—Diomed's pretty, scheming daughter.

The Story

In A.D. 79 the walled city of Pompeii on the Bay of Naples is a luxurious resort for the aristocrats of the Roman Empire. Two of these spoiled young men are Glaucus, an Athenian by birth, and his friend Clodius, a Roman dandy and gambler.

71

Strolling one day toward the fashionable baths, Glaucus tells Clodius of a hauntingly beautiful Greek girl he saw some months before in the Temple of Minerva in Naples, but whom he has since been unable to find.

As they chat lightly about love, the pair pass Nydia, a blind but appealing flower seller. She comes from Thessaly, a region of Greece noted for its witchcraft. Glaucus takes a friendly interest in her.

The young men also meet Arbaces, the powerful priest of Isis, whose vast wealth and magic powers are known and feared by all Pompeii. Unknown to Glaucus, Arbaces is the guardian of Ione, the girl Glaucus saw in the temple, and of her brother, Apaecides, whom Arbaces is training for the Egyptian priesthood with the help of the mercenary priest Calenus.

Glaucus soon meets Ione again at a fashionable party and declares his love, unaware that Arbaces desires the girl for himself. At the same time, Nydia, the slave of the gross and unfeeling innkeeper Burbo, finds herself falling in love with Glaucus who is far above her station in life.

One day Glaucus and Clodius stop at Burbo's wine shop in order to look over the gladiators drinking there. Clodius, an inveterate gambler, wishes to check on the prowess and stamina of the men he will bet on in the gladiatorial combats. One of the few gladiators not yet completely bestialized is Lydon, a youth who hopes to earn enough in combat to buy the freedom of his slave father, Medon. Clodius, however, decides to bet against him because he is young and inexperienced.

While the young men are in the tavern, they hear the cries of Nydia, who is being mercilessly beaten by Burbo's wife. Glaucus buys the slave girl on the spot as a gift for his beloved Ione, but his act of mercy only intensifies Nydia's love for him. Unaware of her love, Glaucus sends the girl to Ione with a letter declaring his passion for Ione and pleading with her not to listen to Arbaces' slanders against him.

Ione returns his love, but is enticed by Arbaces into his palace where with a show of magic the priest tries to force her to marry him. Warned by Nydia, Glaucus and Apaecides rush into the palace just in time to save Ione from rape. Glaucus engages Arbaces in combat. The priest is about to kill Glaucus when an earthquake shakes the palace to its foundations and topples a statue of Isis on Arbaces' head. Assuming that Arbaces is dead, the two young men escape with Ione.

After the earthquake, the people of Pompeii resume their normal lives, heedless of the great volcano, Mount Vesuvius, looming over them. Apaecides is now disillusioned with his guardian and loathes the rites of Isis in which he is being instructed by Calenus. He falls under the influence of the teaching of Olinthus, the humble, eloquent Nazarene who is trying to convert Pompeii to the new religion of Christianity before all its people are engulfed by their sins. Gradually Apaecides becomes converted, while the love of Glaucus and Ione matures.

But Arbaces, who was not killed in the earthquake, but merely stunned, vows revenge on his lovely ward and the Athenian who has stolen her from him. His opportunity comes at a party being given for eighteen select guests by a wealthy parvenu, Diomed. Diomed's daughter Julia, who is in love with Glaucus, comes to the Egyptian's palace a few days before the banquet for a love philter that will win Glaucus away from Ione.

Arbaces takes her to a witch's hovel at the foot of Vesuvius, where he procures a magic draught to drive Glaucus insane. Julia plans to give it to him at her father's dinner, but Nydia hears of the potion and, hoping it will make Glaucus love her, steals it from Julia and gives it to Glaucus when he returns home from the party.

The potion drives Glaucus mad, and he rushes from his house to a cemetery where by chance Arbaces and Apaecides are quarreling over the youth's conversion from Isis to Christianity. Arbaces kills Apaecides and puts the blame on Glaucus who, in his madness, cannot defend himself.

Arbaces then stirs up the mob against the Athenian, claiming he killed Apaecides when the young priest tried to intervene in his affairs with Ione. Glaucus is arrested with Olinthus, the Christian zealot who has tried to defend him. A lion and a tiger have just been brought to Pompeii, and the crowd looks forward avidly to seeing the two prisoners fed to the beasts.

After Apaecides' funeral, Ione tries to save her lover, convinced he is innocent. But Arbaces imprisons her in his palace, along with Calenus, who was an eyewitness to the actual killing. When Calenus tries to blackmail the Egyptian, Arbaces flings him into a dungeon to starve to death.

Nydia, who knows the guilty secrets of his dungeons, is imprisoned, but she bribes her guard to take a letter to Sallust, a powerful friend of Glaucus, informing him of the truth. Sallust is in a drunken stupor when the letter arrives and cannot read it till the morning when the prisoners are to be put to death in the arena.

On the last day of Pompeii a throng has gathered to watch the gladiatorial combats. The bloodthirsty mob is indifferent to the preliminaries, for the main event of the day is to be the slaughter of Glaucus by the lion and Olinthus by the tiger. Young Lydon, outmatched, dies horribly, and Clodius wins his bet while the Christian father mourns for his son.

After this preliminary bloodshed, the lion, who has been starved for days, is let loose in the arena. Glaucus is given only a knife to defend himself. Miraculously, the lion refuses to attack him, slinking back to its cage.

At this moment news comes from Sallust, who has finally read Nydia's letter, that Glaucus is innocent and the murderer of Apaecides is Arbaces. The mob, furious at being cheated out of a spectacle, demands that the Egyptian take Glaucus' place in the arena. Just as this is about to happen, however, all Pompeii is overwhelmed by the great eruption of Vesuvius.

As smoke and ashes billow down upon them, thousands flee the arena, desperately seeking safety in the streets which are rapidly filling with molten lava. The weak are crushed in the panic. Calenus, set free by Nydia in order to be a witness against Arbaces, is killed by the sulfurous smoke as he tries to loot Arbaces' palace. Julia, Diomed, and a group of his friends take shelter in his capacious wine cellar, but to no avail.

Because she is accustomed to finding her way in the dark, the blind Nydia is able to lead Glaucus and Ione through the pitch-black streets of Pompeii toward the waterfront. Eventually they reach a small boat and escape to safety while Arbaces, in hot pursuit, is killed by a second, even greater earthquake.

By nightfall the eruption begins to subside. Asleep in their boat, Glaucus and Ione do not notice that Nydia, despairing

of ever winning the handsome Athenian, has jumped overboard into the sea.

Ten years after the mighty eruption that destroyed the
sinful, pleasure-loving city, Glaucus and Ione, now married
and living in Athens, have become converts to Christianity
which they feel offers them a better life than the one they
knew in Pompeii.

Critical Opinion

While passing through Milan on his trip to Italy, Bulwer-
Lytton saw a painting of the destruction of Pompeii that
inspired him, he said, to reconstruct that fabled city at the
height of its glory as a pleasure resort for decadent Romans.
The basic drama of his book was to be the contrast between
the gay, heedless lives of the Pompeians and their hideous
deaths in the eruption of Vesuvius. Another drama would
emerge from the pagan sensuality of the public baths and the
pagan cruelty of the arena contrasted with the simple, lofty
devoutness of the persecuted early Christians.

Unfortunately, the grand moral drama of Good versus
Evil in Bulwer-Lytton's mind never comes fully to life in the
novel. One reason for this is that his research into the customs
of the period was voluminous, and he had no intention of
letting any stray fact go unnoticed. The result is that the
action often bogs down in a series of pedantic, undramatic
descriptions of daily life in Pompeii. As Disraeli noted, while
Bulwer-Lytton had literary flair, he was no thinker. The
essential meaning of the destruction of a great hedonistic city
eludes him.

Nevertheless, as an entertaining, if turgidly written, historical romance perfectly suited for the movies, The Last Days of
Pompeii has its virtues. When it is not clogged with extra-
neous research, its plot moves with great rapidity and high
suspense. Bulwer-Lytton is a master of plotting, and for
chapters at a time, notably when the "good guys" are menaced
in the palace of Arbaces, he keeps his reader's eyes glued
to the page; no small accomplishment in view of the clumsiness
of the prose style, the lofty unreality of the dialogue, and the
thinness of the characters. Of these, perhaps only Nydia, an
oversentimentalized study in the pathos of hopeless love, and

Arbaces himself, a stock villain with a certain grandeur, endure in the reader's mind. Minor characters, too, such as the vulgar Diomed, the foppish Clodius, and the brutal innkeeper, Burbo, emerge with some liveliness. But as so often happens in historical romances—even those of Scott— the hero and heroine are singularly lacking in individuality or human interest.

The Last Days of Pompeii is not to be compared with such serious historical novels as *The Heart of Midlothian*, George Eliot's *Romola*, or Pater's *Marius the Epicurean*. Rather, it manages to hold its place with such popular romances as *Quo Vadis?* and *Ben Hur*. Alone among Bulwer-Lytton's many novels, it is still read today.

The Author

Parliamentarian and cabinet minister, prolific author and one of the most notable dandies and poseurs of his day, *Edward Bulwer-Lytton* was born in London on May 25, 1805. He was the son of a famous general, Earle Bulwer, and heir, on his mother's side, of one of the great English aristocratic families. Considered a child prodigy, he was educated at Trinity College, Cambridge, where he won the chancellor's medal for a prize poem. He then went into Parliament as Member for St. Ives and later for Lincoln.

Fond of romantic attitudinizing, young Bulwer-Lytton enjoyed reading, boating, and carrying on hopeless love affairs, including one with Lady Caroline Lamb, Byron's former mistress. He wrote prodigiously as a youth, mostly in imitation of Byron and Scott, but few of his early poems or plays have survived. When he married against his mother's wishes, however, his allowance was cut off and he was forced to write popular novels to support his and his wife's extravagant tastes.

His early novels, *Falkland* (1827) and *Pelham* (1828), are memorable largely for the light they shed on the life and habits of an aristocratic dandy in the early nineteenth century. Following in the footsteps of the famous Beau Brummell, Bulwer-Lytton made a high art of dress—impressing even the young Dickens with the variety and splendor of his waistcoats.

He followed his early successes with two lurid tales of crime, *Paul Clifford* (1830) and *Eugene Aram* (1832). During a trip to Italy, inspired, no doubt, by the great success of Scott, he turned his hand to writing historical romances, of which *The Last Days of Pompeii* (1834) and *Rienzi* (1835) are the best known.

In 1838 he was made a baronet and, on inheriting the ancestral estate of Knebworth from his mother, took on the name of Lytton in 1843. In 1858 Bulwer-Lytton served as secretary for the colonies; in 1866 he was elevated to the peerage as Baron Lytton of Knebworth.

His familiarity with the highest political and social circles in England enabled him to feed his vast audience the details of high life they craved. A rival of the great Disraeli, who was also a novelist and a dandy, he drew from the prime minister the opinion that "his mind is full of literature but no great power of thought"—a verdict that seems even more just today than when it was made.

Bulwer-Lytton was a man of many talents, none very profound, and an extremely hard worker whose fingers were always on the popular pulse. He died on January 18, 1873, and was buried in Westminster Abbey.

The Pickwick Papers

by

CHARLES DICKENS (1812–1870)

Main Characters

Samuel Pickwick, Esquire—A genial, innocent, middle-aged man with an inquiring mind and a love of adventure.

Nathaniel Winkle—The most timid member of the Pickwick Club.

Tracy Tupman—The fat, amorous member of the Pickwick Club.

Augustus Snodgrass—The poetic member of the Pickwick Club.

Alfred Jingle—A strolling actor and confidence man who talks nonstop in short, telegraphic sentences.

Mr. Wardle—The stout and jovial owner of the Manor Farm near Rochester.

Rachael Wardle—Mr. Wardle's elderly spinster sister.

Emily Wardle—Mr. Wardle's daughter.

Arabella Allen—The love of Mr. Winkle's life though intended by her brother to marry a doctor.

Mrs. Bardell—Mr. Pickwick's London landlady who fancies he is in love with her.

Sam Weller—The resourceful and inimitable cockney, Mr. Pickwick's devoted servant.

Mr. Serjeant Buzfuz—Mrs. Bardell's unscrupulous attorney in her breach of promise suit.

Mr. Bob Sawyer—The lively young medical student rejected by Arabella Allen.

The Story

Mr. Samuel Pickwick, the genial, bespectacled founder and permanent chairman of the Pickwick Club, sets forth on May 13, 1827, for a stagecoach tour of the countryside accompanied by the three members of his Club, Mr. Nathaniel Winkle, Mr. Augustus Snodgrass, and Mr. Tracy Tupman. The members of the club propose to travel to remote parts of England and report on the local customs. While achieving this quasi-scientific purpose, they intend to have a good time together.

No sooner have they set out on their adventures than they are rescued from a gang of bullies by the suave, ingenious Mr. Alfred Jingle who regales them on the road to Rochester with a variety of colorful stories about his many careers. When they arrive at Rochester, after consuming barrels of oysters en route, they discover that a formal ball is planned at the inn for that evening. Mr. Jingle complains that he has no evening clothes because his luggage has been lost, and he intimates to Mr. Tupman that it would be a pity if he missed the ball because he could introduce the fat, shy Tupman to all the pretty girls there.

Mr. Tupman accordingly "borrows" Mr. Winkle's formal suit for Alfred Jingle, who proceeds to offend Dr. Slammer at the party by flirting with the middle-aged lady the choleric doctor has been courting.

The next morning Dr. Slammer's servant calls on Mr. Winkle to challenge him to a duel. Poor Mr. Winkle was too drunk the night before to remember giving offense. Not realizing that the culprit was Mr. Jingle wearing his clothes, the timorous Pickwickian arrives, shaking with fear, at the field of honor. His second is Mr. Snodgrass, the poet of the Pickwick Club. When Dr. Slammer arrives, he immediately sees that Mr. Winkle is the wrong man, and the affair is settled amicably. No one knows where Mr. Jingle is.

That afternoon the Pickwickians are invited to visit Manor Farm where the stout, jovial Mr. Wardle lives with his two daughters and his plump spinster sister, Rachael. The next afternoon, after a rather harrowing ride, the disheveled

Pickwickians arrive at the farm, some ten miles from their inn.

Mr. Tupman falls in love with the elder Miss Wardle and Mr. Winkle falls in love with the beautiful Arabella Allen. To prove his valor Mr. Winkle goes hunting although he is totally inexperienced with guns, and manages only to shoot Mr. Tupman accidentally in the arm.

During a cricket match, Mr. Pickwick meets Jingle again. Mr. Wardle invites the actor and mountebank to Manor Farm. Ever the opportunist, Jingle decides that Miss Wardle must be a rich heiress, poisons her mind against Mr. Tupman, and elopes with her. Mr. Wardle and Mr. Pickwick set off in hot pursuit and apprehend the pair in London, thanks to the intelligence of Sam Weller, a cockney servant in the White Hart Inn. Jingle is bought off for a tidy sum, and poor Miss Wardle is brought back in tears to Manor Farm.

Impressed by the wit of Sam Weller, the son of a London coachman, Mr. Pickwick hires him for his manservant, and they return to his lodgings in Gosling Street, where the widowed landlady, Mrs. Bardell, conceives the strange notion that Mr. Pickwick is in love with her and is proposing marriage. She manages to faint compromisingly in the innocent old gentleman's arms just as his three friends come in the door.

Deciding that London is no place for him with Mrs. Bardell in her present mood, Mr. Pickwick and his friends next journey to Eatanswill, where a hotly contested election between the Blues and the Buffs is in progress. The Honorable Samuel Slumkey of Slumkey Hall, a Blue, is triumphant, after a good deal of dirty politics, over his Buff rival, Mr. Horatio Fizkin of Fizkin Lodge. During the election excitement, Mr. Pickwick meets Jingle again and is led to think he has foiled Jingle's plan to elope with a rich young girl in boarding school.

When he returns to London, Mr. Pickwick is startled to be served by the firm of Dodson and Fogg with a legal writ informing him he will be sued by Mrs. Bardell for breach of promise. But before the trial opens, Mr. Pickwick spends a happy Christmas holiday with the Wardle family, and Mr. Winkle's romance with Arabella Allen prospers under the mistletoe.

Back in London for the trial, Mr. Pickwick must defend himself against the machinations of Mr. Serjeant Buzfuz, the attorney for Dodson and Fogg. The unscrupulous lawyer convinces the judge that a note Mr. Pickwick had written to his landlady requesting chops and tomato sauce for his dinner was really a love letter. Mr. Pickwick's case is not helped by the well-meaning but hopelessly inept Mr. Winkle who manages to antagonize the judge. Sam Weller rises to the defense of his master, but his shrewd wit is only interpreted as cockney impudence. While the judge dines handsomely on chops and sherry, the jury returns a verdict of guilty. Outraged at this patent miscarriage of justice, Mr. Pickwick refuses to pay even a penny of the £750 damages, insisting on going to prison instead.

Before being sent to the Fleet Street jail for debtors, Mr. Pickwick is allowed to spend a month quietly enjoying the waters at Bath. Here Mr. Pickwick tries to advance his friend Winkle's suit with Arabella Allen. When he learns that the lovely Miss Allen has rejected the medical student, Mr. Bob Sawyer, proposed as her mate by her brother, Mr. Pickwick arranges for her to have a lovers' meeting in a garden with Mr. Winkle.

Still refusing to pay damages (against the advice of his lawyer and Sam Weller), Mr. Pickwick is trundled off to prison. He makes his cell as comfortable as possible with the aid of Sam, who manages to get himself locked up in order to continue serving his master. In prison, Mr. Pickwick once again meets the irrepressible Jingle, now in a sorry financial state. He benevolently forgives the rascally actor his past sins and gives him money for food and clothing.

Mr. Pickwick is startled one day to find that Mrs. Bardell and her son have also been thrown into the Fleet Street jail. Dodson and Fogg, who took her case without a fee, expected to collect from Mr. Pickwick's damages. When she refused to pay, they sent their client to prison. Ever warmhearted, Mr. Pickwick gives the Bardells money, too, and promises to help them on his release from jail.

Meanwhile, against her brother's wishes, Arabella has married Mr. Winkle. The pair visit Mr. Pickwick in his cell and beg him to pay his damages so that he may be released in order to bring about a reconciliation between Arabella and her brother. Mr. Pickwick cannot refuse this appeal. After three months in jail, he pays Mrs. Bardell her damages and is released. He manages to bring Arabella's brother around, but finds that now Mr. Winkle's father objects to the marriage and threatens to cut his son out of his will. Furthermore, Mr. Wardle comes to Mr. Pickwick with his daughter, Emily, claiming that the girl is hopelessly in love with a poor poet, Mr. Snodgrass.

Mr. Pickwick soon resolves all these difficulties. The elder Mr. Winkle becomes reconciled to his daughter-in-law when he sees what a charming girl she is. Mr. Snodgrass marries Emily Wardle, and even Sam Weller gets married—to a housemaid who joins him in Mr. Pickwick's service.

Dissolving his club after his exhausting adventures, Mr. Pickwick retires to the country with the Wellers and serves as benevolent godfather to all the children of the Winkles and Snodgrasses.

Critical Opinion

One day in 1836 an artist named Robert Seymour approached the twenty-four-year-old Dickens to write captions for a series of hunting prints he was designing. The prints would jocularly show the misadventures of a group of amateur sportsmen, somewhat in the manner of the popular novels of Surtees. With the cockiness of youthful genius, Dickens agreed to the more experienced Seymour's suggestion, but with the proviso that the drawings should take second place as mere illustrations to the text he would write. Without really knowing where the book was heading, he began work immediately on *The Pickwick Papers* which was to appear, as was then the custom, in monthly installments.

The Pickwick Papers got off to a slow start, and not until the introduction of Sam Weller did the book catch fire with the reading public. The suicide of Seymour left Dickens in mid-novel without an illustrator. One of the men he interviewed for the job was the young Thackeray, then trying to make a career for himself as an artist. The job went, however, to Hablot K. Browne, who as "Phiz" became the illustrator for many of Dickens' early books, his place being taken later on by the brilliant George Cruikshank.

Meanwhile, as Dickens' genius took over, the original, rather trivial plan for *The Pickwick Papers* was forgotten. No longer bound to recount the misadventures of cockney "sportsmen," Dickens turned instead to his favorite childhood reading, the picaresque novels of Cervantes, Fielding, and Smollett, and shaped a great panoramic novel of English life in the early nineteenth century.

The most loosely constructed of his books, *Pickwick* nevertheless became one of the most famous. At the time he wrote it, Dickens had little experience or awareness of novel form. Writing in monthly installments, he pretty much made up the plot as he went along. Only later in his career did he learn how to impose formal order on a serialized novel.

The haphazard plotting, the interpolated stories that bog down the action, the superabundant wealth of characters all fail to detract from Dickens' vast imaginative powers. *Pickwick* remains a great delight. The glories of the inns and coaches of preindustrial England, the delight in eating and drinking, the sentimental pleasures of a family Christmas are balanced by the indignation at the absurdity and injustice of the law and the horrors of debtors' prison. Most of Dickens' themes make their first appearance in the sprawling, humane pages of *The Pickwick Papers*.

David Copperfield

by

CHARLES DICKENS

Main Characters

David Copperfield—The youthful narrator, who experiences many vicissitudes before he becomes a successful novelist.
Betsey Trotwood—David's eccentric but kind-hearted great-aunt.
Mr. Murdstone—David's cruel and saturnine stepfather.

Jane Murdstone—Mr. Murdstone's grim sister.

Peggotty—David's fat, jolly nurse.

Barkis—A quiet, reserved carrier.

Daniel Peggotty—Peggotty's staunch, simple brother.

Little Emily—Peggotty's innocent orphan niece.

Ham—Peggotty's sturdy and good-natured orphan nephew.

Mr. Creakle—The brutal headmaster of Salem House school.

James Steerforth—David's passionately romantic but deeply selfish boyhood friend.

Tommy Traddles—Another school friend, good-natured and open-hearted.

Wilkins Micawber—Eternally optimistic, certain "something will turn up" to pay his huge debts.

Mr. Wickfield—Betsey Trotwood's Canterbury solicitor.

Agnes—His daughter, a beautiful, sensible girl.

Mr. Spenlow—Senior partner of the law firm of Spenlow and Jorkins, who takes David on as an apprentice.

Dora—Mr. Spenlow's pretty, loving, and silly daughter.

Uriah Heep—Mr. Wickfield's unctuous clerk.

The Story

Shortly before David Copperfield is born at Blunderstone, in Suffolk, his father dies, leaving his young widow Clara with an annual income of £105 and a devoted servant, Peggotty. The night David is born, his great-aunt, the eccentric Betsey Trotwood, is present, but she leaves in a huff because she had hoped for a girl to be named after her.

David's early years are happy ones. His pretty, young mother dotes on him. Once Peggotty takes him on a wonderful excursion to the port of Yarmouth where her brother, Daniel, a simple fisherman, lives in a cozy boat beached on the shore. Daniel has an orphan nephew, Ham, and an orphan niece, Emily, who become David's friends.

On his return from Yarmouth David discovers that his mother has married Edward Murdstone, a darkly handsome, tight-fisted tyrant. Mr. Murdstone brings his pious, gloomy sister Jane to live with them, and together the Murdstones try to break the spirits of David and his mother. When David can stand the bullying no longer, he bites Mr. Murdstone on the hand and is instantly dispatched to the Salem House school, where he is put under the care of Mr. Creakle, the inept and sadistic headmaster.

David's one comfort at Mr. Creakle's ill-run school is the friends he makes there: handsome, aristocratic James Steerforth and the always cheerful Tommy Traddles. But his schooldays end abruptly with his mother's death in childbirth. Even the devoted Peggotty leaves to marry a taciturn carrier named Barkis. David is left alone, neglected by his stepfather.

When he is ten years old, David is sent to London to earn his living in the counting house of Murdstone and Grinby where he is almost starved to death. His job is to wash and label wine bottles in a rat-infested warehouse. His colleagues are the raffish Mick Walker and Mealy Potatoes. David lodges in London with Mr. Wilkins Micawber, an improvident husband and father, who tries to keep his brood of four children alive in spite of the creditors who constantly hound him. Mr. Micawber, an incurable optimist, keeps reassuring David that "something will turn up." But eventually Mr. Micawber is thrown into debtors' prison and David finds himself without a home.

Sick of his soul-destroying job and refusing to seek other lodgings because he has come to love the happy-go-lucky Micawbers, David leaves London for Dover, where his great-aunt Betsey Trotwood lives. Beaten and robbed on the way, David arrives dirty and penniless. Miss Betsey, who has always disapproved of him for not being a girl, nevertheless washes and feeds him. On the advice of her gently mad boarder, Mr. Dick, she decides to give David a permanent home, a decision which is enforced when the odious Murdstones arrive and highhandedly try to take David away.

This time, David is sent to a much better school than Mr. Creakle's, the good Mr. Strong's school in Canterbury. He lodges with his great-aunt's lawyer, Mr. Wickfield, and meets Mr. Wickfield's unctuous clerk, Uriah Heep, to whom David takes an instant dislike. David becomes very fond of Mr. Wickfield's pretty daughter, Agnes, who treats him as if she were his sister.

When David graduates with honors from Mr. Strong's school, he decides to become a lawyer, but first he goes to Yarmouth to visit the Peggotty family. On his way he meets his old school comrade, Steerforth, now an elegant, charming young man. David takes Steerforth with him, and in the two weeks they spend at Yarmouth, Steerforth and little Emily fall in love. Emily, however, is engaged to Ham.

David then returns to become apprenticed to the law firm of Spenlow and Jorkins. He falls in love with Mr. Spenlow's charming, silly daughter, Dora. Soon he receives the bad news that his aunt has lost all her money, and that Uriah Heep has wheedled his way into a partnership with Mr. Wickfield. On another visit to Yarmouth—for word has come that Barkis is dying—David is shocked to learn that Emily, despite her engagement, has run off with Steerforth. Broken-hearted, old Daniel Peggotty has gone in search of his niece.

David begins studying shorthand reporting in order to help out his aunt, who is no longer able to pay for his apprenticeship to Mr. Spenlow. Despite his change in fortune, David continues to see Dora. When Mr. Spenlow learns they wish to marry, he strongly disapproves. Before very long Mr. Spenlow dies, penniless. David and Dora marry on his meager income from reporting. David tries to get his adoring but inefficient young wife to manage the household carefully, but Dora is incapable of any economy, and the couple find themselves hard-pressed. They are still able, though, to prepare cheerful meals for their jolly bachelor friend, Tommy Traddles.

On a trip back to Canterbury, David finds his old friend Mr. Micawber now working for Uriah Heep who has gained complete control over him by giving him advances on his salary. Worse yet, Mr. Wickfield, too, seems strangely under his former clerk's greasy thumb. David is further appalled to learn that the odious Mr. Heep plans to marry Mr. Wickfield's lovely daughter, Agnes.

Eventually Mr. Micawber's basic honesty compels him to tell David that Uriah Heep has been embezzling money from Mr. Wickfield. His thefts have been responsible for the decline in Betsey Trotwood's fortunes. With the clerk exposed, some restitution is made, and Miss Trotwood finances Mr. Micawber's emigration to Australia where, he is sure, something good is bound to turn up. Traveling with him on the ship are Emily and her uncle. Emily, who had returned in disgrace when Steerforth callously abandoned her, is forgiven by the magnanimous Daniel Peggotty, and together they hope to find a new life in the colonies.

Gradually Dora's health—always precarious—begins to

fail. David sorrowfully watches his child wife declining. During these sad days, Agnes is a constant solace to him. When Dora dies, Agnes suggests that David seek consolation abroad. He first visits Yarmouth, however, where a great storm is in progress. A ship is foundering offshore. Ham Peggotty swims out to save a man caught in the wreckage. He drowns trying to save Steerforth, who has gone under in the storm.

For three years David wanders about Europe. On his return to England, he learns from Miss Trotwood that Agnes is about to be married. Although he has always considered Agnes a sister, he is pained by the news. Under his aunt's matchmaking instigation, he goes to pay Agnes a visit. When they are together Agnes confesses she has never loved anyone but him. They marry, to Miss Trotwood's great delight, and have a large family. David becomes a highly successful author.

Critical Opinion

Among the best-loved novels of Dickens, *David Copperfield* is a huge, sprawling autobiographical work filled with characteristic Dickensian touches. Out of his unhappy career in a London blacking factory, Dickens shaped David's nightmare apprenticeship to the firm of Murdstone and Grinby. Mr. Micawber is a half-critical, half-affectionate portrait of Dickens' own improvident father. Superimposed on the autobiographical elements is a portrait gallery of a vast range of eccentrics, from the cryptic Barkis to the oily villian, Uriah Heep. These could have come only from Dickens' incredibly fertile imagination.

But the real strength of the book is the passionate honesty and indignation with which Dickens comes to grips with his early childhood. His six months in the blacking factory had been such a ghastly nightmare to him that in later life he completely suppressed the memory, never even telling his immediate family about it. Only through the medium of art was he able to cope with that nightmare. In *David Copperfield*, he shows us his early childhood—idyllic and innocent; his expulsion from this Eden by the cruel Mr. Murdstone; and his plunge, at an early age, into the grime of lower-class London.

Another early memory which haunts the pages of *David*

Copperfield is that of Dickens' love for Maria Beadnell, whom he knew before his marriage. She is the Dora of the novel. Dickens vividly imagines what marriage would have been like with a weak, silly but affectionate girl rather than with the stolid woman he actually married. The section describing David's young married career is immensely touching; but as he gradually becomes successful, the emotional impetus behind the first half of the novel begins to subside. Dickens' concern with tying the numerous plot threads together now becomes stronger than his interest in confession and self-analysis.

The plot becomes incredibly involved as Dickens introduces a wealth of characters, combining them in all sorts of fortuitous ways. As David, having passed through his childhood crises, becomes less interesting, the novel is largely given over to the galaxy of minor characters. When they are imaginatively conceived, like Micawber or Uriah Heep, the novel is lively. When they are romantic stereotypes of Byronic passion, like Steerforth, or Victorian stereotypes of saintly, betrayed womanhood, like Emily, the novel flags.

David Copperfield is typical of middle-period Dickens. The high humor and fierce indignation, the almost uncontrolled complexity of plot, the sheer number of characters, and the concentration on eccentrics are all Dickensian hallmarks, never combined to better effect than in this interpretation of the novelist's own youth.

A Tale of Two Cities

by

CHARLES DICKENS

Main Characters

Dr. Alexandre Manette—A once-strong, brilliant physician, almost destroyed by eighteen years in the Bastille.
Lucie Manette—Dr. Manette's tender, golden-haired daughter.
Jarvis Lorry—The "man of business" of Tellson's Bank, deceptively gruff.

Charles Darnay—The Marquis St. Evrémonde's handsome nephew who has turned his back on the tyranny of the aristocrats.

Sydney Carton—A self-destructive but brilliant lawyer who looks like Charles Darnay.

Madame Defarge—A woman obsessed with vengeance against the aristocrats.

Ernest Defarge—Mme. Defarge's "dark, angry, dangerous" husband, owner of the wine shop in Paris where the revolutionists frequently meet.

Miss Pross—Lucie's brusque servant and companion.

Jerry Cruncher—A bristly haired man-of-all-jobs, employed by Tellson's bank and on the side a "Resurrection Man," or supplier of corpses to medical students.

The Story

On a freezing November night in 1775, Mr. Jarvis Lorry, agent for the old, respected banking firm of Tellson and Company, is riding on the mail coach to Dover where he is to meet pretty, blonde Lucie Manette, a French refugee recently summoned from London. Together they set off for Paris where Lucie's father, Dr. Manette, is being kept in hiding in a tiny garret above the wine shop run by the Defarges. Dr. Manette has spent eighteen years in solitary confinement in the Bastille. Now, his mind failing, he is to be taken to sanctuary in England. Lorry and Lucie Manette are accompanied on their trip to Paris by Jerry Cruncher, a loyal, odd-looking employee of Tellson's bank.

The Defarges' wine shop is a center for revolutionary activities in Paris. Sworn enemies of the old regime, the Defarges have sheltered Dr. Manette in their attic, where he has sat long hours before a carpenter's bench, trying to recall his past. Mme. Defarge, meanwhile, knits away at a strange scarf inscribed with the names of all the aristocrats she hopes to see executed when the revolution comes.

Five years after Lucie and Jarvis Lorry bring old Dr. Manette back to London, where they are looked after by the faithful Jerry Cruncher, they attend the trial of Charles Darnay, a handsome young French language teacher accused by a man called John Barsad of spying against England. The

Manettes testify that they met Darnay on the boat returning from France five years before. Darnay is saved by the brilliant lawyer Sydney Carton who so closely resembles the accused man that the attorney, Mr. Stryver, is able to shake the testimony of witnesses who "recognize" him.

After the trial, Darnay and Carton become frequent visitors at the humble Manette home. Darnay, it turns out, is the heir of the St. Evrémondes—a family of coldly selfish French aristocrats. Refusing to have anything to do with them, he has preferred to eke out a living in London as a French tutor.

Carton, brilliant but unstable, prepares Mr. Stryver's cases for him but is often too drunk to appear in court himself. Both young men court Lucie. When she chooses Darnay, Carton nobly assures her that he will always be ready to lay down his life for her or for one she loves.

Darnay and Lucie marry. Their little girl is six when the revolution breaks out in France with the storming of the hated Bastille and the release of its pathetic prisoners. One of the last provocations to the long-suffering French peasantry was the killing of a child run down by the coach of the callous Marquis St. Evrémonde, Charles Darnay's uncle. The child's father, having protested in vain, had murdered the Marquis in his bed and was subsequently hanged.

One day a letter arrives in England for the new Marquis St. Evrémonde. From it Darnay learns that an old family servant has been imprisoned by the revolutionaries. He begs the Marquis to intervene on his behalf, for he had been following Charles' orders to make restitution to the people when he was arrested. Darnay honorably determines to return to France to see what he can do.

Accordingly, he leaves for Paris with Jarvis Lorry, who has business to transact in the French branch of Tellson and Company. Darnay is arrested soon after his arrival and accused of being a returned aristocrat. When news of his imprisonment reaches England, Lucie and Dr. Manette go to France to help. Dr. Manette feels that his long imprisonment in the Bastille should count for something in his defense of his son-in-law.

The Manettes find Paris in the grip of the Reign of Terror. Although the old doctor is respected by the bloodthirsty revolutionaries, so implacable is the hatred of the Defarges for any member of the St. Evrémonde family that Charles Darnay is allowed to languish in prison for nearly a year and a half before he is tried. All this time Lucie is prevented from seeing her husband.

Finally Darnay is brought to trial. Mme. Defarge sits in the front row of the courtroom knitting her sinister scarf and demanding the death penalty. Charles insists that he had nothing to do with the St. Evrémondes, and, in fact, had ordered that all their wealth be returned to the people they had injured for so long. When the popular Dr. Manette testifies in his son-in-law's behalf, a cheer goes up in the courtroom. Darnay is freed.

Although the tribunal has freed him, Darnay is forbidden to leave France for England. No sooner have the Manettes held a victory celebration, than Darnay is arrested again, accused by the Defarges and a mystery witness of unspecified crimes against the people. While Darnay, wondering who his new accuser could be, is disconsolately awaiting his new trial, Miss Pross, Lucie's devoted old servant, meets her long-lost brother in the streets of Paris. He is John Barsad, the slippery, treacherous witness against Darnay during his Old Bailey trial years before.

Sydney Carton, now in Paris, interviews Barsad who has become a revolutionary spy. Carton manages to make a secret deal with him by threatening to expose him to the revolutionaries as a former English spy.

At Darnay's new trial, M. Defarge produces a paper accusing the St. Evrémondes of vile crimes. He names Dr. Manette as the other witness against Darnay, because the important, damning document was written by the old doctor during his years of imprisonment in the Bastille. When the notorious prison fell to the revolutionaries, Defarge had found the manuscript in Dr. Manette's old cell.

The paper tells how Dr. Manette was arrested because he had learned of a terrible crime committed by the Marquis St. Evrémonde against an innocent family. By the right of *"le droit du seigneur,"* the Marquis had raped a poor peasant girl—the sister of Mme. Defarge. Called in when the girl was dying, Dr. Manette became a witness to St. Evrémonde's guilt, and hence was thrown into the Bastille. In his document he calls for a curse on the whole house of St. Evrémonde.

The long-forgotten document has its effect on the tribunal. Despite his disclaimers and pleas for mercy, Dr. Manette is ignored. Darnay must pay for the sins of his ancestors. He is condemned to be guillotined within twenty-four hours.

But now Sydney Carton, long steeped in apathy and dissipation, prepares to act in behalf of the husband of the woman he loves. Aided by Barsad, whom he has blackmailed, Carton manages to gain admittance into Darnay's cell. On the pretense of having a farewell drink with him, Carton drugs Darnay, exchanges clothes with him, and gets Barsad to lead his friend out of the cell. Because he closely resembles the prisoner, Carton will be able to take Darnay's place at the guillotine. The mob outside is fooled by the deception, and Darnay is reunited with his family.

Meanwhile Mme. Defarge has made her way to the Manette lodgings in order to denounce the whole family, including Lucie's little daughter. Mme. Defarge meets her match in the stalwart Miss Pross, who keeps the French-woman at bay while the Darnays make good their escape from France.

Furious at being balked in her revenge and dismayed at missing even for a minute the terrible scene at the guillotine, Mme. Defarge struggles with Miss Pross and is shot to death when her own pistol goes off. The explosion deafens Miss Pross for the rest of her life.

As the tumbrels bring their prisoners to the place of execution, the absence of Mme. Defarge is noted and commented upon. In one of the tumbrels, Sydney Carton, noble to the last, is comforting a poor, innocent seamstress, also doomed by the vengeful tribunal.

"It is a far, far better thing that I do, than I have ever done," Carton declares before the guillotine descends; "it is a far, far better rest that I go to, than I have ever known."

Critical Opinion

Although its intricate, exciting plot has always made *A Tale of Two Cities* one of Dickens' most popular novels, he was never particularly comfortable writing historical fiction. His only other major attempt in the genre, *Barnaby Rudge* (1841), is perhaps his least successful novel. As in the later book, *Barnaby Rudge* deals with retribution for a crime committed years before, and takes place against a turbulent background of mob violence—the Gordon Riots, a lurid anti-Catholic episode in English history.

Deeply impressed, however, by a reading of Thomas Carlyle's *French Revolution,* Dickens determined to try his hand once again at historical romance. Carlyle sent the novelist two cartloads of books for research in the period, but Dickens probably ignored most of them. He did not wish to rewrite the history of the revolution which he thought Carlyle had recounted as well as it could be done. Instead, he tried to capture the atmosphere of the time in a tale that would point the moral that Carlyle had found in those events: that blood begets blood; revenge is self-perpetuating; and only the kindness and selflessness of the individual human heart can terminate a series of bloodlettings as ferocious as those unleashed in revolutionary France.

The result is essentially a melodrama, curiously lacking in the high humor of Dickens' fiction. At the time he was writing *A Tale of Two Cities,* Dickens was involved, too, in some amateur stage productions and was fascinated by the dense plotting and heroic characterizations of Victorian melodrama. Thus *A Tale of Two Cities* is not as diffuse and leisurely as such earlier novels as *Pickwick Papers* or *David Copperfield.* Dickens' main concern here was to devise a fast-moving plot.

The theme of the novel is essentially the theme of Carlyle's *French Revolution.* Selfish and tyrannical, the aristocracy has brought upon itself the horror of revolution. But then the revolutionaries, carried away by revenge and cruelty, created the Reign of Terror—a match for the oppression before the revolution. At the end of the novel, Sydney Carton goes to his execution with a poor seamstress who has never harmed anybody but who is the pathetic victim of mob rule and blood-lust.

Only in the heroic self-abnegation of the redeemed Carton and in what Dickens saw as the essential goodness of the long-suffering French people does the novel hold out any hope for the future of humanity.

Great Expectations

by

CHARLES DICKENS

Main Characters

Pip—A lonely and imaginative orphan boy who receives an unexpected and unexplained education.

Joe Gargery—The decent, honorable village blacksmith who looks after Pip.

Mrs. Joe Gargery—Pip's shrewish older sister.

Miss Havisham—The eccentric mistress of Satis House, who was deserted years ago on her wedding day.

Estella—Miss Havisham's ward, beautiful and cold-hearted.

Herbert Pocket—Pip's warm-hearted and loyal friend in London.

Bentley Drummle—A clumsy, ill-tempered snob.

Abel Magwitch—An escaped convict with the assumed name of Provis who is obsessed with the idea of giving Pip a better chance in life than he (Magwitch) had ever had.

Arthur Compeyson—Magwitch's bitter enemy, sworn to his destruction.

Mr. Jaggers—The solicitor who informs Pip of his great expectations in life.

Biddy—Joe Gargery's gentle second wife.

The Story

Young Pip is an orphan boy being brought up by his older sister and her good-natured husband, Joe Gargery, the village blacksmith. In his loneliness, Pip often wanders about the forbidding moors and marshes of the neighborhood, sometimes stopping to mourn over the gravestones of his dead mother and father. One day, while out on the bleak moors, Pip is startled by a hulking, menacing man who threatens him if he does not bring him some food immediately. The stranger is apparently an escaped convict, for he also demands that Pip bring him a file with which to cut the chains binding his legs.

Too terrified to refuse, Pip steals a pork pie from his sister's kitchen and a file from a tool box, and returns to the spot where the prisoner had accosted him. Here he sees another strange man, engaged in a fierce fight with the first man. The second man eventually disappears into the fog. Soon after, the escaped convict, whose name is Abel Magwitch, is recaptured, but before being returned to jail he promises to reward Pip for helping him.

Pip soon forgets the incident. Before long, the eccentric Miss Havisham requests Pip's sister to send the lad to gloomy Satis House. Long ago, Miss Havisham had been jilted on her wedding day. Ever since, she has had all the clocks stopped in the great house where she lives in seclusion with her ward, the beautiful, haughty Estella. The wedding breakfast, complete with decorated cake, has for years been lying on a table, moldering. When Pip visits Miss Havisham, he is startled by her extreme eccentricity.

The lonely Miss Havisham insists that Pip come often to play with her ward. Estella torments him, however, and is encouraged by Miss Havisham to tease him. In spite of himself, Pip is awed by Estella, the most beautiful girl he has ever seen.

A studious lad, Pip hopes eventually to leave the limited life he knows in the blacksmith shop. His opportunity comes soon. One day Mr. Jaggers, a pompous London lawyer, arrives with the news that money has been secretly provided for Pip to go to the city and become a gentleman. Pip, elated at this prospect, assumes that the money is coming from Miss Havisham with the hope that it will make him into a desirable husband for Estella.

In London Pip is befriended by Herbert Pocket, a distant relative of Miss Havisham and a dashing young man about town, who shares the small but cozy rooms that have been rented for Pip. Jaggers refuses to answer Pip's questions about the identity of his benefactor, assuring the lad that in due time he will know who has provided the money for him.

Before long Pip takes to the idle life of a London dandy. He becomes friends with an overbearing aristocrat named Bentley Drummle and learns the sophisticated ways of London society so well that he is embarrassed and irritated by the occasional visits of the simple, loyal Joe Gargery.

After Joe leaves, however, Pip feels remorse at the high-handed way in which he has treated him. Once, at Miss Havisham's request, Pip goes back home with Joe. The elderly recluse and her ward are impressed by the way in which Pip has outgrown his humble beginnings. Miss Havisham even goes so far as to tell Pip that she expects him to fall in love with Estella. Pip is more than willing.

Estella comes to London herself. Soon her dark good looks and aristocratic manner bring her a circle of suitors including Bentley Drummle. Although she still sees Pip occasionally, she obviously is not in love with him.

On Pip's twenty-first birthday, he receives a surprise visit from Magwitch, the convict he helped years before on the moor. A coarse, unprepossessing man, Magwitch at first repels the fastidious Pip, but when he reveals that he is Pip's secret benefactor, Pip is horrified. Magwitch tells him that he has made a great deal of money in the colonies where he had been transported, and has now secretly returned to London to see how Pip, whom he regards as a kind of son, has turned out. All he wants is for Pip to become a gentleman, something circumstances never allowed Magwitch to do. He is in England under the assumed name of Provis. If the police ever find out he has escaped from the convict colony, he will be condemned to death.

Pip reels at his dilemma. While he knows he should feel grateful to Magwitch, he is too snobbish to feel much sympathy for this brutalized man. He is also bitterly disillusioned that his benefactor is not Miss Havisham. Nevertheless, Pip vows to help Magwitch who tells him that the man who struggled with him on the moor was a sworn enemy named Arthur Compeyson. Pip learns from Herbert Pocket that Compeyson is the very man who jilted Miss Havisham on her wedding day.

Angry at his own folly in assuming Miss Havisham to be his benefactor, Pip goes to the gloomy mansion once more to upbraid the old woman for leading him on. With deliberate cruelty she informs him that Estella is soon to marry Bentley Drummle. Pip's anguish is precisely what Miss Havisham has counted on. Since her jilting, she has vowed vengeance on all men. In playing with Pip's affection for Estella, she satisfies her vow.

After Estella's marriage, Pip visits the Havisham mansion again. A fire starts in the mansion. Pip tries to rescue Miss Havisham. He is too late. The house is so filled with the dust and rubble of the past that it goes up like a tinderbox. Miss Havisham dies in the flames.

Back in London Pip learns that Magwitch is in fact Estella's father; her mother is apparently Jaggers' strange house-keeper. Even more startling is the news that Compeyson is in London, hunting down Magwitch to kill him. With Herbert Pocket's aid, Pip attempts to smuggle his benefactor out of England to safety in France, where Pip will join him. But just as they go aboard the boat that will take the convict across the Channel, Compeyson catches up with them. The two enemies lock in fierce hand-to-hand combat. Magwitch kills Compeyson. For this murder the old convict is once again returned to jail where he dies while awaiting trial.

Under the stress of recent events, Pip falls ill and is nursed by the faithful Joe Gargery. Pip's sister has died and Joe has married Biddy who really loves him and doesn't henpeck him. Pip finally realizes how wrong he has been to despise the humble, loyal Joe. He returns with him to his blacksmith shop and, while recovering from his illness, makes amends to Joe for having treated him so shabbily and snobbishly.

Still brooding over the loss of Estella, Pip joins Herbert Pocket in a business venture in London. Many years later he pays his final visit to the place where Miss Havisham's mansion once stood. He meets Estella there. Together they walk about the grounds where they had once been children together. Estella is now widowed. The surly Bentley Drummle, whom she had married for his aristocratic background, was kicked to death one day by a horse that he had been mistreating with his customary brutality. Her experiences with Drummle and her solitary widowhood have considerably softened the once cold and aloof Estella. As she walks hand in hand with Pip, the two understand that they will never part from each other again.

Critical Opinion

In many ways, *Great Expectations* is Dickens' finest novel. Although it lacks the high spirits and wild inventiveness of his earlier fiction, it is less diffuse and better organized. Above all, it has a real theme—the corrosive effect of snobbery—treated in a serious and profound way.

Pip is early subjected to the snobbery of others. Although he smarts under the contempt that Estella (ironically, the illegitimate daughter of a convict and a housemaid) takes no pains to disguise, when he is given the means to live in London, he, too, falls easily into the ways of the snob. Once a good, promising lad, Pip is so ruined by money that he now callously condescends to his real friend, Joe Gargery, while making his way in the superficial world of Bentley Drummle.

Because he has become a snob, Pip is appalled to learn that the source of his wealth is not the respectable Miss Havisham, but the crude, ill-mannered convict, Magwitch. Painfully, his early training under Joe Gargery breaks through the superficial manners Pip has acquired in London, and he vows loyalty to the hunted Magwitch.

Great Expectations, then, is an ironical title. The expectations of wealth that Jaggers presents to Pip seem great indeed, but turn out to be ashes in the mouth as Pip scorns his old friend Joe, loses Estella to Drummle (an even more consummate snob than he is), loses Magwitch, and is unable even to rescue Miss Havisham.

It is only after these blows that Pip begins to realize his duty to the dead Magwitch—to live up to the convict's expectations of him as the true gentleman he might become given the necessary wealth and leisure. Pip must live the good life that the haunted Magwitch was never able to attain for himself.

Great Expectations is also a brilliant commentary on the deadening influence that the past can exert on the present if one allows an ancient injury to poison one's life. Because she was jilted by Compeyson on her wedding day, Miss Havisham has vowed vengeance on all men. For a time she seems successful—her soured love nearly wrecks Pip's life. But ultimately Miss Havisham's perverted will is thwarted. Symbolically, her mansion—a museum of the dead past—is consumed in purifying flames which destroy her, too. It is Estella, not Pip, who suffers most from the marriage made for snobbish reasons.

The psychological insight into these thwarted lives shows Dickens at the zenith of his powers. The plot of this novel is more spare and austere than most of his others. Gone are the digressions and superfluous characters with which Dickens tended to pad his earlier novels. All is subordinated in *Great Expectations* to the theme: a devastating commentary on the moral perversions that wealth and the expectation of it can create in the human heart.

The Author

Charles Dickens, the best loved and most widely read of English novelists, was born into a lower-middle-class family at Portsea on February 7, 1812. His father, who later appears as Mr. Micawber in *David Copperfield,* was an ineffectual naval clerk whose fortunes continually fluctuated. When Charles was nine years old, the family fortunes took a catastrophic turn for the worse. Dickens' father was imprisoned in the Marshalsea debtors' prison, and the boy suffered the humiliation of working in a London blacking factory pasting labels on bottles in full view of passers-by.

These early experiences left an indelible mark on the sensitive, ambitious boy and shaped much of the fiction he was later to write. An improvement in the Dickens' fortunes enabled the boy to continue his interrupted schooling.

In 1835 he became a parliamentary reporter for a newspaper and began to contribute sketches of London life which were published in 1836 as *Sketches by Boz* (Dickens' early pen name). It was not until later that year, when the *Pickwick Papers* began appearing in monthly installments, that the name Dickens became a household word. The success of *Pickwick* enabled Dickens to marry Catherine Hogarth, the sister of the girl he really loved. Catherine, who bore him numerous children, was apparently a rather dull, unimaginative woman. The unhappy marriage ended in a separation in 1856.

Pickwick was followed by *Oliver Twist* (1838) and

Nicholas Nickleby (1839), both of which solidified Dickens' reputation to such an extent that when he visited the United States in 1842 in order to plead for a universal copyright law, he was greeted as a conquering hero. Loathing slavery, irritated by American piracies of his novels and by crude American manners, Dickens pilloried the United States in the middle section of *Martin Chuzzlewit* (1844) and in his *American Notes* (1842).

In 1856 Dickens' public readings from his works enhanced his reputation even further. A born actor, he put so much of himself into these dramatic readings that they totally exhausted him and contributed to his death.

The novels of Dickens' middle period, *David Copperfield* (1850), *Bleak House* (1852), *Hard Times* (1854) and *A Tale of Two Cities* (1859), show the exuberance and high spirits of the early works giving way to a more serious concern with social injustice and the evils of industrialism. A more somber, deeply symbolic style and a tighter and more effective structure are evident in the last novels Dickens wrote, the highly complex and haunting *Great Expectations* (1860), *Our Mutual Friend* (1865), and the unfinished mystery tale, *Edwin Drood*.

Dickens' later life was complicated by overwork and by an unhappy affair with a young actress, Ellen Ternan. In 1867 he paid a second visit to the United States which he liked better this time and which heaped even greater adulation on him than it had done before. The following year he returned to England totally exhausted. On June 9, 1870, a world famous but bitter man, he died in the mansion he had built for himself, Gadshill Place, in Kent.

By the Same Author

Oliver Twist: Dickens' second novel is as somber as his first is high spirited. Born in a workhouse of unknown parentage, Oliver Twist is apprenticed to an undertaker by Mr. Bumble, a monument of cruelty and hypocrisy. The lad then makes his way to London where he falls in with a group of pickpockets including the Artful Dodger. Such notorious figures of the London underworld as the greasy Fagin and the violent Bill Sikes exploit Oliver and kidnap him when he is temporarily rescued by the kindly Mr. Brownlow. Eventually, after Oliver finds a haven and Sikes brutally murders his wife, Nancy, the criminals are caught and punished. Oliver is adopted by Mr. Brownlow.

A Christmas Carol: This short tale of 1843 is one of Dickens' most sentimental and popular works. It tells of the old miser, Scrooge who in a series of dreams learns about the true Christmas spirit. Scrooge has always mistreated his impoverished but cheerful clerk, Bob Cratchit. When the Ghost of Christmas Present takes him to the Cratchit house, Scrooge sees himself through the Cratchits' eyes and realizes that his miserly, unloved life has been a waste. A changed man after his terrifying dreams, Scrooge contributes generously to the Cratchits' Christmas dinner and is blessed by the clerk's crippled son, Tiny Tim.

Jane Eyre

by

CHARLOTTE BRONTË (1816–1855)

Main Characters

Jane Eyre—An orphan who grows up to be a resourceful, self-reliant schoolmistress.

Mrs. Reed—Jane's cold-hearted aunt, mistress of Gateshead Hall.

Edward Fairfax Rochester—The brooding master of Thornfield Manor.

Adele Varens—Rochester's beautiful, precocious, half-French ward.

Mrs. Fairfax—A relative of Rochester, chief housekeeper of Thornfield Manor.

Grace Poole—A servant under Mrs. Fairfax.

Blanche Ingram—Beautiful, snobbish, and self-assured, she fancies herself in love with Rochester.

Mr. Mason—A mysterious visitor to Thornfield from the West Indies.

St. John Rivers—Clergyman of the parish of Morton who befriends Jane Eyre.

The Story

Orphaned as a baby, Jane Eyre is placed in the care of a cold-hearted aunt, Mrs. Reed of Gateshead Hall. Mrs. Reed's husband, a brother of Jane's mother, instructs his wife on his deathbed to care as tenderly for Jane as for her own three children. But Mrs. Reed, a somber and severe woman, ignores this request for the ten miserable years that Jane spends under her roof. She pampers her own spoiled children and brings Jane up as little better than a servant. One day, as punishment for a bit of childish willfulness, she puts Jane into the room in which Mr. Reed died. The highly imaginative child falls into a faint and becomes very ill.

After being nursed back to health by Bessie Leaven, a sympathetic nurse at Gateshead, Jane is sent to the Lowood School, fifty miles away. Although life in this school is very austere, it is generally a relief after Gateshead Hall. Jane is befriended by a Miss Temple and learns her lessons rapidly. Tragedy strikes when an epidemic kills some of the girls at Lowood. This leads to an investigation into conditions at the school and some subsequent improvements.

Jane becomes a teacher at the school, but leaves at eighteen to become governess to the precocious Adele Varens who lives in isolated Thornfield Manor near Millcote.

Jane does not at first meet Edward Rochester, the girl's guardian. She is engaged by the kindly, capable Mrs. Fairfax, chief housekeeper and relative of the lord of the manor. Jane finds contentment in the quiet, rustic life at the manor and in her imaginative young charge, but she is puzzled when Mrs. Fairfax warns her that she is never to enter a mysterious, locked room on the third floor. One day, Jane hears a shrill, blood-curdling laugh coming from the room, but Mrs. Fairfax pretends that the maniacal noise was made by Grace Poole, a rather dumpy, unprepossessing servant.

One January afternoon, while out walking, Jane meets her employer, Mr. Rochester. Rochester has been thrown by his horse, and his dog comes to Jane seeking help. But the gruff, surly Rochester insists on getting home unaided although he is in great pain. He questions Jane and learns she is the new governess. Rochester's manner to her becomes more gracious when she is obviously not cowed by his overbearing manner. In confidence, he tells her that little Adele is his daughter by a French ballerina who deserted both father and child long ago.

One night Jane is awakened by the same shrill scream she had heard before. Opening her door, she sees smoke billowing from Rochester's room. His bed on fire, Rochester is awakened just in time by Jane. He refuses to allow her to awaken the household, telling her the fire may have been set by Grace Poole, who has periodic fits of insanity. The rest of the servants are told the fire was accidentally caused by a candle falling.

Jane, sensing that her employer is suffering from the consequences of some mysterious sin of the past, gives him all her sympathy and gradually finds herself falling in love with him. But her hopes are thwarted when Rochester begins going to parties in the neighborhood where he is courting the beautiful, frivolous Blanche Ingram. At a party Rochester gives in Thornfield Manor, the aristocratic Blanche and her friends treat Jane with haughty condescension. Jane feels she can never compete with these snobbish, elegant people.

While the house guests are staying at Thornfield, Rochester receives a mysterious caller—a Mr. Mason from the West Indies. That night Jane hears a scuffle and a cry for help in the room just above hers. Rochester quiets the household's alarm but asks Jane privately to help nurse Mr. Mason who is bleeding and unconscious. Before dawn the wounded man is spirited away from the house.

One day soon after, Jane is enjoying the lovely midsummer evening in an orchard when Rochester comes upon her and informs her he is shortly to be married. Jane, miserable, assumes he intends to marry Blanche Ingram. She asks him tearfully how he can expect her to remain on at Thornfield under the circumstances. Rochester kisses her and tells her it is she whom he wishes to marry.

Jane's happy excitement before the wedding is interrupted one night when she awakens in horror to see a strange, ugly woman trying on her bridal veil and then tearing it to pieces. Rochester assures her it is only a bad dream, but in the morning Jane finds the ripped fragments of the veil.

On the wedding day the service is interrupted by Mr. Mason who has slipped into the church to announce that the marriage is illegal because Rochester still has a living wife. Forced to reveal the truth at last, Rochester takes Jane to the forbidden chamber on the third floor where Jane sees a hideous creature, crawling on all fours in her madness. It was she who had attacked Mason and torn Jane's wedding veil. Rochester explains that the creature is Mason's sister Bertha whom he had been tricked into marrying fifteen years before in Jamaica and who comes from a family of lunatics and degenerates. His married life has been an un-mitigated hell, with the insane Mrs. Rochester kept under lock and key in the care of Grace Poole.

Jane is filled with sympathy for the misanthropic Rochester. Nevertheless, she realizes she must now depart. Taking just a little money with her, she wanders about the Midland moors, vainly seeking employment. Close to starvation, she is finally befriended and nursed back to health by a clergyman named St. John Rivers and his two sisters, Mary and Diana. Under the new name of Jane Elliott, she finds a job as village school-mistress and tries to forget her seemingly hopeless love for Rochester.

One day Rivers learns that an uncle of Jane's, John Eyre, has recently died in Madeira and has left Jane £20,000. Jane insists on sharing this legacy with Rivers and his sisters who, a lawyer discovers, are really her cousins. St. John Rivers asks Jane to be his wife and to go with him to India where he plans to become a missionary. Although he is not in love with her, he feels she would make an admirable assistant in his mission.

While Jane is considering the offer, she has a dream that Rochester is calling for her. Failing to find him in the neighbor-hood the next morning, she journeys back to Thornfield where she is shocked to find the great manor house gutted by fire and completely in ruins. Making inquiries at the local inn, she discovers that Mrs. Rochester one night succeeded in setting the house on fire. Rochester managed to lead the servants to safety and then went back into the burning mansion to rescue his wife. She eluded him, was able to climb to the roof, and was then killed in a plunge to the ground.

Rochester barely managed to get out of the burning house alive himself. A flaming staircase had fallen, blinding him and crushing one arm so badly it had to be amputated. Rochester is now living in morose solitude at the lonely nearby manor of Ferndean. Jane hurries to see him.

Overjoyed that she has come to him, Rochester asks her to become his wife. She happily accepts and they are married. They soon have a child. Two years later, Rochester regains the sight of one eye.

Critical Opinion

Unlike her great predecessor, Jane Austen, Charlotte Brontë never possessed the ironic aloofness from the world that distinguishes such works as *Pride and Prejudice* or *Emma*. Instead, *Jane Eyre* is infused with passionate involvement and poetic imagination, sometimes bordering on the melodramatic. While Charlotte Brontë's hopeless love for M. Héger is undoubtedly the basis for Jane's love for Rochester, the figure of Rochester is larger than life; his sorrows and furies are titanic.

Rochester is a typical romantic hero, sharing some significant traits with the doomed heroes of Byron and with Heathcliff in Emily Brontë's *Wuthering Heights*. A man of great sorrow and great passion, a man too noble to be seduced by the superficialities of society, he is at the same time tormented and tormenting, tender and ruthless, and very much the figment of a lonely, romantic girl's imagination.

Although much of *Jane Eyre* is autobiographical, especially the scenes in the Lowood School, much is taken from the tradition of gothic romance popularized in the late eighteenth century by such shockers as Walpole's *Castle of Otranto* and Ann Radcliffe's *Mysteries of Udolpho*. Such elements in *Jane Eyre* as the lord of the manor haunted by a mystery from the past, the isolated, ghost-ridden mansion hiding its guilty secret, and the innocent but self-reliant girl trying to unfathom the mystery, are stock devices of the gothic novel.

Jane Eyre triumphs by giving these melodramatic devices a new lease on life and by investing them with unique personal passion and energy. They are no longer fictional clichés, but living facts in Charlotte Brontë's treatment. Because the Brontës' actual lives in lonely, haunted Haworth Parsonage really contained much of the "gothic," *Jane Eyre* is more convincing than most of its predecessors.

Rochester may divert attention from the book's modest, unassuming heroine; but the novel really centers on Jane's moral growth from the impudent, unhappy girl rebelling against her aunt's oppressive religiosity to the woman of delicate sensibility and strong character who eventually marries the crippled Rochester. Such experiences as those in the Lowood School (very Dickensian in tone), the teaching of the spoiled but adorable Adele, and the interrupted first marriage to Rochester give Jane strength to endure the blows of fate that eventually bring her to serene womanhood. *Jane Eyre* is in some respects a Cinderella-like fantasy of wish fulfillment, but one infused with an original and powerful romantic genius.

The Author

Charlotte Brontë was born on April 21, 1816, shortly before her family moved to bleak Haworth Parsonage in Yorkshire. Her father, Patrick Brontë, was a highly eccentric Irish clergyman. Her mother died when Charlotte was five, after bearing six children in all—three of whom, Charlotte and her sisters Emily and Anne, were to become famous novelists. The only son in the family, Patrick Branwell, showed considerable artistic gifts which he dissipated in drink.

In 1824 all the girls except Anne were sent to a school rather like the Lowood School in *Jane Eyre*. Here the two older daughters died, probably of tuberculosis. Charlotte and Emily then returned to Haworth where they were left on their own to roam the wild moors and make up stories for their own entertainment. Out of these tales and poems about a mythical northern kingdom called Angria came the *Gondal Chronicle*, an immature but fascinating saga in prose and verse on which the girls collaborated.

In 1831 Charlotte was sent to a boarding school where she was trained, like Jane Eyre, to become a governess. She hoped to open a school with Emily. In order to perfect their French, the two sisters traveled to Brussels, where they studied at the Pensionnat Héger. They were called back to England in 1842 by the death of their aunt. Shortly thereafter Charlotte returned to Brussels alone, spending a year as a teacher there and falling hopelessly in love with Constantin Héger, the married master of the establishment.

Discovering that her sisters Emily and Anne had been writing poems, Charlotte added some of her own. These poems were published in 1846 as *Poems by Currer, Ellis, and Acton Bell*, the pseudonyms the three girls used. The volume attracted no attention, but soon the three were writing novels. Although Charlotte's first effort, *The Professor*, was rejected, she was encouraged by a sympathetic publisher's reader. Her second work, *Jane Eyre*, became a great success on its publication in 1847.

Shaken by the deaths of Emily and Branwell and forced to care for her now blind father, Charlotte nevertheless managed to write two other novels, *Shirley* (1849) and *Villette* (1853). *Shirley* solidified her success. It was with the publication of that novel that she revealed the true identity of "Currer Bell." In London she met such literary lights of the day as Thackeray, Matthew Arnold, and Mrs. Gaskell, who was later to be her friend and biographer.

In 1854 she married her father's curate, the Reverend Arthur Bell Nichols. The marriage was tragically brief. Charlotte died on March 31 of the following year.

By the Same Author

Shirley: Shirley is a generally successful attempt to treat something Charlotte Brontë had only read about—the strife between workers and mill owners in Yorkshire in 1807–1812. Shirley Keeldar, its heroine, is concerned with the social changes brought about by the Industrial Revolution. She is a lively heiress whose character is partly modeled on Emily Brontë's. Shirley marries a man with a spirit like her own, Louis Moore, brother of a mill owner whose newly installed machinery provokes the laborers to riot. The novel is filled with keenly observed and sharply satirized clergymen whose moral rigidity in the face of changing times draws Charlotte Brontë's scornful fire.

Villette: This is a semi-autobiographical account of Charlotte Brontë's lovesick years as a teacher in the Pensionnat Héger in Brussels. The loneliness and despair she felt in her love for the married Constantin Héger is transmuted into the yearning of Lucy Snowe for Paul Emmanuel. Written after her brother and sisters had died, and while she herself was in ill health, the prevailing mood of *Villette* is the darkest of Charlotte Brontë's novels.

Wuthering Heights

by

EMILY BRONTË (1818–1848)

Main Characters

Mr. Earnshaw—the kindly owner of Wuthering Heights, a storm-beaten house on the moors.

Catherine—His intense and passionate daughter.

Hindley—His weak-willed, snobbish son.

Heathcliff—An orphan boy adopted by Mr. Earnshaw.

Mr. Linton—The owner of neighboring Thrushcross Grange.

Edgar—His highly civilized son who deeply loves Catherine Earnshaw.

Isabella—Edgar's sister who becomes infatuated with Heathcliff.

Frances Earnshaw—Hindley's sickly, childish wife.

Hareton Earnshaw—The son of Hindley and Frances, brought up by Heathcliff to be crude, ignorant, and dirty, who is nevertheless affectionate and loyal.

Cathy—Daughter of Edgar Linton and Catherine Earnshaw, who has her mother's willfulness and pride.

Ellen Dean—The devoted housekeeper at Thrushcross Grange, who narrates much of the story to Mr. Lockwood.

Mr. Lockwood—A tenant at Thrushcross Grange, who hears most of the tale of the Earnshaws and the Lintons while laid up with a cold.

Joseph—A sour, bigoted servant at Wuthering Heights.

The Story

One winter day in 1801 Mr. Lockwood, a tenant at Thrush-cross Grange, decides to pay a visit to his landlord, Mr. Heathcliff, whom he has never met and who lives in the storm-battered old farmhouse nearby known as Wuthering Heights. He gets a surly reception from Heathcliff's dogs and from the landlord himself, a powerfully built, darkly handsome man, extremely sullen and abrupt in manner. Fascinated, Mr. Lockwood returns for a second visit to Wuthering Heights and meets Heathcliff's widowed daughter-in-law, a pretty but silent and haughty young woman, and a clumsy and unkempt young man named Hareton Earnshaw.

While Mr. Lockwood is at Wuthering Heights, it begins to snow heavily and it becomes obvious that he will have to stay the night. Heathcliff inhospitably tells him he will have to share a bed with Joseph, a dour and ill-tempered servant. Un-willing to do this, Mr. Lockwood is about to set forth in the snow when Zillah, a kindly cook, finds him an unused room in the house.

That night Mr. Lockwood has a nightmare in which he thinks he hears the branch of a tree knocking against his window. He tries to open the window to remove the branch. In the attempt, he breaks the window. He reaches for the branch but, instead, finds himself holding the icy hand of a woman. Crying that her name is Catherine Linton, she tries to get in through the window. Mr. Lockwood's screams bring Heathcliff rushing into the room, and in a fury the landlord orders him out of the haunted chamber. Heathcliff then throws himself on the bed and implores the spectral woman to come back to him.

His curiosity aroused by these strange events, Mr. Lockwood returns to Thrushcross Grange and asks the wise old housekeeper, Nelly Dean, to tell him about his landlord, for she has known Wuthering Heights from earliest childhood.

Mrs. Dean tells him that years before Mr. and Mrs. Earnshaw lived at Wuthering Heights with their daughter, Catherine, and their son, Hindley. Returning from a trip to Liverpool one day, Mr. Earnshaw brings back with him a filthy, ragged, dark-complexioned orphan boy whom he found in the slums. He christens the boy Heathcliff and tells his children they are to treat him like a brother. Soon Mr. Earnshaw and Catherine grow to love young Heathcliff, for he is brave, sturdy, and self-sufficient. Hindley grows jealous of Heathcliff for stealing his father's affections. The atmosphere at Wuthering Heights becomes so tense that Hindley must be sent away to school because he is constantly baiting Heathcliff and making him perform menial chores.

Soon after, Mr. Earnshaw dies, and Hindley returns to Wuthering Heights with a sickly, vapid bride named Frances. As master of Wuthering Heights, he now behaves even more cruelly to Heathcliff who vows that he will one day make Hindley pay for his brutality. Heathcliff's one joy in life is roaming about the wild moors with Catherine who finds in him the ideal companion for her own wild, restless spirit.

One night, when Heathcliff and Catherine are mischievously spying on a grand ball being given at Thrushcross Grange, they are set upon by a watchdog, and Catherine is bitten in the leg. She is taken into the house where she stays for five weeks until her leg is healed. There she meets the kindly, civilized Lintons, their charming son, Edgar, and lovely daughter, Isabella. When Catherine returns home, she is full of stories about the Lintons' life of ease and gaiety. Her tales make Heathcliff wildly jealous.

Tragedy soon strikes Wuthering Heights. Hindley's delicate wife, Frances, dies giving birth to a son, Hareton. Hindley drowns his sorrows in drink and continues to torment Heathcliff. Meanwhile, Catherine confides in Nelly Dean that although she really loves Heathcliff, she thinks she will marry Edgar Linton, for she is tired of being a tomboy and it would degrade her to marry a servile orphan who is content to take orders from her brother. Heathcliff, overhearing the last part of the conversation, leaves Wuthering Heights that night in a fury, determined to make his way in the world before he returns to claim Catherine for his wife. Realizing what has happened, Catherine searches for him on the moors in a rainstorm but cannot find him.

While Heathcliff is away, Catherine eventually succumbs to Edgar Linton's charm and good manners. Not hearing from Heathcliff for three years, she marries Edgar and goes to live in the peace and tranquillity of Thrushcross Grange with Nelly Dean as housekeeper. There life proceeds placidly until one day Heathcliff returns and startles the Lintons with his elegant clothes and fine manners. Heathcliff does not reveal what he has been doing over the years, but he has obviously prospered, and now wants to become a tenant at Wuthering Heights. Edgar suspects his motives, but Catherine, over-joyed to have Heathcliff back, urges her husband to consent. Hindley, overwhelmed by gambling and drinking debts, is happy to have anyone pay him some rent for Wuthering Heights, which has now fallen into a state of disrepair.

Accordingly, Heathcliff moves in and begins taking his revenge on Hindley by inveigling him into more and more gambling and drinking. Ultimately Heathcliff becomes the real master of Wuthering Heights. He avenges himself on Edgar Linton for marrying Catherine by getting Edgar's sister, Isabella, to fall in love with him. Edgar, appalled at this turn of events, assaults Heathcliff and orders him thrown out of Thrushcross Grange. Heathcliff later persuades the flighty Isabella to elope with him to Wuthering Heights.

Now Thrushcross Grange is barred to Heathcliff. But one day he hears that Catherine, who is about to give birth, is suffering from a fever. He forces his way to her bedside. She confesses to Heathcliff that she was wrong in marrying Edgar when she really loved him. There is a tender reconciliation between the lovers a few hours before Catherine dies giving birth to her daughter, Cathy Linton. Heathcliff, consumed with guilt and frustrated love, calls upon Catherine's ghost to haunt him forever.

Meanwhile Isabella Linton, completely disillusioned with Heathcliff and aware of his true motives in marrying her, leaves for London where she bears his son, Linton. Eventual-ly Hindley dies of drink, having mortgaged all of Wuthering Heights to the unrelenting Heathcliff.

Now, as complete master of Wuthering Heights, Heathcliff is prepared to carry his revenge into the second generation as he brings up Hindley's son, Hareton, in the most squalid and brutal fashion. Poor Hareton, as rightful heir to the Heights, is denied everything but meager subsistence and is never allowed to forget that as the son of Heathcliff's mortal enemy, he lives at the Heights only by Heathcliff's charity.

Twelve years after her son Linton's birth, Isabella dies brokenhearted in London. Edgar Linton adopts the frail lad. Heathcliff, however, demands that his son live with him at Wuthering Heights. Heathcliff's plan, pathetically opposed by the ineffectual Edgar Linton, is for young Linton and young Cathy eventually to marry. Linton's health is precarious, and Cathy comes to the Heights to visit him. Heathcliff imprisons her for five days until she consents to marry the invalid.

These events hasten Edgar's decline. He dies before he can disinherit Cathy and thwart Heathcliff's plans. Cathy inherits Thrushcross Grange. Soon after, the sickly Linton Heathcliff dies, and Cathy becomes dependent on Heathcliff who now controls both Wuthering Heights and Thrushcross Grange.

After a business trip to London, Mr. Lockwood returns one autumn to Wuthering Heights where he learns that Heathcliff has died three months before after deliberately starving himself for four days, sick of his vengeance and yearning to be united in death with his lost Catherine. Now Cathy and Hareton are alone at the Heights, and the girl takes upon herself the task of bringing out the long-submerged, finer elements in Hareton's character, giving him the education that Heathcliff had denied him.

When Mr. Lockwood visits the local cemetery, he finds Catherine's grave between her husband's and Heathcliff's. Local legend has it that on stormy nights the erstwhile lovers, Catherine and Heathcliff, are seen to roam the bleak moors they loved so much when they were young.

Critical Opinion

Wuthering Heights is one of the supreme masterpieces of English romanticism. In it, Emily Brontë explores two worlds: the world of the passoniate emotions of love and revenge as symbolized by Wuthering Heights ("wuthering" is a Yorkshire dialect word for stormy weather), and the rational, civilized world symbolized by Thrushcross Grange. If the world of Wuthering Heights is often cruel and barbaric, as in Heathcliff's monstrous revenge against Hindley and the Lintons, it is also capable of a passionate love that transcends even death. If the world of Thrushcross Grange is cozy, comfortable, and civilized, it is also somewhat bloodless and ineffectual. The pitting of these two worlds of passion and reason against each other over the course of three generations is the essence of the book.

The novel really centers on Heathcliff, perhaps the most fascinating hero-villain in English fiction. A true figure of the Romantic Age, Heathcliff is consumed with a demonic passion which destroys all less vigorous life around him until he himself is destroyed by it.

Realizing that the demonic passions of the novel could easily turn into melodramatic rhetoric, Emily Brontë controls events through an enormously complex structure involving time shifts, shifts in point of view, and a highly sophisticated method of narration, all of which point to the style of such modern novelists as James, Conrad, and Joyce. Most of the events in *Wuthering Heights* are given a credibility they would not otherwise possess by being filtered through the common sense of Nelly Dean and Mr. Lockwood.

Thus, while the emotions of the book hark back to the romanticism of Byron and the gothic novel, the form looks forward to the control and sophistication of the modern novel. Somehow Emily Brontë manages to avoid completely the conventions of Victorian fiction. If the typical scene of the Victorian novel is a rectory garden or a middle-class drawing room (and this is true even of *Jane Eyre*), the typical scene of *Wuthering Heights* is a storm-swept, infinitely lonely moor. In this sense the novel is imaginatively closer to the world of *King Lear* than to the comfortable and commonplace world of Victorian fiction.

The Author

Although the tragically brief life of *Emily Jane Brontë* was highly circumscribed, her inner life must have been extremely rich. She was born on July 30, 1818, at Thornton, in Yorkshire, before the Brontë family moved to the famous Haworth Parsonage. Although she had very little formal schooling, Emily Brontë went to Halifax for a brief period as a governess in 1836, but returned home discouraged with teaching and homesick for the barren moors she loved. Like Catherine Earnshaw and Heathcliff, Emily Brontë felt an almost mystic passion for this bleak area of England. Except for brief excursions with her sisters, which always resulted in homesickness, she never left the moorland.

Emily seems to have been rather different from the placid Anne and the passionate but practical Charlotte. Perhaps she was closest to her doomed brother, Branwell, who may have been a model for Hindley Earnshaw in *Wuthering Heights*. From what one can gather in brief family glimpses of her and in the character of Shirley, Charlotte's portrait of her, Emily was fiercely independent, stoically accepting loneliness, disease, and privation, and always infused with a transcendental mysticism which gave special significance to the world around her.

Of the three sisters, Emily was the most talented novelist and poet. Her strange, metaphysical poetry somewhat resembles that of the American mystical recluse Emily Dickinson. The prose of *Wuthering Heights* is the most poetic to be found in the English novel before Virginia Woolf.

Wuthering Heights was published in 1847 under the pseudonym of Ellis Bell. Each of the Brontë sisters chose pseudonyms of ambiguous gender in the hope of avoiding what they felt was a prejudice against female authors. Its original critics misunderstood the book and were shocked by its intensity of feeling. Gradually, however, the novel came to be accepted for the masterpiece it is.

Fame, however, came too slowly for Emily Brontë to enjoy. Like her two sisters, she died of tuberculosis on December 19, 1848, in the parsonage at Haworth.

Vanity Fair

by

WILLIAM MAKEPEACE
THACKERAY (1811–1863)

Main Characters

Becky Sharp—A clever, attractive, ruthlessly self-seeking orphan.

Amelia Sedley—Becky's kind and gentle friend.

Joseph Sedley—"Jos," Amelia's lazy brother.

Sir Pitt Crawley—The penny-pinching, slovenly baronet of Queen's Crawley, Hampshire.

Rawdon Crawley—Sir Pitt's second son, an army captain and "man about town."

George Osborne—Amelia's fiancé, but selfish and forgetful of his duty to her.

William Dobbin—Osborne's steadfast friend and Amelia's long-time admirer.

Lord Steyne—A rich, lecherous old aristocrat.

The Story

In the early days of the nineteenth century, two close friends are graduating from Miss Pinkerton's genteel academy for girls. They are Amelia Sedley, the gentle, well-brought-up daughter of a rich London businessman, and Becky Sharp, the poor orphaned daughter of an artist and a French opera girl, who is kept at the snobbish finishing school only because she can teach the other girls French. Amelia is kind-hearted and innocent. Becky is totally selfish and determined to make good in the world by fair means or foul.

As the girls leave the school, Becky, who hates the mean, penny-pinching life she has been subjected to, defiantly tosses a copy of Johnson's *Dictionary* at the headmistress' sister. Then the coach takes the girls to the Sedley home, where Becky is introduced to Amelia's fat, shy older brother, Jos, home on leave from the army in India. Becky decides that although Jos is lazy and an absurd fop, she will marry him for his wealth and position.

Her plan is balked, however, at a party she arranges with Amelia's matchmaking help at the famous Vauxhall Gardens. There Jos drinks too much punch, makes a fool of himself, and is persuaded by Amelia's old friend, George Osborne, to return to India as soon as possible. With Osborne at the party is his faithful friend and admirer, Captain William Dobbin, also stationed in India. Dobbin has long loved Amelia in secret but is willing to stand aside for his more dashing friend, George.

After the disaster of the Vauxhall party, Becky tearfully leaves her friend Amelia to serve as governess to the two small girls at Queen's Crawley in Hampshire. The miserly, thoroughly nasty Sir Pitt Crawley, baronet, tyrannizes over his family. Becky instantly decides to have little to do with the mousy wife or the girls she is supposed to care for. The object of her attention and flattery will be Sir Pitt and Miss Crawley, the rich spinster aunt of the family.

Miss Crawley's favorite is the young rakehell, Rawdon Crawley, Sir Pitt's son by his marriage to the late Lady Grizzel Crawley. Rawdon is a dashing army captain whose many gambling debts his aunt gladly settles. Becky captures Rawdon's heart and manages to ingratiate herself with the entire Crawley family. When old Miss Crawley falls ill, she will allow nobody to care for her but Becky. When the second Lady Crawley dies, Becky receives a startling marriage proposal from the smitten Sir Pitt.

Tearfully, Becky informs the old man that she cannot accept his proposal, flattering though it is, since she is already married. The announcement that she is married to Rawdon throws the haughty Crawleys into consternation. While Becky and Rawdon go off to Brighton on their honeymoon, Sir Pitt rages impotently and old Miss Crawley cuts her favorite nephew out of her will in favor of his older brother, Pitt.

Meanwhile, knowing that Amelia is pining for George Osborne, Dobbin tells the regiment of his friend's intention to marry Amelia. George is furious. He wants to marry the girl, but he wants his freedom, too. Now he feels honor-bound to marry and senses that he has been trapped into it by the loyal Dobbin.

The steady decline in Amelia's father's fortunes raises further difficulties. When Mr. Sedley finally goes bankrupt, George Osborne's father forbids his son to have anything to do with the now penniless Amelia. Egged on by Dobbin, however, George defies his father's will and marries Amelia, and the couple honeymoon in Brighton. There they meet Rawdon and Becky, who are deeply in debt as a result of living handsomely on "nothing a year."

Dobbin undertakes to reconcile George's father to the marriage but is peremptorily dismissed by the bitter old man. He arrives in Brighton with this sad report and with the exciting news that Napoleon has escaped from Elba and his forces are sweeping into Belgium. George, Rawdon, and Dobbin must proceed at once to Brussels. Meanwhile, George, after only six weeks of marriage to the docile but unexciting Amelia, has made overtures to Becky Sharp. The Battle of Waterloo interrupts his adulterous plans, however, and at the battle's end, George Osborne lies dead with a bullet through his heart.

Rawdon fares better in the battle. Promoted to a colonelcy for courage in action, he takes Becky to Paris for the gay and extravagant winter season following Napoleon's final banishment. Rawdon is highly successful for a time at cards and gambling, and Becky, as usual, attracts a host of admirers. She even finds time to bear Rawdon a son, to whom he immediately becomes passionately attached.

Amelia, too, has a son, but her life is hardly as glamorous as her friend's. Despite his son's death on the field of Waterloo, old Osborne still refuses to see Amelia or his grandson. Amelia, living in penury with her bankrupt parents, has only her baby to console her.

After two years of living beyond their means in Paris, Becky manages to buy off Rawdon's many creditors and both return to London to amass some new debts. Unlike her husband, Becky cares nothing for their little boy. She is preoccupied with adorning herself and flirting with rich men. Unable to live on what Rawdon wins at gambling, Becky begins circulating among the London aristocracy and catches the experienced eye of the rich, unscrupulous Lord Steyne. Steyne manages to have Becky presented at Court where she meets her husband's older brother, Pitt Crawley, now the wealthy member of the family, who falls in love with her.

While Becky is teetering on the verge of adultery, poor virtuous Amelia has finally been forced to consent to let her unrelenting father-in-law rear her baby in order to take the financial burden from her impoverished family. Old Osborne refuses to let the heartbroken mother see much of her son after he becomes the guardian.

Although Rawdon has been getting progressively deeper into debt, Becky sports fine new jewels and trinkets. When Rawdon asks her for money, she refuses him. Finally, Rawdon is hauled off one day to a "sponging house," a kind of debtors' prison for gentlemen. He appeals to his brother, who has him released. On unexpectedly returning home that night, Rawdon finds Becky alone with Lord Steyne. It is his final disillusionment. He leaves, never to see Becky again.

Ten years after Jos Sedley and Dobbin leave for India, they return home to find Mrs. Sedley dead and little George Osborne tyrannizing over his doting grandfather. Dobbin once again proclaims his love for Amelia, but she is still faithful to her dead husband. Jos helps out his family, and old Mr. Osborne's eventual death provides for little George. Together Joseph, Dobbin, and Amelia tour the continent, meeting Becky Sharp in a tenth-rate German spa. Amelia, softhearted as ever, wants to give her old friend a home, despite Dobbin's warnings about her character. Becky's life, after Rawdon's departure, has been hard. She allows Sir Pitt Crawley to adopt her child. Excluded from the London aristocracy, which fears a scandal, she journeys from one watering place to another, picking up men and living off them for a while, then going somewhere else where she is not known.

When she meets Jos, she once again manages to entrance him and becomes his mistress. She persuades the naïve, blundering Jos to take out a large insurance policy in her name. When Jos dies a few months later under mysterious circumstances, Becky is at last a rich woman—wealthy enough now to play the part of a widowed Lady Bountiful, a role she greatly enjoys. Despite her conniving, there is some good in Becky after all. When she learns that Amelia has been steadily refusing the suit of the steadfast Dobbin because she insists on remaining faithful to the memory of her dead husband, Becky shows Amelia a letter that George Osborne had written her on the eve of Waterloo, begging her to elope with him. This evidence finally opens Amelia's eyes, and she accepts Dobbin's proposal. They marry and live happily in the country.

Critical Opinion

Vanity Fair is perhaps the greatest English comic novel of manners, embracing in its many pages a vast spectrum of English life during the Napoleonic period. Thackeray, whose burlesques of historical fiction showed his awareness of the dangers inherent in that genre, nevertheless chose to write of the past—albeit the immediate past—rather than the present. Nevertheless, in the tradition of Fielding and Jane Austen, he managed to portray a society filled with hypocrisy and greed that is recognizable even today.

Thackeray's manner in *Vanity Fair* is that of an urbane, sophisticated, slightly cynical man of the world talking at ease to his fellows. Where Fielding interposed his comments on the characters and actions of *Tom Jones* in prefatory essays before each book, Thackeray injects his comments to the reader throughout *Vanity Fair*. These comments tell the reader essentially what to think about the characters, but never in a condescending or peremptory manner.

One of Thackeray's faults is his tendency to veer from the cynical to the sentimental, never quite hitting reality en route. Thus his experience as a caricaturist, both with pen and pencil, makes him portray the Crawleys as monsters of snobbery and selfishness. On the other hand, Amelia, whose name derives from the heroine of Fielding's last novel, is too saccharine for modern tastes. Perhaps only in Becky Sharp was Thackeray entirely successful in portraying a real human being. It is Becky's indomitable scheming for which the novel is best remembered.

The novel's brilliant structure follows the rise and fall in the fortunes of Becky Sharp and Amelia Sedley. At the beginning, Amelia is the daughter of a wealthy merchant; Becky a poor charity girl. Then as Mr. Sedley's fortunes decline and Becky's schemes mature, the positions are reversed. Mr. Sedley goes bankrupt and Becky marries Rawdon Crawley.

When Becky overplays her hand, however, and, in seeking a grander position in society, compromises herself with Lord Steyne, her fortunes begin to plummet, while Amelia's slowly rise again. It is through this dramatic graphing of social success and failure that Thackeray provides his memorable fleshing-out of Ecclesiastes and of the marketplace in Bunyan's *Pilgrim's Progress*.

The Author

William Makepeace Thackeray was born on July 18, 1811, in Calcutta, the son of a British civil servant. When his father died, young Thackeray was sent to England, where he was a miserable schoolboy at Charterhouse and later an indifferent scholar at Trinity College, Cambridge. He left there in 1830 without a degree.

After his undistinguished school career, Thackeray traveled on the continent for a year and returned to England to study law. He also began drawing caricatures and writing little comic magazine sketches, some of which are hilarious burlesques of the prevailing modes of popular fiction. In 1836 he made a tragic marriage with Isabella Shawe whose subsequent fits of insanity darkened Thackeray's later life.

After several years of struggling as a comic journalist, contributing to *Fraser's Magazine* and *Punch*, Thackeray settled down in 1847 to writing his masterpiece, *Vanity Fair*, which was published serially. He followed this triumph of Victorian fiction with the autobiographical *Pendennis* (1849) and with a historical novel of the eighteenth century, *Henry Esmond* (1852).

The research that went into *Henry Esmond* began during a series of lectures Thackeray delivered in 1851 on the English humorists of the eighteenth century. He repeated these lectures on a money-making tour of the United States in 1852, and gave a series of popular talks on the four Georges during a second tour in 1855. Thackeray enjoyed his tours of the United States more than Dickens enjoyed his, being in general a more tolerant and urbane man than his great contemporary.

America inspired a sequel to *Henry Esmond, The Virginians* (1859). After standing unsuccessfully for Parliament in 1857, Thackeray took over the editorship of the *Cornhill Magazine* in 1860, a job he found irksome. He died on December 24, 1863, in London.

Never quite as popular as Dickens, Thackeray appealed to fewer but more sophisticated readers. Unlike Dickens, he had firsthand acquaintance with the English aristocracy, about whom he wrote more convincingly and less melodramatically. Although the care of his insane wife and his two daughters prevented Thackeray from ever attaining financial security, his urbanity, wit, and easy good manners made him far more comfortable in society than the tormented Dickens ever was.

By the Same Author

Henry Esmond: More controlled but less vivacious than *Vanity Fair, Henry Esmond* is an account of the brilliant society of England in the time of Queen Anne. Such actual historical figures as Marlborough, Addison, and Swift appear in its pages. The style is a triumphant imitation of Augustan prose. Esmond himself, the allegedly illegitimate dependent of the house of Castlewood, persistently woos Beatrix, the flirtatious daughter of Lady Castlewood. Like Dobbin in *Vanity Fair,* he is patient and stalwart in his wooing, but unlike Dobbin, he finally decides he has had enough of Beatrix's haughty rejections. When she helps thwart the Jacobite Restoration plot in which he is involved, he marries her mother, Lady Castlewood, instead and emigrates with her to Virginia.

Pendennis: This autobiographical novel traces the growth to maturity of Arthur Pendennis, nephew of the suave Major Pendennis. Arthur Pendennis falls in love with two women, Emily Costigan, an Irish actress older than himself, and Fanny Bolton, a naïve servant girl. Both women are outside his social caste. The novel chronicles the ways in which Arthur is extricated from what would be a misalliance and becomes the mature husband of Laura, his adoring adopted sister. Thackeray's experiences at college, his gambling debts, his flirtations and jiltings are all amusingly recounted in this vast, sprawling novel.

Barchester Towers

by

ANTHONY TROLLOPE (1815–1882)

Main Characters

Bishop Proudie—The pompous new Bishop of Barchester.

Mrs. Proudie—The Bishop's strong-minded wife.

The Reverend Obadiah Slope—Bishop Proudie's self-centered and power-hungry chaplain.

The Reverend Septimus Harding—Former warden of Hiram's Hospital, a kindly, morally scrupulous old man.

Mrs. Eleanor Bold—Mr. Harding's newly widowed younger daughter.

Dr. Grantly—Mr. Harding's son-in-law, competent, ambitious, and opposed to the Proudie faction in Barchester.

The Reverend Vesey Stanhope—A clergyman who has just returned after several years in Italy.

Charlotte Stanhope—His scheming spinster daughter who professes great friendship for Eleanor Bold.

La Signora Madeline Vesey Neroni—Charlotte's vain, affected sister, a semi-invalid and a flirt.

Bertie Stanhope—The Stanhope brother, a weak-willed dabbler in the arts.

The Reverend Quiverful—Poor father of a very large family, who becomes a candidate for warden of Hiram's Hospital.

The Reverend Francis Arabin—A cultivated, well-mannered Oxford divine and friend of Dr. Grantly's.

Squire Thorne of Ullathorne—Most notable member of the Barchester local gentry.

The Story

One summer in the 1850's the placid old cathedral town of Barchester is in a turmoil about who will succeed the dying Bishop Grantly as Bishop of Barchester. As he watches over his father's deathbed, Dr. Grantly, the local "high-church" archdeacon, yearns to fill the post. But just as the old man peacefully expires, the government in which Dr. Grantly has powerful friends also falls, and the new government selects Dr. Proudie, a stranger to Barchester, for the coveted post.

Dr. Proudie arrives with his strong-minded wife, a woman with low-church sympathies, and a conniving, self-seeking chaplain, Obadiah Slope, who preaches the first sermon of the new bishop's regime. The sermon shocks the conservative elders of the church with its puritanical objections to ritual, to the chanting and intoning of services, and to church music.

Soon the lines of battle are drawn. Dr. Grantly quickly realizes that the new bishop is completely dominated by his wife—an intolerable state of affairs—and that she has insisted on giving power in cathedral affairs to the odious Mr. Slope who proposes to make radical changes in the way things have always been done at Barchester.

Aside from doctrinal differences, another point of dispute between the old and new factions at Barchester is the wardenship of Hiram's Hospital, a charitable institution for destitute old men, which is controlled by the diocese. Everyone assumes that the Reverend Septimus Harding, Dr. Grantly's father-in-law, who resigned from this post when a government scandal connected with it persuaded him he could no longer serve in good conscience, will now resume the wardenship. Mr. Slope, however, has different ideas. Seeing another opportunity to impose his clerical ideas on Barchester, Mr. Slope, unknown to Dr. Proudie, attaches such demeaning conditions to Mr. Harding's resumption of his post that the old gentleman feels he must refuse. Dr. Grantly is furious, but momentarily powerless to do anything about it.

Another "reform" of the new bishop's party is to force absentee clergymen to return to the diocese. This decree affects Dr. Vesey Stanhope, an elegant dilettante who has been living in Italy all these years, leaving his parish in the hands of his curates. Dr. Stanhope is head of a remarkable family: a sick wife; a sour spinster daughter, Charlotte; an affected, semi-invalid daughter who, after an unfortunate Italian marriage, calls herself La Signora Madeline Vesey Stanhope Neroni; and a hopelessly lazy and irresponsible son, Bertie, who has taken up a series of professions—never for very long—and has even gone to Palestine to convert the Jews. (He was himself converted for a time.)

One day the entire Stanhope family descends on Barchester for Bishop Proudie's first formal reception, and causes quite a stir. La Signora Neroni, borne by four men to the bishop's sofa, holds court there. With her exotic beauty and fine continental manners, she enthralls poor Mr. Slope who has never seen so glamorous a woman before. His attentions to her infuriate the jealous Mrs. Proudie who determines from then on to keep her husband's chaplain as well as her husband more carefully under her thumb. At the party, too, Bertie Stanhope irritates Bishop Proudie with his asinine opinions on religion.

Soon Dr. Grantly has a chance to strike back at the odious Proudies. The living of St. Ewold's becomes vacant, and Dr. Grantly travels to Oxford to ensure that his high-church friend, the Reverend Francis Arabin, will accept the appointment. Mr. Arabin, a suave, well-bred bachelor of about forty, can be counted on, Dr. Grantly feels, to awe the presumptuous Proudie faction.

Meanwhile, however, Eleanor Bold, Mr. Harding's younger daughter, a widow with an infant son, becomes the object of Mr. Slope's designs. The young clergyman sees a chance to defeat the high-church party, while gaining Mrs. Bold's inheritance for himself, by wooing the lovely young widow. Mr. Slope mistakes Eleanor's native politeness for encouragement and continues to press his attentions on her. Hoping to impress her, he decides to back Mr. Harding for the post of warden.

Unfortunately for his plan, Mr. Slope discovers that his patroness, Mrs. Proudie, has her own plans for the wardenship. She wants to give it to Mr. Quiverful who could certainly use the extra income. Desperately trying to rear a family of fourteen children on £400 a year, the naïve Mr. Quiverful proves no match for the intrigues of Mr. Slope, who easily persuades him to refuse the post by promising him something even more lucrative in the near future.

When she hears of this latest maneuver by her overly

ambitious protégé, Mrs. Proudie is furious, for she has already promised the wardenship to Mrs. Quiverful and has graciously received that humble lady's blessing. Mrs. Proudie stalks into her husband's study, expecting to lay down the law to him, but finds him in conference with Mr. Slope, who refuses to leave. Temporarily frustrated but by no means defeated, Mrs. Proudie breaks the sad news to Mrs. Quiverful.

Mr. Slope's attentions to Eleanor increase, much to the chagrin of Dr. Grantly. But the chaplain soon has a rival in Bertie Stanhope, encouraged by his sisters to woo the well-to-do widow in the hope that her inheritance will pay his debts. In order to help her inept brother in his suit, La Signora Neroni starts exercising her charms on Mr. Slope, not realizing that Eleanor had never even considered him as a possible mate.

Dr. Grantly, under the same misapprehension, hopes to take Eleanor's mind off Mr. Slope by inviting her and her father to visit with him at Plumstead Episcopi. There she meets Mr. Arabin who falls in love with her but, through lack of experience with women, does not know how to press his suit. When Eleanor receives a note from Mr. Slope at Dr. Grantly's home, her brother-in-law furiously assumes she is about to marry his arch-enemy. Mr. Harding shares this feeling, and wistfully prepares to accept Mr. Slope as a son-in-law. But when even Mr. Arabin believes she intends to marry Mr. Slope, Eleanor angrily leaves the house and returns to Barchester.

Affairs come to a head at a splendid lawn party given by the rich and old-fashioned Thornes of Ullathorne, the local country squire and his eccentric spinster sister. Eleanor, driven to the party in a carriage with the Stanhopes, finds herself seated next to Mr. Slope who decides to propose to her. When he does so later in the day, Eleanor slaps him in irritation.

Then Bertie, egged on by his sisters, tries half-heartedly to propose, but he naïvely tells Eleanor that his sister Charlotte has convinced him he should marry the widow to repair his broken fortunes. Eleanor is now furious with the entire Stanhope family, especially when she sees Mr. Arabin being played up to by the Signora Neroni. When Dr. Stanhope learns that Bertie has failed once again, he orders him out of the house. A few days later Bertie sets out for Italy, hoping to make his fortune as a sculptor.

Now Dr. Trefoil, the old Dean of Barchester, has a stroke and is on his deathbed. This means a new ecclesiastical position to fill—and the final test of strength between the warring factions. Mr. Slope, who would like the deanship for himself, plunges into action, writing letters to powerful friends in journalism and the government. He gets his newspaper friends' support and assumes he has Bishop Proudie's blessings. He does not, however, count on the unrelenting fury of Mrs. Proudie who has not forgotten how he danced attendance on the Signora Neroni and thwarted his patroness in the Quiverful affair.

Mrs. Proudie has made her husband's life so miserable that he has completely surrendered to her. He offers the deanship to Mr. Harding to preserve domestic peace. Mr. Slope's defeat is complete. Not only does he not get the deanship, but Mrs. Proudie also sees to it that he is no longer her husband's chaplain, and he must leave Barchester to try his luck elsewhere. He is also subjected to a scornful dressing-down by the Signora Neroni.

Now that Mr. Slope has left, the relieved Stanhopes feel they can safely return to Italy, but before leaving, Signora Neroni summons Eleanor to her home to tell her that Mr. Arabin is deeply in love with her but lacks the courage to make his feelings clear.

Mr. Harding decides he is too old for the deanship. Mr. Arabin is appointed instead, a great victory for the high-church faction, comparable only to the ousting of Mr. Slope from Barchester. Mr. Quiverful finally gets the wardenship of Hiram's Hospital, and Dr. Grantly is content.

With his new power, Mr. Arabin is emboldened to speak to Eleanor, and a meeting is arranged at Ullathorne, where Miss Thorne, a great matchmaker, sees to it that Mr. Arabin proposes. Eleanor accepts him, and peace once again returns to Barchester.

Critical Opinion

Henry James once said of Trollope that "his great, his inestimable merit was a complete appreciation of the usual." Unlike Dickens, his great contemporary, Trollope generally avoided writing about the grotesque, the bizarre, or the desperately poor people of this world. His novels describe in detail the average middle-class lives of mid-Victorian English-men going about their business in a normal way. A keen observer of the niceties of social behavior, Trollope is comparable to the Dutch genre painters who rendered middle-class life in faithful detail, uncharged with passionate emotion.

Thus *Barchester Towers*, although it is about the clergy, can hardly be said to seethe with religious emotion. Trollope's clergymen are average men with average ambitions and desires. The doctrinal disputes between high and low church factions are treated not as genuine theological issues but rather as counters in a political chess game. A religious zealot would be ludicrously out of place in Barsetshire.

Trollope's satire in *Barchester Towers* is milder than the indignant humor of Dickens or the sophisticated wit of Thackeray. It is best exemplified in his portraits of Mrs. Proudie and her henpecked husband, and in such scenes as the bishop's reception and the Ullathorne fete.

Trollope tries to be fair-minded in his judgment of people. None are wholly virtuous or wholly wicked. Mr. Slope, odious as he is, is described neither as a fool nor a coward. Trollope's satire, in short, unlike Dickens' or Meredith's, has nothing in it of the "corrective." He is not a campaigner for any radical change in society. He tends to accept life as it is. This is not to say that Trollope does not moralize. Like Thackeray, George Eliot, and other Victorian novelists, he addresses the reader directly, giving his opinions of the characters at crucial moments in the action.

Trollope's attitude toward his characters is almost remorselessly sane and reasonable. He never attains any grandeur, but neither does he ever become ridiculous or absurd. Although some of his later political novels probe deeper beneath the surface of Victorian society, it is the six-novel Barsetshire series that stands as Trollope's finest achievement. Like Balzac in his *Comédie Humaine*, Hardy in his Wessex novels, and Faulkner in his Yoknapatawpha novels, Trollope, by means of characters who reappear from novel to novel and by means of geographical and thematic unity, brings alive a whole area of human experience. Because the society he depicts is seen in such detail, many of his readers today still find his novels, especially the Barchester group, remarkably real and engrossing.

The Author

Anthony Trollope, born in London on April 24, 1815, attended Harrow and Winchester sporadically until the family, plagued by his father's mismanagement of the family fortunes, moved to Belgium to escape their creditors.

In 1834 Trollope entered the General Post Office as a clerk, but rapidly rose through the ranks. In his travels as postal inspector he began to write his extensive series of novels, beginning with two novels of Irish life in 1847 and 1848, and proceeding to the first of the famous Barsetshire series, *The Warden,* in 1855.

Aside from this series, of which the most famous novels are *Barchester Towers* (1857) and *The Last Chronicle of Barset* a decade later, Trollope's major novels are *The Eustace Diamonds* (1873) and *The Way We Live Now* (1875), an inveighing against the ills of Victorian England. Most of Trollope's novels deal either with clerical or political life.

Trollope was able to write a great number of novels (most of them quite long), indulge in his favorite sport of fox hunting, and travel extensively while performing his duties in the postal service because he worked so systematically at his writing. He planned and wrote his novels in trains while going from one postal inspection job to another, keeping himself to a rigid schedule of literary production. He even set a fixed number of words to write every quarter hour and kept a watch constantly in view. In his fascinating *Autobiography,* published posthumously in 1883, Trollope confessed that up to 1879 he had earned the staggering sum of £70,000 from his writing.

Enormously popular during Trollope's lifetime, his books began to decline in popularity almost immediately after his death, perhaps because the unromantic, businesslike revelations of his *Autobiography* shattered his readers' notions about how his novels were written. Interest in Trollope revived, however, shortly before World War II, when readers under wartime pressures found satisfaction in his leisurely, mildly humorous accounts of everyday life in a more stable world. One modern novelist, the late Angela Thirkell, was so entranced by the world of Barsetshire that she also wrote a series of novels about it.

By the Same Author

The Warden: The first of the Barsetshire series, coming just before *Barchester Towers*, this brief work introduces us to Dr. Grantly and Mr. Harding, who has been happily performing the functions of warden of Hiram's Hospital. When his daughter, Eleanor, falls in love with John Bold, an idealistic, rather priggish young physician, trouble begins. Bold has found out that according to the original stipulations of John Hiram's will, Mr. Harding has been getting a stipend much larger than he should. The kindly, cello-playing old choirmaster of Barchester is willing to resign his post, but Dr. Grantly will not hear of it. He finds it disgraceful that an outsider should meddle in church business, and he opposes Mr. Harding's resignation as a matter of principle. Mr. Harding becomes a pawn in a battle between Dr. Grantly and Mr. Bold, a conflict that raises a furor in the London newspapers. All ends well, however, when Mr. Harding is finally allowed to resign.

The Last Chronicle of Barset: This huge conclusion to the Barsetshire series was considered by Trollope to be his best novel. It deals with the events that follow when the Reverend Josiah Crawley is unjustly accused of stealing £20. Mr. Crawley finds himself in conflict with Mrs. Proudie over the affair (she tries to replace him in his own church). Before he is cleared, Mrs. Proudie, the most fascinating and, in her peculiar way, one of the most lovable characters in the series, dies of an apopletic fit. Old Mr. Harding dies, too.

Adam Bede

by

GEORGE ELIOT (1819–1880)

Main Characters

Adam Bede—A strong and upright young carpenter.
Seth Bede—Adam's brother, in love with Dinah Morris.
Dinah Morris—A serious-minded Methodist preacher.
Martin Poyser—A neighborhood landowner who runs prosperous Hall Farm.
Mrs. Poyser—His voluble wife, Dinah's aunt, filled with folk wisdom and a sense of her own importance.
Hetty Sorrel—Another niece of Mrs. Poyser's, a vivacious, curly-haired girl of seventeen.
Arthur Donnithorne—The selfish, aristocratic grandson of the local squire.
Jonathan Burge—The master builder and carpenter who employs Adam Bede.

The Story

Adam Bede is a powerfully built young carpenter working for the builder Jonathan Burge in the small village of Hayslope in the year 1799. Adam is universally admired, and counts among his friends young Captain Arthur Donnithorne, grandson of the local squire.

One evening as Adam leaves his spacious workshop, his

brother Seth goes courting the earnest Dinah Morris, a gentle Methodist who is preaching on the village green. Escorting Dinah home after her sermon, Seth asks her to become his wife, but she replies that although she likes him she cannot marry because she is called to preach the word of God. When Seth returns home, disconsolate, he finds Adam working on a coffin that their father was commissioned to make but neglected to finish. Old Matthias Bede has of late become a frequenter of the local inn, and his wife, Lisbeth, complains bitterly about his irresponsibility while Adam hammers vigorously at the coffin.

On his way home from the tavern that night, the drunken Matthias Bede falls into the Willow Brook and drowns, leaving Lisbeth more than ever dependent on her two sons who will have to wait before they can think of getting married.

Mr. Burge is so pleased with Adam's work that he wishes he would marry his daughter, Mary. But Adam is in love with Hetty Sorrel, a pert, flirtatious girl of seventeen who lives with her aunt, Mrs. Poyser, at Hall Farm. However, the dashing Arthur Donnithorne visits the Poyser dairy one day, and since then Hetty thinks of no one but him. Her uncle, Martin Poyser, would like Hetty to marry the stable, honest Adam, but she dreams of the luxuries that the heir to Squire Donnithorne can offer her.

During the summer, Donnithorne leaves with his regiment and Adam hopes that Hetty will now turn her attention to him. But when Donnithorne returns to celebrate his twenty-first birthday, the whole village is astir with excitement over the feast that is to be held on the Donnithorne estate. Adam is honored with a place at Donnithorne's table. This act of friendship worries Adam's mother. She fears that it may give him notions above his station in life. The feast is a great success and Donnithorne becomes more than ever a glamorous figure in Hetty's romantic eyes.

Three weeks after the birthday celebration, Adam is returning home when he sees two figures in intimate embrace. His dog frightens them and the girl runs off, but Adam has seen that they are Arthur Donnithorne and Hetty Sorrel.

Knowing that the young aristocrat has no intention of marrying Hetty, Adam calls him "a coward and scoundrel," and soon the two former friends are exchanging blows. Adam easily defeats Donnithorne and makes him promise that he will write a letter to Hetty calling off the affair which Arthur insists was only a harmless flirtation. He gives the letter to Adam to deliver the next day, hoping that this action will prejudice Hetty even further against the carpenter.

When Adam gives the letter to Hetty, she is plunged into despair. After Adam is offered a share of Mr. Burge's business, he proposes marriage to the flighty Hetty. Again the Poysers urge her to accept, and this time, to her joy, she gives in. The wedding is put off for a while so that the Bede house can be enlarged to receive the newlyweds.

In February, Hetty, pretending that she is going to visit Dinah Morris in the mill town where she is currently preaching, impulsively leaves in search of Donnithorne. She learns to her dismay that his regiment has gone off to Ireland. She gives birth to his baby and abandons it in a wood. Then, filled with remorse, she returns to the spot where she left the infant and finds it dead.

When Donnithorne's grandfather dies, the young squire returns to Hayslope. He learns that Hetty is in prison awaiting execution for the murder of her child. He tries desperately to win her release, apparently to no avail. Dinah returns to Hayslope and visits the condemned girl, trying to ease her misery and get her to make a full confession. Hetty breaks down and says she did not intend the baby to die, and in fact was overcome with guilt when she learned what had happened. For a while she even considered killing herself.

Just as Hetty is about to die on the scaffold, Donnithorne, remorseful at his role in the tragedy, wins a reprieve for the girl. Instead of imposing the death sentence, the court orders that she be exiled to the colonies. Donnithorne leaves for a new life in Spain. He later learns that Hetty has died after serving her sentence.

Meanwhile, Adam Bede tries to find solace at his workbench. The following autumn Dinah Morris returns to the Poyser farm but leaves soon after to preach in the town. One day she accompanies Adam to his house, where his mother is ailing. On the way there, Adam shyly confides that he wishes Dinah were his sister so they could be together always. Dinah blushes at this but keeps her silence. Then her mother hints outright that Adam ought to propose to the good, earnest Methodist girl.

Adam first consults with his brother Seth who, he feels,

has a prior claim to Dinah's hand. Seth assures him, however, that all is over between them and that Adam can lose nothing by proposing to her.

Adam finally asks Dinah to marry him. She tells him that, although she is strongly attracted to him, she must await divine guidance. Accordingly, she goes back to the town to live. After a while Adam comes to see her and he learns that Dinah will marry him after all.

Critical Opinion

Although *Adam Bede* is the first of George Eliot's novels, it was written when she was forty years old and is consequently more mature than the first work of most novelists. From its initial publication in 1859—the year also saw the appearance of *A Tale of Two Cities*, *The Ordeal of Richard Feverel*, and *The Origin of Species*—it became a favorite with readers, including Dickens, Charles Kingsley, and Alexandre Dumas.

All of George Eliot's characteristic concerns and skills appear in *Adam Bede*. Her brooding compassion for weak humanity caught in moral traps of its own devising is movingly set forth in the tragedy of Hetty Sorrel, a sensuous girl of great sensitivity to life whose sin and expiation form the moral backbone of the novel. As one who had herself "sinned," or at least flouted the conventions of society, George Eliot was keenly aware of the temptations of love and at the same time sharply perceptive of its morally destructive qualities.

Another achievement of George Eliot's in *Adam Bede* is her ability to portray with gentle, uncondescending humor the uncomplicated lives of the rural lower middle class. Mrs. Poyser, Hetty's bumbling, officious aunt, is a triumph of comic art. Her sayings, folk wisdom mingled with self-important sententiousness, remain a delight. In her portrayal of rural types, George Eliot is matched in English literature only by Shakespeare and by her follower, Thomas Hardy, whose *Tess of the D'Urbervilles* in many ways resembles *Adam Bede*.

Central to George Eliot's moral doctrine is the influence of one soul on another. It was here that George Eliot touched upon themes that made her so unpopular for years after her death. The purity of Dinah and of Adam himself tends to be less acceptable to the modern reader than to George Eliot's contemporaries. In the story of Hetty she refurbished the stock Victorian cliché of the sinning girl, seduced and abandoned by an aristocratic weakling.

George Eliot transcends the limitations of her period, however, by the keenness of her analysis of a man who is amoral and basically selfish but who nevertheless has considerable charm and who redeems himself. She is most expert at outlining the conflict between the weakness of the flesh and one's moral duties to oneself and to others, a theme richly explored by her for the first time in *Adam Bede*.

The Author

George Eliot was the pen name of Mary Ann Evans, who was born in Warwickshire on November 22, 1819. Her father was an estate agent of somewhat conventional religious and social views which Mary Ann rebelled against. At an early age she had come under the influence of a Coventry manufacturer named Charles Bray.

Characteristically, the first work of this gentle, intensely serious and intellectual girl was a translation of the controversially rationalistic *Life of Jesus* by the German scholar, D. F. Strauss. Her father died in 1849, unreconciled to his daughter's views of religion.

Between 1851 and 1853, she was assistant editor of the *Westminster Review* and did further translations of significant German works. As an editor of this important liberal publication, she met the leading intellectual and artistic lights of her day, including the philosopher Herbert Spencer and the author of a standard biography of Goethe, George Henry Lewes. She fell in love with Lewes who was separated from his wife but could not obtain a divorce.

From 1854 until Lewes' death in 1878, George Eliot lived unconventionally with him. They never married. Although this step was initially shocking to Victorian morality, the rectitude and high moral tone of the match soon silenced most scandal, but the ambiguous social position George Eliot occupied shaped her later thinking about morality in the novels she began to write, of which *Adam Bede* was the first.

She followed this success with *The Mill on the Floss* (1860) and *Silas Marner* (1861). During the composition of these works, George Eliot visited Florence, where she did research in Renaissance life for her historical novel, the vast, somewhat inchoate *Romola* (1863). She returned to England for the subject matter of *Felix Holt* (1866) and her master-piece, *Middlemarch* (1871–1872), the most complex and artistically successful of her novels.

After *Middlemarch*, George Eliot's talents seemed ex-hausted. Her final novel, *Daniel Deronda* (1876), is more noteworthy for its moral philosophy and for its prophetic treatment of Zionism (the hero, unique in Victorian fiction, is a Jew) than for any unusual qualities as fiction.

In May 1880, George Eliot married John Walter Cross. She died on December 22 of the same year. At the time of her death she was widely recognized as one of the outstanding novelists of the day, but her reputation underwent an eclipse from which it only recently has begun to emerge.

By the Same Author

Silas Marner: Silas Marner is a brief tale, told in classically simple style, of the redemption of an embittered miser through love. Falsely accused of theft in a small religious community, Silas Marner, a linen weaver, settles in Raveloe, where he lives for a while only to accumulate wealth. After fifteen years of loneliness, Marner is accused of a new theft, but his troubles begin to disappear when he discovers and adopts a pretty stray child named Eppie. As Eppie grows up, her selfless, unquestioning love for the old man purges his soul of the crabbed suspicion of his fellow beings which had formerly consumed it. The real culprit is discovered eventual-ly, and Silas is allowed to live out the rest of his days with Eppie in peace and contentment.

Middlemarch: This, the most complex and richest of George Eliot's novels, was once cited by Virginia Woolf as one of the few English novels written for adults. Several stories are intertwined in it, the central "hero" really being the outwardly placid small English town of Middlemarch. In it Dorothea Brooke, an idealistic young woman, makes a bad marriage with the dry pedant Casaubon and later falls in love with his charming, irresponsible cousin, Will Ladislaw. At the same time, an idealistic young doctor, Lydgate, marries the shallow, spendthrift beauty, Rosamond Vincy, whose unceasing demands for a more luxurious life destroy him as a pure scientist. Out of these unhappy marriages, George Eliot weaves an immense tapestry in which the material life is seen in constant battle with the life of the spirit, and in which the social fabric of a town is scrupulously but compassionately analyzed.

The Ordeal of Richard Feverel

by

GEORGE MEREDITH (1828–1909)

Main Characters

Sir Austin Feverel—The embittered, possessive Lord of
Raynham Abbey, suspicious of women and determined to
protect his son from the world by a strict but eccentric
system of education.

Richard Feverel—Sir Austin's only son, the "Hope of Raynham," a headstrong, idealistic, and thoroughly aristocratic
youth who chafes at his father's "System."

Adrian Harley—Sir Austin's nephew, the "Wise Youth," a
parasitical and cynical young man who reports to Sir Austin
on Richard's doings and enjoys trading epigrams with the
Lord of Raynham.

Austin Wentworth—Richard's sensible, humane uncle who
thinks the "System" is all nonsense.

Ripton Thompson—Richard's middle-class playmate and
friend who joins him in his youthful escapades.

Tom Bakewell—A local farmhand who becomes Richard's
loyal servant.

Blaize—The neighboring farmer, blunt, straightforward, and
totally unimpressed by the grandeur of the Feverels.

Lucy Desborough—Blaize's Catholic niece, who loves Richard
despite Sir Austin's disapproval and Richard's infidelity.

Lord Mountfalcon—A debauched aristocrat who flirts with Lucy after her marriage to Richard.

Bella Mount—A "fallen woman" who seduces Richard when he tries to have her accepted by society.

Clare—Richard's cousin, secretly and hopelessly in love with him.

Lady Emmeline Blandish—A wise, sophisticated woman whose admiration for Sir Austin Feverel does not prevent her from trying to intervene on Richard's behalf.

Heavy Benson—Sir Austin's serpentine butler.

The Story

When Sir Austin Feverel's wife ran off with a minor poet, the Lord of Raynham Abbey vowed that he would bring up his only son, Richard, according to a system that would spare him such disagreeable experiences. A confirmed woman-hater and author of the cynical book of anti-feminist epigrams. *The Pilgrim's Scrip*, Sir Austin is determined that Richard should have no serious contact with women until he is twenty-five.

Placing Richard's education in the hands of his worldly-wise nephew, Adrian Harley, Sir Austin takes great pains to ensure Richard's innocence of the world and tries to instill in him a fine moral sense. He brings Richard up to be everything a young aristocrat should be: honorable, chivalrous, and high-spirited. But as he approaches adolescence, Richard becomes impatient with the kind of life he is leading. Sir Austin decides he must have a safe companion for his son, one he can trust not to lead Richard astray. He selects Ripton Thompson, the rather plodding son of his lawyer, who proves a willing follower in all of Richard's youthful pranks.

One of these escapades gets Richard into the first serious trouble of his life. Out hunting one day with Ripton, he unintentionally trespasses on the neighboring estate of Farmer Blaize, a political enemy of his father, and illegally shoots a pheasant. Blaize accuses the boys of poaching and orders them off his land. When Richard, insulted that a mere farmer should address him in this way, refuses to leave, Blaize horse-whips him.

On Richard's return, his father sends him to his room after dinner. Unrepentant, Richard meets Ripton and they plot a suitable revenge on Farmer Blaize. The boys set fire to Blaize's hayricks, with the aid of Tom Bakewell, a local farm laborer. Sir Austin suspects the truth, but does not accuse his son because he wants to see whether the boy will behave honorably without any prompting, as the system has taught him to do. Ripton, however, is immediately sent back to his father.

Tom Bakewell is arrested for arson, but he protects Richard by not mentioning the bribe Richard gave him to set the ricks on fire. When he hears of Tom's courage, Richard immediately goes to Farmer Blaize to confess. He does not know that his father has already quietly paid for the damage. Humiliated by Blaize's refusal to take his confession seriously, Richard stalks out of the house, failing to notice the farmer's pretty, young orphan niece, Lucy Desborough. Tom is acquitted at the trial and becomes Richard's lifelong loyal servant.

When Richard turns eighteen, his father decides to go to London to find a suitable wife for him. When Richard reaches the age of twenty-five, Sir Austin plans to let him marry a girl worthy of his fine upbringing.

But while Sir Austin is away, Richard meets the lovely Lucy Desborough, and they have an idyllic, innocent love affair. Richard had been earlier attracted to his cousin Clare, who passionately but secretly loves him. Now, however, he can think only of Lucy. The pair meet frequently in the meadows and woods surrounding the abbey to swear their love to each other. Lucy unfortunately has, in the eyes of the Feverels, one major defect. She is a Catholic.

In their innocence Lucy and Richard are unaware that they are being spied upon by Heavy Benson, Sir Austin's woman-hating butler. When Richard learns of this, he beats Benson nearly to death, but it is too late. Sir Austin has been informed of the affair and summons Richard to London to meet the girl he has chosen for him, Carola Grandison.

When Richard, unwilling to part from Lucy, puts off going to London, Adrian tells him his father is ill with apoplexy, and the dutiful son then hurries to London. Here, he finds his father quite healthy, but angry with him for carrying on with Lucy behind his back. Sir Austin lectures his son about the dangers of women, pointing out that every Feverel is doomed to an ordeal brought about by a woman. He insists on Richard's meeting Carola Grandison, who is nice enough but hardly the girl to drive Lucy from Richard's mind. Soon, however, Lucy stops writing him, and Richard, distracted, insists on returning to Raynham. There he discovers that Farmer Blaize, who also disapproves of the affair, has sent the unwilling Lucy off to a distant school.

Now Richard determines to take matters in his own hands. He persuades his old friend, Ripton Thompson, to procure lodgings in London for Lucy, and then, accompanied by his dyspeptic and inefficient Uncle Hippias, sets off for London himself. Giving his uncle the slip, Richard secretly establishes Lucy in a lodging house run by Mrs. Berry, his childhood nurse. He persuades the seventeen-year-old Lucy to marry him; but just as he is hurrying to the church, he accidentally meets Adrian Harley, Cousin Clare, and her mother. In his embarrassment, he drops his wedding ring which Clare picks up. Aware now of what Richard is about to do, Clare loyally keeps his secret, even though it is an agony for her to know that Richard is marrying another girl.

Delegating Ripton to break the news to Sir Austin, Richard marries Lucy and the pair go to the Isle of Wight for their honeymoon. Sir Austin's reaction to the news is cold and philosophical. He recognizes that the elopement means the defeat of his system. His old friend and admirer, Lady Blandish, tries to persuade him to meet Lucy, for she knows that the lovely girl will surely captivate him. But Sir Austin refuses even to answer Richard's conciliatory letters.

Efforts made by Lady Blandish and by Adrian, who has visited the honeymooning couple, to reconcile father and son fail. Sir Austin is deeply hurt by Richard's deception. Journeying from the Isle of Wight to London in the hope of meeting his father there, Richard innocently leaves Lucy in the care of the wicked Lord Mountfalcon. Mountfalcon arranges with a friend of his, the notorious Mrs. Bella Mount, to seduce Richard in London and to keep him there while Mountfalcon has his way with Lucy. Disregarding the warnings of friends, Richard falls into the trap by determining to rescue the reputation of Mrs. Mount while he is in London. After three months of waiting for his father to show up, Richard finally succumbs to Mrs. Mount's charms, unaware that his own Lucy, now staying with Mrs. Berry in London, is about to bear his son.

Meanwhile Richard's cousin Clare, having realized the

hopelessness of her love for him, has consented to marry an old man chosen by her mother. She dies soon after, leaving a diary telling of her love for Richard which fills him with remorse for his callousness. He feels further guilt about his relations with Mrs. Mount and goes wandering vaguely about Europe, unsure of himself and unable to face Lucy.

While Richard is wallowing in self-pity and guilt, his reasonable uncle, Austin Wentworth, returns to England after five years abroad. Wentworth, who never approved of the system, learns of the unhappiness it has produced and brings Lucy to Raynham to meet Sir Austin. In his loneliness Sir Austin has relented somewhat. He is charmed by his daughter-in-law and the handsome grandson she has borne him. Richard, informed that he is a father, returns to England. But before he can get to Raynham, he receives a letter from Mrs. Mount divulging Lord Mountfalcon's plot to seduce Lucy. He challenges Lord Mountfalcon to a duel, not realizing that whatever his original intentions may have been, the old roué never succeeded in undermining Lucy's virtue.

Then Richard returns to Raynham. He embraces the ecstatic Lucy and sees his son for the first time. Overcome with remorse, he confesses his infidelity and receives Lucy's forgiveness. Leaving a distraught Lucy behind, Richard rushes off to France for his duel. He is only slightly wounded by Lord Mountfalcon. But Lucy, in her anxiety for his safety, contracts brain fever and dies. When Richard hears of her death, his spirit is completely crushed. Lady Blandish wonders if Sir Austin, in his grief at the double tragedy, realizes that he has destroyed his boy with the rigors of his system.

Critical Opinion

The Ordeal of Richard Feverel is a strange and not altogether successful novel, a fact Meredith tacitly admitted when he revised it twenty years after its first publication. The plot is often incoherent and cluttered with minor characters, many of whom disappeared in the revised version. Its outstanding quality is its mingling of sophisticated comedy with passionate lyricism and somber tragedy. Many readers have felt, for instance, that the death of Lucy and the ruin of Richard's future are insufficiently motivated by that unimportant last-minute duel. The novel oscillates between high comedy (the court of admiring females hoping to marry Sir Austin, the determined but attractive woman-hater) and lyricism (Richard's love for Lucy, couched in a style that reminds us that Meredith thought of himself primarily as a poet).

Much of *Richard Feverel* is autobiographical. The desertion of Sir Austin by his wife before the book begins is a reflection of Meredith's own loss of his first wife. The tragi-comic efforts of Sir Austin to educate his only son represent Meredith's own nagging fears of the kind of father he might prove to be.

The greatness of the book lies in its ironic sense of the difference between reality and romance, and in its perception of the folly of trying to force a young, independent spirit into the rigorous, life-denying mold of an egoistic system of education. Warm-hearted and idealistic, Richard genuinely wants to help the "fallen woman," Bella Mount, but only succumbs to her charms and neglects the wife who really needs him. Similarly, Sir Austin's adoration of his son ironically leads to the most tragic consequences. For all Sir Austin's witty aphorisms and Adrian Harley's cynical appraisal of life, *The Ordeal of Richard Feverel* is a profoundly pessimistic book, underscoring the tragic consequences that flow from any effort to mold another human being after one's own sterile image.

The Author

George Meredith was born on February 12, 1828, the son and grandson of prosperous naval outfitters in Portsmouth. A consummate snob, he kept his ancestry secret throughout his life. His mother died when he was a child, and Meredith was sent to a German school where he received a thorough education. In 1849 he married the widowed daughter of Thomas Love Peacock, the distinguished satiric novelist.

It was an unhappy marriage, but it had one bright aspect: the friendship between Meredith and Peacock. The older novelist's sparkling wit and cosmopolitan view of the world strongly impressed Meredith and was later to influence his own fiction.

In 1858 his wife ran off with a lover, leaving Meredith, like Sir Austin Feverel, to bring up their son alone. The next year he published *The Ordeal of Richard Feverel*, his first real novel. Although the book did not sell well, it caught the attention of Swinburne, Rossetti, and others of the Pre-Raphaelite group of artists and writers. From that point on Meredith became the darling of the English intelligentsia although his novels never won the vast audiences that Dickens and Thackeray reached.

In 1861 Meredith's estranged wife died. Brooding over the failure of his marriage, Meredith wrote the great, tragic *Modern Love*, one of the finest long poems of the nineteenth century. At the same time he became a reader and editor for Chapman and Hall, a job he kept until 1894. He made some strange mistakes as a reader, rejecting, for instance, Samuel Butler's *Erewhon* and the early works of George Bernard Shaw, but he was also responsible for the encouragement of his great contemporary, Thomas Hardy.

In 1864 Meredith married again, this time more successfully. With his new wife, Marie Vulliamy, the novelist settled down at Box Hill in Surrey, where he lived the rest of his life. There he wrote some of his most famous novels, *The Adventures of Harry Richmond* (1871), *Beauchamp's Career* (1876), *The Egoist* (1879), and *Diana of the Crossways* (1885).

Meredith's second wife died in 1885, but Meredith lived on for another quarter century. Lonely and ailing, his productive powers waning, Meredith became the recipient of many honors, including the highly coveted Order of Merit. His brand of intellectual comedy had not won him a vast audience. Only a small, fiercely loyal group mourned his death, on May 18, 1909.

By the Same Author

The Egoist: Like Sir Austin Feverel, Sir Willoughby Patterne of Patterne Hall, the hero-villain of *The Egoist*, is a man consumed with a sense of his own importance. Again, like Sir Austin, Sir Willoughby is hounded by women who are at once attracted and repelled by his arrogance. After he is jilted by one of them, Constantia Durham, he falls in love with the beautiful and intelligent Clara Middleton, who stays with her father at Patterne Hall during a six-month engagement.

Sir Willoughby meanwhile maintains an interest in another

intelligent young lady, Laetitia Dale. His great fear is that he will be jilted a second time, something his ego could never bear. This inevitably happens when, in his blind conceit, he fails to see that Clara has fallen in love with Vernon Whitford, Willoughby's scholarly cousin and secretary. After a series of brilliant maneuvers and intrigues, Clara and Vernon marry, and poor Laetitia ends as the wife of the man she knows to be a "vindictive and incorrigible egotist." *The Egoist* is probably Meredith's richest and most complex novel. It is consistently comic, although tinged with pathos.

Diana of the Crossways: Meredith's last important novel, and during his lifetime one of his most popular, *Diana* is based on an actual scandal that shook early nineteenth-century England. The scandal concerned Mrs. Caroline Norton, the grand-daughter of the famous playwright and parliamentarian, Richard Brinsley Sheridan. Mrs. Norton was unjustly accused of selling to a newspaper an important political secret she had obtained from her lover. In the novel, Mrs. Norton becomes the beautiful, witty, and misunderstood Diana Merion. Diana, trying to escape a loveless marriage with Augustus Warwick, becomes involved in a trial over her innocent but suspect relation with the powerful Lord Dannisburgh. Her beauty and wit make her a popular hostess, but she arouses the jealousy of most society women whose rumor-mongering nearly brings her to ruin.

Alice in Wonderland

by

LEWIS CARROLL (1832–1898)

Main Characters

Alice—A well-mannered little Victorian girl, full of curiosity.
The White Rabbit—Nervous, elegant, and very anxious about
   missing an appointment with the Duchess.
The Duchess—An extremely ugly creature, in mortal fear of
   the Queen.
The Queen of Hearts—Her favorite expression is "Off with
   his head!"
The Cheshire Cat—With its broad grin, it can appear and
   disappear at will.
The Mad Hatter—The host at the Mad Tea Party.

The Story

One drowsy summer afternoon, Alice is sleepily reading over
her sister's shoulder when all at once she sees a White Rabbit,
dressed for a party, consulting his pocketwatch and fretting
about being late. Curiously she follows the Rabbit across a
field and suddenly tumbles down the hole into which he has
scuttled, falling and falling until she comes to a stop on a pile
of leaves. There she sees the Rabbit again, but before she can
question him he scurries away, leaving her in a long hall
bounded by many locked doors.

Spotting a golden key on a glass table, Alice manages to unlock the smallest of the doors. Although she sees an inviting garden with a cool fountain through the door, she is too tall to get in. On a table she spots a bottle labeled "Drink me." When she drinks, Alice finds she has shrunk to ten inches— but she still cannot get into the garden because she has foolishly left the key on the table, and it is now far above her reach.

On a dish beneath the table, however, Alice finds a cookie labeled "Eat me." Alice does and immediately becomes nine feet tall.

Now Alice sees the White Rabbit again, but when she tries to talk to him, he scampers off, dropping his gloves and fan. Alice picks them up and begins to fan herself, only to discover that it is the fan that is reducing her height again. The White Rabbit reappears, frantically searching for his gloves. Under the impression that she is his maidservant, he curtly orders Alice to fetch new ones. Alice dutifully obeys and runs through a wood until she comes to a small white house with a doorplate reading "W. Rabbit."

In the Rabbit's house she finds the new gloves and fan, and also a very tempting-looking bottle. Unable to resist, Alice drinks from it and immediately begins growing again. This time she grows to such a size that she barely saves herself from being crushed by the house by putting one leg up the chimney and her elbow out the window, with her head drawn up to her chin.

Suddenly, Alice hears someone throwing pebbles against the window of the house. These become little cakes, which she eats, and soon she is small enough to emerge from the Rabbit's house. Running through the wood, Alice comes to rest beside a giant mushroom. Perched lazily on it is a caterpillar smoking a hookah. After rudely insulting her intelligence, the caterpillar tells Alice that she will grow if she eats from one side of the mushroom; she will shrink if she eats from the other. At first Alice shrinks so much that her chin hits her foot. In a panic, she quickly eats from the other side, and her neck becomes so long it reaches up to the treetops where an indignant pigeon scolds her for being an egg-stealing serpent.

Finally Alice is the right size. Proceeding through the wood, she comes upon the Duchess' cottage where a fish-like servant is handing to a frog-like servant an invitation to the Duchess to play croquet with the Queen of Hearts. Without knocking, for she cannot be heard above the din, Alice enters the cottage and finds the Duchess rocking her infant in her lap while a cook is sprinkling pepper into some soup. The noise is deafening. The baby is squalling, and the Duchess is sneezing violently from the pepper. At the hearth is the Cheshire Cat grinning enigmatically from ear to ear.

The Duchess gives Alice her baby to hold for a while and disappears. As Alice tries to quiet the infant, its cries gradually become grunts, and she suddenly finds herself holding a little pig in her arms. It slips out of her arms and runs into the forest. Alice looks up and sees the Cheshire Cat grinning at her from the treetops. He tells Alice to go to a tea party being given by the Mad Hatter and then disappears in sections, his grin remaining to the last.

At the tea party, Alice meets the Mad Hatter, the March Hare (who is also mad), and a drowsy dormouse who keeps falling into the teapot and has to be rescued. Everyone is very rude to Alice, asking her unsolvable riddles and making personal comments. Finally, the Dormouse is persuaded to tell a long, involved story that puts even him to sleep.

Alice escapes from the party and comes to a garden where gardeners are painting talking flowers to please the Queen. The Queen catches the gardeners painting some white roses red and immediately orders them away to be executed, but Alice saves them by hiding them in a flowerpot. Now a royal procession begins, with soldiers and courtiers made out of playing cards followed by the Duchess, the White Rabbit, and the Queen of Hearts herself.

The royal croquet game gets under way. Live flamingoes are used as mallets and hedgehogs as balls. The wickets are formed by the card soldiers bending over. The Queen hands Alice a flamingo and peremptorily orders her to start playing. The game is impossible. Everyone plays at once. The hedgehogs crawl away just as the players are about to strike them. The flamingo keeps turning its head up to stare at Alice. Since the Queen shouts "Off with his head!" every time someone's playing displeases her, the soldier-wickets keep leaving their positions.

The Cheshire Cat materializes on the scene and asks Alice how she likes the game. Alice says she does not, and the Cat then looks at the King of Hearts and grins his famous grin. The King complains to the Queen who orders the Cat beheaded; but since, by now, only the Cat's head is in view, nobody knows how to go about executing him, and he is ignored.

When Alice is ready to give up the game in despair, the Duchess corners her and takes her to the seaside. Here Alice meets the Mock Turtle and the Gryphon, two lugubrious characters. The Mock Turtle describes his education, which has consisted of Reeling, Writhing, and all the parts of Arithmetic: Ambition, Distraction, Uglification, and Derision. These creatures invite Alice to join them in the Lobster Quadrille, a very complicated dance performed on the sands.

While they are dancing, they hear news that a trial is in progress. The Knave of Hearts has stolen the Queen's tarts and is being tried for his life. The Queen is all for delivering the verdict before the jury can deliberate. Several witnesses, however, give their testimony, none of which has anything to do with the case. (The jurymen are the dormouse, a ferret, a frog, a hedgehog, and other animals.)

Alice is finally called upon to give her testimony, but she denounces the trial as unfair, and the Queen orders, "Off with her head!" By now Alice has grown to such size that she inadvertently upsets the jury box, and all the creatures in it spill helter-skelter on the floor. After returning them to the box, Alice tells the Queen her procedure of "sentence first— verdict afterwards" is stuff and nonsense.

Screaming for Alice's head, the Queen becomes wild with fury, but Alice, now her full size, retorts, "Who cares for you? You're nothing but a pack of cards!" The cards all rise in the air and start flying at her. With a little scream, Alice awakens and finds that the cards are really dead leaves that have fallen on her face. Her sister shakes her and tells her she has been asleep all the time. Alice has been to Wonderland in a dream.

Critical Opinion

The Alice books (*Alice in Wonderland* and *Through the Looking-Glass*) appeal to adults and to children alike. A century after they were written, they remain as popular as ever. Children are delighted by the magic changes in size, the strange creatures Alice meets, and the perfectly sustained fairy-tale atmosphere. Adults find in the books witty social satire and profound commentaries on illusion and reality and on the relations between children and the adult world.

Most of the creatures Alice meets are abominably condescending. The White Rabbit, the Caterpillar, the Mad Hatter, and the Queen all believe devoutly in the topsy-turvy logic which they hold superior to Alice's simple, pragmatic values, and which they are usually too busy or too full of their own superiority to explain. To a child the rigid rules and seemingly meaningless regulations of the adult world must be what they seem to Alice—arbitrary, unreasonable, and foolish.

The world in both Alice books is essentially a looking-glass world (although the image is explored more consistently in the second work). Holding a glass up to the foibles and conventions of society, the very conventional Carroll shows how absurd they must appear to the clear, unspoiled intelligence of a child.

In a sense, then, *Alice in Wonderland* is as much a book about the problems of growing up as is *David Copperfield, The Way of All Flesh,* or *Sons and Lovers.* Alice must learn in the course of her dream what to take seriously about the adult world and its standards and what to ignore. Significantly, she achieves her full physical height in the trial scene, when she is no longer upset by the ludicrous behavior of the adults around her. When she tells the Queen and all the court that they are nothing but a pack of cards, she has made the difficult journey from childhood, which is abashed by adult standards, to maturity, which is able to judge them.

Two particularly delightful contributions to the Alice books are the now classic illustrations by Sir John Tenniel and the poems that Carroll scatters through the stories. Carroll delights in wickedly distorting into sheer nonsense scraps of the sickly sweet verse that good Victorian children were taught to spout to their approving elders. Even the great Wordsworth is parodied in the White Knight's song in *Through the Looking-Glass,* the book that contains the verbal fireworks of "Jabberwocky."

The Author

Lewis Carroll was the pen name of the Oxford mathematician Charles Lutwidge Dodgson who was born on January 27, 1832, in Darebury, Cheshire. He was educated at Rugby and Christ Church, Oxford, where he took a first in mathematics in 1854, and was appointed lecturer the following year—a position he held until 1881.

A shy, retiring bachelor, Dodgson wrote many books on mathematics, the most important of which is *Euclid and his Modern Rivals* (1879). Indeed, when Queen Victoria, delighted with *Alice in Wonderland,* asked the professor for more of his books, she received a crateful of recondite tomes on mathematics.

One trait, however, colored Dodgson's otherwise conventional life. He found small girls charming and would entertain them by the hour with tales, puzzles, and magic tricks, and loved to photograph them. (Carroll was a highly gifted amateur when photography was in its infancy.) One of the girls of whom he was especially fond was Alice Liddell, daughter of the Dean of Christ Church.

On July 4, 1862, Dodgson and a clergyman friend took Alice—who was ten at the time—and her two sisters on a rowing trip up the Thames near Oxford. To repeated demands for a story to beguile the afternoon, Dodgson told what was in essence the tale of *Alice in Wonderland* which, at Alice's insistence, he later wrote down and illustrated as a little book entitled *Alice's Adventures Underground.* Three years later, expanded and altered somewhat, it was published. It was an immediate success and its popularity has grown over the years.

Dodgson's personality presents a fascinating paradox. The author of the most delightful and durable children's book in English was in private life a dry, convention-ridden man. He was handsome, although his face was rather asymmetrical, but he suffered from partial deafness and a pronounced stammer that prevented his delivering many sermons (although he was ordained a deacon) and made his lectures excruciating to hear. In addition, he was an orthodox member of the Church of England, a devout Tory, and a considerable snob.

The other Dodgson—the Lewis Carroll whom he kept

rigidly separate from the Oxford don—delighted in tricks, magic, and games, and published the great sequel to *Alice,* *Through the Looking-Glass* (1872), and one of the finest comic poems in the language, "The Hunting of the Snark" (1876).

Dodgson died at Guilford on January 14, 1898. In our Freud-ridden age, his personality may inspire some psychiatric interest, but children play around the statue of Alice in the Children's Zoo at Central Park, and no shadow falls on the Carroll Wonderland.

By the Same Author

Through the Looking-Glass: Disproving the unwritten law that all sequels must be inferior to their originals, Carroll wrote in *Through the Looking-Glass* a child's fantasy that is, if possible, even better and richer than *Alice in Wonderland.* Where the first book consists of an adventure in an underground world peopled partly by characters from card games, the second deals with a looking-glass house where everything is turned backward, and the characters are chessmen. Alice is a pawn. She meets the Red and White Queens, and the country through which she travels is a giant chessboard. Some of the most memorable things in the book are the meeting with Tweedledee and Tweedledum who sing the profound song "The Walrus and the Carpenter," and the brilliantly punning parody of songs of knight-errantry, "Jabberwocky." Ultimately, Alice reaches the eighth square of the chessboard and is made a queen herself. When she shakes the Red Queen, it turns into her kitten, Dinah, and Alice once more awakens to reality.

Erewhon

by

SAMUEL BUTLER (1835–1902)

Main Characters

George Higgs—A priggish, conventionally religious young
  sheep rancher who adventures over the range into Erewhon.
Chowbok—A native guide baptized but not converted by
  Higgs.
Yram—Daughter of Higgs' jailor in Erewhon.
Senoj Nosnibor—An Erewhonian gentleman of great fortune
  found guilty of defrauding a widow.
Zulora—Mr. Nosnibor's unappealing elder daughter.
Arowhena—The Nosnibors' beautiful younger daughter.
Thims—A cashier in the Musical Banks who takes Higgs to
  visit the Colleges of Unreason.

The Story

In 1868, when George Higgs is twenty-two years old, he emigrates to New Zealand to seek his fortune as a sheep rancher.
He soon finds a position in sparsely settled country.

One day, while tending his sheep, Higgs sees a series of
mountain peaks in the distance and wonders what lies beyond
them. He questions a drunken old native, Chowbok, about
the land beyond the range. Chowbok merely says it is forbidden territory into which no man dare venture. Higgs, never-

theless, prevails upon him to act as his guide. The mountains seem impassable, and Chowbok keeps trying to dissuade Higgs from completing his expedition. One day Higgs finds a pass that he thinks will lead him through the tall peaks. When he returns to camp for Chowbok, the old native runs away, and Higgs is left to explore the terrain alone.

The pass is rugged. A swollen, treacherous river bars his way, but Higgs fashions a crude raft and makes the crossing. On the other side he is startled to hear strange music of what sounds like a giant Aeolian harp. The source of the music, he finds, is a number of grotesque statues equipped with organ pipes on which the wind plays. These gave rise to Chowbok's superstitious fears.

Next morning Higgs is discovered by some girls who are tending goats. The girls, more beautiful than any he has ever seen, lead him to the local town where Higgs is closely inspected by the men and his clothing confiscated. The men, too, seem a handsome, superior race, but they are shocked when they discover Higgs' watch. They immediately take it from him and show him a museum where all sorts of dilapidated machinery is kept in glass cases. The men of Erewhon (for this is the name of the country) seem impressed by Higgs' blond hair and fair complexion, for they themselves are all swarthy. After a close physical examination, Higgs is put in jail.

He is well treated by the jailor and his pretty daughter, Yram, who teaches Higgs the language of the country. Hoping to win Yram's sympathy, Higgs one day complains of a cold. Instead of being sympathetic, Yram berates him severely for his illness. Higgs learns that in Erewhon illness and disease are considered serious crimes, one reason for the health and vigor of the people. Conversely, people who in England would be considered criminals are hospitalized and treated carefully by so-called "straighteners" until their moral defects disappear.

A conventional Christian, who even baptized the crude Chowbok, Higgs decides that the Erewhonians are really the ten lost tribes of Israel, whom it is his duty and privilege to convert to Christianity.

Higgs learns from his jailor that he is to be summoned to the King and Queen who are curious about him. He is to travel blindfolded a great distance across Erewhon to the capital city where he will live in the house of Senoj Nosnibor who has cheated an impoverished widow of her inheritance. According to Erewhonian justice, Nosnibor is still considered a respectable member of society although he is under the care of the straighteners. The widow, however, was tried and convicted for being unfortunate enough to be victimized. The Erewhonians, Higgs learns, worship success and have little patience with gullible people.

At Mr. Nosnibor's house, Higgs meets his devout wife and his two daughters, the overbearing, ill-mannered Zulora and the fair young Arowhena. Higgs learns that he is well thought of in Erewhon because he is so fair-skinned and healthy although he is the object of some suspicion because he was found with a watch.

Higgs is introduced to society by the Nosnibors, who also take him to the Musical Banks—the Erewhonian churches. At the Musical Banks one pays the cashiers or priests with a strange, valueless sort of money and receives equally valueless change. Although all respectable Erewhonians profess great devotion to the Musical Banks, Higgs notices that only a few women attend them, and the cashiers are a disconsolate lot. He makes friends with a cashier named Thims who takes him on an expedition to visit the Colleges of Unreason where young Erewhonians are instructed at great cost in Hypothetics —dead languages and obsolete science. This education assures the youths of a place in society but makes them unfit for any useful work.

The religion the Erewhonians really follow is Ydgrunism, a conforming creed governed by a fear of what the neighbors will think. Higgs learns that the Erewhonians have experienced epidemics of puritanism ever since an Erewhonian prophet 2500 years before wrote a book on "The Rights of Animals," in which he condemned the eating of meat unless the animal had already died of natural causes or had committed suicide. The Erewhonians usually ignored these laws unless there was some plague or national disaster. Then they enforced them. A professor of botany at the College of Unreason decreed that since there was no real distinction between the animal and vegetable worlds, the killing and eating of plant life should also be forbidden. The Erewhonians, starving for their beliefs, eventually overthrew both laws and became a healthy, happy race again when instinct triumphed over reason.

Higgs also reads "The Book of the Machines," in which an ancient Erewhonian claimed that machines evolved as animals and plants did, and with great ingenuity demonstrated that the day would come when men would be slaves to their machines as dogs are to men. This so appalled the Erewhonians that they destroyed all their machines, saving only a few for the museum. (This was followed by an unsuccessful counter-revolution of the lazy who did not want to live in a machineless society.) Now the Erewhonians live a simple life without tools or appliances invented more recently than 271 years before the laws were originally adopted.

Although Higgs dislikes the Nosnibors, especially Zulora, he falls in love with Arowhena. Unfortunately, according to Erewhonian law a younger sister cannot be married before the older sister, and so Higgs must either wait until someone else marries the disagreeable Zulora (an unlikely prospect), or try to elope with Arowhena. He resolves to elope, when rumors reach him that he is no longer in favor at court. The King is still suspicious of Higgs because he was found with a watch in his pocket; his health is showing signs of strain, and Mr. Nosnibor suspects he is having an affair with Arowhena. Higgs carefully plans his escape.

Erewhon has not had rain for some time. Higgs persuades the Queen that if she will have a balloon built for him he will ascend and speak to the air god about the drought. The Queen and King both agree to this plan. (The King hopes Higgs will fall and be killed.)

When the balloon is ready to be launched, Higgs bribes Arowhena's maid and the chief mechanic and spirits Arowhena into the cabin. Arowhena is missed at breakfast by her family, however, and Higgs sees Mr. Nosnibor running toward the balloon. Without waiting for the King and Queen to appear, he cuts the ropes and they ascend. For days and nights they are propelled through the air by the trade winds. One day they find themselves descending over the ocean. Desperately Higgs drops their ballast overboard and wins some more time. Eventually he must even throw overboard "The Book of the Machines" which he hoped to bring back to England with him.

At the last moment, when the balloon is in the sea, the

pair are rescued by an Italian liner which transfers them to a ship bound for England. Higgs and Arowhena are married on board.

Back in England, Higgs determines to organize an expedition to return to Erewhon and enslave the people for work in Queensland, converting them to Christianity at the same time.

Critical Opinion

Erewhon is a complex and often ambiguous satirical utopia in which Butler both approves and disapproves of Erewhonian beliefs which are sometimes the same as those of Victorian England and sometimes radically different. Just as the word "utopia" is Greek for "nowhere," so "erewhon" is "nowhere" spelled backward. (Similarly, Yram is Mary, Senoj Nosnibor is Jones Robinson, Thims is Smith, and the goddess Ydgrun is Grundy, symbol of English middle-class morality.)

Never at ease in writing fiction, Butler barely clothes his ideas with plot and characterization. After the prosaic account of Higgs' trek over the range, the novel becomes an intellectual fantasy, its characters essentially mouthpieces for ideas. Many parts of the book, such as the chapters on "The Book of the Machines," were written earlier as essays. In essence Arowhena is a stock Victorian heroine, vapid and colorless, whose only function in the book is to listen to what the hero has to say.

In the character of Higgs, however (we first learn his name in the sequel, *Erewhon Revisited*), Butler creates a masterpiece of self-satisfied Victorian piety. Unable to accept the validity of another way of life, Higgs is primarily interested in converting the obviously happy and healthy Erewhonians to the life-denying perversion of Christianity in which he has grown up. It does not even strike him as odd to propose an expedition that will simultaneously enslave and convert the Erewhonians who ask only to be left alone. The Erewhonians are happy because they have found an ideal social system. Since pain and sickness are punishable by imprisonment, few hypochondriacs exist. Immorality is treated as a disease, not as a crime.

Butler is most prophetic in his vision of the "straighteners" who talk to criminals and try to "cure" them of their crimes. The shadowy borderland between the sick and the immoral, blurred even further in today's psychiatry, is explored with vivacity and wit in *Erewhon*.

Originating as a satire on Darwinism, "The Book of the Machines" is also oddly prophetic. Butler ironically foresees in it the subjugation of men by machines. The Erewhonian solution to the problem—destruction of all machinery—has, in more desperate moments, been entertained by the victims of automation in our time.

The Way of All Flesh

by

SAMUEL BUTLER

Main Characters

Mr. Overton—The narrator, a friend of the Pontifex family, who tries to make young Ernest's life endurable.
Ernest Pontifex—Brought up in a strict religious household, Ernest struggles against all the forces of Victorian hypocrisy and narrow-mindedness in order to find his own identity.
John Pontifex—The founder of the Pontifex family, a humble carpenter and music lover.
George Pontifex—Ernest's grandfather, publisher of religious books, and the first of the money-minded, joyless Pontifexes.
Theobald Pontifex—Ernest's father, a priggish clergyman who represses all his natural instincts and nearly ruins his son.
Christina Pontifex—Theobald's hypocritical wife.
Alethea Pontifex—Ernest's sensible, good-natured aunt.
Ellen—The Pontifexes' drunken maidservant.

The Story

The founder of the Pontifex family is old John Pontifex, a carpenter and music lover, who leaves his son George moderately well off. George, however, inherits none of his father's love of music nor any of his simple, humane spirit. Apprenticed to a printer uncle, George amasses a fortune printing religious books for the great religious revival of the Victorian age now in full swing. George has five children whom he thrashes and bullies, determined to rid them of their "self-will."

One of George's children, Theobald, is so shy and ill at ease that George decides he can make a living only in the clergy. Accordingly, Theobald is sent to Cambridge, against his will, to prepare for ordination. He bows to his father's repeated threats of disinheritance and takes holy orders. He becomes curate to Mr. Allaby, rector of Crampford, near Cambridge, and Mr. Allaby's daughter Christina, who is four years older than Theobald, decides she will marry the young clergyman. She "wins" him in a game of cards with her other unmarried sisters.

The naïve and unsuspecting Theobald easily succumbs to Christina's wooing. His father disapproves of the match. But Theobald feels he is too deeply committed to Christina to terminate their relationship. After a five-year courtship, they are married, and Theobald gets a fairly remunerative post at Battersby. George settles £10,000 on his son and daughter-in-law.

Immediately after the wedding, Theobald asserts his position as master and by the time their first son, Ernest, is born on September 6, 1835, five years later, Christina is entirely subject to Theobald's every whim.

The birth of Ernest so pleases old George Pontifex that he settles some money on the infant. Theobald, who feels he has satisfied his father's expectations of him for the first time in his life by producing a male heir, is piqued that the boy should receive this bequest and never forgives him for the independence it implies. Soon another boy, Joseph, and a girl, Charlotte, are born into the Pontifex family. Both take after their parents far more than Ernest does.

The upbringing of the children is harsh, rigorous, and typical of the Victorian middle class. At the age of three Ernest begins his studies and is learning Greek and Latin by the time he is five. Lessons are driven home with frequent beatings. Sunday is the worst day of all, when the children are forbidden to play but must spend a dismal day in religious observance.

An old friend of the Pontifex family, Mr. Overton, remembers his boyhood affection for old John Pontifex. Now he is appalled at the harsh, dreary life John's grandson Theobald is imposing on his children. One day he sees Ernest beaten within an inch of his life—for his own "good," of course—when he mispronounces a word. Mr. Overton tries to improve the boy's condition, but he is essentially powerless against the Pontifex philosophy of breaking a child's spirit.

At twelve, Ernest is sent to school at Roughborough and placed under the discipline of Dr. Skinner, an incompetent teacher and a bully like Theobald Pontifex. At Roughborough Ernest is as miserable as he was at home. Puny, gloomy, and indecisive, Ernest has one great consolation, music, a love inherited from his great-grandfather.

The only human warmth the boy knows at school is the affection of his Aunt Alethea who moves from London to be with him. She is a kind, generous woman who sees great potentialities for happiness in her nephew and refuses to allow him to succumb to his father's discipline. She helps the boy to build an organ, thus giving him exercise, skill in carpentry, and encouraging the love for music that his father considers degenerate and sinful. When Alethea dies a year later, she leaves £15,000 to Mr. Overton with the understanding that he keep it secretly in trust for Ernest until he is twenty-eight.

Ernest's last scrap of respect for his parents disappears one school holiday when he sees them summarily dismissing Ellen, a pregnant maidservant. In a moment of pity for her, he gives her his watch and pocket money. For this he is severely punished. Indeed, his mother suspects that he is responsible for Ellen's condition.

Ernest is in such disgrace at home that Theobald journeys to Roughborough to find out all he can about his son's behavior. He learns that Ernest is guilty of occasionally smoking, drinking, and running up insignificant debts for lack of pocket money. He informs Dr. Skinner, and Ernest, ignominiously punished, becomes a martyr to his schoolfellows.

After Roughborough, Ernest is sent to Cambridge to prepare for the ministry. Although the boy has no interest in religion, he finds the freedom and intellectual liveliness of the great university refreshing after the stultifying atmosphere of Dr. Skinner's school. For the first time he makes friends and participates in sports. He writes an original article attacking the Greek dramatists and wins some notoriety and a small scholarship.

After leaving Cambridge, Ernest dutifully continues to prepare for a church career although his heart is not in it. As a social worker in the London slums, he has many misadventures. He entrusts the legacy he received from his grandfather to a Mr. Pryer who promises to increase it in the stock market. Instead, Mr. Pryer cheats him out of all the money.

Totally innocent about the world and unprepared by his education to cope with people, Ernest idealistically moves into a slum district to be close to the real poor. Attempting to convert an articulate freethinker to belief in God, Ernest is himself converted to atheism. His greatest blunder, however, comes when he visits the room of a girl he believes to be a prostitute. She is really respectable and Ernest is summarily arrested, charged with assault, and sentenced to six months in prison.

Ernest's fortunes are now at their lowest. Unable to emigrate to Australia for lack of funds and barred from the clergy, Ernest decides to set up a modest tailoring shop in London upon his release. At least he will not have to endure the middle-class life he now loathes. But just as he emerges from jail, he is met by his parents who are filled with pious forgiveness and high moral sentiments. Finally Ernest has the courage to tell them he never wants to see them again. With Mr. Overton's help, he is able to set up his tailoring establishment.

Soon after his release from prison, Ernest meets Ellen (his parents' dismissed maid) in the streets of London. In his loneliness, he falls in love with her, partly because he sees in her another helpless victim of his parents' way of life. Against Mr. Overton's advice, Ernest and Ellen marry and have two children. But it is soon apparent that Ellen is a hopeless drunkard. Her drinking puts a great drain on Ernest's modest income, and she becomes more sluttish and slatternly every day. Utterly miserable at the way his marriage has turned out, Ernest despairs of ever making his way in life.

One day Ernest meets John, his family's old coachman, who tells him that he is the father of Ellen's illegitimate child; soon after she left the Pontifex family he had married her. Since Ernest's marriage is thus bigamous, Mr. Overton is able to make an arrangement with Ellen under which she receives a weekly stipend on condition that she never bother Ernest again. Fearing to become as bad a parent as his own, Ernest boards his two children with the simple, happy family of a bargeman utterly free of any middle-class pretensions. The children will be allowed to live their own lives.

On Ernest's twenty-eighth birthday, Mr. Overton tells him of his Aunt Alethea's bequest, which through wise investment now amounts to £70,000. The money enables Ernest to fulfill his real ambition—to be a writer—which has lain dormant in his troubled mind ever since the publication of his successful article at Cambridge. A few years traveling abroad provides him with experiences and background for a book.

When he learns that his mother is dying, Ernest tries to become reconciled to his family. But his father is resentful that Ernest has become independently wealthy despite his follies. No real reconciliation is possible. Ernest never marries again but spends his days writing iconoclastic books and living a decent, civilized life. Although he becomes a prolific author, he never gets around to writing his own story. This is done for him by Mr. Overton.

Critical Opinion

The Way of All Flesh is one of a number of autobiographical novels which were highly popular in late Victorian and Edwardian England. Written between 1873 and 1885, it was not published until after Butler's death because he was fearful lest it give offense to his still-living sisters. Indeed, it is one of the most brilliantly devastating attacks in all literature on religious hypocrisy and on the family as an institution.

Theobald and Christina Pontifex are cruelly and wittily portrayed by Butler as monuments of complacency, smugness, false religiosity, and unfeeling brutality to their children. In almost every particular, they match Butler's own parents. Butler sees himself partly as Ernest and partly as Mr. Overton, the wise, civilized, easy-going man of wide culture.

The book begins unpromisingly with a long, somewhat tedious account of the early Pontifexes—John and George. Ernest is not even born until Chapter 17. One of Butler's deepest interests in the story was the question of heredity. A disciple of the biologist, Lamarck, Butler had several notions of heredity (at variance with the prevailing Darwinian doctrine of his day) which he wished to explore in *The Way of All Flesh*. One of these ideas is that inherited characteristics can skip one or even two generations. Thus Ernest is interested in carpentry and music, like his great-grandfather John and unlike his grandfather and father. Because traits can skip generations, Butler felt that parents and their children may have little in common and thus rarely understand each other.

The book's appeal, however, hardly depends on its biological assumptions or on its autobiographical core. Generations of rebellious youths, feeling themselves trapped in an oppressive home environment, have drawn spiritual aid and comfort from Butler's furious assault on the hypocrisies of parents and the life-denying rigors of a puritanical household. The "way of all flesh" is to seek freedom and self-fulfillment, Butler feels, but too often in practice it is to tyrannize over the young.

The Way of All Flesh is Butler's only full-fledged novel, and the number of years required for its composition are testimony to the pain it cost him. This arose not merely from the psychological difficulty of contemplating his own wretched childhood and youth but from the esthetic problems posed by the novel as well. Because Butler was primarily a controversial essayist and not a novelist, *The Way of All Flesh* is a far from perfect novel. Whole chapters are merely extended diatribes on the follies of Victorian life with very little plot holding them together. The end, where Ernest's story diverges widely from Butler's, tends to disintegrate into a series of connected essays.

Nevertheless, if a fertile Dickensian imagination was not one of Butler's gifts, he shared with the earlier novelist a lively sense of humor, at once bitterly indignant and humane. The brilliantly rendered portrayal of Ernest's soul-destroying youth and education remains the classic picture in English of family life at its worst.

The Author

Like the hero of *The Way of All Flesh, Samuel Butler* came from a religious family. Born on December 4, 1835, Butler was the grandson of Dr. Samuel Butler, the famous headmaster of the Shrewsbury School and bishop of Lichfield. Butler's father was a domineering clergyman—cruelly portrayed as Theobald Pontifex in *The Way of All Flesh*—who made the boy's life a nightmare.

Educated at Shrewsbury and St. John's College, Cambridge, Butler was headed for the clergy but revolted against that fate and decided to become a painter. Butler's father could not accept this career for his son. So they reached a compromise. Butler went to New Zealand in 1859 to take up sheep breeding. In time he became quite wealthy. His first book, *A First Year in Canterbury Settlement* (1863), is really a series of letters to his father describing his life in New Zealand.

In 1864 Butler returned to England and settled for the rest of his life in Clifford's Inn, London. *Erewhon* was published in 1872 and brought Butler more fame and notoriety than any other book he wrote. His father was mystified and enraged by the irreligious irony of *Erewhon* and of its successor, *The Fair Haven* (1873), which ironically defends the evidence for the Resurrection. On one occasion, he told Butler that the books had killed his mother. Butler's father claimed he never read any of his son's works.

A lonely, eccentric bachelor, Butler lived with a lawyer named Pauli who defrauded him of nearly all his income. Butler also became friends with a Miss Savage, a crippled artist who was the model for Aunt Alethea in *The Way of All Flesh* and who probably nurtured an unrequited love for the author.

Butler's interests were many and varied. He continued with his painting, played Handel on the piano, and even collaborated with another friend, his eventual biographer, Henry Festing-Jones, on two mock-Handelian oratorios. He traveled a good deal, especially in Greece and Italy, in search of evidence to support his theory that the author of Homer's works was a woman—specifically Nausicäa in the *Odyssey*—and that Odysseus' trip could be precisely charted in the neighborhood of Sicily.

Science, too, was a major interest of Butler's. He wrote several books, of which *Unconscious Memory* (1880) and *Luck or Cunning?* (1887) are best known as challenges to Darwin's theory of heredity. A man ahead of his time, Butler remained a sort of Don Quixote tilting at the windmills of Victorian ideas. He died on June 18, 1902. The masterpiece on which he had been secretly working for several years, *The Way of All Flesh*, was published in 1903. It was not until World War I, when Bernard Shaw became a passionate proselyte for them, that Butler's works began to be widely known.

By the Same Author

Erewhon Revisited: In this sequel to *Erewhon*, written thirty years later and published the year of Butler's death, Higgs returns to Erewhon to find himself worshiped as a child of the Sun God for his miraculous ascent long ago in the balloon. A cathedral has been consecrated in his name, old Chowbok has become Bishop Kahabuka, and the dominant religion in Erewhon is no longer Ydgrunism, but Sunchildism, explained and preached by Professors Hanky and Panky. Higgs finds that he has a son by Yram, the jailor's daughter. Eventually he must escape from the country once again. Less inventive and vivid than *Erewhon*, the sequel is very much the book of an old, disappointed man. It, nevertheless, contains some entertaining blasts at the evidence for miracles and revealed religion.

The Return of the Native

by

THOMAS HARDY (1840–1928)

Main Characters

Diggory Venn—An itinerant seller of reddle, a dye used for marking sheep.

Damon Wildeve—A romantic ex-engineer who has become the restless proprietor of the Quiet Woman Inn.

Thomasin Yeobright—A fair, simple, birdlike girl engaged to Wildeve.

Mrs. Yeobright—Thomasin's aunt, a strong-willed, middle-aged woman.

Clym Yeobright—Her son who returns to Egdon Heath after becoming successful in the diamond business abroad.

Eustacia Vye—A dark, passionate girl who hates Egdon Heath and yearns for a glamorous life.

The Story

Across somber, barren Egdon Heath in the south of England only the cart of Diggory Venn, the reddleman, is visible as it slowly makes its way late one November night. The scene is illuminated, however, by a series of bonfires lit by the local peasants to celebrate Guy Fawkes Day, the fifth of November.

In the cart, worn out and sick, is young Thomasin Yeobright, who two years before had refused to marry Venn. She is now being taken home to Blooms-End. They meet a group of peasants who assume that Thomasin has just married Damon Wildeve, the proprietor of the Quiet Woman Inn. But the marriage has not taken place because at the last moment the license was found to be technically invalid. Thomasin has asked the faithful Diggory Venn to take her home.

Thomasin's aunt, Mrs. Yeobright, is disturbed because she knows of Wildeve's weak character and fears that the invalid license was merely an excuse for him to get out of marrying her simple, trusting niece. Indeed, Wildeve is secretly in love with the wild, mysterious Eustacia Vye, granddaughter of a retired sea captain. Eustacia has lit her own bonfire on Guy Fawkes Night to signal Wildeve to meet her, although all she has in common with him is a loathing for the brooding, impersonal heath on which they live. Eustacia has always hoped for a great love which would take her away from Egdon Heath; she now feels she must accept Wildeve as a poor substitute.

Meanwhile, Mrs. Yeobright goes to Wildeve and asks him not to stand in the way of Thomasin's marrying another man, for she knows that Diggory Venn is still in love with her niece. When Wildeve learns that Thomasin has another suitor, he is torn by indecision and proposes to Eustacia that they leave the heath together and go to America. But now it is Eustacia who is indecisive. She has heard that Clym Yeobright is returning to the heath after a brilliant career in the diamond business in Paris.

Unsuccessful in her attempts to meet Clym in a casual encounter, Eustacia bribes one of the boys taking part in a Christmas pageant at the Yeobrights' to let her substitute for him. Clym notices her and is piqued by her daring disguise as a boy. He asks her to remove her mask, but she coquettishly refuses. Feeling she has finally attracted Clym, Eustacia finally breaks off with Wildeve, who marries Thomasin to spite her.

Eustacia hopes that if she can persuade Clym to marry her he will take her to Paris, which she longs to see. But Clym has left his successful business there precisely because he is sick of the sophisticated life. He now wishes only to live on his native heath and open a school, teaching the ignorant yeomen to give up their superstitious beliefs. He is strengthened in this purpose when he hears that Eustacia has been attacked as a witch by a local woman.

Mrs. Yeobright also thinks Clym is wrong to stay on the heath, but for a different reason; she fears that her son will fall into Eustacia's clutches. The mother's concern comes too late, for Clym has fallen in love with this strange, unhappy girl. He asks Eustacia to join him in teaching, but she refuses because she wants to leave the heath entirely.

Against his mother's advice, Clym marries Eustacia and begins studying to be a schoolteacher. Through overwork he strains his eyes and, unable to read any more, becomes a furze cutter to keep from dipping into his savings. Eustacia becomes increasingly disillusioned with her moody husband as she sees her chances of going to Paris fading.

Reconciled somewhat to her son's marriage, Mrs. Yeobright entrusts some money to a local rustic, Christian Cantle, to be equally divided between Clym and Thomasin. Christian loses the money gambling with the unscrupulous Wildeve, but the money is won back by Diggory Venn who loyally gives it all to Thomasin. Thinking Wildeve has given the sum to Eustacia, Mrs. Yeobright accuses her daughter-in-law of receiving it from the innkeeper. Furious, Eustacia tells Mrs. Yeobright of her disillusionment with her son, and they part bitter enemies.

Bored with her existence as the wife of a humble wood-cutter, Eustacia one night goes to a gypsy camp where she meets Wildeve, and once more feels attracted to him. They are seen by Diggory Venn who tells Mrs. Yeobright that she must become reconciled to her son and daughter-in-law before disaster strikes their marriage.

Mrs. Yeobright agrees and trudges across the vast heath in the burning sun to visit them. When she knocks at the door, however, there is no answer, for while Clym is asleep in one room after his morning's hard labor, Eustacia is entertaining Wildeve in another. Fearing that the knocking will awaken her husband, Eustacia shows Wildeve out the back door. When she returns, Clym is still asleep, but Mrs. Yeobright has left. Making her way back across the heath, Mrs. Yeobright, parched, exhausted, and grief-stricken at what she imagines is a rebuff from her son, is bitten by an adder.

When Clym wakes up, he sets forth across the heath to visit his mother, and discovers her dying in agony. Eustacia tells Clym that she did not open the door to his mother because she did not know he was asleep and assumed he would open it. Eustacia conceals from her husband the real reason, her fear that Mrs. Yeobright would discover her and Wildeve together.

At first Clym is consumed with grief and guilt. But when he learns the truth, he turns on his wife and demands that she leave his house. Remorse-stricken, she agrees, feeling that the only salvation for both of them is for her to leave Egdon Heath.

Eustacia returns despondently to her grandfather's house and tries to commit suicide, but is prevented by Charley, Captain Vye's servant. She knows that Wildeve is still willing to run away with her. When the innkeeper unexpectedly comes into a considerable fortune, flight becomes a possibility. One night Eustacia leaves the house for a tryst with Wildeve without seeing on the mantelpiece a letter that Clym, at Thomasin's instigation, had written in the hope that it might bring them together again.

Searching in the dark for the spot where she is to meet Wildeve, Eustacia loses her way and drowns in Shadwater Weir. Nearby, Clym meets Wildeve who is searching for Eustacia. The two men who loved her see Eustacia's body in the lake. Wildeve jumps in to save Eustacia. He, too, drowns. In turn Clym tries to rescue him, and is saved from the treacherous waters only by the arrival of Diggory Venn.

Several months later, Diggory marries the widowed Thomasin, and Clym becomes a preacher wandering about the heath in the hope of bringing light to the dark lives of its people.

Critical Opinion

As in all Hardy's major fiction, man in *The Return of the Native* is seen as the plaything of the gods, buffeted about by fate and ultimately destroyed by an uncaring universe. The blind, heedless power of nature is symbolized in the novel by Egdon Heath, a forbidding, uninhabited stretch of land that quite literally consumes its victims; by heat and the serpent's bite in the case of Mrs. Yeobright, by darkness and drowning in the case of Eustacia and Wildeve. The insignificance of struggling man in the face of a cosmic order he does not understand is thus embodied in the heath.

But novels are primarily about people, not about scenery, and Hardy's real interest is in the struggles of his characters against their destiny which Hardy views with a unique combination of irony and compassion. Like her famous French prototype, Emma Bovary, Eustacia Vye is a passionate romantic at odds with the dull, commonplace world around her. In revolt against the slow, plodding natural world of the heath, she yearns for a life of excitement in Paris. A perverse fate links Eustacia with a man who longs only for peace and solitude, having been disillusioned with the worldly life she so admires.

Thus, the tragedy of Eustacia and Clym is only partially caused by fate and coincidence. Essentially it stems, as all great tragedy does, from character. The wild coincidences of which Hardy is so fond merely contribute a touch of the grotesque to something foreordained by the very nature of the characters involved.

In the subtle interplay between predestination and free will, then, Hardy finds the philosophic basis for his fiction much as the Greek dramatists had done centuries before. Man is foredoomed to tragedy, according to Hardy, but the seeds of doom lie in his character—constantly striving, never at peace with the universe or with other human beings.

The plot of *The Return of the Native* is carefully organized, each section of the novel having its individual climax, starting slowly and building inevitably to the final disasters. The reliance on coincidence, for which Hardy has been taken to task, has come into its own today in a period that relishes the drama of the absurd. For the point of Hardy's coincidences (all the mislaid letters in his novels, for instance) is that life is not rational; events do not happen as in a "well-made" novel, but blind chance constantly intervenes in man's fate.

The only comforting note in Hardy's fiction is provided by his peasant types, like Christian Cantle. Inured to the blows of fate by centuries of experience, they live more or less at one with nature, refusing, in their folk wisdom, to make the mistake the major characters make—of trying to impose their puny wills on an unseeing, indifferent universe.

The Mayor of Casterbridge

by

THOMAS HARDY

Main Characters

Michael Henchard—The passionate and self-destructive grain merchant who becomes mayor of Casterbridge.

Susan Henchard—Henchard's long-suffering wife whom he sells to a sailor.

Richard Newson—The sailor who buys Susan Henchard for five guineas and takes her to Canada.

Elizabeth-Jane—Henchard's beautiful, loyal stepdaughter, who falls in love with Henchard's rival in Casterbridge.

Donald Farfrae—A bright, easy-going Scotsman who makes his fortune in the grain business in Casterbridge.

Lucetta Le Sueur—A young lady from Jersey who compromises herself in a love affair with Henchard.

Joshua Jopp—Fiercely envious of Farfrae.

The Story

Three dusty, tired travelers arrive late one summer afternoon at the small farming village of Weydon Priors: Michael Henchard, a bitter young man looking for work, his wife, Susan, and their little girl, Elizabeth-Jane. Arriving in time for a country fair, the youthful parents seek refreshment in the tent of a woman selling furmity, a kind of rustic milk punch. Henchard persuades the woman to spike his furmity with rum, and before long he becomes drunk and abusive.

In his drunkenness, Henchard, who is resentful at having married too young to be able to make his way in the world, publicly offers to sell his wife and daughter to any buyer. Richard Newson, a sailor, out of pity buys the downcast

Susan Henchard from her drunken husband for five guineas and leaves the refreshment tent with his new "family."

When Henchard awakes the next morning, he is appalled at what he has done. Swearing never to drink liquor for the next twenty years, he sets off in search of his wife and daughter. He learns at a seaport town that they have just emigrated from England with Newson, and he gives up the search. Arriving ultimately at the ancient town of Casterbridge, Henchard decides to make his fortune there in the grain business.

When Newson takes Susan Henchard and her daughter to Canada, he convinces the docile, unquestioning young woman that she is no longer legally bound to the husband who has so mistreated her. Susan's daughter dies soon after, but Newson and Susan have a daughter of their own. Susan and Newson live together as man and wife, but eventually Susan learns that she is still legally married to Henchard. Before she can act on this knowledge, Newson is reported drowned in a shipwreck, and Susan sets out for England with her daughter, now eighteen, in search of Henchard.

A meeting with the old furmity woman leads Susan to Casterbridge. In the intervening years, Henchard, true to his vow, has not touched liquor. By sheer energy and force of will he has become the leading citizen of Casterbridge. When his wife and stepdaughter arrive, he is mayor of the town.

Another recent arrival in Casterbridge is an ambitious, personable young Scotsman, Donald Farfrae. Overhearing Henchard's complaint about some rotten grain he has inadvertently sold, Farfrae makes an ingenious suggestion about how to make the grain edible. Although Farfrae is bent on seeking his fortune overseas, Henchard is so enthusiastic about the corn expert that he persuades the young man to stay in Casterbridge and become his manager.

When Susan meets Henchard, she does not tell him that Elizabeth-Jane is not really his daughter. The two women are set up in lodgings nearby so that Henchard can "court" his wife and "marry" her before the whole town. But in his loneliness, Henchard has confided to Farfrae that he once had an affair with a beautiful girl named Lucetta Le Sueur who became an object of scandal in her native Jersey because of Henchard's attentions.

Eventually, Henchard marries Susan and brings his wife and Elizabeth-Jane to live with him. The beautiful Elizabeth-

Jane finds Farfrae intensely attractive. When Henchard wants the girl to take his legal name, he is surprised at Susan's refusal.

Relations between Henchard and Farfrae become strained as Henchard grows envious of the popularity of his employee. Farfrae has none of the harshness at the root of Henchard's character. When the two men set up rival festivities at a country dance, Henchard is infuriated to see the townspeople flock to Farfrae's entertainment.

Realizing that his association with Henchard is ending, Farfrae begins his own grain business, but is so ethical that he refuses to take any trade that might otherwise go to his former employer. Henchard refuses to allow Elizabeth-Jane to see Farfrae.

One day Henchard receives word from his former love, Lucetta, that she will visit Casterbridge to obtain the love letters she had written to him. He goes to meet her, but when Lucetta fails to appear, Henchard puts the incriminating letters into his safe. Meanwhile, Susan, who has fallen mortally ill, writes a letter to Henchard which he is not to open until the day of Elizabeth-Jane's marriage.

When Susan dies, Henchard, hoping to draw Elizabeth-Jane closer to him, tells the girl the story of how he had lost his wife and daughter twenty years ago. Searching among his documents for evidence to convince the girl, he finds Susan's deathbed letter and discovers that Elizabeth-Jane is the daughter of Newson. Shocked, Henchard immediately becomes cold and abrupt with the girl who cannot understand the reason for this sudden change in him.

In one of her lonely excursions to the village graveyard, Elizabeth-Jane meets a handsome, rich woman who comforts her and offers to employ her as a companion. Having just inherited property in Casterbridge, the woman intends to live in the ancient town. She gives her name as Lucetta Templeman, but in reality she is Henchard's former love, Lucetta Le Sueur. Having Elizabeth-Jane in her house is designed to provide a convenient pretext for Henchard to visit her.

One day when Farfrae comes to the house to see Elizabeth-Jane, he meets Lucetta who is immediately drawn to him. In her new love for Farfrae, Lucetta completely forgets about Henchard. As Elizabeth-Jane sees her former lover falling in love with Lucetta, Henchard becomes infuriated with Lucetta for refusing to see him any more.

Determined to ruin Farfrae for this latest affront, Henchard buys immense quantities of grain when a weather prophet forecasts a rainy harvest. The weather stays fine, however, and Henchard is forced to sell his grain at a loss while Farfrae buys it very cheaply. The rains eventually do come, and Farfrae becomes wealthy overnight selling his cheaply bought grain at high prices.

In despair at this financial setback, Henchard warns Lucetta that unless she marries him he will expose her past to Farfrae. She agrees. She leaves the town, however, when the old furmity seller arrives in Casterbridge and reveals that many years before Henchard had sold his wife and daughter. Lucetta learns the truth for the first time. While she is away from the town, Lucetta secretly marries Farfrae. Elizabeth-Jane, heartbroken, leaves her employ and Henchard repeats his threat to reveal Lucetta's past.

Henchard's ruin is completed when creditors, hearing the furmity woman's story, demand their money from him. Henchard becomes ill and is reunited with Elizabeth-Jane who nurses him through his illness. When he finally recovers, he is bankrupt and must become a common laborer in Farfrae's employ. Having kept his vow to stay away from drink for twenty years, Henchard once again takes to drink, even more violently than before. The crowning blow to his pride comes when Farfrae, richer and more popular than ever now, is elected the new mayor of Casterbridge.

Now Joshua Jopp, who used to work for Henchard and who knows Lucetta's past, begins to blackmail Lucetta into getting him a good job with her husband. Henchard, whose own misery has made him relent, decides to send the incriminating love letters back to Lucetta, but he makes the mistake of asking Jopp to deliver them. Jopp first regales his cronies at the inn with a reading of the spicier portions of the letters.

When the Duke of Windsor visits Casterbridge, Henchard makes a last attempt to become a power once again in the town. He drunkenly attempts to join the pillars of Casterbridge society who are entertaining the royal visitor, but is humiliated anew when Farfrae brusquely pushes him aside. When Henchard later gets Farfrae alone in the warehouse, he is tempted to kill his former friend and manager, but, shamed by Farfrae's contemptuous pity, he lets him go.

Jopp's malicious reading aloud of Lucetta's letters has its tragic consequence. The townspeople place models of Henchard and Lucetta on a donkey which they lead through the streets of Casterbridge. Farfrae is away at the time of this mummer's parade, but Lucetta, appalled when she sees it, dies later that night of a miscarriage.

Richard Newson, the sailor who was thought lost, arrives in Casterbridge looking for Susan and Elizabeth-Jane. Henchard, who cannot bear the thought of losing his stepdaughter, the last prop of his life, tells the sailor that both women are dead. With Elizabeth-Jane, Henchard opens a fairly successful seed shop, but soon the widowed Farfrae begins to court the girl again.

Newson, too, returns, now aware of the truth. Henchard sees a lonely old age confronting him, for Newson is Elizabeth-Jane's father. Now she is to be married to Farfrae. Bereft of the only person in the world he loves, Henchard goes into a decline and dies. In his will he stipulates that he is not to be buried in consecrated ground.

Critical Opinion

Of all Hardy's novels, *The Mayor of Casterbridge* most closely resembles a classic Greek tragedy, for it is concerned with the downfall of a great man resulting from a combination of flaws in his character and repeated, ironic blows of fate. Henchard's initial act, selling his wife and child, so typical of his headstrong, unthinking temperament, comes back years later to haunt him with classic inevitability, when he has reached the heights of prosperity and honor in his little world of Casterbridge. Relying more heavily than ever on coincidence, Hardy, bit by bit, tears away the props that have raised Henchard to power in Casterbridge, until he is a completely broken and disillusioned old man.

For all his savagery when drunk, Henchard is a man of many fine qualities. He is open-hearted and generous, incapable of sustained guile or malice, and a man of abundant energy. When he has the power to blackmail Lucetta with her love letters, he is unable to bring himself to use it even though she has betrayed him by marrying his rival, Farfrae. But with typical Hardyesque irony, Henchard's well-intentioned return of the letters backfires. In the malicious hands of Jopp they have their full evil effect.

Henchard, like Heathcliff in *Wuthering Heights*, is a typically romantic figure—a single-minded, almost demonic man possessed of vast energy. He is deeply passionate and capable of inadvertently doing much harm. He seems always doomed to kill whatever he loves.

In contrast Hardy draws the thoughtfully energetic young Farfrae whose star inevitably rises while Henchard's sinks. Farfrae is like Horatio in *Hamlet*: a good, whole man always in control of his passions, emotional but capable of coolly intelligent behavior. Virile and energetic as Farfrae is, he is not the stuff of tragedy because his character is almost flawless. The disaster of his life—the death of his wife in a miscarriage—is not the result of his own passion or folly but is imposed on him by the trickery of the gods. He can later marry Elizabeth-Jane with a clear conscience.

The Mayor of Casterbridge is one of Hardy's most tightly knit novels and also one of his most blatantly coincidental. As if managed by a puppeteer, characters appear and disappear, always in time to bring more disaster crashing down on Henchard's head. The book's magnificence stems in large part from the stoic grandeur with which Henchard accepts the consequences of his early folly.

Jude the Obscure

by

THOMAS HARDY

Main Characters

Jude Fawley—An intensely serious, self-educated stonemason who yearns for a higher intellectual life.
Drusilla Fawley—Jude's great-grandaunt.

Arabella Donn—A coarse peasant girl who initiates Jude into the world of sex.

Richard Phillotson—The country schoolmaster, Jude's sole contact with the world of education.

Sue Bridehead—Jude's neurotic, self-assertive cousin, one of the restless "new women" of the late nineteenth century.

Little Father Time—The prematurely sad and wizened son of Jude and Arabella.

The Story

Young Jude Fawley, an orphaned baker's boy, gets his first taste of what his life will be like when he is hired by a local Wessex farmer to frighten the rooks away from the farmer's garden. When Jude takes pity on the birds and feeds them instead of scaring them away, the farmer beats him unmercifully. Some light comes into the lad's life, however, when the local schoolmaster, Richard Phillotson, introduces him to the magic world of learning. Jude decides to emulate his teacher; but when the boy is eleven years old, Phillotson leaves Marygreen to go to the great university town of Christminster in order to get an advanced degree.

Jude wishes to go, too, but must content himself with the Latin textbooks that Phillotson sends him from Christminster, for Jude's great-grandaunt, Drusilla Fawley, insists on his helping her in her bakery. Jude eagerly studies the grammar books that Phillotson sends him but realizes they are no substitute for a formal education.

As he grows into young manhood, Jude, who secretly yearns to study religion, is apprenticed to a stonemason whose job is to restore local medieval churches. One evening, while returning home from work, the nineteen-year-old Jude, who is still innocent in the ways of love, passes three peasant girls who are washing pigs' chitterlings. The boldest of them, Arabella Donn, attracts Jude's attention by throwing a bit of pig's flesh at him and provoking him into agreeing to meet her later. In his inexperience, Jude fancies himself in love with the lusty Arabella. Before long she traps him into marriage.

The marriage becomes a nightmare. Arabella, who is all coarseness and vulgarity, derides Jude's yearning for higher things. After a series of quarrels, Arabella leaves him and emigrates to Australia.

Free at last of the shackles of marriage, Jude determines to journey to Christminster and try somehow to enter the academic community. Denied admission, he takes a job there as a stonemason, for that is as far as the hidebound university authorities will permit him to enter the life of Christminster.

Jude knows that his cousin, Sue Bridehead, is living in Christminster, but at first he avoids her because his Aunt Drusilla had warned him against her, pointing out with some justice that "the Fawleys were not made for wedlock."

In his loneliness, however, Jude eventually seeks out Sue Bridehead who is working as an artist in a shop that sells religious articles. An agnostic, Sue seeks relief from her job by reading Gibbon and by keeping large plaster casts of Venus and Apollo in her room. Jude is immensely impressed by his cousin's nervous, restless intelligence and suggests that she leave her job to assist his old schoolmaster, Phillotson.

Before long Phillotson, too, is captivated by Sue and becomes intimate with her. In his unhappiness Jude takes to drink and loses his job. Discouraged, he returns home to Marygreen but is soon attracted to the town of Melchester where Sue is studying at a teachers' college. Jude abandons his own tentative studies for the ministry in order to be near her, and once again turns to stonemasonry for a living.

Their lives in Melchester end disastrously when Sue is expelled from her college for her innocent relationship with Jude. She then marries Phillotson, leaving Jude to return, again defeated, to Christminster. There Jude encounters his wife Arabella who has returned to England and is working in a local bar. Gradually tales come to Jude of Sue's intense unhappiness with Phillotson. At the funeral of Jude's Aunt Drusilla, he and Sue decide that she should come and live with him since she has already left the schoolmaster. Phillotson, who is too "civilized" to make much of a fuss, allows his wife to live with Jude in the city of Aldbrickham where nobody knows them. He willingly grants Sue a divorce. Jude, too, divorces Arabella. Sue, however, will hear nothing of a formal church wedding with Jude; her deep-rooted anticlericalism and her fear of binding herself permanently to any man make her prefer to live out of wedlock with Jude.

For a while the pair live in reasonable happiness which is

shattered when Arabella arrives and tells Jude that she has remarried and is unhappy. She sends to Jude a pathetically aged-looking young son she claims to have had by him after she arrived in Australia. The wizened boy is nicknamed Little Father Time. Soon word that Jude and Sue are not really married begins to circulate, and Jude loses one job after another. He is forced to travel about the countryside looking for work, living an unhappy gypsy life with Sue, Little Father Time, and two children of their own. Jude's health begins to fail. Since the arduous work of stonecutting is bad for his lungs, he is reduced to becoming a baker. Sue sells his cakes at local fairs.

In his discouragement Jude is more than ever unable to pry himself away from the old university town that has figured so largely in his dreams of a better life. Unfortunately, Christminster is so scandalized by his irregular relationship with Sue that they are forced to live in separate lodgings. One day, in her bitterness, Sue lectures Little Father Time about the sin of bringing children into an already over-populated world. The unnatural child takes her tirade to heart. When Sue returns to her rooming house after dining with Jude that evening, she finds that Little Father Time has hanged her two children and himself in a gesture of despair. The shock of finding their bodies sends Sue into a dead faint, and in a premature delivery she loses the baby she has been carrying.

Once an outspoken agnostic who did all she could to destroy Jude's simple, innate faith and who finally succeeded in making him an agnostic, too, Sue now becomes a religious fanatic. Filled with a sense of sin, she tells Jude she can have no more to do with him but must return to her first (and, as far as she is concerned, only legal) husband, Phillotson.

She remarries the schoolmaster, and once again, for the last time, Jude takes to drink. In a drunken daze he is again tricked into marrying Arabella whose husband has died. By now, Jude is near death. Years of masonry work have eaten into his lungs. Despite his precarious health, however, he goes out into the rain to see Sue once more, for Arabella has cruelly refused to summon her to Jude's bedside. The meeting is a failure. Sue will have nothing to do with Jude.

Returning home, Jude curses the day he was born. While Arabella is enjoying herself with a new lover at a sporting meet, Jude dies tasting the final bitter irony as he hears through the window the shouts and cheers from the nearby theater where the Christminster faculty are conferring honorary degrees on a group of undeserving aristocratic dilettantes.

Critical Opinion

With *Jude the Obscure*, his last novel, Hardy reached the pinnacle of his art and the depths of his pessimism. Unlike his other novels, *Jude* is not illuminated by the faintest ray of light or hope. Even the rough peasant humor that relieves the tragedy of *The Return of the Native* is missing here.

The novel's publication led to such a hue and cry in the press about its outspoken treatment of sex and the so-called "new woman" that Hardy decided to return to his first love, poetry, which he felt would give him a freer hand in expressing his tragic view of life. But although the critical blast that greeted the publication of *Jude* was ostensibly directed at its "immorality," it is difficult not to believe that the critics were really disturbed at the novel's unalloyed pessimism, for, from the first to the last, Jude's life and the lives of those who come into contact with him are blighted. The world view of the novel is symbolized by the grotesque suicide of Little Father Time.

Much of the novel's disturbing effect stems, too, from the savagery of its assault on the institutions of marriage and the university as Hardy saw them operating in Victorian England. His own first marriage, to a snobbish, empty-headed woman who fancied herself his superior, was a desperately unhappy one. Hardy brooded over the cruelty inherent in the difficulty of obtaining an annulment when a couple is patently mismated and over the cruelty society inflicted on people living together illicitly. He offers no glib solution to this problem, however, for Sue Bridehead, the believer in free love who is opposed to binding contracts between men and women, is scathingly portrayed as a frigid, deeply neurotic woman who can hardly solve her own personal problems, let alone those of society. As always in genuine tragedy, a panacea is neither suggested nor does one seem remotely possible.

The other major target of *Jude*, academic snobbery, was a subject of much concern in Hardy's day. Christminster is a combination of Oxford and Cambridge, toadying, in Hardy's view, to the inept sons of aristocrats instead of offering education to those genuinely desiring it and capable of appreciating it. *Jude the Obscure* is a powerful document for higher education based on merit rather than on social position. For if anyone deserves as good an education as his society can provide it is the serious-minded Jude, always striving to better himself and always excluded by a society that closes ranks at his approach.

By the time he wrote *Jude*, Hardy had become the complete master of his art. Although his reliance on coincidence is as strong as ever, he builds the book in blocks of chapters like a great gothic cathedral. The symmetry of plot and action that never obtrudes itself gives the book a seemingly inevitable structure and design. It is the ultimate triumph of the architect who became a novelist.

The Author

Thomas Hardy was born of old yeoman stock on June 2, 1840, in a small hamlet in Dorsetshire. His father was a builder and Hardy was trained to be an architect specializing in church restoration. As a youth, he was fascinated by the lore of old churches and by the centuries-old folk music and dances of the countryside, which he later immortalized as the "Wessex" of his novels.

After working five years as an architect in London, Hardy feared his eyes would not stand the strain of architectural drawing. Self-educated, he had read the great classics, especially the Greek tragedians, and he considered turning his hand to literature. He thought briefly, too, of entering the Church, but his readings in modern science and philosophy and his interest in architecture turned him in other directions.

His first novel, *The Poor Man and the Lady*, was rejected by George Meredith, then a publisher's reader, who encouraged Hardy to continue writing. A second novel, *Desperate Remedies*, was published in 1871. The novel that followed, *Under the Greenwood Tree* (1872), was the first in which Hardy's "Wessex" country appeared—a region of

England closely resembling his native Dorsetshire but stamped with the imprint of Hardy's own brooding, compassionate genius.

It was not until 1878, with *The Return of the Native*, that Hardy really hit his stride as a novelist. It is one of the four masterpieces that capped Hardy's career as a novelist, the others being *The Mayor of Casterbridge* (1886), *Tess of the D'Urbervilles* (1891) and *Jude the Obscure* (1896).

The bleak view of the human predicament expressed in these novels, combined with an honesty about sex unique at the time, brought a storm of criticism down on Hardy. The uproar over *Jude the Obscure* was responsible for Hardy's giving up the writing of fiction and spending the last three decades of his life writing poetry, his first love.

From 1898 until his death in 1928, Hardy wrote poetry exclusively, publishing seven distinguished volumes of sharply ironic lyrics, and rounding out his poetic achievement with a massive verse drama about the Napoleonic wars, *The Dynasts* (1904–1908).

As Victorian prudery subsided in the twentieth century, Hardy came to be appreciated as one of the master novelists of his day. In 1910 he received the Order of Merit as well as honorary degrees from the leading British universities. Reviled as a pornographer during his middle years, Hardy found himself revered as a grand old man in his old age. When he died on January 11, 1928, his ashes were buried in the Poets' Corner of Westminster Abbey, an irony Hardy would have been the first to appreciate.

By the Same Author

Tess of the D'Urbervilles: Tess is the story of the seduction, betrayal, and destruction of an innocent girl, Tess Durbeyfield, who is led by her foolish parents into thinking she comes from an ancient noble family, the D'Urbervilles. Encouraged to claim kinship with the family, Tess is seduced by the suave, plausible Alec D'Urberville, who abandons her when she bears his baby. The child dies, and Tess finds a new love with the egotistic, self-righteous Angel Clare. When he hears her story on their wedding night, he too abandons her. In despair, Tess murders Alec. She finds a few fleeting days of happiness with

Clare, who returns to her before she is captured and hanged. In the famous last lines of the novel, which could fit any other of Hardy's works almost as well, " 'Justice' was done, and the President of the Immortals . . . had ended his sport with Tess." *Tess* exemplifies Hardy's tragic irony which views through compassionate eyes the difference between the fate human beings deserve and the one that they suffer.

Treasure Island

by

ROBERT LOUIS STEVENSON (1850–1894)

Main Characters

Jim Hawkins—The brave young narrator of the story who
  becomes cabin boy aboard the *Hispaniola*.
Dr. Livesey—A physician friend of Jim's.
Squire Trelawney—A country squire with a love of adventure.
Captain Smollett—The highly capable, no-nonsense captain of
  the *Hispaniola*.
Billy Bones—A mysterious guest at the Admiral Benbow Inn.
Pew—A blind, bloodthirsty pirate.
Long John Silver—A plausible, shrewd, treacherous pirate who
  signs up as cook on the *Hispaniola*. He has a wooden leg and
  a pet parrot named Captain Flint.
Ben Gunn—A half-crazed pirate marooned for three years on
  Treasure Island.

The Story

Young Jim Hawkins has been helping his parents run the
Admiral Benbow Inn, near Black Hill Cove, a secluded spot in
the English west country. One day a mysterious seaman appears looking for room and board. The stranger's name is
Billy Bones. Presumably a retired sea captain, he makes him-

self at home in the inn, drinking vast quantities of rum, nervously scanning the coast, and singing the strange chantey:

> "Fifteen men on the dead man's chest
> Yo-ho-ho, and a bottle of rum."

Bones offers Jim a fourpenny piece every month if he will keep his eyes peeled for strangers, particularly a one-legged sailor who might appear at any moment.

When Bones fails to pay his board, Jim's father tries to get rid of him, but the old salt is so rough and terrifying that Mr. Hawkins, a sick man, never evicts him.

Soon another old sailor, Black Dog, appears at the Admiral Benbow, and he and Billy Bones get into a terrible fight in the parlor. Bones chases Black Dog away from the inn. He then falls on the floor in a fit and is treated by Dr. Livesey who has been caring for Jim's sick father.

Jim's father dies; and on the day he is buried, still another mysterious stranger shows up, ominously tapping his cane. It is the blind beggar called Pew, and he forces Jim to lead him to Billy Bones. He gives Bones the Black Spot—a note informing him he is to be killed at ten that night—and leaves. Billy Bones is so frightened at receiving this traditional pirate's death notice that he has a second stroke and dies.

Jim and his mother take the key to Billy Bones's old sea chest, hoping to find money to pay the old sailor's back rent. They plan to take only as much as is due them, but are interrupted by the sound of Pew's stick tapping along the walk. Quickly taking the dead sailor's account book and a sealed packet that they find in his trunk, Jim and his mother leave the inn to search for help. Eventually they find some revenue officers who arrive at the inn in time to scatter a host of Pew's friends. One of the officers on horseback crushes Pew to death.

Jim shows the sealed packet to the local squire, Squire Trelawney, who, with the help of Dr. Livesey, discovers that it contains a map showing the location of buried treasure left on an island by Captain Flint, a notoriously bloodthirsty old pirate. Apparently Billy Bones was to be murdered for holding out on his former friends. Excited by the prospect of high adventure, Squire Trelawney decides to equip a ship and sail for the island with Dr. Livesey and Jim. Trelawney has a reputation as a gossip so Dr. Livesey warns him to keep silent about their mission.

In Bristol, Squire Trelawney buys and outfits the *Hispaniola*, a fine schooner, and engages Captain Smollett. He also hires Long John Silver, a Bristol innkeeper and an old sea dog, to be ship's cook. Silver eagerly helps in the selection of the rest of the crew.

When Jim arrives at Bristol and visits Silver's inn, *The Spyglass*, he is surprised to see Black Dog drinking there. Silver persuades Jim that he does not know his guest's identity, and Black Dog escapes.

Soon the *Hispaniola* is ready to sail. Captain Smollett tells Trelawney that he does not like the idea of the cruise. He complains that he is the only one aboard who does not know the ship's destination. All the hands seem to know exactly where they are bound in search of treasure. Trelawney quiets the captain's fears, and off they sail.

The cruise is uneventful. But one night, just before arriving at Treasure Island, Jim, who is looking for an apple in the apple barrel on deck, is surprised by the approach of Long John Silver. Jim hides in the barrel, where he overhears Long John Silver planning mutiny with Israel Hands, one of the crewmen. Jim learns that in reality the crew look to Silver as their real leader. Most of them have known him since they sailed together with Captain Flint. Their plan is to slay Trelawney and the loyal members of the crew as soon as the treasure is taken off the island.

Jim tells his friends the news as they reach the island. Captain Smollett, his worst suspicions confirmed, cleverly sends most of the crew ashore, and Jim sneaks along with them to find out what they are up to. He hears the screams of two of the loyal crewmen whom Silver has put to death for refusing to go along with his plans.

Exploring the island, Jim comes across Ben Gunn, a poor half-mad hermit who had been aboard Captain Flint's ship when the old buccaneer buried the treasure. On a later trip Gunn had tried to find it but failed, and was left on the island by his shipmates.

In Jim's absence Captain Smollett, Squire Trelawney, and Dr. Livesey decide to leave the *Hispaniola* with the few loyal crew members and occupy Captain Flint's old stockade on the island. They make several trips to take supplies ashore. On the last trip they are fired upon by the pirates remaining aboard the ship.

Despite attacks from the pirates on shore, the loyal party is able to hold the stockade. Jim, who has left Ben Gunn, takes his position in the old fort. The next morning the wily Long John Silver, carrying a truce flag, comes to parley. He offers the men safe conduct back to the ship if they will surrender the treasure map. Captain Smollett contemptuously sends Silver back empty-handed, and soon the pirates attack again. There are casualties on both sides.

After this attack is repulsed, Jim sneaks off again, this time in search of the coracle (a small, one-man boat) which he knows Gunn has built and hidden on the island. He finds it and sets off at night to cut the *Hispaniola*'s anchor hawser. He succeeds in setting the ship adrift, but it bears down on him, smashing the little coracle. Jim is forced to go aboard the *Hispaniola* to escape drowning. Aboard he finds Israel Hands, wounded after killing the only other pirate left on the ship. Hands, in a drunken stupor, pretends to allow Jim to run the ship; but suddenly, just as Jim is bringing it into safe harbor, he goes after him with a dirk. He hurls the knife at him, pinning Jim to the mast, but the boy is just able to fire his pistols in time and kills the pirate.

With a wound in his shoulder, Jim manages to anchor the *Hispaniola* safely in a secret spot and make his way back to the stockade. There Silver and the other pirates have now taken over. Jim learns that his friends have abandoned the stockade and given the pirates the treasure map.

Jim is held captive by the pirates who want to kill him and depose Silver as their leader. But the old sea dog bullies the men and promises Jim safety on condition that when they get back to England Jim will stand up for him at his trial. Since most of the pirates now are wounded, drunk, or sick with swamp fever, Silver keeps the upper hand even after they give him the Black Spot.

Carrying the flag of truce, Dr. Livesey arrives to treat the men's wounds. He is curt with Jim who he thinks has deserted to the pirates. Jim cannot understand why Dr. Livesey gave the pirates the chart, but Dr. Livesey tells him he had a secret reason. When Jim recounts his adventure aboard the *Hispaniola*, Dr. Livesey is convinced of his loyalty and tries to get the boy to escape with him, but Jim has given Silver his word not to leave.

Now the pirates go in search of the treasure. The route is

arduous. When they reach the hiding place, they hear a mysterious voice singing "Yo-ho-ho, and a bottle of rum" and taunting them with the final curses of the terrible Captain Flint. Sick with superstitious fear, the men panic, but they finally realize that the mysterious voice is that of poor old Ben Gunn hiding in a tree.

When the men reach the place, they find that the treasure is gone. Furious, they want to kill Silver and Jim, but at that moment Jim's companions come to the rescue and rout the pirates. They bring Jim and Silver to Ben Gunn's cave where the treasure had been hidden by the lonely castaway long before the *Hispaniola* ever arrived. That was why Squire Trelawney was willing to abandon the stockade and give the pirates the now useless map.

With a few days' labor the treasure—thousands of pounds in the currency of almost every nation in the world—is safely stowed aboard the *Hispaniola*, and she leaves the blood-soaked island, abandoning the three remaining buccaneers as they had once abandoned Ben Gunn.

When the ship puts in at a West Indies port, Long John Silver escapes with his share of the treasure and is never heard of again. With a fresh crew hired at the port, the adventurers finally reach Bristol where they divide the remainder of the fortune. Jim decides he has had enough adventure to last him the rest of his days.

Critical Opinion

It would be absurd to read any solemn significance into *Treasure Island*, a book conceived to delight a boy. Stevenson himself, speaking of the treasure map he drew for his stepson, once said that the second voyage of the *Hispaniola*, when Israel Hands and Jim Hawkins are fighting for control of the ship, was written because he had drawn two ports on his map and wanted to make literary use of both of them. Freely admitting his debt to Washington Irving and Charles Kingsley, he pointed out that he got "a parrot from Defoe, a skeleton from Poe (indeed, "The Gold Bug" deeply influenced *Treasure Island*), a stockade from Marryat." The book was first serialized in a boys' magazine.

Treasure Island has nevertheless endured while much of the boys' fiction of its time has been relegated to the dust heap. Stevenson came at just the right moment in English literary history. With the death of Dickens, Thackeray, and Trollope, English fiction had more or less run out of steam. The novels of the 1880's tended to be either absurdly snobbish accounts of "high society" or dreary, naturalistic imitations of Zola, sordidly detailed accounts of the stifling commonplaces of lower-middle-class life. Stevenson, with his superb tale-spinner's imagination, gave English fiction a lift and a new dimension.

A romanticism rare in the novel after Scott makes *Treasure Island* memorable. The opening scenes in the Admiral Benbow Inn, nestled in its sea cove, have never been surpassed for imaginative re-creation of mood and local color. The sinister figures who invade the inn—Billy Bones, Black Dog, and Pew—lightly but unforgettably sketched, bring color and adventure as well as terror into the lives of Jim Hawkins and his stouthearted English friends.

Later on, in the re-creation of the island, Stevenson surpasses even Defoe in the use of imaginative detail that makes a highly romantic yarn altogether convincing. We know the geography and climate of *Treasure Island* more intimately than we know Crusoe's island.

Finally, *Treasure Island* lives because Stevenson, it is said, was incapable of writing a slipshod or ineffective sentence. Seldom has prose as supple and evocative been lavished on a mere "boy's book." Stevenson's keen ear for the rhythm of a sentence gives the style of *Treasure Island* a classic beauty that transcends the simple characterization, the "thriller" plot, and the modest intentions of the book.

The Author

Born on November 13, 1850, in Edinburgh—the home of that other great romancer, Sir Walter Scott—*Robert Louis Stevenson* was intended by his family to be either an engineer or a lawyer. Young Stevenson was educated at Edinburgh University and admitted to the bar in 1875, already determined to be a writer.

Falling in love with Fanny Osbourne, an American woman estranged from her husband and living in France, Stevenson followed her to California where he nearly starved to death waiting for her divorce to come through. In 1880, having broken with his puritanical family over his affair with Mrs. Osbourne, he was at last able to marry her. In order to support her, he began writing magazine essays, some of which were published the following year in the notable collection *Virginibus Puerisque*. Stevenson's first venture into fiction was a group of stories called *The New Arabian Nights* (1882).

One day, hoping to entertain his stepson, Lloyd Osbourne, Stevenson drew an imaginary treasure map which so intrigued him that he composed a novel to explain it—*Treasure Island*. Although it was unsuccessful in serial form, it made a great sensation when published as a book in 1883. Stevenson was even more successful three years later with the "shocker," *Dr. Jekyll and Mr. Hyde*, which appeared at about the same time as his great romance about the Jacobite uprising in Scotland, *Kidnapped*.

Afflicted with tuberculosis, Stevenson spent much of his life traveling for his health. He spent a winter at the tuberculosis sanatorium in Saranac. In 1888 he set out for the South Seas which had always intrigued him.

On the island of Samoa Stevenson, revered by the natives, recovered his health. In 1889 he published *The Master of Ballantrae*, his most ambitious work. Stevenson also enjoyed collaborating on stories with his stepson, and together they wrote *The Wrong Box* (1889), a fascinating puzzle, and *The Wrecker* (1892).

Although he was usually ill, Stevenson was always a great rebel and adventurer. In Edinburgh he had shocked staid society by his debauchery. In the South Seas he feasted with cannibal chiefs and was able to govern a tribe of savages. Forced to write "penny dreadfuls," or cheap shockers, for a living, Stevenson nevertheless brought a lively romantic imagination and a finely wrought prose style to everything he wrote. When he died in Samoa on December 3, 1894, he left behind an unfinished book, *Weir of Hermiston*. His flair for romance was deeply admired not only by his young readers but by such astute critics of the art of fiction as Henry James and Joseph Conrad.

By the Same Author

Kidnapped: Another exciting tale in the manner of *Treasure Island, Kidnapped* relates the efforts of young David Balfour to recover his rightful inheritance from his miserly Uncle Ebenezer. After the uncle's attempt to murder David fails, Ebenezer tries to sell him into slavery in America. David is kidnapped and taken aboard the brig *Covenant,* where he has the good fortune to meet the dashing Jacobite Alan Breck, who helps David defeat the crew and return to Scotland to wrest his inheritance from his uncle. *Kidnapped* ends abruptly because Stevenson fell ill while writing it. A sequel, *David Balfour,* was published in 1893. Both are rousing adventure stories, filled with vivid descriptions of the Highlands.

The Strange Case of Dr. Jekyll and Mr. Hyde: The idea for this psychological study of a split personality came to Stevenson in a nightmare. The highly respected Dr. Jekyll finds a drug that can reduce him to a hideous, evil, dwarf-like being whom he calls Mr. Hyde. The same drug will change him back to Dr. Jekyll, but the good doctor finds himself drawn beyond his control to the life of pure evil and power he knows as Mr. Hyde. One night, as Mr. Hyde, he commits a shocking murder and finds himself unable to return to his other self. The truth of his split personality is discovered, and with the police on his trail he kills himself. Written merely as an entertaining "penny dreadful," *Dr. Jekyll and Mr. Hyde* nevertheless reveals a psychological subtlety and insight Stevenson rarely achieved in his other books.

The Picture of Dorian Gray

by

OSCAR WILDE (1856–1900)

Main Characters

Dorian Gray—A young, rich, extraordinarily handsome, debauched dandy in the sin-ridden London of the 1890's.

Lord Henry Wotton—Dorian's witty, cynical mentor in sensuality.

Basil Hallward—A serious artist whose haunting portrait of Dorian is his masterpiece.

Sibyl Vane—A naïve young actress who catches Dorian's fancy.

James Vane—Sibyl's vengeful brother, a sailor.

Alan Campbell—A tormented young scientist being blackmailed by Dorian Gray.

The Story

Lord Henry Wotton, a cynical man about town, pays a visit to the luxurious studio of his painter friend, Basil Hallward, where he sees the full-length portrait of an exquisitely handsome young man whose features are marked by purity and innocence. Lord Henry asks Hallward who the model is. The artist replies that the young man's name is Dorian Gray, but that he does not want Lord Henry to meet the lad for fear he will corrupt him. He says that young Dorian has inspired him to do his finest work.

While they are talking, Dorian Gray arrives and Hallward is forced to introduce him to Lord Henry who engages the youth in charming, cynical banter while he poses. He begs Dorian to make the most of his youth and beauty while he has it, and deeply impresses the young man with his sophistication and epigrammatic wit.

Before long the portrait is finished and the three men admire it. Dorian is disturbed because the picture will remain eternally young and handsome while he himself will grow old and ugly. He says he would give his soul if only the portrait would age, and he remain perpetually young.

In the next few months, against the wishes of Basil Hallward, Lord Henry takes Dorian under his wing. The youth, who comes from a wealthy but unhappy family, is completely unspoiled. Lord Henry begins to change him. He takes him about London—to parties, plays, and operas—introducing him to society and to a life of pleasure and self-indulgence.

Lord Henry's influence is checked, however, when Dorian falls in love with the innocent seventeen-year-old actress, Sibyl Vane, whom he sees playing Juliet in a tenth-rate theater. At first Dorian is hesitant about letting Sibyl know his name, so she calls him "Prince Charming." Her mother, a faded, somewhat vulgar actress, entirely approves of the affair, but Sibyl's brother, James, becomes furious when he hears of it. James, a sailor, is soon to leave England, but first he warns Sibyl against her mysterious admirer, threatening to kill him if he ever betrays her innocence.

Lord Henry and Basil Hallward react coolly when Dorian tells them he is engaged to Sibyl. They see it as the unfortunate but necessary first affair of an inexperienced youth, and are sure that he will soon leave Sibyl for someone more worthy of his wealth and social position. Dorian insists that they come with him to the theater where she is acting Juliet to see what a paragon she is. That night Sibyl gives a stiff, unimaginative performance. Bored and embarrassed, Lord Henry and Basil Hallward leave the theater before the final curtain. When Dorian goes backstage to see Sibyl, she tells him that she acted badly because art means nothing to her now that her life has become fulfilled by his love. Suddenly Dorian realizes that his friends are right: Sibyl is "common."

He brutally tells her he no longer loves her, leaves her weeping in the dressing room, and storms out of the theater.

At home Dorian receives a terrible shock. Looking at the portrait of himself, he sees it has changed slightly. Although in the mirror his features are as fresh and innocent as ever, in the portrait a cruel grimace distorts his mouth. Dorian hastily writes a letter begging the girl's pardon and assuring her of his love. The next afternoon Lord Henry arrives with the news that Sibyl Vane had taken poison in her dressing room immediately after Dorian had jilted her. The girl is dead, but Lord Henry assures Dorian that he is well rid of her; she was unworthy of him anyway. Furthermore, he will be spared any scandal because nobody connects his name with hers.

Basil Hallward calls to offer his sympathy and asks to see the portrait which he is thinking of exhibiting. Dorian refuses to let him see the picture which he conceals behind a screen. Later he hides the portrait in an unused upstairs room. Fascinated by the idea that the picture will be a mirror of his soul, Dorian is terrified lest anyone else learn of its power.

During the next few years, Dorian falls deeply under the spell of Lord Henry Wotton. The older man gives him a "poisonous" French book to read (J. K. Huysmans' *À Rebours*) which details the infinite variety of sins and sensual pleasures in which a rich, selfish young man can indulge himself. Under its influence, Dorian collects rare gems and perfumes, flirts with Catholic ritual, and even frequents low haunts and opium dens. He takes pleasure in leading young men into a life of debauchery and soon finds himself barred from London society where evil rumors about him are circulating.

Dorian's greatest interest in life is to compare his still youthful, unravaged face in the mirror with the coarse, cruel face emerging in the portrait. Nobody else in London can understand how Dorian manages to remain physically unmarred by his vices.

Late one night, Dorian is visited by Basil Hallward. The artist tells him he is leaving for Paris where he will spend at least six months painting, trying to recover the inspiration that left him when Dorian and he became estranged. Before he leaves, however, he feels he must make one last attempt to talk Dorian out of his evil ways. He harangues him about his evil reputation and begs Dorian to assure him that the rumors are unfounded. Instead, Dorian angrily reveals the picture to the artist who painted it. Basil is appalled by the loathsome visage of evil staring insolently at him from the canvas. He pleads with Dorian to pray for his soul, but Dorian, in a sudden fury, grasps a knife and stabs Hallward to death.

Since Hallward was supposed to be going to Paris, Dorian is sure the murder will not be discovered if he can only dispose of the corpse. To do this, he enlists the aid of an old friend, Alan Campbell, a chemist whose life Dorian had ruined. Campbell has not been on speaking terms with him for years, but Dorian pleads with him to help destroy the body of Basil Hallward. When Campbell angrily refuses to do so, Dorian threatens to blackmail him for some secret sin of the past. Resigned to his fate, Campbell orders large quantities of nitric acid and in a few hours destroys every vestige of the artist's body. While this grisly work is going on, Dorian indulges in witty banter with Lord Henry at a fashionable dinner party.

One night in an opium den, Dorian comes close to death. James Vane, returned from his voyages and single-mindedly stalking his prey, has overheard a woman calling Dorian "Prince Charming," which he remembers as his sister's name for her lover. When Dorian emerges from the den into the fog, Vane is waiting for him with a pistol. Only Dorian's quick thinking saves him from the brother's vengeance. He reminds Vane that Sibyl had died eighteen years before, and then asks the sailor to look at his face under a street lamp. Since Dorian has not aged at all, he seems to be only twenty, and the would-be avenger slinks away. Later Vane realizes his mistake and stalks Dorian at a fashionable hunting party where Vane himself is accidentally killed.

Dorian now thinks himself completely safe. The minor flurry of interest about the disappearance of Basil Hallward has subsided. Sibyl's embittered brother is dead, and Alan Campbell has committed suicide. No one can possibly accuse Dorian of murder. Sick of the past and grateful for his new lease on life, Dorian tells Lord Henry that he is determined to lead a better, less selfish existence. When Lord Henry laughs, Dorian insists that he has begun by refraining from seducing a peasant girl he could easily have had. Filled with good intentions, Dorian wonders if his noble acts will also be recorded on the portrait. Perhaps it will not be so horrible now. He looks again at the picture, but to his horror the face is even worse. In addition to its grossness and cruelty, he can see a hypocritical smirk on the lips and blood dripping from the hand.

Seizing a knife, he slashes passionately at the picture which he feels has betrayed his good intentions and ruined his life. When the servants below hear an agonized cry, they break down the locked door and see on the wall the picture of Dorian Gray as it looked originally—godlike in its beauty and purity. But on the floor is the real Dorian Gray who, in stabbing the portrait, has actually killed himself. Old, debauched, and withered, he is unrecognizable to his own servants until they identify him by the rings on his gnarled, grasping fingers.

Critical Opinion

The Picture of Dorian Gray is Wilde's only full-length novel. It is a curious reworking of the Faust legend in which Dorian is Faust; Lord Henry Wotton, Mephistopheles; Sibyl Vane, Gretchen; and her brother, Valentine. The major difference is that while Faust wishes for eternal youth in order to experience all that life has to offer—including unselfish work for good—Dorian wishes to remain young only to be admired and to experience all the lusts of the flesh. A very debased Faust, his end is appropriately sordid and essentially meaningless.

Like Dorian's portrait, the novel has aged badly. After its first notoriety as an exhibit used by the prosecution in Wilde's trial, it became a great favorite. Wilde, however, had very little talent for fiction: the plotting is heavy-handed, the characters one-dimensional. Whatever vigor the novel has today stems not from its allegorical treatment of the wages of sin but from its sparkling epigrams and its charm as a period piece of late-Victorian London.

Lord Henry's epigrams and paradoxes are still entertaining. "The only way to get rid of a temptation is to yield to it," he says to Dorian, and (later in the novel), "A man can be happy with any woman, as long as he does not love her."

Obviously, Lord Henry's wit is Wilde's own, and he may have seen himself in the novel as the cynical roué who debauched the "innocent" Lord Alfred Douglas. The pervasive sense of sin is largely unconvincing today, however, because Wilde is too conventionally Victorian to be specific about it. We are not told, for instance, just why Dorian can blackmail Alan Campbell, although we may assume that much of the sin talked about in the book is pederasty.

As a period piece, *The Picture of Dorian Gray*, like the Sherlock Holmes stories, paints the fog-muffled streets, the dandies, and the languors of London in the 1890's. The atmosphere of the book is still entrancing even if the basic plot has less impact today.

The Author

No other sensation in the literary and social world of the 1890's matched the meteoric rise and fall of *Oscar Fingal O'Flahertie Wills Wilde*. Born in Dublin on October 15, 1856, Wilde inherited his artistic tastes from his eccentric mother, a minor literary luminary of the time. He went to Oxford in 1874, where he came under the influence of the esthetic theories of John Ruskin and Walter Pater.

On leaving Oxford, Wilde made it his mission in life to bring a simplified version of the doctrine of art for art's sake to the philistine middle class, not only by means of brilliant essays, plays, and stories but by his own behavior. Dressed extravagantly, and usually clutching some such "esthetic" object as a lily in his hand, Wilde propagandized for an art free of any moral considerations. His lecture tour of the United States in 1882 was a great success largely because of Wilde's genius for self-advertisement. He was parodied as Bunthorne in the Gilbert and Sullivan comic opera *Patience*.

Wilde published a volume of poems that increased his notoriety, although they were little more than pastiches of Swinburne and the Pre-Raphaelite poets. In 1891, under the influence of the French decadent writer J. K. Huysmans, he published *The Picture of Dorian Gray*.

Wilde's real popularity came, however, from the series of comedies he wrote, starting with *Lady Windermere's Fan*, produced in 1892, and reaching a climax with perhaps the most brilliant farce in the English language, *The Importance of Being Earnest*, in 1895. Here all of Wilde's gifts for self-dramatization, for scintillating, sophisticated dialogue, and for gay absurdity reached fruition. He revitalized the English stage, which had lain dormant for over a century, and laid the groundwork for the plays of Bernard Shaw.

But disaster closed in on Wilde in the same year. Married and the father of two sons, Wilde had for some years been indulging in homosexual practices with a variety of young men ranging from the elegant, spoiled Lord Alfred Douglas, who resembled Dorian Gray, to male prostitutes in the lowest strata of the London underworld. When Lord Alfred's father, the Marquess of Queensbury, insulted Wilde at his club one day, Wilde sued him for slander. He lost the suit and in turn was prosecuted by the crown for his sexual crimes. The trials became the scandal of the age. Wilde answered flippantly to the prosecution's charges, rejected the advice of his friends to escape to France, and was condemned to two years at hard labor.

A broken man when he was released from Reading Gaol in 1898, Wilde went to France to live. His wife had left him, his plays had been immediately taken off the stage, his property had been sold at auction, and many of the powerful friends who had been delighted with his repartee at social gatherings now deserted him. Wilde's spirit was broken by the years in prison. Only two more works worth noting came from his pen: the long, self-explanatory letter *De Profundis*, written to Lord Alfred Douglas, and the poem "The Ballad of Reading Gaol."

In France, Wilde lived two years in squalor and poverty, and died on November 30, 1900, a broken man, victim both of his own weakness and folly and of a hypocritical, vengeful society.

The Twentieth Century

The Time Machine

by

H. G. WELLS (1866–1946)

Main Characters

The Time Traveler—An adventurous scientist who journeys
millions of years into the future by means of his time
machine.
Weena—A girl of the race of Eloi whom the Time Traveler
discovers inhabiting England in the year AD 802,701 and
who becomes his trusting and affectionate companion.

The Story

In the waning years of the nineteenth century, the Time
Traveler is entertaining some friends after dinner with a
discussion of time as the fourth dimension. All things, he says,

exist not only in length, breadth, and thickness, but in time as well. The only reason we cannot properly perceive the dimension of time is that we ourselves are moving in it.

To correct this condition and to test his theories, the Time Traveler has constructed a machine designed to help him move backwards or forwards through the centuries. He jolts his skeptical guests (a politician, a doctor, and a psychologist) when he shows them an actual model of the machine, which has taken him two years to construct. He persuades the psychologist to press a lever, and suddenly the model disappears. The Time Traveler tells his astonished guests that as soon as his machine is perfected he hopes to launch himself into the future.

The next week the same group gathers at the Time Traveler's house, joined by a newspaper editor. Their host is late for dinner, and his guests wonder what is keeping him. Can he actually have traveled into the future?

Suddenly the door bursts open and the Time Traveler appears, dirty, disheveled, and bedraggled, with a nasty cut on his chin. After he has cleaned up and dressed and they have all dined, he tells the guests his extraordinary story.

In the week after demonstrating his model, the Time Traveler perfected his machine. That very morning, strapping himself into the time machine, he took off like a rocket into the future. Travel was very uncomfortable, for the days and nights sped past in such rapid succession that his eyes hurt from the alternating light and dark. Eventually, in the misty, strange world of the future, he brought his machine to a jolting halt and found himself in the year AD 802,701.

Hoping to find a greatly advanced civilization, the Time Traveler sees in the misty, warm air only an ominous, giant white sphinx on a huge pedestal. Before long, some men approach. They are frail and delicate and only about four feet tall. One of them, childlike, asks the Time Traveler if he has come from the sun in a thunderstorm. Then these feeble creatures deck the Time Traveler with garlands of flowers and sing and dance around him. They are mildly curious about his time machine, and he allows them to touch it after taking the precaution of removing the operating levers. Together they dine on fruit and vegetables—animals have become extinct— and the Eloi, as they are called, teach the Time Traveler the rudiments of their language.

The Eloi, he decides, are an overcivilized race. Easily fatigued, like children they rapidly lose interest in things. They are extremely lazy, but beautiful, peaceable, and friendly. The Time Traveler realizes that this is the end of human evolution. In a world freed from the struggle for existence by better and more efficient machinery, the people have become unambitious and unassertive. Because the Eloi are no longer struggling with nature, which has long since been entirely subdued, they have become reasonable and cooperative. Having achieved the apparent goal of civilization, they seem to be leading a happy if uneventful life.

As night falls, the Time Traveler is dismayed when he discovers that his machine has disappeared. He tries to awaken the Eloi, but they are terrified of the dark and refuse to help him search for his machine. Uneasy, the Time Traveler finally falls asleep. The next morning he finds a path leading to the huge white sphinx, and realizes that his time machine is inside the statue. He tries vainly to open the door of the sphinx. The Eloi are uncooperative. The Time Traveler begins to despair of ever getting back to his own century.

At this point, however, the Time Traveler makes a special friend among the Eloi, Weena, an affectionate, childlike girl whom he saves from drowning. Like the other Eloi, Weena is easily fatigued and fearful of the dark, but she loyally joins the Time Traveler in his adventures.

On the fourth day of his sojourn, the Time Traveler understands why the Eloi are terrified after nightfall. In the dark ruins of an ancient building, he becomes aware of strange eyes staring at him. Following them, he discovers that they belong to a loathsome, ape-like creature that lopes along before him, eventually disappearing down a ladder into a shaft. The Time Traveler cannot believe that this creature is as human as the Eloi until he realizes that the Morlocks, as they are called, are also descended from the human beings of his time. The world has been divided between the fragile, helpless Eloi, who inhabit the surface of the earth, and the fierce, obscene Morlocks, who clamber about in the darkness of their underground tunnels, like human spiders, emerging only at night. The Eloi, obviously the masters, are descended from the nineteenth-century ruling class in England. The Morlocks, descended from the working class, do all the physical labor, but their brutality and savagery keep the Eloi in mortal terror of the day these servants will revolt.

Certain now that the Morlocks, and not the Eloi, are responsible for hiding his machine, the Time Traveler determines to follow them into their subterranean caverns, despite Weena's warnings. Clambering laboriously into one of the caves, the Time Traveler sees a group of the creatures gnawing at a chunk of meat. He is attacked by them, but by lighting matches before their eyes, he manages to escape above gound. Later the horrible realization comes to him that the Morlocks live on Eloi meat, carrying off their victims at night.

The only safeguard against these obscene creatures is light, which they fear as much as the Eloi fear darkness. As the Time Traveler is running out of matches, he goes exploring the next day with Weena to find some other sources of light. He discovers an ancient palace of green porcelain, apparently a science and natural history museum long forgotten by the Eloi. There he fortunately finds some matches and wax from which he can fashion a candle.

Weena is exhausted after the long trek to the museum, so the Time Traveler decides to camp out with her that night, building a fire to keep the beasts away. But when he sees some Morlocks crouching in the woods, he decides it would be safer to spend the night up on a hill where he builds a new campfire. During the night he awakens to discover that his new fire has gone out, his matches are missing, and Weena is no longer there. Fearing that she has been abducted by the Morlocks, he searches for her without success. He finds that his first fire has spread through the forest, killing thirty or forty Morlocks.

Sleeping by day and traveling by night, he makes his way back to the sphinx, which he is determined to open with a crowbar from the science museum. The door, however, is already open when he gets there, and, not suspecting a trap, the Time Traveler enters.

Inside he discovers his machine. But at that instant a group of Morlocks pounce upon him, and it is all he can do to fend them off while he starts the machine. Just as the Morlocks are about to carry him off to suffer Weena's fate, the machine hurtles him out of their grasp and far into the future.

Millions of years later, the earth has stopped rotating on its axis. The machine lands on a desolate beach where the Time Traveler discovers the only inhabitants are giant, evil-looking crabs. He sets the machine in motion again, and now, thirty million years after leaving the safety of his laboratory, he finds the world a cold, still hulk, faintly lit by a dying sun.

Horrified, the Time Traveler sets the machine back for the return journey, and eventually reaches home where he tells his story to his friends. Disillusioned though he is with the future, the Time Traveler has not lost his scientific curiosity. The next day he sets off again on a journey through time. Three years later he has still not returned, and his friends can only speculate about what misadventure has overtaken him in the depths of time.

Critical Opinion

The Time Machine is a scientific romance with philosophical and political overtones. More serious than Jules Verne, Wells in his first successful book set the tone for contemporary science fiction.

Wells has often been accused of having an over-optimistic faith in what science and intelligent planning could do for the human race. Recent critics have complained that his faith in science as a panacea failed to take into account the side of human nature which would pervert scientific learning into weapons of destruction like the nuclear bomb. In *The Time Machine*, however, Wells shows that he is far from being a facile optimist.

Essentially, this brief book is a speculation about the future of a race which rapidly, through science, finds itself less and less challenged by the physical universe. The soft, lazy, hypercivilized Eloi are as degenerate in their way as the bestial Morlocks who represent an aspect of human nature that can never be entirely suppressed. Wells merely extends into the future the existing society of his day, with its sharply divided ruling and serving classes. In AD 802,701 the rulers find themselves on the brink of being annihilated by their servants whom they depend on for physical sustenance but fear as their potential destroyers.

The only hope for human society, as Wells sees it in *The Time Machine*, is in a humane, intelligent blending of the vigorous and the contemplative life, and in an amicable, just relationship between the classes until such time as class lines disappear.

Tono-Bungay

by

H. G. WELLS

Main Characters

George Ponderevo—The narrator of the story who is interested in aeronautical engineering but gets sidetracked by his uncle into the patent medicine business.

Edward Ponderevo—George's enthusiastic, ambitious pharmacist uncle, who invents the patent medicine Tono-Bungay.

Susan Ponderevo—George's sweet and unassuming aunt, who humorously tries to keep Edward's ambitions in perspective.

Beatrice Normandy—The aristocratic love of George's life.

Marion Ramboat—The grasping, unimaginative girl George marries.

Gordon-Nasmyth—A reckless soldier of fortune who interests the Ponderevos in stealing a pile of radioactive material from an East African island.

Cothorpe—An idealistic, self-educated engineer who helps George in his flying experiments.

The Story

Young George Ponderevo spends his childhood learning at first hand about the rigid class system that dominates late Victorian England. As the son of the housekeeper of Bladesover—a large ancestral estate—he sees that everyone has his predestined rank, from the regal Lady Drew down to the lowliest tradesmen and servants. It is impossible to move from one rank to another, and George quickly perceives that his is near the bottom.

When he is twelve, George falls in love with a high-spirited, aristocratic neighbor, Beatrice Normandy. Little Beatrice seems to return his puppy love; but when George gets into a fight with her overbearing half brother, Archie Garvell, Beatrice not only fails to help him, but betrays him to Lady Drew, pretending that he started the fight. It is George's first disillusioning experience with the clannishness of the English aristocracy, and he never forgets it.

Forced to leave Bladesover, George works for a while in a bakery run by his dull, pious maternal uncle, Nicodemus Frapp. But again the lad disgraces himself by uttering blasphemies before his hypocritically religious young cousins who inform against him to his uncle.

Finally, George finds a place with his paternal uncle, Edward Ponderevo, a pharmacist in the sleepy little town of Wimblehurst. His uncle is a sympathetic spirit. After his mother's death George is well brought up by his patient, humorous aunt, Susan Ponderevo. Uncle Edward, however, is constantly chafing at the dullness of life in the small village. He has great dreams of making a fortune with a single invention that would cater to the wants of the expanding middle class. He sees himself getting a monopoly on some commodity that industry desperately needs and thus becoming a captain of industry.

In his haste to make money, Edward Ponderevo invests his savings foolishly and loses the little he has as well as his small chemist's shop. He even dips into the money entrusted to him for George's upbringing. Unable to bear the sarcastic comments of their neighbors, the Ponderevos leave town to seek their fortune. George is reunited with his uncle and aunt in London when he gets a Bachelor of Science degree at the university.

Although he is angry with his uncle for appropriating his inheritance, George is still fascinated by his restlessness and eccentricity. One day Edward Ponderevo hints to George that he has come upon a great invention with the cryptic name "Tono-Bungay," but that is all he will divulge at the time.

While he is studying science, George meets Marion Ramboat, who helps him forget his childish love for Beatrice. George is naïvely smitten with Marion's wholly commonplace charms and wants to marry her, but she keeps reminding him that he is too poor to set up a household.

Just at this point, Edward Ponderevo summons George to a momentous meeting. Tono-Bungay has been perfected and is being advertised and sold all over England. Will George help him in the production of this unique product? As far as George can discover, Tono-Bungay will neither kill nor cure the people who swallow it. It is a secret formula, cheap and easy to make, but the demand for it has far exceeded Edward's ability to manufacture it. When his uncle offers him £300 a year to come in with him, George, seeing in this offer his chance to get married, agrees.

George's natural efficiency and scientific training enable him to expand the production of Tono-Bungay. He collaborates with his uncle on increasingly vulgar and ludicrous advertisements, and notes, to his amazement, that his uncle really believes in the product and is hurt to hear any criticism of it. The nostrum sweeps England, and the Ponderevos prosper. George's qualms about wasting his scientific skill on a perfectly useless and fraudulent product are assuaged by the fact that he can now finally afford to marry Marion. The marriage is a ghastly failure, however. Marion is interested only in material possessions and is intellectually and temperamentally unsuited to George. Before long George is seeking solace in a temporary affair with Effie Rink, his uncle's secretary.

Once Tono-Bungay is well launched, George can spare the time and money to cultivate his real interest—building and experimenting with gliders and balloons. While he is devoting himself to science, his uncle, ever on the alert to increase his fortune, has been giving to almost anyone who comes to him with a scheme for making money a favorable hearing and capital to go ahead with the project. One of these projects, which is eventually to bring disaster, is the stealing of some "quap," or radioactive slag, from the barren shore of an East African island. This scheme, broached by a soldier of fortune named Gordon-Nasmyth, hangs fire for a while because both Ponderevos are too busy to pursue it.

Meanwhile Edward Ponderevo moves from one elaborate home to another. Still restless, but by now immensely wealthy, he can find no home sufficiently grand to suit his Napoleonic concept of himself. His wife, Susan, tries vainly to keep a check on his pretensions by her quiet humor and by the example of her unaffected personality. Edward is determined to become one of the leading social figures of his time. As long as he has the money to spend, he seems able to break through the rigid class barriers. He tries to learn French and to be a wine connoisseur. The results are ludicrous. Ultimately he buys Crest Hill, as splendid a mansion as Bladesover, and employs a hundred workmen to "improve" it.

Meanwhile, with the money pouring in from Tono-Bungay, George continues his glider experiments with a talented assistant named Cothorpe. Once again he meets Beatrice Normandy, and their love is rekindled when she nurses him back to health after George is nearly killed in a flying experiment.

Edward Ponderevo's massive speculations backfire. Overextended financially, he finds himself dangerously close to bankruptcy. The public begins to lose confidence in him, his powerful friends refuse to help him, and he must call on George to take up Gordon-Nasmyth's scheme, to sail to Mordet Island in search of the mysterious quap. If he can bring back a substantial amount, the Ponderevos will have a monopoly of radioactive substances which are becoming vital in science and industry, and Edward may be able to recoup his losses in other enterprises.

Reluctantly but dutifully, George leaves Beatrice and his flying experiments to set sail aboard the leaky brig *Maude Mary*. George struggles to keep the mutinous crew in order. When they reach the barren island, the heat is nightmarish; stealing the heaps of quap is dangerous and backbreaking work. One day George spots a native staring at him. Afraid of being discovered in the illegal operation, he draws a gun and kills him. Loading the last of the quap aboard ship, he heads for home. In mid-ocean the boat springs a leak and sinks with the entire cargo of quap. George is rescued by a passing ship and returns to England only to learn that Edward Ponderevo has gone bankrupt.

Hounded by creditors and afraid of arrest, Edward decides to leave England. He and George take off in George's latest flying ship, a huge dirigible, and successfully cross the channel at night, landing near Bordeaux, where they pretend to be ordinary tourists. But the excitement and physical rigors of the trip prove too much for the broken-spirited Edward

Ponderevo. With all his grand financial schemes in ruins about him, he falls ill and dies in a little inn near Bayonne with only George at his side.

When George returns to England, he has a two weeks' idyl with Beatrice Normandy. He sees no reason why they cannot marry now, but Beatrice tells him she can never step outside her class. She has become too accustomed to luxury and easy living to share her life with a man who is starting from scratch even though she admits that she loves him.

Disillusioned, George, now forty-five, becomes a designer of warships and sets out to write his first and only book, *Tono-Bungay*.

Critical Opinion

Although *Tono-Bungay* is often amusing, it is a deeply serious analysis of the breakdown of values in pre-World War I England. The character of George Ponderevo is much like Wells's own, down to the details of being a housekeeper's son and receiving a scientific, technical education rather than the classical education of the upper class.

Three major symbols in the book illustrate Wells's theme. The first is Bladesover, the great estate on which George is raised and a symbol of the hidebound, snobbish England of the late nineteenth century. Bladesover, and the whole system of life implied by its existence, nevertheless had its good points, George realizes. At least it was based on tradition and an ordered way of life, not on exploitation and advertising. Lady Drew belonged there, but after her death the estate was taken over by members of the newly rich class—uneducated, vulgar people who cared about its traditions only because they enhanced their own status.

The second major symbol is the patent medicine, Tono-Bungay. Utterly valueless, through saturation advertising it makes a fortune for George and his uncle. Scientific experiment, which Wells felt should be subsidized by the government, is dependent on the financial success or failure of such goods. As the first major satire on modern advertising techniques, *Tono-Bungay* is still an effective novel.

Finally, the mysterious radioactive quap symbolizes the folly of imperialism and industrialism, and the plunder of the natural resources of the earth to satisfy men's greed. In order to get this substance, which is nauseating to smell and dangerous to hold, George, who is normally decent and honest, must lie, steal, and even kill. The quap is finally lost—returned to nature where it always belonged.

Although Wells never sermonizes in *Tono-Bungay*, it is clear that he is sharply criticizing the vulgar commercialism in the England of his day. Neither the self-destructive snobbery of Bladesover, symbolized by Beatrice's refusal to marry George, nor the aggressive unscrupulousness of the middle class, traditionless and socially unsure of itself, strikes Wells as good. The aristocracy dies because it is weak, insular, and self-indulgent. The middle class is rising to take the aristocracy's place, but its only system of values is a relentless materialism.

At first, science seems to be the only legitimate human concern in the book. But it is science that has taught the world the uses of quap, and we last see George putting his scientific training to use in designing destroyers. Fundamentally only the good-humored patience and bravery of George's Aunt Susan, like the spirit of Weena in *The Time Machine*, is worth anything. Underneath its ebullient humor and Dickensian high spirits, *Tono-Bungay* is a darkly prophetic book, richer in detail and human warmth than *The Time Machine* but every bit as pessimistic about the future.

The Author

Like his Time Traveler and like George Ponderevo, the narrator of *Tono-Bungay*, *Herbert George Wells* was fascinated all his life by the power of science to shape man's destiny. It was science that lifted Wells from the undistinguished, lower-middle-class world into which he was born on September 21, 1866. His father had tried his hand unsuccessfully at gardening and shopkeeping; his mother was a lady's maid and later housekeeper at Up Park in Hampshire, an establishment like the Bladesover of *Tono-Bungay*. Wells, who called himself "a typical Cockney," learned early what it meant to be a member of the lower social orders of Victorian England.

Determined to rise in the world, Wells rejected all attempts to make a shopkeeper or pharmacist of him. Instead, in 1881, he became a pupil-teacher at Midhurst Grammar School.

Wells's preoccupation with science won him a scholarship in 1884 to study biology under Thomas Henry Huxley at the Royal College of Science. Poor health and a foray into journalism cut short his career as a science teacher. By 1895, with the publication of *The Time Machine,* he had established himself as one of England's most popular and successful authors.

Wells was extraordinarily prolific—there are at least a hundred titles to his credit—in three genres. First are the scientific romances, precursors of modern science fiction, of which the most successful, besides *The Time Machine,* are *The Island of Dr. Moreau* (1896), *The Invisible Man* (1897), and *The War of the Worlds* (1898). Then come the novels about lower-middle-class eccentrics, filled with Dickensian humor and keen social observation. Among these the best known are *Kipps* (1905), *Tono-Bungay* (1909), and *The History of Mr. Polly* (1910). The third group is by far the largest, if the least enduring, of Wells's fiction and includes novels of ideas— ideas about love and sex, politics, war, religion, and education. They include *Ann Veronica* (1909), *Mr. Britling Sees It Through* (1916), and *The World of William Clissold* (1926).

With the publication in 1920 of his vastly successful *Outline of History,* Wells attained world-wide fame as a political and social pundit. Like his friend George Bernard Shaw, he had always been interested in Fabian socialism, which to Wells meant the only rational way of organizing the world in order to prevent waste, poverty, and war.

Never particularly interested in the esthetics of fiction, Wells, as he grew older, turned more frequently to the writing of popularized history, philosophy, and science, sometimes thinly disguised as fiction but more often straightforward expository or argumentative tracts. A lifelong hater of war, he found himself propagandizing for England in the two major wars of the century.

Before he died, on August 13, 1946, the Labour Party whose program he had done much to formulate had risen to power in England.

By the Same Author

The War of the Worlds: This grim tale of a savage, destructive invasion of earth by ruthless, super-intelligent Martians shocked a good many Victorian readers out of their complacency about man's inevitable progress. In it Wells describes the invasion, starting with the landing of a single, mysterious spaceship which is mistaken for a meteorite, and leading into a universal panic through wholesale destruction of the English countryside and of London itself. The Martians are all brain and no heart. They are the scientific superiors of men on earth, but finally, after literally sucking the blood of human beings for food, they succumb to the bacteria of earth for which their systems are unprepared. In the light of the immense accumulation of scientific knowledge about outer space since the book was written, it may seem rather primitive to sophisticated modern readers. Wells's vision of a universal holocaust destroying man's complacency, however, has in recent years become even more pertinent than at the time he wrote this short, terrifying book.

The History of Mr. Polly: This is a delightful novel about an especially charming lower-middle-class draper's apprentice's frustrations and glorious escape from a humdrum existence. After fifteen years of trying to run an unsuccessful shop and to cope with a shrewish wife, gentle, mild-mannered Mr. Polly decides to escape. He sets fire to his shop so his wife can collect insurance, pretends to commit suicide, and then takes off for high adventure as a tramp. Eventually he meets an unpretentious woman who runs a country inn and joins her in that more cheerful enterprise. *The History of Mr. Polly* reflects Wells's compassion for the average man who leads what Thoreau called a life of "quiet desperation" but who nevertheless refuses to close his eyes to the beauty and romance in life. Mr. Polly, however, is no stereotype for the "little man": he is one of the "originals" in our literature, and the novel is a gem, mined in the Dickensian vein.

Heart of Darkness

by

JOSEPH CONRAD (1857–1924)

Main Characters

Charles Marlow—An old, experienced seaman telling the
story of a nightmarish youthful adventure.
Fresleven—A Danish captain, Marlow's predecessor in the
Congo.
The Russian—An enthusiastic sailor Marlow meets deep in
the Congo.
Mr. Kurtz—The mysterious European ivory trader whom
Marlow is sent to search for.
Kurtz's "Intended"—His idealistic, loyal fiancée back in
Brussels.

The Story

The experienced old sea dog, Marlow, is perched one evening
like a Buddha on the deck of the cruising yawl *Nellie*, which
is anchored in the Thames estuary. He is talking to a group of
his boyhood friends. They are now grown to be important
people—a director of companies, a lawyer, and an accountant
—but between them there has always existed the "bond of the
sea." Marlow, looking at the great city of London enveloped
in the gloom of dusk, makes a cryptic remark to his friends.
"And this also," he says, "has been one of the dark places of
the earth."

Seeing London, now the apex of civilization but at one time a barbaric port where Roman legionaries came in fear and trembling, reminds Marlow of his experience many years before, sailing up the Congo River in search of the mysterious ivory trader, Mr. Kurtz.

As a boy, Marlow had always been fascinated by maps, especially those of unexplored continents. The map of Africa particularly intrigued him, with its gaps of uncharted land deep in the Congo. After growing up to be a sailor and spending some six years in the East, Marlow one day decides to take a job aboard a steamer headed for the Congo River. He visits an aunt in Brussels who has influence with one of the continental trading companies that are exploiting Africa and need brave men to sail their fresh-water steamers.

Marlow learns later that his predecessor in the company's employ was a Dane named Fresleven, who had been brutally murdered in an argument with some natives about a couple of chickens. Still full of the spirit of adventure, Marlow impresses his future employer. A strange, disquieting medical examination follows, performed by a doctor who measures Marlow's skull with calipers, all the time remarking ominously, "The changes take place inside, you know." The doctor also, significantly, asks Marlow if there is any history of insanity in his family.

Ultimately Marlow ships aboard a French steamer which follows the forbidding African coast past such bizarre places as Gran' Bassam and Little Popo. One day he sees a French man-of-war firing shells futilely into the continent; a nameless war is in progress, but the jungle has swallowed up the combatants.

Landing finally at the company's seaboard station, Marlow sees wretched Negroes engaged in slave labor. There is general apathy among the whites, and everything is going to ruin in the implacable grip of the jungle. One accountant, however, has managed to keep up European standards. To Marlow's delight and surprise, he wears a formal business suit, keeps up appearances, and even tries to do his job efficiently despite the general rot and decay surrounding him.

Marlow also begins to hear rumors of the great Mr. Kurtz who operates the company's inner station deep in the heart of the Congo. Mr. Kurtz is renowned, even on the coast, for the vast quantities of ivory he sends back. Nobody quite knows how he gets it, but they are all pleased that their agent is so efficient, even if his methods may be slightly unorthodox.

Trekking two hundred miles in two weeks through dense forest, Marlow reaches the company's central station on the shore of the river where he is to find his steamer. Here he learns that his boat has sunk, and it will take at least three months to dredge it up and make it seaworthy again. He is greeted with cold disdain by the inscrutable manager of the central station, who, like everyone else there, is obsessed with the profits to be made from ivory.

Again Marlow hears the name of Kurtz, as he waits for his boat to be repaired and meets the various people of the station, most of whom are intensely jealous of the great ivory trader. The rumor is that Mr. Kurtz is seriously ill. It will be Marlow's job to pilot the steamer up the river until he reaches Kurtz's station, and there to bring the sick man—and his accumulated ivory—back to the central station.

Eventually Marlow's boat is made seaworthy, and he begins the voyage, joined by a company manager, some pilgrims, and a few cannibals who have been paid by the company with useless little bits of wire to man the ship.

As Marlow penetrates deeper and deeper into the jungle, his boat is in constant danger of hitting snags, his cannibal steersman is enthusiastic but unreliable, and the trigger-happy pilgrims aboard are ready to fire at any natives they see ashore.

About fifty miles from the inner station, Marlow comes upon an abandoned hut where he finds a note urging him to hurry but to approach cautiously. He also finds an old English maritime manual with strange, cipherlike annotations in the margin. The sight of this book, a touch of sanity in the midst of the oppressive madness of the jungle, encourages him.

When the boat approaches Kurtz's station, however, the natives on the shore open fire on it with arrows. Marlow's cannibal steersman is killed. Marlow saves the situation by pulling on the boat's steam whistle. This sends the superstitious natives scurrying for shelter. At last the boat reaches the inner station.

There Marlow is greeted by a Russian sailor whose clothing is so patched that he looks like a tattered harlequin. The Russian had left the naval manual behind. (The strange notations were in Russian script.) He is a personable, enthusiastic young man who fills Marlow's disbelieving ears with hero-worshiping talk about Mr. Kurtz. The great ivory merchant is mortally ill, the Russian confides sadly. Marlow looks around and spots what seem to be highly polished wooden balls decorating the picket fence surrounding the compound. But when he looks more closely he realizes they are native heads impaled on poles and grinning hideously.

Gradually Marlow begins to learn the truth about the remarkable Mr. Kurtz. Entering the jungle as an idealist who thought that European commercial exploitation would bring culture and civilization to the natives, Kurtz had eventually succumbed to the savage lure of the jungle where he became all-powerful.

Although Kurtz has a fiancée back home in Brussels, whom he loftily refers to as "my intended," Marlow sees a savage native girl wailing on the shore. She is obviously Kurtz's mistress. As the jungle has taken its inexorable toll of Kurtz, he has allowed savage rites to be performed in his honor and has ruthlessly slain anyone who has stood in the way of his single-minded pursuit of ivory.

By the time Marlow actually meets the moribund Kurtz, he is filled with ambivalent feelings about him. On the one hand he detests him for being a hollow egomaniac who has lived for plunder while giving it the sweeter name of progress. But on the other hand Marlow realizes that at one time Kurtz had elements of genuine greatness in him. He was many cuts above the tawdry merchants of the central station. At least he started out his career in Africa with some ideals, even if they did ultimately disintegrate.

It is too late now, however, to bring Kurtz to any kind of justice. The dying man is placed on Marlow's steamer, and back they head down river, to the menacing hoots of the natives ashore. Soon after the return journey has begun, a native contemptuously comes to Marlow with the news, "Mistah Kurtz—he dead." The last words Marlow had heard him utter had been "The horror! The horror!" as the darkness of the jungle, of death, and of his knowledge of his own terrible sin had closed in on him.

Back in Brussels, Marlow resists the attempts of various interested parties to get at the papers Kurtz had entrusted to him. Physically and spiritually shaken by the experience and by the curious sense of identification he felt with Kurtz,

Marlow goes to see his bereaved fiancée. He discovers that she has remained loyal to the idealistic Kurtz who first went to Africa. Marlow decides that even though he hates nothing more than a lie, he cannot tell the girl the truth about her dead lover's last hideous moments. Instead, Marlow agrees with Kurtz's "intended" that he was a great man, and tells her his last word had been her whispered name.

Critical Opinion

On the surface, *Heart of Darkness* is a short novel about a long voyage into the depths of the Congo. It is, however, an allegory, like Bunyan's *Pilgrim's Progress* or Dante's *Divine Comedy*. The narrator's actual, literal voyage is symbolic of the more profound voyage of the soul on which it discovers that the heart of man is dark and capable of monstrous evil.

Like Christian and Dante, Conrad's narrator, Marlow, in the course of his nightmare journey, makes discoveries about himself and his relation to good and evil.

As in *Lord Jim*, the narration proceeds by means of complicated time shifts. The prose style is lushly romantic and richly suggestive, the words "dark" and "black" recurring with haunting suggestiveness. Conrad says of Marlow that "to him the meaning of an episode was not inside like a kernel but outside, enveloping the tale which brought it out only as a glow brings out a haze." This is the esthetic theory that underlies the writing of *Heart of Darkness*, which is mysteriously suggestive and allusive rather than explicit or realistic.

The real "facts" of the story stem from a voyage like Marlow's that Conrad made into the Congo in 1890 just after he had begun to write *Almayer's Folly*. The voyage was every bit as harrowing as Marlow's. The Mr. Kurtz who died aboard Conrad's boat was in reality a Georges-Antoine Klein whom Conrad had picked up at Stanley Falls. Eventually Conrad fell ill, and the whole experience effectively ended his career as a sailor.

What is significant about the story is not its foundation in actual fact but the implications that Conrad draws from the facts.

"All Europe contributed to the making of Kurtz," Marlow

tells us, and indeed he is a representative figure of the lust for plunder which ravaged Africa in the nineteenth century and which attempted to conceal its rapacity under the guise of idealism.

The true horror of the story lies not in Kurtz's degeneration and ultimate despair but in Marlow's growing realization that he, too, is capable of undergoing the moral regression that destroyed Kurtz. He is made painfully aware of the savagery pulsating behind the most civilized façade.

Lord Jim

by

JOSEPH CONRAD

Main Characters

Jim—The ruggedly built sailor son of an English country parson.

Charles Marlow—The main narrator of the tale, a sympathetic, experienced seaman who tries to help Jim.

Stein—A philosophical German trader and butterfly collector.

Cornelius—A corrupt white trader living on the island of Patusan.

Jewel—Cornelius' fanatically loyal, beautiful daughter.

Doramin—A stern old native chieftain on Patusan.

Dain Waris—His son, a loyal friend and comrade of Jim's.

"Gentleman" Brown—A bloodthirsty pirate fleeing the law.

The Story

Spotlessly clean and immaculately dressed, Jim at first glance is more prepossessing than any other water-clerk in the Eastern ports. But the job of water-clerk, which entails rowing out in a small boat to sell ship's supplies to vessels reaching port, does not seem to agree with him, for after doing satisfactory work for a while he will suddenly and mysteriously take off for a distant port.

Charles Marlow, an experienced old sailor, is intrigued by the tall, blond English lad with the haunted look. Although Jim, the son of a country parson, seemed to all the world "the right kind," a gentleman, he was involved in the disgraceful *Patna* affair, which Marlow learns about while attending the Court of Inquiry investigating the affair.

Twice in Jim's apprenticeship to the sea he had shown moments of indecisiveness that could easily have been interpreted as cowardice. Then he ships aboard the *Patna*, an old, unseaworthy vessel commanded by a drunken, cowardly old captain, and carrying eight hundred Malayan pilgrims. The crew, with the exception of Jim, is rough, disorderly, and mercenary. Jim is the only true gentleman aboard.

One supernaturally still night, while the pilgrims are sleeping in squalor on the deck of the overcrowded ship, the *Patna* runs into an unidentified, submerged object. One of the officers notices a bulging bulkhead and spreads the word among the crew that the ship is about to sink. With only seven lifeboats aboard, there is no hope of saving any of the eight hundred Malayans in the mad scramble that would follow a general alarm. So the crew, fearing the ship will go down at any moment, jump into the lifeboats, without even sounding an alarm lest the pilgrims awaken and panic.

Jim stays on deck for a moment, shocked at the crew's cowardice. After checking the rusty bulkheads, he is convinced that the ship will sink. The captain and crewmen call to him from the lifeboats and Jim impulsively jumps, not because he is afraid of dying but because he visualizes how helpless he would be when the horrified pilgrims awake.

The lifeboats reach shore, and tell the appalled British colonials what happened. The colonials had expected nothing better from the captain and crew but are embarrassed that one of them, Jim, should also have behaved so dishonorably. They even offer him money to flee before the Court of Inquiry meets, but Jim proudly insists on taking the consequences of his cowardly action.

It is this stubborn sense of his worth as a man responsible for his acts that attracts Marlow to the sailor. One day, for instance, after a particularly grueling session of the court, somebody refers to a dog ambling along as a "wretched cur."

Jim spins around, assuming the remark is meant for him, and Marlow realizes how deep the shame must have burned into the youth's soul.

Ironically enough, the *Patna* does not sink after all, but just drifts, crewless, until she is spotted by a French gunboat. The French captain orders the *Patna* secured by a rope to his own boat and, staying on the wretched ship all the time, sees her into port. The French captain, too, gives evidence. He tells the court that he was frightened to death himself while aboard the *Patna* but was merely doing his job. The board deprives all the officers of the *Patna* of their sailing certificates and closes its hearings.

Gradually, through his blunt, realistic sympathy, Marlow manages to make friends with Jim. He sees in the unfortunate young sailor a mirror of what might well have happened to him in the crises he has somehow managed to survive. He gets Jim a job with the owner of a rice mill. For a time Jim seems well-suited to his work. But one day a former officer of the *Patna* shows up, and at this reminder of his disgrace, Jim bolts without saying a word. He leaves one job after another, constantly heading east in the hope that somewhere far enough from civilization his disgrace will not be known. But by now everyone knows Jim's story. He is never able to stay on any one job for long, for, although people are too polite to mention the *Patna* affair to him, his own conscience keeps tormenting him.

Marlow, beginning to despair that Jim will ever find peace and salvation for his troubled soul, goes to visit an old German friend, Stein, the wealthy, widely respected head of Stein and Company, who is also an ardent butterfly collector and an amateur philosopher. Stein diagnoses Jim's trouble immediately: Jim is a romantic, unrealistic about human limitations in this world, with too noble a concept of himself. Thus he cannot forgive himself for his momentary, all-too-human lapse into cowardice.

Stein's solution for Jim's problem is to send him to the remote island of Patusan, where Stein and Company have a trading post. There, far from any white men who might know his story, perhaps Jim can forget the past and reclaim himself. Stein gives Jim a ring to present as identification to his old friend Doramin, an island chieftain, and Marlow bids Jim an emotional farewell.

At first Jim runs into trouble on Patusan. He is jailed by a tyrannical rajah who is fearful of the trade competition Jim may bring. But Stein's friend Doramin intervenes when Jim escapes from prison. Together with his stalwart son, Dain Waris, Doramin helps Jim defeat the rajah in a pitched battle.

Jim also meets his predecessor in Stein's employ, a corrupt old man named Cornelius, who first tries to persuade Jim to leave the island and then, when he is unsuccessful, watches with growing, impotent hatred as Jim falls in love with his beautiful daughter, Jewel. When Marlow pays him a visit two years after Jim has come to Patusan, all seems to be going well. Jim and Cornelius' daughter are deeply in love with each other, so much so that Jewel is cold to Marlow, whom she suspects of trying to lure Jim away from Patusan. She cannot believe that her strong, respected lover could never find acceptance in the outside world. Indeed, to the natives, Jim has become a hero for defeating the hated rajah and bringing prosperity to the island. They call him "Tuan" or "Lord" Jim. Marlow leaves the island satisfied that Jim's reclamation is proceeding well.

Trouble comes to the island in the ominous person of "Gentleman" Brown, a pirate fleeing from the law, who harbors his boat in Patusan, hoping to find provisions, money, and sanctuary. Jim is on a trip up-river when Brown and his crew attack the stockade, now temporarily commanded by Dain Waris. The natives manage to repel the attack, for Brown and his men are half-dead with exhaustion and hunger. Dain Waris drives Brown and his crew to take shelter on a hilltop. The stronghold they build there proves impregnable.

When Jim returns from his expedition, he goes himself, at considerable risk, to interview Brown. Brown cravenly begs Jim for a chance to escape—after all, did not Jim ever need a second chance in life? The words hit home. Jim sees himself as no better really than this cutthroat. He had been given a second chance; who was he to withhold one from "Gentleman" Brown? He returns down the hill and persuades the natives to lift the siege.

They do so reluctantly. The savage Brown repays Jim's benevolence by descending on the natives and slaughtering several of them, including Dain Waris. Heartsick at what he considers this second great betrayal, Jim presents himself before the slain warrior's father. Native justice demands that

Jim be punished for the slaying of Dain Waris, which was, after all, the result of his own misjudgment of character. Stoically, feeling this is the only way now to recapture his lost honor, Jim allows the heartbroken old native chieftain to shoot him through the chest. His tragic death, Marlow believes, was the only possible salvation for Jim.

Critical Opinion

Lord Jim has been called Conrad's *Hamlet,* for it is the complex tragedy of an indecisive man of great inherent nobility who nevertheless, with "the stamp of one defect," manages to bring death and destruction upon those he loves. In form, this novel of Conrad's greatest period is no less rich and complicated than *Hamlet*. Using constant changes of point of view, narrations within narrations, kaleidoscopic time shifts, and other highly sophisticated and masterly fictional techniques, Conrad weaves around the anecdote of Jim's desertion of the *Patna* a complex moral skein. A basically simple adventure yarn thus becomes a great parable of man's fate.

Originally, Conrad had intended to write a short story around the *Patna* incident. When he decided to develop it into a novel, he found great difficulty welding it together with the Patusan story into a single, coherent narrative. Realizing this was the "plague-spot" of his novel, Conrad once told a friend that the cleavage at the middle of the book made him feel "as if he were left with a lump of clay into which he had failed to breathe the right sort of life." He need have had no worry on that score, however, for *Lord Jim* ranks with his finest achievements.

A thoroughgoing romantic, Jim can never come to grips with reality, can never accept his limitations as a human being who is often indecisive, sometimes even cowardly. Only Stein and Marlow realize that in Jim's single-minded quest for redemption he is heroic as well as absurd and "wrongheaded"; his romanticism is his glory as well as his dilemma.

Jim is on the point of redeeming himself from the disgrace of the *Patna* affair by becoming a trusted and beloved native leader when the invasion of Brown and his crew of cutthroats leads him to make an unrealistic, foolishly chivalric error of judgment which destroys his friends. He would not have made this error had not Brown insidiously appealed to his sense of guilt. Thus, as in the greatest tragedies, Jim's character —haunted by the sin of his past and lost in his search for absolution—brings the ultimate catastrophe down upon him.

The Author

A great paradox of English fiction is that one of its supreme masters was born in the Ukraine, of Polish parents, and was totally ignorant of the English language until he was twenty years old. Born on December 3, 1857, the future novelist's full name was *Teodor Józef Nalecz Konrad Korzeniowski*. His father was a poet and revolutionary, a translator of Shakespeare who ended his life a political prisoner in Russia where Conrad's mother died, too, a brokenhearted exile.

The young Conrad was brought up by his conventional but understanding uncle, Tadeusz Bobrowski. Like Marlow in *Heart of Darkness*, Conrad as a youth was fascinated by maps and was filled with a desire to explore the world. Accordingly, he signed aboard a French vessel in 1874 and had some extraordinary adventures, including a duel while he was a gunrunner for the Carlist cause in Spain. Eventually he joined the English merchant marine in 1878, became a naturalized British subject, and gained his master's certificate in 1884.

For the next few years, Conrad sailed over much of the world, especially in the Far East. He taught himself English by reading the plays of Shakespeare and the novels of Trollope. Eventually he began trying his own hand at fiction. The result, *Almayer's Folly*, was shown to John Galsworthy, who encouraged the sailor to continue writing. In 1894, the year before *Almayer's Folly* was published, Conrad settled in England and became a struggling, full-time author.

Writing was always difficult for Conrad, who once said he wrote in English, thought in French, and dreamed in Polish. Nevertheless, with a wife and growing family, he struggled hard, publishing a sequel to *Almayer's Folly*, *An Outcast of the Islands*, in 1896; the masterful *Nigger of the 'Narcissus'* in 1897; and *Lord Jim* in 1900. Although he was immediately appreciated as a master by the novelists of his day—James, Galsworthy, and Wells in particular—the difficulty of his style, his psychological subtleties, his handling of time, and his somber, dry irony baffled the general public. At best, he was considered the author of unduly complicated boys' sea yarns.

Annoyed by this reputation, Conrad embarked on the writing of three political novels that had nothing to do with adventures afloat: *Nostromo* (1904), his longest work, about South American politics; *The Secret Agent* (1907), a completely ironic tale about anarchists in London; and *Under Western Eyes* (1911), a bitter look at Russian psychology.

Politically conservative, morally at one with the stern maritime traditions of loyalty and honor, Conrad was a unique voice in English fiction. A late starter as a novelist, he was more or less worn out by the time of World War I, although it was only with *Chance* (1913) and *Victory* (1915) that he really achieved a wide audience. Conrad died of a heart attack after a visit to the United States on August 3, 1924.

By the Same Author

Nostromo: Conrad's largest canvas and the work that was written with the greatest pains, *Nostromo* was inspired by Conrad's brief visit to South America during his days in the merchant marine. In the book, Conrad describes a typical Latin American country named Costaguana. The corrupt nation is beset by revolution, during which Nostromo, a virile young Italian working for the Gould silver mine, hides some silver treasure for safekeeping on a desert island. He spreads the rumor that the ship carrying the treasure has sunk and keeps the silver for himself. He is, however, found out and destroyed by the father of the girl he loves. Many subplots are woven around the central one to make *Nostromo* the richest and most complex of Conrad's novels. As an analysis of Latin American politics and character, it remains unmatched.

Victory: The last of Conrad's important novels, *Victory* is about a disillusioned, Hamletesque Swede named Axel Heyst who tries to escape involvement with other human beings and retreats to an island of his own. He becomes involved against his will with Lena, a girl being mistreated by the heavy-handed, coarse German hotel keeper, Schomberg. Heyst spirits Lena off to his island but is pursued by Jones, who, like "Gentleman" Brown in *Lord Jim*, is the incarnation of evil. In the ensuing battle, Heyst thinks Lena has betrayed him to Jones but learns, too late, of her moral victory in keeping unto death a faith and trust he had never been capable of returning.

Kim

by

RUDYARD KIPLING (1865–1936)

Main Characters

Kimball O'Hara—An impish and ingenious thirteen-year-old orphan educated in the teeming streets of Lahore.

Teshoo Lama—An ancient priest of Such-zen in Tibet, he is searching for a mystic, all-healing river.

Mahbub Ali—A crafty Indian horse trader working for the British secret service.

Colonel Creighton—Ostensibly a member of the Ethnological Survey, actually the chief of secret service operations.

Hurree Chunder Mookerjee—A Bengali educated in English schools, a wily secret service agent.

Father Victor—A kindly Catholic chaplain attached to the Maverick regiment.

The Reverend Arthur Bennett—The Mavericks' blunt, unimaginative Anglican chaplain.

Mr. Lurgan—A gem dealer and "healer of sick pearls" who trains Kim in the art of spying.

The Story

Kimball O'Hara, known as Kim in the crowded, colorful streets of Lahore, is the orphan son of a dissolute sergeant in the Mavericks, an Irish regiment in India, and an Irishwoman who died when he was a baby. He has been carelessly brought up by a half-caste woman who lets him roam the streets at will. Deeply bronzed by the burning Indian sun, Kim looks more Asiatic than European and is more proficient in Hindustani than in English.

One day, idly perched on the great cannon of Zam-Zammah, Kim sees a Tibetan lama obviously lost in the bustling city of Lahore. The lama is searching for the River of the Arrow, which reputedly washes away all sin. Kim, sensing a chance for adventure, joins forces with the old man and promises to take him to Benares, the holy city. He begs food for him and protects him from the jeers of the other street boys.

But Kim now receives an assignment from Mahbub Ali, a crafty horse peddler, to deliver a secret message to the British command at Umballa. Although the message seems to be about horses, Kim senses that it really is a code. His hunch is confirmed that night when Mahbub Ali's house is unsuccessfully ransacked.

Kim and the lama arrive by rail at Umballa. After delivering his message, Kim hides in the grass and overhears the conference among the officers. The coded note from Mahbub Ali is the signal for eight thousand armed men to destroy some far-flung native potentates who are planning a rebellion.

Then Kim and the old lama begin their travels along the Grand Trunk Road, which stretches 1500 miles across India and offers an unparalleled cross section of native life. The holy man and his *chela*, or servant boy, are adopted by a rich old Kulu woman traveling to visit her daughter. The old lady is very talkative and nearly bores the lama to death with her demands for religious talismans. But she feeds the two wayfarers handsomely during their search for the mystic river.

One evening the Irish regiment of the Mavericks encamps near the road. Kim is attracted by their flag, displaying a red bull on a green field. He recalls a prophecy that his fortunes will rise when he finds a red bull on a green field. Stealing closer to the camp, Kim is discovered by the Anglican chaplain, the Reverend Arthur Bennett, and his Catholic cohort, Father Victor. The chaplains find an amulet hanging from Kim's neck in which his birth certificate is kept. They are astonished to learn that this Indian ragamuffin is the son of the late Sergeant O'Hara.

For Kim the discovery spells disaster. He will be separated

from his beloved lama and sent to school, which he loathes. He assures the lama that he will escape from the soldiers in a few days. Meanwhile the old holy man is to follow the rich dowager lest he get into trouble without Kim to aid him.

But when the lama hears that the regiment will send Kim to school, he asks for Father Victor's name and address and promises to send some money for the boy's education. Kim astonishes the soldiers with a prophecy that soon eight thousand men will go into action. At first they laugh at his prediction, but soon it comes true, and they are ordered to march against the rebel potentates.

Meanwhile a letter comes from the lama enclosing three hundred rupees with a promise to send the same amount yearly for Kim's tuition at the fine St. Xavier's school. Father Victor is amazed that the lama, who looks like a woebegone beggar, should be able to command such a sum.

Kim is beaten by the drummer boy charged with seeing that he does not escape. He is desperately unhappy with the orderly, military routine of the regiment. He manages to get a scribe to send a letter to Mahbub Ali begging for help. One day the horse trader arrives and snatches Kim away with him. Kim thinks he is to be rescued from the military life, but Mahbub Ali turns him over to Colonel Creighton, a member of the Ethnological Survey, who extracts from Kim a promise that he will go to St. Xavier's. Kim recognizes the colonel as the man who gave the order for the eight thousand men to march.

Kim is unhappy at school, but he works hard and slips out from time to time to meet his lama. When vacation time comes, Kim dyes himself a dark brown, puts on a turban, and escapes to more adventure. He begs Mahbub Ali to let him travel with him, proving his worth to Mahbub by spying on some men who are planning to kill him and exposing the plot.

Mahbub Ali turns Kim over to a mysterious Mr. Lurgan at Simla. Mr. Lurgan, who calls himself the healer of sick pearls, has gems, totems, and even a phonograph in his shop. Mr. Lurgan is actually a member of the British secret service in India. He trains Kim to observe, to remember, and to be secretive, pitting Kim against his son in contests of observation and disguise. At Mr. Lurgan's house Kim meets fat Hurree Chunder Mookerjee, a babu or Indian who has been educated by the English. Mookerjee, also employed by the secret service, tells Kim that if he stays in school and learns well, he, too, may become a secret agent or join the "Great Game," as spying is called.

Accordingly, Kim returns to St. Xavier's where he studies for two more years to become a geographic surveyor, a useful occupation for spies. One day, when Mahbub Ali assures Colonel Creighton that the boy is ready, Kim leaves school and resumes his Indian color and costume. He joins the lama, who has kept his promise to pay Kim's tuition every year. Together they head for Delhi in search of the River of the Arrow.

On the train Kim meets E. 23, another Indian spy playing the Great Game, who is frantically trying to escape from some enemies waiting to kill him in Delhi. Kim disguises the spy so well that when they get off the train nobody knows who he is. Kim is praised for his skill and ingenuity and once again he and his lama ply the roads of India.

They meet the garrulous old Kulu woman again and Mookerjee, who tells Kim he is needed for more spy work. Two Czarist agents, one a Russian and the other a Frenchman, have penetrated the north country, bribing the treacherous kings there to let them do some secret surveys. Orders are to capture them. Kim and the lama head for the steep foothills of the Himalayas. Kim tells the simple old man he will find his river there. The lama is pleased to be in mountainous country once more, but the steep passes and heavy snow baffle Kim, who can barely keep up with his friend.

Meanwhile the babu encounters the Russian and the Frenchman and offers his aid as a guide. He finds their maps and some letters incriminating the local kings. He leads the two spies to Kim and the lama, and the foreigners begin to fight with the holy man, tearing the sacred drawing that he keeps with him at all times.

In a fury, Kim wrestles with one of them and wounds him. In the confusion sliding down the mountain, Kim makes off with the agents' basket, which he examines in the nearby village of Shamlegh. Keeping all the written evidence in an oilskin pouch next to his body, Kim tosses the spies' other belongings into a deep ravine.

Their mission a dismal failure, the spies are escorted out of the Himalayas by Mookerjee. But the adventures and the strange climate of the North have taken their toll of Kim.

The lama, too, is ill. They are both cared for by the old woman of the Grand Trunk Road, who adopts Kim as her son. When Kim awakens from a long, feverish sleep, he sees the babu at his bedside. He delivers the papers stolen from the Russian to Mookerjee, who compliments him on his fine work. Mahbub Ali also praises the lad.

The lama, who in his innocence has never realized that Kim is playing the Great Game, receives his reward, too. A stream on the old lady's property turns out to be the sacred river, and the holy man is washed of his sins.

Critical Opinion

Kim is a boys' book in much the same way as *Huckleberry Finn* is a boys' book—that is to say, it resonates far more deeply than the usual adventure tale. There is even some similarity in the character of the two protagonists. Both Kim and Huck are resourceful, mischievous, but open-hearted boys who hate the restrictions and confinements of "civilization" and seek adventure in the great world: Huck on his raft in the Mississippi, Kim on the Grand Trunk Road winding through India. Like *Huckleberry Finn*, *Kim* is a great, nostalgic evocation of its author's youth. The similarity in name between Kim and Kipling is not fortuitous.

The plot of *Kim* is rather halting and tenuous. It consists of separate episodes not really welded together either by the lama's search for the great river or by Kim's apprenticeship in the secret service. The episodes are so individually exciting, however, that the looseness with which they are strung together is barely noticeable. (Kipling's real forte was the short story, a form in which few Englishmen have excelled. Somerset Maugham—one of the few—has called Kipling the great English master of the art; and indeed he is, rivaled perhaps only by D. H. Lawrence.)

The sporadic plotting of *Kim*, which reveals Kipling's essential uneasiness in the novel form, is more than compensated for by the book's richness of local color and detail. Kipling loved India and understood it as few other Englishmen have. He reveled in its sights, sounds, and even smells. All of these he richly explored in *Kim*.

It is this love for India that the critics who assailed Kipling for his jingoism during the 1920's and 1930's failed to take into account. Although in *Kim* he is interested in observing the clash of temperaments and cultures between East and West, Kipling never asserts that the Western values are superior. The reverse would seem to be true, for such crafty Orientals as Mahbub Ali and Mookerjee can outwit practically any sahib in India. The natives, too, speak in a colorful, proverb-strewn language far more flexible and attractive than the stiff, correct English taught at St. Xavier's.

When the novel opens, Kim, at thirteen, is clever, self-sufficient, and warm-hearted. But he must learn discipline in order to become a man, and he does this by assimilating the best of both East and West.

The Author

Rudyard Kipling, born on December 30, 1865, in Bombay, was the son of a connoisseur of Indian art. As a boy, he spent most of his time, like Kim, learning the ways and languages of India. This idyllic period in his life came to an abrupt halt in 1871. The weak and nearsighted Kipling was sent to England in charge of a cruel and imperceptive guardian. He went to a Devon public school for Anglo-Indians, where he was a poor student and worse athlete. His adventures there he later recounted in *Stalky and Co.* (1899), a classic of English school life.

Deciding against going to a university, Kipling returned to India in 1883 and joined the Lahore *Civil and Military Gazette*, becoming a first-class journalist. Discontented with mere newspaper work, however, Kipling began writing tales for the paper about three wildly exuberant and eccentric soldiers in the British Army in India, the famous "soldiers three": Ortheris, Mulvaney, and Learoyd. These stories, collected in *Plain Tales from the Hills* (1888), were an instant success in England. They were followed the same year by *Soldiers Three* and *Under the Deodars*, and by an equally successful volume of verse, *Barrack-Room Ballads* (1892). Before long, Kipling's name became a household word in the English-speaking world.

He continued with journalism on the Allahabad *Pioneer*, returning in 1889 to England, where he settled down near

Fleet Street. In 1892 Kipling married Caroline Balestier and emigrated to his wife's home in Brattleboro, Vermont, where they lived four years until a quarrel with his brother-in-law sent Kipling back to England. In 1900 he covered the Boer War where his staunch imperialistic defense of British action in South Africa became widely known.

After two not entirely successful novels, *The Light That Failed* (1890) and *Captains Courageous* (1897), Kipling produced his fiction masterpiece, *Kim*, in 1901. With such poems as "If" and "Gunga Din," it remains his best-known work.

For all his wide success, Kipling was a truculent and combative man. He became increasingly shrill and embittered after World War I, in which his son was killed in action. An ardent propagandist for the war, Kipling afterward helped form the Imperial War Graves Commission.

Although the 1920's saw the rise of a generation that found Kipling's chauvinism and imperialism repugnant, honors continued to be heaped on him, including the Nobel prize (1907) and the Order of Merit, which he rejected. He died in London on January 18, 1936, on the eve of the destruction of the colonialism he had praised for so long.

By the Same Author

The Light That Failed: This sentimental, semi-autobiographical tale is about Dick Heldar, an artist, who wins fame during the fall of Khartoum, but who tragically begins to lose his vision as a result of a sword wound suffered at the same time.

Dick is brought up in England by Mrs. Jennett, a dour religious woman who starves the boy for love. He finds sympathy with a fellow orphan, Maisie, who encourages him in his study of art. As a correspondent at Khartoum, Dick sends back drawings of General Gordon's heroic action which (like Kipling's stories) take England by storm.

After the war, however, Dick's vision begins to fail. The model for what is to be his masterpiece ruins the painting in a fit of jealousy, and Maisie, too, deserts him now that he is going blind. Dick goes to Egypt, where fighting has broken out, and deliberately exposes himself to deadly enemy fire.

Captains Courageous: Like *Kim*, this is a story about a

youth growing up. However, its hero, Harvey Cheyne, is totally unlike Kim. A spoiled American boy, Harvey falls overboard from an ocean steamer and is rescued by some Gloucester fishermen. All his father's wealth cannot protect him from the rough life he must endure with the fishing fleet, but the experience with wind and waves—and heroism— makes a man of him. When he is reunited with his father, Harvey is no longer a spoiled brat but a youth ready to face the vicissitudes of the world.

Green Mansions

by

W. H. HUDSON (1841–1922)

Main Characters

Abel Guevez De Argensola—A twenty-three-year-old Venezuelan aristocrat who finds a tragic love and ultimate self-
knowledge in the dense jungles of South America.

Rima—Mysterious and elusive, half girl and half bird, friend
and protectress of all wildlife in the Green Mansions.

Nuflo—Rima's crafty old guardian.

Runi—The chief of an Indian tribe.

Kua-ko—An Indian youth who teaches Abel the ways of the
forest.

The Story

Abel Guevez De Argensola, known in Georgetown, British
Guiana, as "Mr. Abel," tells the story of his youthful passion
to an old friend. A member of a wealthy Venezuelan family,
Abel flees into the densely forested territory south of the
Orinoco River when a political coup in which he is involved
fails. Intending to cross the Rio Negro into Brazil, he is
diverted by tales of gold to be found in the Parahuari mountains in southern Venezuela.

Failing to find the gold, the young adventurer joins an
Indian settlement led by Runi, whose suspicions of the white

youth are allayed when Abel gives him a precious tinderbox. Abel is adopted by the Indians, particularly by Kua-ko, who promises to teach him how to hunt with blowpipe and bow and arrow. These primitive people fear only two things: Managa, the chief of a hostile tribe, and the enchanted forest, which Abel discovers some two miles west of the village. Although this lovely woodland is filled with wildlife, the Indians refuse to hunt there for they believe a malevolent spirit—the mysterious daughter of the Didi—lives there.

Abel laughs at their superstitions and explores the forest, which he calls his green mansions. He hears a seductive bird-like voice calling to him and vainly pursues it, until one day he sees a delicate girl, Rima, playing with a bird. Rima is a lovely, elfin sprite, shy and yet alluring, who constantly eludes Abel's attempts to capture her. Kua-ko tells Abel that someday he may be proficient enough with the blowpipe to kill the girl, who has prevented them from hunting in the forest. Abel, who has already fallen in love with her, rejects the idea in horror.

One day Abel comes upon a poisonous snake in the forest and is about to crush it when Rima appears, dressed in a gossamer gown, with her lovely, iridescent hair reflecting the sun. She upbraids him for trying to kill the snake which slithers to safety at her feet. When Abel tries to embrace Rima, the snake bites him. He runs panic-stricken through the forest and falls down a precipice. When he regains consciousness, Abel finds himself in the hut of Nuflo, an old man dark as an Indian, who tells him that he is really Spanish. He calls for his seventeen-year-old granddaughter—Rima. In the hut, however, the girl is listless and spiritless—totally different from the wild wood sprite Abel had encountered in the forest. It was Rima who rescued Abel when he fell down the precipice. She nurses him back to health.

When Rima speaks to Abel in Spanish, he asks her about the lovely bird speech he had heard from her lips in the forest; but, resentful because he does not know the bird language, she runs away. Abel learns that Rima is so fond of the creatures of the woods that she will not allow Nuflo to kill any of them for food. So the strange pair exists on plants and berries. Nuflo, however, kills and eats animals on the sly.

Since Rima flies from Abel when he touches her hand, to teach her a lesson he leaves her grandfather's hut and returns for a few days' visit to the Indian village. There he finds that the Indians have given him up for dead and have gone to a neighboring settlement. Only the toothless old hag, Cra-Cra, is there to greet him. Abel, stricken with remorse for his treatment of Rima, returns to the forest.

There he and Rima spend an idyllic day on top of a mountain, where Abel tells the girl of the unimaginable vastness and diversity of the world. Lonely for people who can speak her language, Rima asks him if there are people like her anywhere on earth. Abel tells her she is unique. He mentions a faraway mountain called Riolama, which Rima suddenly recognizes as the place for which she was named, and where her mother had come from. She is furious with Nuflo for having kept Riolama a secret from her and descends the mountain to upbraid the old man. She insists that they make an expedition to Riolama immediately.

Although old Nuflo is unwilling to make the arduous trip, he fears that Rima, who is constantly communicating with her dead mother, is really a spirit who will damn him in the next world if he does not obey her. So he makes preparations for the long march.

Before they leave, however, Abel returns once again to the Indian village. The natives regard him with suspicion for having consorted with the daughter of the spirit Didi. In effect a prisoner, he is able to elude his captors after a week, and he returns to Rima and Nuflo.

As the three take the eighteen-day trek through the jungle to Riolama, Nuflo finally tells Abel the true story of Rima: Nuflo was a member of a group of outlaws. One day, he found a lovely woman hiding in a cave. She was weeping and was soon to give birth. Thinking her a saint and hoping for her intervention in heaven on his behalf, Nuflo went to her aid. She had slipped down a precipice. Nuflo rescued her, tended her broken ankle, and brought her back to health. The woman could speak neither Spanish nor Indian but only the bird language.

Nuflo took her to the nearby settlement of Voa, where she gave birth to Rima and taught her the bird language. When the girl was seven, her mother died. Since Rima, too, seemed sickly, Nuflo took her to the Parahuari mountains where she was restored to health. At first they lived near Runi's tribe, but Rima shared her mother's fear and loathing of the Indians.

She constantly balked their attempts to hunt in the forest, thus acquiring her reputation as an evil spirit.

When the trio reaches Riolama, Abel feels he must disillusion Rima. He tells her she will never find the tribe that bore her because if they were still in existence her mother would have told her about them. What must have happened, Abel sadly tells her, is that her people, a delicate, exotic breed, must long ago have fallen victims to an Indian assault. Rima, the last of the bird people, must accept her loneliness and seek comfort only in him, for he will be her protector. When she senses the truth of Abel's conjectures, Rima faints. Nuflo fears she is dead. When she recovers and moans that no one in the world can ever understand her, Abel once again swears his love and eternal constancy.

They set off on the long return trip, but Rima, impatient, gets far ahead of the two men. When Nuflo and Abel reach the old hut, they find it burned to the ground. Rima is nowhere to be found. Searching for her in the forest they both knew and loved so well, Abel meets an Indian hunting. He knows Rima cannot be around or else the Indian would never have dared invade her sanctuary.

Abel returns to Runi's tribe, hoping to get some news of what has happened to his beloved. He is greeted with even greater suspicion than before. A council of war is held to decide what to do with him. The Indians consent to accept him back into the tribe when Abel tells them he had merely been out searching for gold. With great patience he finally manages to elicit from the surly Kua-ko the story of what has happened to Rima.

When the Indians realized that Rima had left the forest, they began to hunt there again. A week before Abel returned, however, they caught Rima in a tree in the enchanted woods. Superstitiously fearing that arrows would be powerless against her, they had heaped wood around the tree and set it on fire. Her last despairing cry had been "Abel, Abel!" before she plummeted, like a great white bird, into the smoke and flame where she was burned to ashes.

Barely able to restrain himself from killing Kua-ko on the spot, Abel pretends to fall asleep and then leaps from the campfire and escapes through the woods with Kua-ko in hot pursuit. Half-crazed with grief and without his revolver, Abel kills the Indian in hand-to-hand combat. He then goes to the tribe of Managa, persuading the savage enemy of Runi to slaughter everyone in the village.

When Abel returns to the charred hut where he had once been so happy, he finds the bones of Nuflo, who had also been slaughtered by the Indians. A search through the forest reveals the tree where Rima met her death. Reverently Abel collects her remains and brings them in an urn to another part of the woods.

Here he tries to live as a hermit but finds he is unable to and fears he is going mad. So, Abel makes the great trek to Georgetown, carrying with him the ashes of his beloved Rima.

Critical Opinion

The modern attitude toward Hudson is perhaps best expressed by Ernest Hemingway in *The Sun Also Rises*. One of the characters in that novel yearns to go to South America after reading *The Purple Land*, which, Hemingway says, "is a very sinister book if read too late in life. It recounts splendid imaginary amorous adventures of a perfect English gentleman in an intensely romantic land, the scenery of which is very well described. For a man to take it at thirty-four as a guide-book to what life holds is about as safe as it would be for a man of the same age to enter Wall Street direct from a French convent, equipped with a complete set of the more practical Alger books."

In the romantic tradition, Hudson is obsessed with the oneness of all nature. Rima is part bird, part girl, speaking, or rather warbling, in birdlike tones incomprehensible to mortals. Completely at one with nature, she is unable to understand how man can plunder the Green Mansions which are her home. The tragedy of the book is that she herself dies horribly at the hands of savages who, although they too live intimately with nature, fail utterly to see any higher spiritual meaning in it.

Rima's impact on Abel is that of a powerful natural force. Coming to the jungle as a city-bred sophisticate, disgusted with the life of politics in which he has dabbled with unfortunate results, disillusioned with his early search for gold, Abel is ripe for a conversion to the gospel of nature. At first he mistakenly thinks he has found the happy natural life with Runi's Indians, but in the course of the book, beginning with Kua-ko's suggestion that he kill Rima, Abel's attitude toward these primitives begins to sour.

After the tragedy of Rima is complete, Abel, half-crazed, wreaks bloody revenge on his former friends and finds himself reverting to savagery as a hermit. He does not really come to grips with nature and himself until he abandons his primitive hut and returns to civilization.

What he emerges with is a kind of stoicism based on a profound acceptance of man's relatively puny place in the natural scheme of things. Abel's ultimate acceptance of the hard facts of existence, coupled with Hudson's keen observation of nature rendered in classically simple prose, does much to redeem a novel whose lush romanticism has proved generally alien to the modern spirit.

The Author

William Henry Hudson was a descendant of one of the families that came to America on the *Mayflower*. His father, however, after an injury sustained while working in a New England brewery, became a sheep farmer near Buenos Aires, where the future poet-naturalist and romancer was born on August 4, 1841.

Hudson got his education on the wild pampas of Argentina, which he loved as a boy and which sharpened his unique gift for the observation of nature. At fifteen, however, he suffered a debilitating attack of rheumatic fever after driving some cattle through a blizzard. His health thereafter was always frail.

In 1870 Hudson emigrated to England, where he entered into an unhappy marriage with a dull, unimaginative older woman, Emily Wingreave. For many years the couple struggled for a livelihood, as Hudson's books went largely unnoticed by the public. It was not, in fact, until *Green Mansions* was reissued in 1916 with an enthusiastic preface by John Galsworthy that Hudson won any measure of recognition outside his immediate circle of friends and other writers.

One of his most influential friends, Joseph Conrad, sponsored Hudson for British citizenship in 1900, and said of this strange, irascible man, "Hudson writes as the grass grows. The good God makes it be there. And that is all there is to it."

While Hudson was struggling to make a living in London, his wife kept a boardinghouse. In 1901, however, a civil service pension was granted the author, and he moved to the isolated Cornish town of Penzance. He had begun his literary career as a writer of ornithological books, but his first important work was *The Purple Land* (1885), the narrative, in Hudson's words, "of one Richard Lamb's adventures in the Banda Oriental, in South America, as told by himself." This romantic work was followed in 1904 by *Green Mansions*, and in 1906 by *A Crystal Age*, Hudson's not entirely successful attempt at a utopian romance. He was never really a writer of fiction. Hudson's most readable book today is an autobiography he wrote late in life, *Far Away and Long Ago* (1918), describing his boyhood experiences on the pampas and setting forth his pantheistic religious beliefs.

Ill health and lack of recognition made Hudson a rather crusty man given to abrupt, savage laughter. Among his many antipathies, the killing of wildlife for sport ranked high. Despite his illnesses, Hudson managed to live past eighty, dying of a heart attack on August 18, 1922, a decade after his wife's death. He was buried in his beloved Sussex Downs. A fitting memorial to him is Sir Jacob Epstein's controversial statue of Rima standing in the Hyde Park bird sanctuary.

The Man of Property

by

JOHN GALSWORTHY (1867–1933)

Main Characters

James Forsyte—The stiff-necked, strait-laced founder of the
firm of solicitors, "Forsyte, Bustard, and Forsyte."

Soames Forsyte—James' son, also a solicitor and man of
property, who considers himself a connoisseur of art.

Irene—Soames' most beautiful possession, his unhappy wife.

Old Jolyon Forsyte—James' older brother who has become
immensely wealthy as a tea merchant, the only Forsyte
with a true appreciation of beauty.

Young Jolyon Forsyte—An artist disinherited by Old Jolyon
for a scandalous love affair.

June Forsyte—Young Jolyon's impetuous, strong-willed
daughter who has lived with her grandfather ever since
Young Jolyon's elopement, a close friend of Irene.

Philip Bosinney—A talented, headstrong young architect,
June's fiancé.

The Story

On a fine June afternoon in 1886, the formidable Forsyte
family has gathered in Old Jolyon's home in London to toast
the engagement of Old Jolyon's granddaughter, June, to a
poor but talented young architect, Philip Bosinney. The elder

Forsytes, entrenched in wealth, are highly suspicious of the young man whom they call "the Buccaneer."

They justify their suspicions on the grounds that June is to be sole inheritor of her grandfather's vast wealth. (Old Jolyon had adopted her when his son, June's father, brought disgrace to the Forsyte name by running off with a governess whom he married after the death of June's mother. Perhaps even worse, Young Jolyon became an artist—an unheard-of calling in the Forsyte family—and an unsuccessful one at that.)

Now that June is to be married, Old Jolyon fears he will be left all alone in his vast, dark old house, now reverberating with the gossip and malicious small talk of the Forsyte clan. Fearing the loneliness of old age, Old Jolyon determines to pay a visit to his son's club. After the engagement party he sees Young Jolyon for the first time in years.

Old Jolyon is pleased that his son bears him no grudge for disinheriting him. Although he is leading a hand-to-mouth existence as an underwriter for Lloyd's and in his spare time is painting his unsuccessful water colors (which his father secretly collects), Young Jolyon is blessed with a happy family. The governess has proved a good wife and has borne him two lovely children, Holly and Jolly, who immediately capture Old Jolyon's fancy when he visits their cottage. Nevertheless, Old Jolyon feels guilty; the Forsytes would look upon this reconciliation as unseemly weakness.

Now that Philip Bosinney is engaged to June, he must call on all the Forsytes. They are a great family of upper-middle-class lawyers and businessmen who have amassed considerable fortunes and who live for their wealth and for the luxury the wealth has brought. The women of Old Jolyon's generation are crotchety old spinsters. They all look down upon the arts except possibly as profitable investments.

Bosinney, who lives for his architecture, finds little in common even with Soames, Old Jolyon's nephew, who fancies himself a connoisseur and collector. Irene, Soames' wife and the most beautiful "object" in his collection, immediately attracts Bosinney. At the many teas, dinners, and receptions given by the Forsytes, Bosinney sees more and more of Irene.

The Forsytes have long suspected that all was not well between Soames and Irene. Having bought her just as he bought his various art treasures, Soames regards her as a good investment reflecting credit on himself. When Irene agreed to marry Soames, she stipulated that she should have full freedom of action if the marriage proved unsuccessful. In his egoism Soames was unable to imagine such a possibility. In fact, however, Irene's aversion to the Man of Property has increased through the years. Rumor has it that Soames and Irene now occupy separate bedrooms.

Hoping to please his wife, whose "whims" he cannot understand, Soames decides to build her a great house worthy of her beauty. He buys some property at Robin Hill, outside London, and hires Philip Bosinney as architect. This, Soames feels, will be a fine opportunity for June's fiancé to make a name for himself. Soames wishes to please June because she is Irene's only close friend.

Immediately a contest of strong wills begins over the house. Bosinney refuses to listen to Soames' conventional ideas about what he wants. The architect is determined to build a masterpiece regardless of cost, but Soames, a typical Forsyte, wants showy magnificence at not too high a price. Soames realizes he has met his match in the young architect, whom he cannot bully, and gives him a more or less free hand in the planning and construction of the great country house.

One day Soames's Uncle Swithin takes Irene out to see the house under construction. Bosinney is there. While the old man dozes, Irene and Philip discover that they have fallen passionately in love with each other. For all their discretion in meeting later on, in out-of-the-way parts of London, June and the rest of the Forsytes soon learn of their affair. A full-fledged scandal is in the making. But Soames remains unaware of what is happening. Blinded by his self-esteem, he still cannot understand why his wife is so cold to him even though he lavishes expensive gifts on her.

As the house progresses, Soames and Philip begin to quarrel bitterly about the mounting costs. Philip agrees to decorate the house only if he is given a completely free hand, but Soames sets a limit to the amount of money he can spend. Philip finally agrees.

Meanwhile, Old Jolyon, troubled by the rumors of an affair between Philip and Irene, finds increasing comfort in the simple, unaffected lives of his son and grandchildren. He decides to take the trusteeship of his estate away from James and Soames Forsyte, who would ridicule his change of heart, and alter his will to leave Young Jolyon and his family in more comfortable circumstances. He asks Young Jolyon to speak to Bosinney about the rumors. Young Jolyon does so but realizes there is nothing he or anyone else can do to break up the architect's affair with Irene.

By the time the house is completed, Soames learns from the old gossips in the family that his wife has been seeing Bosinney. Furious, he decides to sue Bosinney for spending too much money on the house. If Bosinney loses the suit, he will have to pay Soames £350, which will bankrupt him. When she hears of Soames's intentions, Irene refuses to move to the house built for her. She locks her bedroom door against Soames. One night, consumed with jealousy and frustration, he manages to get in and forces himself on her.

Soames's suit comes to trial uncontested by Bosinney. June, who is in the courtroom, sees that her fiancé is not there, and, wondering what has become of him, she sets out for his apartment. He is not there either. But, while June is waiting for him, Irene enters, also worried about her lover. She tells June that she has left Soames; the two former friends argue bitterly and Irene leaves.

The next morning a policeman brings the horrible news that Bosinney has been run over and killed by a cab in the thick London fog. It was apparently suicide, for Bosinney had been seen earlier wandering distraught through the city. He had just learned from Irene of Soames's brutal act, and in the state of mind that this news produced he seemed not to care what happened to him.

In the wake of this final tragedy, Irene, numb with grief, returns to Soames, and June persuades Old Jolyon to buy the house at Robin Hill. She knows that Soames and Irene will never live in the mansion created by her dead fiancé.

A short epilogue, called "Indian Summer of a Forsyte," ties up the strands of the story. Some years after Bosinney's death, lonely Old Jolyon, now eighty-five, is living at Robin Hill. June, still unmarried, and Young Jolyon are away on vacation. One day Irene pays him a secret call. She has left Soames permanently now, supporting herself in a meager way by giving music lessons and occupying her time in charity. Gradually, through the hot summer, Irene wins the affection of Old Jolyon. He tacitly forgives her for stealing June's fiancé, and they are reconciled. He provides for her in his will and tries to persuade her to give music lessons to Holly and Jolly, but Irene cannot bear to see June again.

One day, sitting in the garden waiting for Irene's last visit, Old Jolyon, the only Forsyte ever to have known through suffering the values of love and beauty, dies in his sleep.

Critical Opinion

"This long tale," Galsworthy wrote of *The Forsyte Saga,* "is no scientific study of the period; it is rather an intimate incarnation of the disturbances that beauty effects in the lives of men. The figure of Irene, never present except through the sense of the other characters, is a concretion of disturbing beauty impinging on a possessive world."

Like Thomas Mann's *Buddenbrooks, The Forsyte Saga* is a magnificently detailed account of upper-middle-class morality, mentality, and tribal customs. One of its great appeals, despite its author's disclaimer, is unquestionably its almost scientific delineation of the world of business and professional men between 1886, when *The Man of Property* opens, and World War I. The later novels in the *The Forsyte Saga,* dealing with the postwar world, are not nearly as successful.

The conflict in *The Man of Property* results, as Galsworthy suggests, from the clash of two very different temperaments. The first is that of Soames Forsyte, self-assured man of the world, secure in his wealth, and a great "collector" of beauty. Yet his most beautiful possession, Irene, is drawn to the architect, Bosinney, because he is a creator of beauty rather than a mere collector and sees her as a living person rather than a museum exhibit. Soames's esthetic judgments depend mainly on the monetary value of a work of art. In a sense he cannot distinguish between his collection of "dead" beauty—his paintings and *objets*—and the live woman who is his wife. The climax of the book comes when Soames asserts his property rights to a wife who cannot abide him, thus destroying her lover and removing any affection or pity she might have had for her husband. Soames, however, becomes a more and more sympathetic figure, eventually dominating the story completely, as Galsworthy grows more and more disenchanted with the modern world and looks with increasing nostalgia at the good, stable, late-Victorian society so scandalized by

Irene's behavior. If it was a smug, self-satisfied world, if its values were essentially materialistic and philistine, it at least had some guiding principles, and principles of any kind, Galsworthy felt, were rapidly disappearing from the postwar world.

The Author

The seething passion that underlies the social satire in *The Man of Property* and makes it the finest of Galsworthy's many novels comes from the author's personal identification with the story. For just as Philip Bosinney, an honorable man, finds himself wooing another man's wife, so did *John Galsworthy* love his cousin Ada, whose relationship to her husband was essentially that of Irene to Soames Forsyte.

Although Galsworthy's love had a happier ending than Bosinney's—his marriage to Ada in 1905 proved a happy one —the difficulties and scandal leading up to the marriage transformed him from a rather superficial young dilettante into a novelist and playwright whose labors were crowned with the Nobel prize in 1932.

Galsworthy was born in Surrey on August 14, 1867, into a prosperous, upper-middle-class family that had risen from yeoman stock, much as the Forsytes had done. His father was a successful attorney. Galsworthy attended one of the finest English public schools, Harrow, and later went on to Oxford. He did not particularly distinguish himself. He was later a barrister without any observable talent or passion for the law.

A good deal of travel abroad opened horizons for him. On one voyage he sailed aboard a ship whose mate was Joseph Conrad, then wrestling with his first novel, *Almayer's Folly*. Galsworthy read the manuscript and persuaded Conrad, who later became a close friend, to become a professional writer.

Between the years 1897 and 1901, Galsworthy himself began writing stories and novels under the pen name of "John Sinjohn," but they are of very minor interest. It was not until 1906, the year after his marriage to Ada, that he produced his masterpiece, *The Man of Property*. Although he had no idea at the time of expanding this tale of the Forsytes into anything as massive as the three trilogies that eventually appeared, the theme of beauty trapped in a world of material complacency haunted him. Interspersed with other novels and plays, *The Forsyte Saga* and its sequels, *A Modern Comedy*, and *The End of the Chapter*, each comprising three novels, gradually emerged.

Galsworthy's fame spread as a result not only of his novels but also of his highly popular plays which dealt with social injustices of the day. Among these were *The Silver Box*, produced in 1906, *Strife* (1909), a play about labor unions, *Justice* (1910), and *Loyalties* (1922), concerned with English snobbery.

In many ways, Galsworthy was the ideal English gentleman. Tall and handsome, fond of animals and country life, gentle and honorable in his behavior to others, and an implacable foe of any manifestation of cruelty or injustice, he became one of the best-loved authors of his time. Since his death on January 31, 1933, however, his reputation has diminished considerably. Often, to the modern reader, his brooding over the vanished splendors of the Victorian past and his compassion for the weak and helpless seem mere sentimentality, and his refusal to take sides in viewing social conflict, mere lack of intellectual power.

By the Same Author

In Chancery: *In Chancery* begins in 1899 and ends two years later with a notable description of the funeral of Queen Victoria, the great monarch of Forsyteism. Soames Forsyte, hoping for a son to inherit his property, tries to effect a reconciliation with Irene but only manages to drive her into the arms of Young Jolyon whose children are now grown up. Irene and Young Jolyon eventually marry and live in the ill-starred house at Robin Hill. They have a son, Jon. Meanwhile Soames, after his divorce from Irene, marries a French girl, Annette. Instead of giving him the longed-for son, she has a daughter, Fleur. But Soames, ever the Man of Property, is able to reflect in pride at the baby's crib, "By God, this thing was . . . his!" *In Chancery* is less complicated emotionally and lighter in tone than *The Man of Property*.

To Let: Now we are in the postwar world of the 1920's. Jon, the son of Young Jolyon and Irene, meets and falls in love with Fleur, not aware of her parentage. Fleur, very much a Forsyte, strong-willed and grasping, determines that she wants Jon; she ignores the protests of the two sets of parents, who are aghast at the possibility of a marriage. Jon and Fleur, like Romeo and Juliet, must love each other against a background of bitter family feuding. Jon, deeply influenced by his mother, gives Fleur up, and she marries the son of a baronet instead. After writing a pathetic letter to Jon about why he had to renounce Fleur, Young Jolyon dies. The famous house at Robin Hill, tied up with so many thwarted lives from the day Soames first decided to build it, is finally "To Let."

The Old Wives' Tale

by

ARNOLD BENNETT (1867–1931)

Main Characters

Mr. and Mrs. Baines—Owners of a humble draper's shop in
  Bursley.
Constance Baines—Their pleasant, placid older daughter.
Sophia Baines—Constance's willful, headstrong sister.
Samuel Povey—The dull, unimaginative manager of the
  Baines' shop.
Daniel Povey—Samuel's cousin, unhappily married to a wife
  who drinks.
Cyril Povey—Constance's selfish, artistically inclined son.
Gerald Scales—A dashing and imprudent traveling salesman
  from Manchester who represents to Sophia the glamorous
  world outside Bursley.
Mr. Critchlow—A Bursley chemist and friend of Mr. Baines.
M. Chirac—A French newspaperman, friend of Gerald's.
Madame Foucault—Owner of a Paris rooming house of ill
  repute.

The Story

In Bursley, one of the Five Towns in the north of England
dominated by the manufacture of pottery, Mr. and Mrs.
Baines operate a humble draper's shop, aided by their two
daughters: Constance, sixteen, and Sophia, fifteen. The two

girls are very different in temperament and outlook. Constance, a good-natured, unimaginative girl, is perfectly willing to remain in the shop all her life. But Sophia, a proud beauty, is full of plans to see the great world. Her first step is to become a teacher, a plan that shocks her parents who see teaching as a profession for widows and spinsters.

Even Mr. Baines, a semi-invalid suffering from a paralytic stroke, tries to put pressure on Sophia to abandon her ideas, but the girl remains adamant and becomes apprenticed to the local schoolmistress. When she is not teaching, she takes turns watching over her sick father.

One day a dashing young commercial traveler from Manchester, Gerald Scales, enters the shop adjoining the Baines home, and Sophia leaves her father for a moment in order to meet him.

While she is talking to Gerald, her father slips off his bed and, unable to move, suffocates. Overcome with remorse at her negligence, Sophia promises to forget about teaching and help run the shop. But her real reason for staying in the draper's shop is that she hopes to see Gerald again on his occasional visits there.

Meanwhile, Constance has fallen in love with the unassuming, unglamorous Samuel Povey, manager of the shop. Mrs. Baines approves of this, but alarmed at Sophia's infatuation with Gerald Scales, she makes inquiries about the traveling salesman and becomes convinced he is not good for Sophia.

The two lovers nevertheless begin writing to each other. When as a last resort Mrs. Baines sends Sophia off on a visit to her Aunt Harriet, the willful girl elopes with Gerald who has inherited £12,000 and has quit his job. Together they go to London where Sophia forces him to marry her against his will. From London the couple move to Paris where Gerald begins spending his inheritance lavishly on fine clothes, elegant dinners, and gambling. Disillusioned with her husband, Sophia, a true Baines, manages to steal £200 from him and hide it against a rainy day.

After years of high living and a descent to increasingly cheaper rooms, Gerald's money is gone and he suggests that Sophia write home for more funds. When Sophia refuses to do this, Gerald abandons her in a wretched Paris hotel room. The shock of abandonment sends Sophia into a terrible fever, and for weeks she hovers between life and death. She is

tended in her illness by a sympathetic journalist friend of
Gerald's, M. Chirac, who brings her to the seedy rooming
house of Madame Foucault. Madame Foucault and two kindly
prostitutes who work for her nurse Sophia back to health.

When Sophia learns that Madame Foucault is badly in
debt, she buys the house from her with the £ 200 she took
from Gerald and makes the place a respectable rooming house.
The Franco-Prussian War of 1870 is raging now, Paris is
under siege, and food is extremely scarce. But with her
determination and acumen Sophia, aided by Chirac, who
keeps asking her to marry him, manages to make a go of it.
Gradually the flighty girl becomes a successful, unsentimental
businesswoman.

After the siege is lifted, Sophia buys the Pension Frensham,
one of the favorite spots in Paris for visiting Englishmen. Here
she is successful, too, and gradually amasses a considerable
fortune. However, she still refuses to marry Chirac, of whom
she has become very fond, because she does not know
Gerald's whereabouts.

Back in Bursley, meanwhile, life has been placid and dull
for Constance. After seven years of gradually increasing
prosperity under Samuel Povey's plodding care, the couple
have a son, Cyril, whom they dote on. Mrs. Baines dies while
the boy is an infant, and young Cyril grows up selfish and
unheeding of his dull parents. He has a talent for drawing,
which he persists in cultivating despite the Poveys' wish that
he enter the draper's shop.

Tragedy enters their life when Povey's cousin Daniel kills
his drunken wife in a fit of desperation. Putting family loyalty
above his own health, Samuel fights unsuccessfully in court
for his cousin's acquittal. Soon after the trial Samuel succumbs
to pneumonia.

Constance, now a widow, is increasingly lonely. Young
Cyril gets a job as designer in the local pottery, which keeps
him away all day. At night he attends art school. At nineteen
the youth wins a national scholarship and goes off to London,
leaving his proud but lonely mother to look after herself in
Bursley. She has not heard from Sophia except for one
Christmas card some years before.

One day a young Englishman comes to the Pension Frensham in Paris. Attracted by the stately, dignified Sophia, he
reveals that he is a friend of Cyril Povey's. On returning to

England, he informs Cyril and Constance that he has found the missing Sophia. Constance immediately writes her sister a long, loving letter, asking her to return to Bursley for a visit.

At first Sophia is unwilling to leave her thriving business even for a short while. Soon, however, she suffers a mild stroke. When she is made a handsome offer for the Frensham by a hotel corporation, she accepts. After a quarter-century in the business, she sells her pension and visits England.

The two sisters are reunited once more. But soon the worldly, sophisticated Sophia begins to urge Constance to leave Bursley—which now seems utterly dingy and third-rate to Sophia—and move to Paris, or, at least, to London. But Constance resents what she considers Sophia's effort to dominate her, and remains stolidly in the decrepit old house where she was born. They live dully together for nine years, hearing infrequently from Cyril who is constantly traveling in pursuit of his art.

One day Sophia receives a telegram informing her that Gerald Scales is dying and wishes to see her. She rushes to his bedside only to find that he has died of exhaustion and malnutrition. Penniless and shabby, the once gay salesman has come to the end everyone predicted. Sophia is shocked not only at the sight of the wizened old man who had once been her dashing lover but at her incapacity to feel anything for him. "My life has been too terrible," she thinks at Gerald's deathbed. "I wish I was dead." Returning to Bursley after this deeply disturbing experience, Sophia suffers a second stroke and dies, leaving all her money to Cyril.

Now Constance is completely alone. At first she is relieved to be free of her sister's nagging domination. She suffers from sciatica and rheumatism. She almost never hears from her son. She is puzzled by the rush of events as Bursley is about to be officially incorporated into the Five Towns. When Constance dies a few years later, Cyril is off in Italy and cannot get home for the funeral. Only her poodle, last in a long succession of Baines's dogs, is there to mourn her.

Critical Opinion

In the autumn of 1903 Bennett used to dine frequently at a

small, undistinguished Paris restaurant. Once he saw the waiters and customers ridiculing a "fat, shapeless, ugly, and grotesque" old woman whose peculiar mannerisms soon "had the whole restaurant laughing at her." Reflecting that her case was a tragedy, Bennett realized that "this woman was once young, slim, perhaps beautiful." With the example of Guy de Maupassant's *Une Vie* in mind, Bennett decided to write a novel in which the hero and villain would be "time" as it remorselessly converts a lovely, spirited young girl into a pathetic old frump. Thus the idea for *The Old Wives' Tale* was born.

But where Maupassant had chronicled one woman's passage from innocent youth to disillusioned old age, Bennett decided to use two, in order to appraise and compare the effect of the forces of heredity and environment. Both Constance and Sophia are Baineses; that is to say, essentially granite-willed, indomitable North of England women. By separating them early in life, keeping Constance in the environment of her birth and sending Sophia to the totally different environment of besieged Paris, Bennett was able to show that, except for superficial differences, a person's character will remain essentially what it was at birth. Constance stoically endures her long, uneventful life in Bursley, while Sophia, as much a Baines as her sister, triumphs over a worthless husband, a totally foreign atmosphere, and even a great famine, to become a success in business. But like Constance, Sophia ends up a lonely old woman.

The triumph of *The Old Wives' Tale*, then, is in its subtle, meticulous study of time's erosions. Ever so gradually the girls become less frolicsome, less self-assured, but better able to take care of themselves and more inured to loneliness in their very different environments. Time works its havoc on them and in the end wins a hollow victory over these two indomitable women.

With quiet confidence in his power to keep two plots moving simultaneously, Bennett set out quite deliberately in *The Old Wives' Tale* to write what he knew would be his masterpiece. He even learned penmanship so that the manuscript itself would be a work of art, as indeed a published facsimile edition of it shows it to be. Following his usual rigid writing schedule, thinking out each episode a day in advance during long walks in the beautiful forest of Fontainebleu, Bennett attained his goal. *The Old Wives' Tale* combines the ruthlessly accurate detail of French realism with the gusto and humor that have always characterized English fiction.

The Author

Enoch Arnold Bennett was born on May 27, 1867, in Hanley, one of the Five Towns in North Staffordshire that he immortalized in his novels and stories. His father was a solicitor. After Bennett attended London University, he became a solicitor's clerk in his father's office. Following a family quarrel, he moved to London in 1893 and took up journalism, editing the magazine *Woman* for six years.

When Bennett began writing novels, with *A Man from the North* (1898), he was deeply influenced by the French realism of Zola and the Goncourt brothers. His second novel, *Anna of the Five Towns* (1901), was an attempt—on the whole successful—to transplant the French realist manner to the material he knew best: the hard, unyielding character of the potteries and their workers in the North of England. It was not, however, until *The Grand Babylon Hotel* (1902), a light detective romance, that Bennett achieved any popular success as a novelist. He maintained his popularity in the three following decades.

In 1900 Bennett moved to France, where he lived for eight years, marrying a French actress in 1907. Like Trollope, Bennett was an assiduous worker, turning out vast quantities of fiction and journalistic writing on a rigid schedule. With financial success he was able to indulge his tastes for high living, buying a succession of yachts and motor cars and staying in lavish hotels.

Aside from theater and book reviews, Bennett's work falls into three main categories. First are the serious novels, of which the most distinguished are *The Old Wives' Tale* (1908), *Clayhanger* (1910), and *Riceyman Steps* (1923). Then there are the lighter works, which Bennett called his "larks," of which the most popular are *Buried Alive* (1908) and *The Card* (1911). Least important, but most successful during his lifetime, are the numbers of self-help books such as *How to Live on Twenty-Four Hours a Day* (published in 1908, the same year as *The Old Wives' Tale* and *Buried Alive*) and *The*

Human Machine (1909). These shallow "pocket philosophies" essentially told readers how to organize their lives as efficiently as possible—as efficiently, in fact, as Arnold Bennett had organized his.

A genial, kindly man whose severe stammer was a lifelong embarrassment to him, Bennett loved what he conceived of as the glamorous life—hotels de luxe (his last major work, *Imperial Palace*, is a massive tribute to such a hotel), yachts, and French cuisine. Although he was popular chiefly with middle-brow readers, no educated taste in fiction could disregard such solid achievements as the *Clayhanger* trilogy. For many years Bennett was in essence the literary dictator of England. He died of typhoid fever in a grand hotel on March 27, 1931, years after a more esthetically oriented younger generation, led by Virginia Woolf, had ceased to take him seriously as a novelist.

By the Same Author

Clayhanger: *Clayhanger* is the first of three novels (the others are *Hilda Lessways* and *These Twain*) that tell of the rise to maturity of Edwin Clayhanger, a boy much like Bennett, living under a domineering father in the Five Towns. Edwin wants to become an architect, but his father insists on apprenticing him in his printing firm. Lonely and artistically inclined, Edwin defies his father's will and falls in love with the strange, free-spirited Hilda Lessways. The second novel tells of the courtship from Hilda's point of view, and *These Twain* details the difficulties of the marriage—difficulties that Edwin, with true Five Towns spirit, determines to overcome.

Riceyman Steps: Written in 1923, long after most critics had stopped considering Bennett a serious novelist, *Riceyman Steps* is the last real triumph of his art. It tells in brilliantly imagined detail—sometimes hilarious, sometimes poignant— the story of a miserly book dealer named Earlforward and his bizarre marriage to Mrs. Violet Arb. Earlforward is so cheap that he literally starves himself to death. The true heroine of the novel is Elsie, his maid and victim of his miserliness, who bears her lot in life with stoical good humor and remains loyal to her eccentric employer.

The Crock of Gold

by

JAMES STEPHENS (1882–1950)

Main Characters

The Philosopher—Kindly, wise, and eccentric, with ideas on
 every subject which he expounds at great length.
The Thin Woman of Inis Magrath—The philosopher's shrew-
 ish wife.
Seumas and Brigid Beg—The philosopher's children.
Meehawl MacMurrachu—A neighborhood farmer who gets
 into trouble with the leprechauns of Gort na Cloca Mora.
Caitilin—Meehawl's lovely daughter.
Angus Óg—A great Celtic god who lives in a cave far away.

The Story

At first there were two philosophers living in peace and contentment in the dark pine forest of Coilla Doraca near the
leprechaun-haunted woods of Gort na Cloca Mora. But they
both took shrewish wives who moved into the hut with them
and constantly interrupted their philosophical discussions.
One was the Grey Woman of Dun Gortin and the other was
the Thin Woman of Inis Magrath. One couple had a boy
named Seumas and the other had a girl named Brigid, but
each wife decided she liked the other's child better than her
own and so they switched children.

When Seumas and Brigid are ten years old, the first philosopher decides he knows everything he wants to know about life and is ready to die even though he is in perfect health. His friend tries vainly to dissuade him. For a quarter of an hour, the philosopher whirls around on the floor like a top and falls dead. Then his wife, the Grey Woman of Dun Gortin, follows suit, spinning about until she is dead. The Thin Woman of Inis Magrath buries the philosopher and his wife under the hearthstone and brings up both children, forgetting which is really her own.

The surviving philosopher is often sought out by the people of the wood to solve problems beyond their limited understanding. A small farmer named Meehawl MacMurrachu asks the philosopher one day what has happened to his wife's scrubbing board, which has mysteriously disappeared. After intensive Socratic questioning, the philosopher decides that the leprechauns must have made off with the scrubbing board and tells Meehawl to go to the woods where they live and steal it back.

Meehawl complies, but instead of the scrubbing board he finds, to his delight, the crock of gold which the leprechauns keep in order to ransom themselves when one of them is captured by a mortal. Since it is very hard work to accumulate a crock of gold by scraping the edges off coins they find in people's houses, the leprechauns are naturally furious when they discover the theft.

Knowing that Meehawl had sought the advice of the philosopher, the leprechauns decide to kidnap the philosopher's two children, Seumas and Brigid Beg. Pretending to teach them games, one of the leprechauns lures the children into their little house inside the root of a great tree. When Seumas and Brigid Beg do not come home for supper, the Thin Woman, who has occult powers, demands that the leprechauns return them, and the Little People, fearing her, obey.

Frustrated, the leprechauns then seek vengeance on Meehawl himself. They send for the Great God Pan, half goat, half man, who has not been seen in Ireland for many years. They persuade Pan to seduce Caitilin, the lovely daughter of Meehawl. With his magic pipes and his tales of the pleasures of the flesh, Pan succeeds in luring Caitilin away from her humble peasant life into his cave.

Once more Meehawl comes to the philosopher for advice.

The wise man sends his children to Pan's cave to beg him to release the girl, but the god refuses to have anything to do with them. Determined now to take matters into his own hands, the philosopher orders his wife to bake him some cakes for his long journey. First he goes to see Pan, but he is unable to persuade him to release Caitilin. Then he sets out to find the great old Irish god, Angus Óg. After a long journey during which he meets all sorts of people—some helpful, others nasty and suspicious—the philosopher finds Angus Óg and urges him to do something.

Angus Óg visits the cave where Pan holds Caitilin a willing captive and wisely leaves it up to the girl to decide whom to follow. Pan represents all that is lusty in man, but only with Angus Óg will Caitilin find love instead of lust, happiness and serenity instead of fear and hunger. The girl soon decides to follow the old god and leaves the cave of Pan.

On his way home from Angus Óg's dwelling, the philosopher delivers several prophetic messages from him to the people he meets. When he eventually comes home, his wife is so happy to see him that she swears never to be ill-tempered with him again or serve his evening stirabout with lumps. All seems well for the present. The philosopher and his wife are blissfully unaware of the troubles to come.

Furious at being thwarted in their revenge and determined to get back their crock of gold, the leprechauns leave anonymous information at the police station about two dead bodies—murdered by the philosopher—lying buried under his hearthstone. The police break into the philosopher's house, find the bodies of the first philosopher and his wife, and accuse the philosopher of murder.

The philosopher, vainly protesting his innocence, is escorted to jail. It is a pitch-dark night, and the police have a hard time keeping watch on their prisoner, who talks them practically to death on such recondite philosophical matters as why only man, of all the social species on earth, needs policemen. Suddenly the police come upon a leprechaun, and in their amazement at this tiny, bearded being, lose sight of both philosopher and leprechaun, who escape.

Meanwhile, Seumas and Brigid, playing in the wood, have found the crock of gold where Meehawl buried it, and they return it to the leprechauns. The Little People are overjoyed, but it is too late to do anything about the information they have given the police. The philosopher, now at home, decides that since he is innocent of any crime, he will give himself up to the police. In grateful surprise they put him in jail, and here he listens to the pathetic stories of two other captives.

While her husband is in prison, the Thin Woman decides to take matters into her own hands. She bakes some cakes and sets off with Seumas and Brigid in search of Angus Óg. On her way she meets the Three Absolutes: the Most Beautiful Man, the Strongest Man, and the Ugliest Man. Terror-stricken at these superhuman figures, the Thin Woman nevertheless answers their questions and succeeds in saving her children from them. Eventually she finds the dwelling of the great Angus Óg. He has been waiting for her to ask his help, for the gods help only those who request their intervention.

Living now with the lovely Caitilin, Angus Óg summons a great conference of the gods of ancient Ireland, and together they dance and sing through the countryside. In the town, moved by the life-affirming joy of the gods, the people are transformed, and the police immediately release their prisoners. The philosopher returns to his house in the pine forest and once again offers his sage counsel to his neighbors.

Having done their good deed, the gods return to the country of Angus Óg and Caitilin to await the birth of their child. Someday they will be able to leave their secret caves for good and again dispense joy and wisdom (which are the same thing) to the people of Ireland, for the gods are beneficent and wise; only people are sometimes misguided.

Critical Opinion

One of the characters in Stephens' *The Demigods* (1914) remarks that "humor is the health of the mind." If this is so, James Stephens must have been the healthiest of the many figures who enriched Irish literature during the Celtic renaissance that began in the late 1880's and flourished until World War I. For although most of the writers of that movement dealt, as Stephens did, with magic, myth, and legend, none did so with as much vivacity and good humor as Stephens, whose books combine the whimsical, fey, moonlit quality of much Irish poetic prose with a gusty, almost Rabelaisian appreciation of the joys of life.

Although the philosopher in *The Crock of Gold* is ludicrously henpecked, he never lets his wife get the better of him but simply ignores her when he is in full spate of eloquence. Similarly, in one of the most hilarious scenes of the book, he lectures his police captors when they come to arrest him, gives them the slip, and then surrenders in his own good time.

Such gods in *The Crock of Gold* as Angus Óg represent to Stephens the good life, which is compounded of simplicity, respect for both the natural and supernatural worlds (which coexist in a miraculous alliance), benevolence, and good humor. The one rebel among the gods is Pan, a foreign deity who mistakes lust for love and is not spiritual enough for Stephens' people.

Essentially a fairy tale for adults, *The Crock of Gold* is a very difficult book to classify. In the words of Frank Swinnerton, "First it is a tale, and then it is a philosophy, and then it is nonsense; but all these qualities are so merged and, for the reader, confounded, that the effect is one of profound laughter."

Indeed, myth, folk tale, patches of poetic prose, domestic comedy, and even social commentary (in the prison scene) all give *The Crock of Gold* its unique flavor. The "philosophy" of the book is deceptively naïve. While Stephens gently mocks the long-winded platitudes of his philosopher, he never lets the reader forget that basically the philosopher is speaking the truth, which so often in our moon-struck world eludes both men and leprechauns.

The Author

James Stephens was born in Dublin on February 2, 1882, in the very hour in which his great compatriot James Joyce was born. This coincidence so impressed the superstitious Joyce that he once said only Stephens could complete his *Finnegans Wake* should he die prematurely.

Stephens' family was poor, and he received his only education in the Dublin slums. He taught himself to be a stenographer, however, and was discovered in an office by George Russell ("AE"), the Irish poet and statesman, who saw some of Stephens' early poems and sketches and encouraged him to become a writer. Recognition did not come to Stephens until 1912, when *The Crock of Gold* was published and won the Polignac Prize. It remained his most popular work, although Stephens began and ended his career essentially as a poet.

A student of Gaelic and an important figure in the Irish literary renaissance of the early twentieth century, Stephens was determined to give his country "a new mythology." He did so in such lyrical, mystic prose works as *Deirdre* (1923), which won the Tailteann Gold Medal, *In the Land of Youth* (1924), in the famous volume of short stories *Etched in Moonlight* (1928), and, of course, in *The Crock of Gold.*

Interested in all aspects of Irish culture, Stephens became an assistant curator of the Dublin National Gallery, a noted collector of Celtic folk songs, and a member of the Sinn Fein working to establish the De Valera government. During World War II, he protested against Irish neutrality, moved to London, and wrote to the *Times* that he was an Irishman who wanted "to elect himself an Englishman for the duration." Grateful for his services, the British government granted him a civil pension in 1942.

Stephens, who was married and the father of two children, traveled widely, living much of the time in Paris and visiting the United States in 1925 and in 1935, when he lectured at the University of California. Appropriately, the author of *The Crock of Gold*, according to his friends, resembled nothing so much as a leprechaun. Under five feet tall, bald, with the long, sad face of a stage Irishman, and speaking in a heavy brogue, Stephens seemed himself to have emerged from the forest of Gort na Cloca Mora rather than from a Dublin slum. He died in his home in London on December 26, 1950.

Sons and Lovers

by

D. H. LAWRENCE (1885–1930)

Main Characters

Walter Morel—A coal miner, crude and uneducated but full
of life and high spirits.
Gertrude Morel—Walter's unhappy wife who seeks a better
life for her children.
William Morel—The fun-loving, sociable, oldest Morel son.
Lily Western—William's snobbish and superficial fiancée.
Paul Morel—Sensitive and artistic, bullied by his father and
doted on by his mother.
Miriam Lievers—The intensely spiritual daughter of a neigh-
boring farm family.
Clara Dawes—A buxom and earthy suffragette who seduces
Paul.
Baxter Dawes—Clara's husband, a blacksmith.

The Story

When Gertrude Coppard, the refined, middle-class daughter
of an engineer, marries the coal miner Walter Morel, she is
twenty-three and he is a handsome, vigorous man in his prime.
But not long after the couple settles down in Bestwood, a
mining town in Nottinghamshire, Gertrude begins to realize
her marriage is a mistake. Her husband is a lazy drunkard,

crude, and ignorant of the things Gertrude considers important in life.

Over the years they have four children: William, Annie, Paul, and Arthur. Mrs. Morel takes comfort in them, protecting them from their father's periodic drunken rages and trying to bring them up to be refined and cultured, despite the family's precarious finances. The oldest of her sons, William, a clerk in Nottingham, is socially ambitious and is always going to dances. When he is only twenty, he leaves the unhappy family to make his way in London. The burden of Mrs. Morel's frustrated love then falls on the next son, Paul, a sensitive, artistically inclined lad who shrinks from his father's crudities and hates him for his rough treatment of Mrs. Morel.

As Paul is growing up, William becomes more and more successful in a London lawyer's office, but his social engagements take up most of his money and time, and he has little of either for his family. One day, however, he brings home to Bestwood, Lily Western, the flighty brunette he has become engaged to. Vain and superficial, Lily snobbishly condescends to the Morels. Mrs. Morel strongly disapproves of her and convinces William she is not the girl for him.

Shortly afterward, Mrs. Morel is summoned to London where William is dying of pneumonia. After his death, Mrs. Morel falls into a deep depression. It is not until Paul, too, becomes ill that she realizes she still has him to live for. Paul is more sensitive than the two younger children, and Mrs. Morel feels he needs her protection against his loutish father more than they do. She begins to smother him in mother love, hoping that he will someday fulfill her frustrated ambitions. Paul easily becomes her favorite, never realizing that his father, too, has good qualities, including a vigorous, realistic acceptance of life that Mrs. Morel lacks.

Paul's first step toward independence is to get a menial job in Nottingham working for Mr. Jordan, a manufacturer of surgical appliances. He travels a considerable distance from home and earns only eight shillings a week; but he continues to draw in his spare time and finds the gossipy, superficial lives of his fellow workers a relief from the dour, passionate life at home.

One day Paul bicycles to neighboring Willey Farm, a lovely pastoral spot far removed from the grimy coal town in which he lives. Paul has become friends with the sons of the farm's owners, the Lievers, but soon he begins to notice their quiet, dark-haired, fifteen-year-old sister, Miriam. The Lievers, who are very religious, have brought up their daughter to be intensely spiritual. Shy and sensitive, Miriam comes to rely heavily on Paul's visits for solace when the crude life of the farm becomes too much for her.

While Paul is recuperating from an illness, he goes more and more frequently to the Lievers' farm, and while he tutors Miriam in French and mathematics, they fall deeply in love. Love to Miriam, however, is chaste and spiritual. She shrinks from any physical expression of love. Paul becomes increasingly frustrated. Mrs. Morel, too, who wants her son all for herself, disapproves of the generally unpopular Miriam and tries to persuade Paul to stop seeing her. Mrs. Morel knows that she is herself slowly dying of cancer. When Paul tells her one day that he is not in love with Miriam, she kisses him fervently and tells him he must live for his art and never let any woman trap him into marriage and prevent him from making something of himself.

Through Miriam, Paul meets Clara Dawes, a beautiful, buxom suffragette five years his senior, separated from her blacksmith husband, Baxter Dawes. Clara is just the opposite of Miriam. Where Miriam is spiritual, fearing any physical contact with men, Clara is sensual and earthy. Before long, she becomes Paul's mistress. Miriam knows of this but is sure that her loftier, platonic love will win out in the end. Clara, however, refuses to divorce her estranged husband. Paul is, in a sense, relieved for he does not really want to marry anyone. No woman, he has been brought up to believe, is as worthy as his long-suffering mother.

Paul's paintings have met with some local acclaim. Annie, after studying to be a teacher, marries; and Arthur, after a brief stretch in the army, marries too, after his fiancée has become pregnant. Mr. Morel suffers a leg injury in a mine accident and, no longer able to get around as he used to, begins to age rapidly. Paul takes his place as breadwinner and tries to buy his mother all the things her husband's irresponsibility has deprived her of.

Sensing that Clara represents less of a threat to her dominance over Paul than Miriam, Mrs. Morel lets her son know she approves of his mistress. But after Clara's husband, the powerful blacksmith, hears of the affair and gives Paul a bad beating, Paul stops seeing Clara for a time.

Paul returns to Miriam and finally possesses her, but without joy, because he realizes she has given him nothing but her body. Meanwhile, Mrs. Morel has come close to death. Visiting her in the hospital one day, Paul meets Baxter Dawes again. He is recuperating from typhoid fever, and, oddly, the two rivals become close friends. But Mrs. Morel's disease grows more painful and hopeless. She is brought home to die. Unable to watch her suffering any longer, Paul gives his mother a lethal dose of morphine. She is found dead the next morning.

Now Paul is depressed and confused. He has broken off with Miriam because of her loathing for sex. Clara has gone back to Baxter Dawes. Paul and his father, who have never understood one another, are unable to live together now that Mrs. Morel is dead, and they take separate lodgings. For a long time Paul wanders about purposelessly, occasionally thinking of studying art abroad and at other times longing to be united with his mother in death.

Slowly Paul's painting begins to find acceptance among art critics, and he feels now that his mother would have wanted him to continue with it. He has one final meeting with Miriam in Nottingham and finally realizes that she is capable only of sacrificing herself to him, never of loving him. They only torment each other when they are together. Leaving Miriam, Paul determines somehow to make his way in life on his own, without his mother to guide or impede him.

Critical Opinion

Sons and Lovers, Lawrence's first really mature novel, remains his most widely respected. It was written before ill health, poverty, and critical misunderstanding had made Lawrence an embittered prophet. Most significant, although it is a classic study of the oedipal relationship between mother and son, it was written before Lawrence had ever read Freud, with whom, as a matter of fact, he later disagreed violently.

The material of *Sons and Lovers* is almost purely autobiographical. Paul Morel is Lawrence. Miriam is actually Jessie Chambers, who knew Lawrence, encouraged him to write, and left a curious book of her own (*D. H. Lawrence:*

A Personal Record) in which she tells "her side" of the relationship so painfully dissected in the novel.

As an autobiographical novel, *Sons and Lovers* ranks with Joyce's *Portrait of the Artist as a Young Man*, Maugham's *Of Human Bondage*, and Bennett's *Clayhanger*. What makes it unique is not only its piercing psychological insights into the highly complex relationships between mother and son and between son and other women, but Lawrence's passionate involvement with the characters and even the landscapes of the novel—an involvement that underlies every page of its richly lyrical prose.

The fault that mars some of Lawrence's later books—a tendency to forget the story in order to harangue his readers —is fortunately missing from *Sons and Lovers*, in which all the ideas are rendered symbolically or in pure fiction.

The sexual ideas for which Lawrence became notorious are presented in full in *Sons and Lovers*. Briefly, he felt that because of the rationalism of the eighteenth century and the industrialism of the nineteenth, a vital force—the individual relationship between man and woman—had been submerged and all but crushed. Social convention, disembodied spirituality, and worship of the machine were Lawrence's enemies. They are embodied in the ghastly coal mine and in Miriam, a crippled being who loves Paul but cannot give herself to him. At the same time, Lawrence disapproved of Clara's promiscuity as he saw sex as an essentially religious function.

Before Paul can fulfill himself as man or artist he must come to grips with the "dark forces" Lawrence worshiped: understand the hold his mother has over him, free himself from the destructive inhibitions of Miriam, and even come to appreciate the animal vitality of his father. By the end of the novel he is on the brink of manhood because he has succeeded in mastering these forces in himself and understanding them in others.

The Author

Like his hero, Paul Morel, *David Herbert Lawrence* was the son of a collier, born in the mining village of Eastwood, Nottinghamshire, on September 11, 1885. His mother, a schoolteacher, was, like Mrs. Morel, determined that her children should rise above the poverty into which they were born. A sickly youth, Lawrence was encouraged by his mother to study. He entered Nottingham High School on a scholarship, later training to be a teacher at University College, Nottingham.

His career as a teacher was short-lived. Encouraged by the prototype of Miriam, he began to write. Ironically, Lawrence's first novel, *The White Peacock*, appeared in 1911, a month after his mother's death. Lawrence then fell in love with Frieda von Richthofen, an aristocrat, married and the mother of three children. He persuaded Frieda to leave her husband and join him in his travels through Europe. Frieda was the sister of the famous German air ace, Baron von Richthofen. When war came, Lawrence and Frieda went to England where they were under constant suspicion as spies.

Suffering from poverty and tuberculosis, Lawrence nevertheless wrote steadily throughout the war. *Sons and Lovers* appeared in 1913, followed by *The Rainbow* in 1915. This novel, with its outspoken views on sex, caused a furor in the press and a whole edition was destroyed by the police. Lawrence did not help matters by his caustic scorn for his critics and his passionate—often absurd—involvements in the literary world of London. Quick to make friends, Lawrence jealously expected absolute loyalty and would reject friends the instant their views failed to coincide with his.

The Rainbow was followed by a sequel, *Women in Love*, in 1920, and by a variety of splendid travel books recounting Lawrence's experiences in his search of health. His travels took him to Australia, Sardinia, Mexico, and the southwestern part of the United States. Among the most notable of these travel accounts are *Twilight in Italy* (1916), *Sea and Sardinia* (1921), and *Mornings in Mexico* (1927). In addition, Lawrence was a talented if eccentric painter, a fine poet, and a first-rate short-story writer.

Recognition came very slowly to the ruthlessly puritanical, bearded prophet of sex. In all his writing, Lawrence combined a painter's eye for natural scenery with fierce polemic about modern man whom he saw as surrendering his natural instincts and functions to an emasculating rationalism and industrialization.

Desperately ill, Lawrence came to Italy for the last time in 1926, after completing his novel about Mexico, *The Plumed*

Serpent. Embittered by his struggles with censorship and public misunderstanding, Lawrence in his last years wrote *Lady Chatterley's Lover* (1928), the most notorious if not the best work of his fiery career. He died of tuberculosis in a sanatorium at Vence, France, on March 2, 1930. The controversies he and his works aroused have continued unabated to the present day.

By the Same Author

The Rainbow: Confiscated by the police when it first appeared, *The Rainbow* is a vast novel about three generations of farmers (the Brangwens) and their sexual and social conflicts, from the tempestuous marriage of Tom Brangwen and a Polish widow, Lydia, to the wedding of his foster child, Anna, and his cousin Will Brangwen on to the third generation. These darkly passionate men of the English soil find themselves locked in combat with their women who, like Mrs. Morel, try to "civilize" them or, like Miriam, withhold themselves in the hope of crushing the occasionally brutal but essentially healthy masculine spirit.

Women in Love: A sequel to *The Rainbow, Women in Love* centers around two sisters, Ursula and Gudrun Brangwen, and their men, Gerald and Birkin. Fiercely individualistic and intent upon primacy in any sexual relationship, the characters torment one another in a series of often bizarre scenes. Lawrence's underrated gift for satire appears here, too, as he describes Birkin's adventures in pseudosophisticated London society. Lawrence's favorite among his own novels, *Women in Love* is the most fully developed example of his penetrating psychological exploration of the war between the sexes and the ills of modern society.

Of Human Bondage

by

W. SOMERSET MAUGHAM (1874–1965)

Main Characters

Philip Carey—A highly sensitive man, orphaned very young.
   He has a clubfoot.
William Carey—Philip's clergyman uncle, a narrow, cold
   man with an inflated sense of his own position.
Louisa Carey—Philip's kindly aunt who longs for a child of
   her own.
Miss Emily Wilkinson—Twice Philip's age and far more
   sophisticated, his first love.
Cronshaw—An egocentric hack poet and amateur diabolist
   who influences Philip in Paris.
Fanny Price—An untalented woman trying to become an
   artist in Paris.
Mildred Rogers—Utterly unattractive and self-seeking, yet she
   is able to enslave the infatuated Philip.
Thorpe Athelny—An eccentric who befriends Philip during
   a wretched period in his life.
Sally Athelny—A direct and warm-hearted girl.

The Story

Philip Carey is only nine years old in 1885 when his mother
dies and he goes to live with his Uncle William and Aunt

Louisa in the vicarage of Blackstable, not far from London. The highly sensitive orphan suffers agonies of self-consciousness and embarrassment about the clubfoot he was born with. His uncle is a "close" man with money and emotion, a self-righteous and smug domestic tyrant. Philip's childless Aunt Louisa gives him the only warmth and affection he knows as a boy.

Philip's schooldays are made wretched by his affliction. Unable to participate in sports and constantly mocked by his callous schoolfellows, Philip learns to retreat into himself and becomes a lonely but independent boy. His uncle is a great collector, if not reader, of books, and soon Philip devours all the books of romance and adventure he can find in the vicarage library.

At the King's School in Tercanbury, where Philip is eventually enrolled, he is forced to show his deformed foot to the other boys, who cruelly imitate his peculiar gait. This horrible experience drives him even further into himself. When a religious revival sweeps the school, Philip, the nephew of a low churchman, takes to reading the Bible avidly. When he learns that faith can move mountains, he decides to try an experiment. One night he prays fervently to God to heal his clubfoot. When he awakens the next morning as deformed as ever, Philip loses whatever faith he may have had and becomes an agnostic for the rest of his life.

At eighteen, Philip persuades his uncle to let him use some of his own inheritance to study in Germany instead of at Oxford. He spends a year at the home of Professor Erlin in Heidelberg where he comes under the intellectual influence of the famous university town. Philip studies German and philosophy and becomes hardened in his agnosticism. The year in Germany is a happy one for Philip. Here he begins to appreciate the great world outside Blackstable.

On his return to England, Philip falls in love with Miss Emily Wilkinson, daughter of a clergyman, who is staying at the vicarage. She is twice his age, but gay and high-spirited, and has little difficulty in seducing the innocent Philip who, at twenty, shyly feels that he ought to have an affair. When she returns to Germany as a governess, however, Philip quickly recovers and settles in London to become an apprentice to a firm of chartered accountants.

Lonely and bored with his job, Philip decides that he must

go to Paris to study art. His uncle strongly disapproves and refuses to subsidize him. But Aunt Louisa gives Philip her savings of £100, and he is launched on the bohemian life of a poor art student.

In Paris he comes under the influence of Cronshaw, an untalented writer but a magnetic speaker with heady ideas about diabolism that intrigue Philip for a while. Although he works hard at painting, Philip learns from his frank instructor that he has no real talent. Affected by the tragic fate of Fanny Price, a fellow art student who killed herself when she discovered she had no talent, Philip decides to return to England and begin life anew as a medical student.

With his uncle's approval, he enrolls in St. Luke's Hospital and studies hard. But he is still lonely. He meets Mildred Rogers, a waitress, pale and consumptive-looking, vulgar and utterly selfish, and becomes obsessed with the desire to possess her. She is coy with him, however. In his frustrated and humiliating preoccupation with her, Philip fails his examinations. Then Mildred tells him she is going to marry a rich German named Miller.

Philip is crushed, but he is consoled by a young widow named Norah. Their love affair is hearty and direct, but Norah cannot take his mind off Mildred. When Mildred reappears, she tells Philip that Miller was already married and poorer than he pretended to be. He has deserted her, and she is pregnant with his child.

Unable to let Mildred fend for herself, Philip pays her medical bills; and when a baby girl is born, he takes mother and daughter into his rooms to live with him. He comes to love the little girl, but Mildred still despises him and taunts him about his clubfoot. She soon leaves him for a lecherous friend of his named Griffiths. The degraded Philip has even paid for one of Mildred's outings with her lover.

Meanwhile Philip has repeated the course he failed in medical school and has become a popular intern. An operation is performed on his clubfoot, and his limp improves considerably. He meets an eccentric patient named Thorpe Athelny, who at forty-eight has a wife and nine children, but little money to support them. When Athelny leaves the hospital, he invites the lonely young doctor to visit his home. Philip is delighted by the happy family life he sees there—so different from the grim atmosphere in which he spent his childhood. He becomes a frequent visitor at the carefree Athelny cottage.

Late one evening Philip meets Mildred again on the streets of London. Deserted by Griffiths, she has become a prostitute. Once again Philip feels he must shelter her, although by now he has gotten over his early infatuation. Mildred, seemingly a sadder and wiser woman, consents to live with Philip as his housekeeper. But now it is she who desires Philip. She is outraged when he refuses to have anything to do with her, and one day in his absence she rips up his furniture and paintings. Philip returns to find his apartment wrecked and Mildred gone.

He takes lodgings across the street and, on the advice of a Scottish friend who works for an investment firm, begins investing the rest of his inheritance in the stock market. At first he is successful, but then the Boer War knocks the bottom out of the market, and Philip loses his inheritance. Again he must quit medical school. For a period he faces starvation. Thorpe Athelny gets him a job in the linen draper's shop where he is employed, but Philip hates being a floorwalker. Eventually things improve a bit as he puts his artistic training to use designing posters and dresses.

Left £500 at his uncle's death, Philip is able to resume his medical studies. Eventually he gets an assistantship with a physician in Dorsetshire. The old doctor wants Philip to become his full partner, but Philip, now thirty, is filled with wanderlust and wants to become a ship's doctor.

Before signing aboard a vessel, however, Philip goes on a holiday to the Athelnys' cottage. There he notices for the first time that the Athelny daughter, Sally, whom he had always thought of as a little girl, has matured into an attractive woman. They walk in the country together, and Philip makes love to her.

A few weeks later, Sally tells Philip that she is pregnant. Philip sees that the only honorable thing to do is to abandon his plans for travel and marry the girl for whose plight he is responsible. But when Sally later tells him that she was mistaken, Philip, far from being relieved, feels disappointed. He realizes that what he really wants in life is not aimless travel as a lonely bachelor but a happy, secure home life with the sympathetic Sally Athelny. Accordingly they are married, and Philip, settling down as a country doctor, is finally released from the bondage of his hopeless love for Mildred Rogers and his lack of faith in himself.

Critical Opinion

In the tradition of *David Copperfield, The Way of All Flesh,* and *Sons and Lovers, Of Human Bondage* is concerned with the growing pains—emotional, intellectual, and spiritual—of a youth on the way to maturity. It is a highly autobiographical record not only of the young Maugham's life and loves but of his intellectual development as well, ranging from the joyless religious upbringing in his uncle's vicarage through the heady philosophic freedom of Heidelberg, the bohemian life in Paris with all its absurdities and tragedies, and finally the coming to grips with the meaning of life in London and in the kindly, sensible home of the Athelny family.

The title, taken from Spinoza's *Ethics,* is a clue to the theme of the work which differentiates it from other autobiographical novels. To Spinoza, human bondage consisted of centering one's being on an inadequate object, that is to say on something transient rather than on something permanent. Freedom came only when one was able to control the lusts of the flesh and the weakness of the spirit and attach oneself to some permanent good.

This is the course that Philip Carey must follow in his youth. He falls into a hideously degrading bondage to Mildred, knowing all the time that she is a vulgar slut. He is, however, too weak-willed to free himself from his passion for her until he has suffered greatly. Mildred nearly wrecks his life on several occasions, but gradually Philip's soul is purged of her influence, and he gains control of his passions. His love for Sally Athelny at the end of the book is perhaps less passionate than his love for Mildred, but it is a saner and healthier emotion, one that will allow him to build a good life rather than destroy himself.

Thus *Of Human Bondage* is essentially a success story in which the hero, after many trials and tribulations, usually self-imposed, emerges happy and in general unscathed. The ideas that have influenced Philip finally evolve into an urbane, reasonable skepticism about life and human motives. From each of his love affairs, beginning with Miss Wilkinson and ending in marriage to Sally, Philip learns something—mostly how to endure the torture of being in love with someone who despises or at best ignores him and how to free himself eventually from the shackles of such love.

If *Of Human Bondage* is psychologically less penetrating than *Sons and Lovers,* or technically less exciting and venturesome than Joyce's *Portrait of the Artist as a Young Man,* it is nevertheless a surely written, well-balanced, and frequently perceptive treatment of the great theme of youth's awakening. In the fifty years since its publication it has been widely and consistently popular.

The Author

William Somerset Maugham, one of the best-loved English storytellers, was born in Paris on January 25, 1874, son of the solicitor to the British Embassy there. A happy boy, he grew up speaking French before he learned English. By the time he was ten, however, he was orphaned, like Philip Carey, and sent to live in his uncle's home in Whitstable.

Maugham's youth was very similar to Philip's. He studied at King's School, Canterbury, and went to Heidelberg instead of the more traditional Oxford. A pronounced stammer produced the psychological effect on Maugham that Philip's clubfoot had on him. Shy and lonely and suffering from incipient tuberculosis, Maugham spent a troubled youth searching for his vocation.

Like Philip, Maugham became a qualified physician, but he always yearned to write. His first book, *Liza of Lambeth* (1897), was a drab but expertly told story of life in a London slum as Maugham had come to know it while interning at St. Thomas' Hospital. Narrated in the then fashionable vein of French realism, *Liza of Lambeth* was not highly successful although it was respectfully received by the critics.

Maugham persisted in writing and for ten years almost starved in Paris until the production in 1907 of his first successful play, *Lady Frederick.* From that point on, Maugham became an immensely popular playwright and novelist. His royalties permitted him to indulge his passion for travel and art collecting. On his voyages around the world Maugham collected the material for his many stories, of which "Rain" became the most famous.

During World War I, Maugham enlisted with an ambulance unit but was soon shifted to the Intelligence Department, where he gained the espionage experience that he used in his tales about the British agent, *Ashenden* (1928). It was the story of his own troubled youth, however, to which Maugham turned for his finest novel, *Of Human Bondage*. Its publication in 1915 was a great success. Maugham followed this with *The Moon and Sixpence* (1919) and *Cakes and Ale* (1930) as well as numerous other novels, stories, and essays. His career as a playwright extended from well before the war right through the 1920's. Such sparkling plays as *The Circle* (1921), *Our Betters* (1923), and *The Constant Wife* (1927) made Maugham the toast of the English stage.

In the early 1930's Maugham settled in the famous Villa Mauresque at Cap Ferrat, in the south of France, where he remained—except for occasional voyages—until his death in 1965.

By the Same Author

The Moon and Sixpence: Based on the life of the great French painter Gauguin, *The Moon and Sixpence* is Maugham's interpretation of the selfishness and single-mindedness that go into the making of a great artist. His hero, Charles Strickland, is a stockbroker with a wife and two children, who becomes possessed by the desire to paint. He abandons his job and family and settles down to an amoral, poverty-stricken life in Paris where he ruthlessly pursues his art. In the process he drives the wife of his friend and admirer Dirk Stroeve to suicide and emigrates to Tahiti where he eventually goes blind and dies, leaving the walls of his primitive hut covered with paintings of great splendor.

A Portrait of the Artist as a Young Man

by

JAMES JOYCE (1882–1941)

Main Characters

Stephen Dedalus—The young Irish artist-hero who struggles against poverty and lack of understanding to find his life's vocation.

Simon Dedalus—Stephen's sentimental, good-natured father, a minor civil servant, fond of drinking and arguing about politics with his friends.

Dante Riordan—Stephen's pious but argumentative aunt, bitterly opposed politically to Simon Dedalus.

Cranly—Stephen's college friend, a sounding board for Stephen's ideas about art and religion.

Father Dolan—The stern prefect of studies at Stephen's school, ever on the lookout for lazy students.

Mr. Tate—Stephen's English teacher who accuses him of committing heresy.

Emma—Stephen's fickle girl friend who also accuses him of being a heretic.

The Story

We first meet Stephen Dedalus, a sensitive Dublin boy, listening to nursery songs and nonsense verses at his mother's knee.

Before long he is enrolled in the Clongowes Wood School, run by strict Jesuit teachers. Young Stephen suffers immensely from his shyness, his nearsightedness, and his strange, un-Irish last name. The other boys also bully him unmercifully because his father is a humble civil servant. One of them, Wells, even shoulders him into a ditch of cold, filthy water crawling with rats, because Stephen will not trade him a valuable little snuffbox for a marble.

As a result of this ducking, Stephen becomes sick and spends some time in the school infirmary. Filled with self-pity, he dreams about how sorry everyone would feel if he were to die. While Stephen is in the infirmary, the great Irish patriot and leader Parnell dies. The wailing of the people outside fixes this date, October 6, 1891, forever in the boy's memory.

Home for Christmas, Stephen finds that the death of Parnell has aroused intense antagonisms in his family. His father, Simon Dedalus, staunchly defends the dead leader, while his aunt, Dante Riordan, attacks Parnell as a heretic who betrayed both the Catholic Church and Ireland by having an adulterous affair with Kitty O'Shea, another man's wife. Simon Dedalus protests bitterly that the church and country for which Parnell fought all his life hounded him to death for one moral slip.

This fierce dispute ruins the first Christmas dinner that Stephen remembers. He feels that he is already being forced to take sides in religious and political disputes that do not really concern him. He sees them dividing his family as they have divided all Ireland.

More misfortunes await Stephen when he returns to school after the holiday. A student on a bicycle collides with him while Stephen is walking on a cinder path, and breaks his glasses. Stephen is excused from work until his father can send him a new pair, but Father Dolan, the prefect of studies, prowling up and down Father Arnall's Latin class looking for lazy and mischievous boys, spots Stephen not doing his lesson. Without waiting for an explanation, Father Dolan accuses Stephen of having broken his glasses intentionally and beats Stephen's hand furiously with a "pandybat." As he fights back his tears, his classmates, even "Nasty Roche," seem to sympathize with him for the first time. Craving excitement, they egg Stephen on to complain to the rector of the school about the unjust punishment. The rector sympathizes with him and promises to tell Father Dolan to excuse Stephen until his glasses arrive. His courage in speaking to the rector makes Stephen a sort of hero to his classmates, and they carry him about the campus in their arms. Later Stephen finds out that the rector and Father Dolan had enjoyed a good laugh over the incident.

As Stephen grows older, he becomes better able to handle bullies. At one point, Mr. Tate, the English teacher, accuses Stephen of inserting a heretical statement into one of his compositions. Stephen immediately apologizes and changes the essay, but later a group of the boys attack him for being a heretic and for liking the "immoral" poet Byron. Stephen sticks to his guns, however, and tells them that a poet's greatness has nothing to do with his private morality. The boys gang up on him and beat him with a cane. It is his first encounter with the bigotry and narrow-mindedness of his schoolfellows, but Stephen does not flinch from their jeers and abuse.

Family embarrassments hound Stephen at this time, too. His father, a shallow, easygoing man, given to sentimental talk about his own youth, takes Stephen on a trip to Cork where he embarrasses his rigorously honest son by treating everyone he meets to sentimental harangues over glasses of beer. From this point on, the fortunes of Simon Dedalus decline, and the family keeps moving to cheaper and drearier quarters.

Stephen is able to improve their financial lot temporarily by winning some prizes at the end of the term. Filled with ambition to live a less grimy life, he buys all sorts of delicacies, decorates his room, and even establishes a family loan service. The money soon runs out, however, and the Dedalus family is plunged again into genteel poverty. With the last of his prize money, Stephen wanders into Dublin's red-light district and, at the age of sixteen, has his first, unsatisfactory experience with sex.

This experience torments him when he is back at school where a religious retreat is being held. During the retreat, Stephen, almost constantly in chapel, hears a priest describe the torments of hell in lurid terms. Stephen is thoroughly frightened and believes that his experience with the prostitute will send him to endless damnation. He has nightmares every night, and yet feels he cannot confess at school. Instead he goes to a Dublin church where nobody knows him. There a kindly, wise old priest hears his confession and directs him on the road to penitence.

Stephen is so relieved by the old priest's comforting words that he studies very hard and resolves to lead a life free of all sensual temptations. He tries to imitate the monks and saints by mortifying his flesh, seeking out disagreeable experiences in order to rise above them. He tries not to dream about girls and plunges into the study of Aristotle, St. Augustine, and St. Thomas Aquinas.

Stephen is so successful at his studies and in his new regimen that the director of the college tries to persuade him to enter the priesthood. The director thinks that Stephen, with his intelligence and will power, must have a vocation. Stephen is flattered by the director's attention. He soon begins to see himself in the role of a priest. In his egoism he enjoys the idea of having all the power of the Catholic Church behind him.

As Stephen grows older, however, religious doubts begin to plague him. The more he doubts the more he studies, and the more he studies the more he becomes confused about the Church and its dogma. He finds some measure of intellectual companionship with his friends, Davin, Lynch, and Cranly, although they cannot match his intelligence. He gives up a girl, Emma, because he thinks he saw her flirting with a priest.

Stephen's friendships are not very successful. Most of his classmates are involved in the Church or in the Irish nationalist movement, now gaining momentum. Many of them are studying Gaelic, hoping it will eventually replace the hated English. But Stephen admires English poetry too much to throw the language overboard. He begins to have his doubts about the wisdom of the Church, and insultingly calls Ireland "the old sow that eats her farrow." He has not forgotten the Christmas dinner discussion of how Parnell was betrayed by his own people. When his fellow students ask Stephen to sign a petition calling for world peace, he rejects it on the grounds that the movement is headed by the Russian czar. Also, he tells them, he has determined to become a writer, and an artist cannot waste his time with politics.

When Stephen meets Emma again, she asks him why he has been staying away from her. He answers that he intends to become a monk. She replies that she thought he was setting out to become a heretic. This finally convinces him that the priestly life is not for him. He must cut himself off from friends, family, church, and country in order to make his own way as a lonely but independent artist. When his friends try to bring him back to the Church, Stephen merely questions them about their ideas of beauty, which is all that now concerns him. To him beauty is largely a matter of "art for art's sake" and has nothing to do with conventional morality. Even if it means breaking his religious mother's heart, he must leave Ireland, where the Church, he feels, has destroyed beauty. He must go in search of his artistic destiny.

As the novel ends, Stephen is about to leave Ireland, certain at last that he has found his true vocation, that of the artist. "Welcome, O life!" he writes in his diary. "I go to encounter for the millionth time the reality of experience and to forge in the smithy of my soul the uncreated conscience of my race."

Critical Opinion

A Portrait of the Artist as a Young Man was Joyce's first novel. Originally he wrote a very long draft of it called *Stephen Hero*, most of which he later destroyed. Then he rewrote the book, intensifying the experiences and selecting those that dealt with Stephen's emotional and spiritual development. A deeply autobiographical book, *A Portrait of the Artist as a Young Man* is in some ways like any number of novels written between 1890 and World War I about the growing up of an artistic young man in an insensitive family and a hostile environment. What distinguishes it, however, from such novels as Butler's *The Way of All Flesh* or Maugham's *Of Human Bondage* is the originality of the style.

Since every incident is filtered through Stephen's sensibility, the prose at the beginning of the book is almost baby talk. As Stephen matures, however, the writing grows more and more complex, keeping pace with the growth of his mind.

Although Joyce seems to be writing from within Stephen's mind, he also manages to comment obliquely to the reader about his hero who often acts foolishly or pompously. This double vision keeps the novel from becoming just another story about a sensitive young man. Above all, Joyce is coolly objective about both his hero and the environment against which the hero is struggling. Throughout the novel Joyce is detached; he never comments or moralizes. The result is a classic of fictional method as well as an intense and exciting account of the development—against all odds—of the artistic mind and soul.

The Author

James Joyce was born into a lower-middle-class family in Dublin on February 2, 1882. There was no hint in his background that he would become one of the most significant writers of his time. His father was an undistinguished civil servant more interested in drinking and arguing about politics than in reading literature. His mother, although more artistically inclined, had, unlike her son, a conventional mind.

Young Joyce got a thorough Jesuit education at Clongowes Wood School and later at Belvedere College and University College in Dublin. While in school, he thought he might become a priest or an opera singer (he had a fine tenor voice), but upon graduation in 1902 he turned his back, like his hero, Stephen Dedalus, on home, religion, and country. He eloped with a simple girl, Nora Barnacle, and went into voluntary, lifelong "exile" on the Continent, determined to become a writer.

Forced to support his wife and two children, Joyce nevertheless refused to write to suit the popular taste of his time. Instead he struggled for a living in Paris, Trieste, and Zurich by doing translations and reviews and by tutoring students in English. The originality of his style and his realistic, anti-romantic view of Irish life, made it difficult for Joyce to get his work published.

Although he completed his volume of short stories, *Dubliners*, in 1905, it was not published until 1914. *A Portrait of the Artist as a Young Man*, which he had worked on from the beginning of his writing career, was finally published in 1916. *Ulysses*, Joyce's crowning achievement in the novel, was published only through the intervention of friends in 1922. For many years it was banned in England and the United States for its alleged obscenity. Joyce's most startlingly original work, *Finnegans Wake*, appeared in book form in 1939, although parts of it had been printed in the "little magazines" throughout the twenties and thirties. Because the increasing complexity of his style attracted only sophisticated readers, Joyce was never able to support himself and his family by his writing.

Joyce was a fantastically erudite man who was never pedantic in company, a heavy drinker who never allowed alcoholism to interfere with his regular work habits, and a professional writer totally indifferent to personal notoriety or popular success.

A highly sensitive man, Joyce was forced to endure a series of extremely painful eye operations, none of which was entirely successful. Although his last years brought him some measure of fame among his more literate contemporaries, they were clouded by his increasing blindness, concern for his mentally ill daughter, and the approach of World War II. Joyce died in Zurich on January 13, 1941, while fleeing from the Nazis.

By the Same Author

Ulysses: Ulysses is an immense and stylistically complex sequel to *Portrait of the Artist as a Young Man*. All the action of the novel takes place in Dublin on June 16, 1904. Stephen is living in a tower on the beach with a medical-student friend, Buck Mulligan. His mother has died tragically after Stephen, in his atheistic pride, has refused to give her benediction. His father, Simon Dedalus, has become a hopeless drunkard.

Closely paralleling Homer's *Odyssey*, the novel concerns itself with Stephen's search for an adequate father, just as Homer's Telemachus searches for his father, Odysseus. Stephen ultimately finds a father in Leopold Bloom, a middle-aged Dublin Jew who also wanders through Dublin trying to sell newspaper advertisements. Bloom and his sensual wife, Molly, represent a modern Odysseus and Penelope who undergo a series of erotic and comic misadventures culminating in Molly's famous long, unpunctuated monologue as she is lying in bed after midnight mulling over the events of the day.

Ulysses is even more of a technical tour de force than *A Portrait of the Artist as a Young Man*. In addition to the close parallels to Homer's *Odyssey* which govern the action of the book, *Ulysses* represents the full flowering of Joyce's stream of consciousness technique. The point of view is restricted to what is seen, thought, and remembered by the three main characters, Stephen Dedalus and Leopold and Molly

Bloom. Since everything is seen through their eyes, the reader must figure out what specific sight or memory is eliciting any particular thought. Flashbacks are used with great virtuosity, necessarily, since the "action" of the book is restricted to a single day. Finally, the novel abounds in puns and word play and alludes to actual Dublin "characters" of the period whom Joyce knew or had heard about but who are largely forgotten today.

Finnegans Wake: Even more complex than *Ulysses* in its mythological framework and verbal experimentation, Joyce's last novel follows the dreams of a single character, the Dublin public-house keeper, Humphrey Chimpden Earwicker, through a single night. The logic of the book is as difficult to follow as that of a dream. Symbolism, free association, and puns in nearly all languages make *Finnegans Wake* the most puzzling as well as the most ambitious of British novels. Earwicker, whose initials also stand for Here Comes Everybody, represents all humanity, and his dream encompasses all human history, myth, and, ultimately, experience.

South Wind

by

NORMAN DOUGLAS (1868–1952)

Main Characters

Thomas Heard—The Church of England bishop of Bompopo who unbends somewhat under the softening influence of Nepenthe's famous south wind.

Mrs. Meadows—The Bishop's cousin, living in mysterious seclusion on Nepenthe and beloved by the natives.

Mr. Muhlen—Alias Retlow, a blackmailing scoundrel come to haunt Mrs. Meadows.

Don Francesco—A fat, jolly, pleasure-loving Catholic priest.

Cornelius Van Koppen—An American millionaire who travels around the world on a yacht filled with beautiful young girls.

Sir Herbert Street—Van Koppen's pompous art expert and adviser.

Freddy Parker—The corrupt proprietor of the Alpha and Omega Club.

Mr. Keith—A rational Scotsman who enjoys the civilized pleasures of Nepenthe.

Ernest Eames—An elderly scholar-recluse who lives only to work on a new edition of Perrelli's *Antiquities*, a quaint old history of Nepenthe.

Count Caloveglia—A poor but aristocratic lover of the good things in life, especially sculpture.

Signor Malipizzo—The anticlerical, corrupt chief magistrate of Nepenthe.

Denis Phipps—A moody young English poet, in love with Angelina, a local serving maid.

Edgar Marten—Denis' chief rival for Angelina, a joyless, unimaginative young geologist.

Commendatore Giustino Morena—Otherwise known as "the assassin," a widely feared lawyer and member of the Black Hand.

The Story

Returning to England after his largely unsuccessful efforts to convert the heathens of Africa, Thomas Heard, the Bishop of Bompopo, stops en route at the idyllic Mediterranean island of Nepenthe. There he plans to pick up his cousin, Mrs. Meadows, whose husband is in India, and take her and her child back to England with him. On the boat the bishop meets Mr. Muhlen, a rather mysterious and disagreeable man, and Don Francesco, a jovial, easygoing Catholic priest who confirms Mr. Heard in his prejudices against Rome and Mediterranean frivolity.

It is Don Francesco, however, who introduces Mr. Heard to local society, which includes a variety of eccentrics ranging from the American Duchess of San Martino, at the top, to the Little White Cows, a group of harmless Russian religious fanatics led by the mystic Bazhakuloff, at, or near, the bottom. Mr. Heard finds that not even his years spent among the happy-go-lucky natives of Bompopo have adequately prepared him for such Nepentheans as Miss Wilberforce, an English lady given to strong drink and undressing in public; Ernest Eames, a hermit scholar devoting his life to producing a new edition of a book of Nepenthean lore; Mr. Keith, the urbane man of pleasure; and Freddy Parker who serves atrociously adulterated liquor to the patrons of his notorious Alpha and Omega Club.

The first days of Mr. Heard's visit are spent calling on his elusive cousin who gives him a chilly welcome, and watching with dismay the pagan celebration of the Festival of Saint Dodekanus, the somewhat bogus patron saint of Nepenthe. The even tenor of life on Nepenthe is soon disturbed, however, by a series of omens, beginning with the drying up of the famous medicinal wells and culminating in a thick, suffocating snowfall of ashes from a nearby volcano. Usually, all the Nepentheans have to contend with from the elements is the enervating south wind, or sirocco, which constantly blows from Africa. But the shower of ashes is more than anyone can bear, least of all Freddy Parker. His stepsister, a malicious old gossip, has just died, but she cannot be buried until the fall of ashes stops. To add to Freddy's troubles, he learns that the Nicaraguan minister, who gave him a sinecure as finance commissioner for Nepenthe, has been thrown out of office. Freddy may now have to look for some new source of graft.

Freddy gets the brilliant idea of enlisting the Church in behalf of his negotiations with Nicaragua. Hinting to the local parish priest, a puritanical enemy of Don Francesco, that he might be willing to become a convert to Catholicism, Freddy suggests that the priest organize a religious procession to implore Saint Dodekanus to stop the fall of volcanic ash. The priest agrees, and miraculously the ashes stop falling and are washed away by a rainstorm.

New excitement comes to Nepenthe with the arrival by yacht of Cornelius Van Koppen, a lecherous American millionaire. Van Koppen's annual visits to Nepenthe are eagerly anticipated because nearly everyone manages to extract some money from him. The parish priest always gets a contribution for unnecessary church repairs, and other Nepenthean causes are liberally financed by the shrewd and benevolent magnate. One such charity broached to Van Koppen is the founding of a rest home for Miss Wilberforce who was last seen undressing in public (contrary to her custom, in *daylight*, albeit the false daylight of the ash fall). Van Koppen, amused at the hypocritical busybodies who hope to make some dishonest money out of the rest home, replies that he will gladly give a vast sum if they can get even a tiny sum of money from Mr. Keith. He knows that his hedonistic friend will react violently to any suggestion that Miss Wilberforce's freedom be curtailed. Van Koppen is right. On the morning of Freddy Parker's step-sister's funeral, a delegation interrupts Mr. Keith at his leisurely breakfast and is sent about its business with a stern lecture on puritanical hypocrisy.

Another scheme to get at Van Koppen's money is more successful, however. Count Caloveglia, a kindly, decayed aristocrat who has but two passions in life (his daughter, Matilda, and sculpture), has not enough money for Matilda's dowry. He tells Van Koppen that he has found a rare antique statue of a faun buried in his estate on the mainland, has smuggled it past the Italian authorities, and is willing to part with it—for a price—to enhance the millionaire's art collection. Van Koppen summons his art expert, Sir Herbert Street, who pronounces the faun a genuine masterpiece of classical art. Although Van Koppen knows Count Caloveglia has sculpted the faun himself and then buried it, he is so amused at Sir Herbert's gullibility and at the count's ingenious story that he buys the piece anyway, thus providing a handsome dowry for Matilda.

Practically the only unhappy islander is young Denis Phipps, a frustrated English college student and poet who is losing out in competition for the favors of Angelina, the duchess' shapely maid. His rival, Edgar Marten, is a sour geologist, more aggressive with women than Denis is. One day Denis calls on Mr. Heard to go mountain climbing with him. Mr. Keith has told him he will get in touch with "elemental powers" atop the cliffs of Nepenthe which will give him a vision of the future, at present somewhat murky. In the blinding midday heat the two men trek up the mountain to a spot near Mrs. Meadows' villa. When they sit down to rest, Mr. Heard sees his cousin in the distance strolling along the cliffside with Mr. Muhlen.

He cannot imagine what she sees in this questionable character whose real name, it is rumored, is Retlow and who is reputed to make his living in shady ways. Suddenly the bishop is appalled to see Mrs. Meadows shove Muhlen off the cliff to his death. He later realizes that Retlow was the name of his cousin's first husband. Retlow was apparently blackmailing Mrs. Meadows because her second marriage is illegal and her child illegitimate. The bishop finds himself in a moral quandary: should he tell the authorities that he has witnessed a murder committed by his own cousin?

Formerly his course would have been clear. Duty would have come first. But the pervasive south wind of Nepenthe has had its effect on him. Now he is no longer so sure that morality is a matter of black and white. Retlow deserved to die. Mrs. Meadows deserves to live happily with her second husband and child. The bishop decides to keep silent.

When Retlow is missed, everyone assumes that he has simply sneaked off to avoid paying his bills. One day, however, a coin belonging to the departed blackmailer is found in the possession of a young cousin of the parish priest. Seeing his opportunity to harass this old enemy, Signor Malipizzo, the anticlerical Freemason chief magistrate of Nepenthe, arrests the boy and doctors the "evidence" against him.

Immediately the parish priest swings into action. He enlists the aid of the powerful Commendatore Morena, a lawyer and political bigwig who is a power both in Church politics and in the much-feared Black Hand Society. Known to his many victims as "the assassin," the great commendatore arrives at Nepenthe to defend the accused murderer. Terrified by his reputation, Signor Malipizzo immediately arrests most of the Little White Cows, too, to show that he was not prejudiced in bringing charges against the priest's cousin. His gesture of impartiality fails, however. Roused by the commendatore's highly emotional eloquence, the jury acquits the boy and everybody tacitly agrees to forget about the murder of Mr. Retlow who was, after all, only a foreigner and a Protestant at that. Justice—after the Nepenthe fashion—has been done, and Mrs. Meadows, now a free and happy woman, will never be accused of the murder she committed.

As he prepares to leave Nepenthe with his cousin, the bishop realizes that he has learned a good deal about civilized life during his two-week stay. Although the local religion is almost pagan, it keeps the natives happy—happier, in fact, than most English people. Although affairs of church and state are handled in a wildly corrupt manner, a kind of rough justice does seem to prevail. The bishop learns that people are made happy not by being harangued into feeling guilty for their pleasures all the time but by being left alone to enjoy their lives as chaotically as they choose.

Critical Opinion

South Wind is both a backward glance at Europe before World War I and a prophetic novel of the breakdown of organized religion and traditional, puritanical morality that took place in the 1920's. In form it is a series of interrelated anecdotes about Nepenthe's ancient history and current population of eccentrics, both local and foreign. Imitating the early nineteenth-century novels of Thomas Love Peacock, Douglas sets his oddly assorted characters in action, or, more often, conversation, and sits back to watch the intellectual sparks fly. In its technique *South Wind* also looks forward to the iconoclastic, witty novels of Aldous Huxley.

A serious vision of life emerges, however, from the absurd behavior of the natives and expatriates on Nepenthe. While Douglas modeled his island on Capri, it must be remembered that "nepenthe" is the name of a drug used by the ancients to dull pain and bring on oblivion. In this sense, *South Wind* is about a utopia where nobody needs to work hard or worry much, where the climate is gentle, and where men can cultivate their leisure in a variety of urbane pursuits. The brunt of Douglas' usually gentle satire falls on those, like Marten, who disregard the physical beauty of life for a humorlessly dogmatic career.

Thus Catholicism in the hands of the jovial, high-living Don Francesco is a fine religion. It becomes odious, however, when practiced by bluenoses like the parish priest. Agnosticism is equally fine to Douglas when expressed in witty conversation by Mr. Keith. In the heavy hands of the aggressive, doctrinaire priest-baiter, Signor Malipizzo, it becomes life-denying and absurd.

If Douglas has a central character in his gallery of eccentrics, it is Bishop Heard who learns the lesson of Nepenthe: to be easygoing, tolerant of one another's foibles, and to enjoy life both sensually and intellectually in the manner of the best pagans of the past. Those who create trouble, like Mr. Muhlen, deserve to reap trouble for their pains. Although some of the conversations in the book are slow and outdated in their schoolboyish irreverence, *South Wind's* wise, tolerant vision of human eccentricity and sensuous yet witty evocation of the best in Mediterranean culture have never been surpassed.

The Author

Norman Douglas was well equipped by temperament and education to write a witty, erudite, and iconoclastic novel like *South Wind.* Born in an ancestral castle in Scotland on Decem-

ber 8, 1868, Douglas studied languages and science in Karls-
ruhe, Germany, for a few years and then entered the British
foreign service, in which he served for three years in Russia.
Primarily interested in science—especially zoology and arche-
ology—he left the foreign service to settle with his wife and
family on the island of Capri, the model for Nepenthe. There
he wrote learned papers on science, eventually departing from
this pattern in 1911 with what was meant to be a "popular"
book, *Siren Land.* Undismayed by its lack of success, Douglas
labored on *South Wind* for several years, finishing it in 1917.
The book was highly successful, providing as it did a nostalgic
look at prewar life at its most sophisticated.

Like Mr. Keith in the novel, Douglas was a man of wide
culture and many interests. He lived the life of an English
gentleman in Capri, producing few works but indulging to
the utmost his cultivated tastes for fine wine, witty conversation, music, and the Mediterranean way of life. One of his
most engaging books is *Old Calabria* (1928), ostensibly a
travel book but actually a compendium of the Italian folklore and customs that so appealed to the author. Other typical
productions of his are his memoirs, *Looking Back* (1933),
and a posthumously published cookbook of allegedly aphro-
disiac recipes called *Love in the Kitchen.*

The only thing Norman Douglas hated was the spirit of
fanaticism, whether religious or political. Christianity and
Communism were almost equally abhorrent to him. He
managed to live as a more or less virtuous pagan, untouched
in his island paradise by the ideological strife of the twentieth
century. Douglas died on February 9, 1952, an Edwardian
gentleman to the last and a delightful anachronism in his own
time.

A Passage to India

by

E. M. FORSTER (1879–)

Main Characters

Dr. Aziz—A sensitive, intelligent young Moslem surgeon attached to the hospital at Chandrapore.

Dr. Callendar—Aziz' coldly condescending superior.

Ronnie Heaslop—The unimaginative but decent young city magistrate of Chandrapore.

Mrs. Moore—Heaslop's mother, an open-minded Englishwoman seeing India for the first time.

Adela Quested—A plain, well-intentioned girl, engaged to Heaslop who has come to India with Mrs. Moore.

Cyril Fielding—The forty-five-year-old principal of Government College, highly suspect among the British colony for his friendliness to Indians.

Professor Narayan Godbole—A high-caste, mystical Hindu teaching at Government College.

The Story

Dining one evening with his friends, young Dr. Aziz, a lonely widower with three children, is interrupted by a summons to the hospital where he serves under the arrogant Dr. Callendar. Aziz regretfully leaves his friends and arrives by cab at the hospital, only to find that Dr. Callendar has departed without leaving him a message. To add insult to injury, just as Aziz is about to leave, his cab is requisitioned by two Englishwomen who do not even bother to thank him.

Upset at this typical treatment at the hands of the English, Aziz drops into a mosque for a moment of peace. Seeing an Englishwoman there, he shouts at her, assuming she has neglected to remove her shoes. But the Englishwoman, Mrs. Moore, is sensitive to Moslem custom, and has entered the mosque barefooted. This pleases Dr. Aziz so much that he starts a conversation with Mrs. Moore who has recently arrived in India and wants to see as much of it as possible. Dr. Aziz is pleased to find that Mrs. Moore shares his low estimate of Mrs. Callendar, the doctor's wife.

A woman in late middle age, Mrs. Moore has come to the dusty, undistinguished town of Chandrapore in order to see her son, Ronnie Heaslop, the city magistrate. She has brought with her Ronnie's rather plain friend, Adela Quested, who is determined to see the "real India," not the superficial India known to most of the British colony. To satisfy what he considers an eccentric and misguided whim, one of the club members suggests to Adela that they hold a bridge party— not to play cards, but to "bridge the gap," so to speak, between East and West.

The bridge party is a dismal failure because, with the exception of Adela, most of the English condescend haughtily to their Indian guests who are not even allowed inside the club house. Instead, the Indians stand, deeply embarrassed, on the lawn, as some of the Anglo-Indian matrons make small talk with them. Dr. Aziz refuses to attend. At the party Adela meets Mr. Fielding, principal of Government College and one of the few Englishmen in Chandrapore genuinely sympathetic to the Indians.

Fielding invites Adela and Mrs. Moore to have tea at his house. He also invites some genuine Indians, Dr. Aziz, a Moslem, and Professor Godbole, a Hindu. Fielding and Dr. Aziz take to one another immediately, and everything seems to be going well until Heaslop shows up to escort the ladies to a polo match. He disapproves of social contact between English and Indians for, although Heaslop is basically a good and sympathetic young man, his experience in meting out justice to Indians has soured him. He curtly interrupts a Hindu song

Professor Godbole is singing and takes Adela and Mrs. Moore away with him.

Adela is annoyed with Heaslop's rude behavior at the tea party and tells him she can never become engaged to him. Ronnie takes the announcement in stride and proposes an automobile ride in the car of the wealthy Nawab Bahadur. In the dark the car runs over an animal. The accident draws Ronnie and Adela together again, and they decide to become engaged after all.

Meanwhile, ignoring Ronnie's stern injunction to have no social contacts with the natives, Adela has accepted an invitation extended to her and Mrs. Moore by Dr. Aziz to visit the celebrated Marabar Caves. Aziz himself has never seen these caves but is eager to show off India to Mrs. Moore. The caves are the most interesting spot near Chandrapore.

Disaster plagues the expedition from the start. First Fielding and Professor Godbole, who were supposed to come along, miss their train because of the professor's extensive morning prayer. The day is very hot, and after seeing one cave, Mrs. Moore begins to feel ill and decides not to see any more. She is disturbed by the number of native servants hired for the occasion who crowd into the cave with her and by the hollow, meaningless echo that seems to mock her.

While Mrs. Moore sits on a rock outside, Adela and Aziz visit the other caves. They become separated for a moment. When next he sees Adela she is racing hysterically down the hill to join a friend, Miss Derek, in a motorcar. Fielding, who had arrived with Miss Derek, returns to Chandrapore with Mrs. Moore and Aziz.

When Aziz arrives at the train station, he is placed under arrest. Adela has charged that he attacked her in the cave, breaking her field glasses. Indeed, Aziz had seen the broken glasses lying on the ground, had picked them up, and is found with them in his possession. Although Fielding insists the charge is nonsense, Aziz is put into jail. The English colony is up in arms at the alleged affront to their visitor who is now suffering a nervous breakdown.

The trial sharpens the animosity between English and Indians as ranks draw together behind Adela and behind Dr. Aziz. When Mrs. Moore tells her son that she is sure Aziz would never have attacked Adela, she is shipped off to England to visit her two younger children. Ever since her experience at the caves, Mrs. Moore is a changed woman. She takes no more interest in the doings of her son or of anyone, but broods about the nothingness of existence as symbolized by the meaningless echo she heard in the cave.

When Fielding supports Dr. Aziz, he is ostracized by the English community and excluded from the English club. Because Ronnie is so personally involved, the case is presided over by his subordinate, a capable but timorous Indian justice, Mr. Das. The English colony crowds the steamy courtroom and tries to intimidate Mr. Das. When the Indians learn that Mrs. Moore has suddenly left India, despite the terrible heat in the Indian Ocean, they assume she has been spirited away because she would have testified for Dr. Aziz. A strange, semireligious chant is heard outside the courtroom as the Indians transmute Mrs. Moore's name into that of a goddess, "Esmiss Esmoor," over and over again.

When Adela is finally put on the witness stand, she breaks down. She is by no means sure that it was Dr. Aziz who followed her into the cave; in fact she is not sure that the whole dreadful experience was not just a nightmare. The trial, of course, ends abruptly. The English colony is furious. Dr. Aziz' lawyer, a violent Anglophobe, demands heavy damages from Adela. In the victory celebration among the Indians after the trial, Fielding is separated from Aziz and thrown together with Adela, to whom he gives sanctuary at his college.

Only after the trial is it learned that Mrs. Moore has died aboard ship, embittered and disillusioned. Adela then leaves for home, her engagement to Ronnie terminated. Fielding succeeds in convincing the now bitterly anti-English Dr. Aziz not to sue Adela for damages.

Two years later, Aziz has left the British state of Chandrapore for an independent Hindu state where he is court physician to an aged rajah. Fielding has returned to England and has written frequently to his old friend, but Dr. Aziz is furious with him because he assumes Fielding has returned home in order to marry Adela on the money that was rightfully Aziz'. Professor Godbole, who in his spiritual indifference to worldly matters refused to take sides during the trial, has poisoned Aziz' mind against Fielding, telling him that the schoolmaster has married Adela when in fact he has married Mrs. Moore's daughter, Stella.

One night during a Hindu religious celebration, Fielding comes to visit Aziz accompanied by Stella and her brother Ralph. Aziz is cold to him even when he learns the truth about Fielding's marriage.

But after the festival, during which Aziz' potentate dies, the doctor and Fielding take a ride together through countryside strange to both of them—to Fielding as an Englishman and to Aziz as a Moslem. They become reconciled to each other although Aziz realizes that their friendship is doomed by India herself. For Fielding, by his marriage, is now committed to the English colony he once despised, and Aziz has become increasingly Indian as a result of his experience during the trial. The friends part, never to see each other again.

Critical Opinion

The title *A Passage to India* comes from Walt Whitman's exuberantly optimistic poem of that name. In a sense, the novel is a wry, ironic commentary on the American poet's hopeful nineteenth-century vision of a world unified by technical progress. Hailing the passage to India made possible by the building of the Suez Canal, Whitman had bravely intoned:

"Nature and Man shall be disjoin'd and diffused no more,
The true son of God shall absolutely fuse them."

And earlier in the poem, Whitman prophesied:

"All affection shall be fully responded to. . . ."

Early in the novel these sentiments are adopted by the liberal Cyril Fielding, who believes that the world "is a globe of men who are trying to reach one another and can best do so by the help of good will plus culture and intelligence." But it is a creed, Forster comments, "ill suited to Chandrapore." The tragedy of the novel lies in the breakdown of communication, both between races and between individuals.

"Only connect!" was Forster's plea in his earlier novel *Howards End*. But more connections are severed than made between the people in Forster's essentially pessimistic work.

The trouble is not merely a basic antipathy and misunderstanding between races, however, because there are also failures to connect among the English and among the Indians. Ronnie Heaslop does not understand his mother's bleak view of the world; Fielding is cut off from his own countrymen because of his humane view of the Indians; and Professor Godbole, a Hindu mystic, refuses to aid Dr. Aziz, the Moslem rationalist. Everywhere Forster sees division between people as well as between races and cultures. Tenuous friendships, like that between Fielding and Aziz, break down under the pressure exerted on both sides.

The center of the novel is in the mysterious caves at Marabar, those uncharted jests of nature that divide people and return only a hollow, echoing laugh to whatever man tries to communicate. To the sensitive Mrs. Moore who has tried to love and understand people, the caves' echo seems to say: "Pathos, piety, courage—they exist, but are identical, and so is filth. Everything exists, nothing has value."

Whatever one says in the caves, the answer is the same: the meaningless "ou-boum" of the echo. Man, Mrs. Moore realizes, is alone in an uncaring universe. All he has for comfort is his fellow man. When Mrs. Moore realizes that the divisions between people cannot be bridged, she dies.

Thus for all its sparkling wit and satiric observation of the social mores of Englishmen and Indians, *A Passage to India* is profoundly pessimistic about the inability of man to communicate with or understand his fellows.

The Author

One of the famous "Bloomsbury Group" of Cambridge-oriented intellectuals which included Virginia Woolf, Lytton Strachey, and T. S. Eliot, *Edward Morgan Forster* was born in 1879 and attended the Tonbridge School and King's College, Cambridge. After college, he went to Italy, which provided the background for two of his early novels, *Where Angels Fear to Tread* (1905) and *A Room with a View* (1908). Quietly effective, with moments of high comedy, these novels deal with the cultural barrier between Englishmen and Italians, just as *A Passage to India* later dealt with misunderstandings between Englishmen and Indians.

In 1907 Forster returned to England, which was the scene for two other novels, *The Longest Journey* (1907) and *Howards End* (1910), his most important work up to that time. Four years after his return to England, Forster set out for India with a Cambridge preceptor and friend, Goldsworthy Lowes Dickinson, whose biography Forster later wrote. A second visit, in 1921, strengthened the impression India had made on Forster. In 1924, after a lapse of fourteen years, he wrote *A Passage to India*, the last novel he published.

Untroubled by financial problems, Forster has published only these five novels in his long lifetime. The meticulous craftsmanship that went into them has made them all modern classics, especially the rich and haunting *A Passage to India*, which stands with *Kim* as Britain's finest perception of the subcontinent she once ruled.

But if Forster's production of novels has been comparatively slight, he has been a prolific essayist. In 1927 he was invited to deliver the annual Clark lectures at Cambridge. These he later turned into his remarkable treatise on fiction, *Aspects of the Novel*. Two collections of essays and reviews, *Abinger Harvest* and *Two Cheers for Democracy*, have also appeared over the years.

An honorary Fellow of King's College, Forster has spent most of his later years residing at his alma mater. Except for occasional lectures and conferences, he has not officially taught there. Ever since his early days in the heady intellectual atmosphere of Bloomsbury, Forster has aligned himself with liberal causes. An outspoken enemy of fascism, he delivered valuable radio talks to India during World War II, enlisting his former friends behind the British cause.

By the Same Author

Where Angels Fear to Tread: Forster's first novel announces most of his future themes. The conflict between English and Italians is represented by the ghastly Mrs. Herriton and her silly, widowed, daughter-in-law, Lilia, on one side, and by the handsome, charming, but unconventional (by English standards) son of an Italian dentist, Gino, on the other. Gino and Lilia marry and have a child, but Lilia's life with her Italian husband is miserable. Mrs. Herriton's son, Philip, is sent to investigate. When Lilia dies in childbirth, the Herritons descend on Italy en masse, in order to "rescue" the baby from Gino. The novel reaches a tragic climax as the baby is killed in an accident while being kidnapped by Mrs. Herriton's odious, small-minded daughter, Harriet.

Howards End: Howards End is the country home near London of the Wilcox family, whose lives become intertwined with those of two intellectual girls, Helen and Margaret Schlegel. Mrs. Wilcox dies, leaving Howards End to Margaret Schlegel, but the family does not acknowledge the bequest and disapproves when the widowed Mr. Wilcox eventually marries Margaret. Finally, after a family tragedy involving the death of Helen Schlegel's lover, a social inferior named Leonard Bast, Margaret gets the mansion, as had been originally intended. *Howards End* is chiefly concerned with class differences in prewar England and with the snobbery and unintentional cruelty these differences produce.

Mrs. Dalloway

by

VIRGINIA WOOLF (1882–1941)

Main Characters

Clarissa Dalloway—A sensitive, imaginative, middle-aged London society woman.

Richard Dalloway—Her husband, a semi-successful member of Parliament.

Peter Walsh—Mrs. Dalloway's former suitor, recently returned after five years in India.

Elizabeth—Mrs. Dalloway's impressionable seventeen-year-old daughter.

Doris Kilman—Elizabeth's embittered, ugly tutor, a religious zealot.

Sally Seton—Mrs. Dalloway's former friend, once full of life and high spirits but now quite matronly.

Septimus Warren Smith—A shell-shocked war veteran haunted by his inability to feel emotion.

Lucrezia—Smith's troubled, affectionate Italian wife.

Sir William Bradshaw—A fashionable psychiatrist, pompous and overbearing.

The Story

One fine, hot June morning Clarissa Dalloway emerges from her handsome home in Westminster to go shopping. She is giving an important dinner party that night. On the street she meets an old friend, Hugh Whitbread, now grown fat and rather pompous. Hugh is in town, Mrs. Dalloway knows, to consult a doctor about his constantly ailing wife, Evelyn. Clarissa wonders what sort of present would be appropriate to take to Evelyn in the nursing home. But first she must buy some flowers for her party.

While she is ordering flowers, Mrs. Dalloway sees a grand limousine pull up to the curb. Its drawn curtains arouse the curiosity of passers-by. Is the Queen inside or an important cabinet minister—perhaps even the Prime Minister? Mrs. Dalloway's husband is a member of Parliament, but for some reason his career has never advanced as it should have. He will never be a member of the cabinet. He is a good man, but rather stuffy and unimaginative. When the limousine pulls into Buckingham Palace, Mrs. Dalloway is sure the Queen is inside.

A plane flies overhead skywriting an advertisement for some toffee. Skywriting is still a novelty in the twenties, and Mrs. Dalloway feels at one with all the Londoners craning to see the marvel.

The bustle and spectacle of London remind her of her past. She was a well-bred girl whose father's house in the country was always filled with guests. Among these, Clarissa's favorite was Sally Seton, a lively, iconoclastic girl on whom Clarissa had a schoolgirl crush. Sally was careless and mischievous. When she made fun of the stuffy Richard Dalloway, with whom Clarissa had fallen in love one evening, the friendship cooled. Now the Dalloways have an almost grown-up daughter, Elizabeth, whose schoolgirl crush on Doris Kilman, an odious, embittered, religious fanatic, worries Mrs. Dalloway.

Before she married Richard Dalloway, Clarissa had been in love with handsome, brilliant Peter Walsh, but he always mocked her family's pretensions and sided with Sally Seton against Richard Dalloway. Then he had left for India, and Clarissa had heard he had gotten married en route. All these memories of the past bring a warm feeling of nostalgia to Clarissa as she is enjoying her shopping, the fine weather, and the thought of the party she is to give.

But another soul wandering the streets of London is not so happy. Septimus Warren Smith is a shell-shocked war veteran with an Italian wife, Lucrezia. Smith is haunted by the memory of Evans, his great friend and commanding officer in the war. Shortly before the armistice, Evans had been killed, and Smith is shocked to realize that he really did not feel one way or another about his closest friend's death.

He himself, idealistically enlisting early in the war, showed valor in action, fighting, as he believed, for the England of Shakespeare. Now he is obsessed with the vileness of human beings and is haunted by the dead Evans. His wife, Lucrezia, lost in foreign London, does not know what to do. Smith, who married her soon after the war, refuses to have any children. Instead, he broods about life and death. The bluff, hearty Dr. Holmes, who is treating him, has warned Lucrezia that at all costs he must avoid shock and excitement. Septimus loathes the insensitive, dull doctor and refuses to see him.

Meanwhile, Clarissa Dalloway has returned home with her flowers to learn that her husband has been invited—without her—to have lunch with Millicent Bruton, a clever, ruthless woman. Mrs. Dalloway is hurt at not being invited (Lady Bruton's luncheons are reputed to be so very entertaining) but she realizes that Lady Bruton cannot abide the wives of her men friends, especially if she thinks they have held their husbands back politically.

While she is sewing up her dress, Mrs. Dalloway receives a surprise visit from Peter Walsh, just back after five years in India. He has not changed at all: he still makes fun of Clarissa for being so caught up with society. He tells her that he has fallen in love with Daisy, a married woman in India, and is in London to consult with lawyers about her divorce. He has been divorced, his career is a shambles, and he hopes that Hugh Whitbread will help find him a job in London to support Daisy and her two children.

When Clarissa introduces Peter to her daughter, Elizabeth, Peter realizes what he has missed in life. But when Clarissa reminds him not to forget her dinner party, Peter Walsh suddenly sees her life, so filled with social events, as empty and trivial.

At Lady Bruton's luncheon, meanwhile, Richard Dalloway and Hugh Whitbread help their hostess compose a letter to the *Times* about some petty matter. Lady Bruton is all for political "causes," but she is too scatterbrained even to write a letter to a newspaper. Hugh Whitbread composes an appropriately pompous and cliché-ridden letter for her.

Meanwhile Lucrezia is deeply worried about her husband. Because he has refused to see the jovial Dr. Holmes, Lucrezia has engaged the services of the wealthy, impressive Harley Street psychiatrist, Sir William Bradshaw; but even the innocent Lucrezia can see that Bradshaw is a selfish, unsympathetic man. Sir William suggests that, to avoid the possibility of suicide, Septimus may have to go to a rest home in the country—where Lucrezia cannot join him—as long as his fits of depression persist.

Late that afternoon, when Dr. Holmes blunders his way upstairs to see Smith in his apartment, the haunted veteran leaps out of the window, impaling himself on the rusty grating outside, and dies. Dr. Holmes cannot understand why a young man with a beautiful wife and a brilliant future should do such a rash, unnatural thing. Lucrezia is completely crushed by her husband's suicide.

During the same afternoon, Doris Kilman comes to take Elizabeth shopping. Mrs. Dalloway cannot help hating the woman Richard hired as a tutor for their daughter. Miss Kilman is a poor woman who despises and envies the Dalloways for their wealth and easy life. A highly intelligent but unprepossessing student of modern history, she had lost her post in a school during the war because of her German ancestry and sympathies. Ugly and lonely, Miss Kilman has turned to religion for consolation. The liberal, easygoing Mrs. Dalloway is shocked to find that Miss Kilman is indoctrinating Elizabeth in church ritual. "Love and religion!" Mrs. Dalloway muses. "How detestable they are!" Why cannot people leave others alone, lead their own lives, and not impose their wills on others? Knowing she is wrong to hate anyone, Mrs. Dalloway nevertheless finds herself loathing the unfortunate Doris Kilman.

By now the hour for the party has arrived. After some initial awkwardness, it proves a great success. The Prime Minister's arrival causes quite a stir. Everyone agrees that Clarissa Dalloway is a remarkable hostess.

Only Peter Walsh is unhappy. An overwhelming sense of age comes over him when he meets Sally Seton, now Lady Rossetter and the mother of five sons. The once vivacious, iconoclastic Sally has become selfish and class-conscious. She still despises Clarissa for marrying the socially acceptable but unromantic Richard Dalloway. Peter, who had reveled in his return to civilized London, begins to wonder if he can bear society again.

In the midst of the party, Sir William Bradshaw and his wife arrive. They are late, he explains, because one of his patients, a war veteran, has just committed suicide. Perhaps, he suggests to Richard Dalloway, Parliament ought to take up the matter of veterans suffering from delayed shell-shock.

Wealthy and self-assured, Sir William has no personal sympathy for the dead Septimus Smith; but when Clarissa hears the story, she feels a sudden sense of identification with the haunted youth although she had never known him. Her life, too, she perceives in an instant, has been a failure; she completely understands any suicide. But after most of the guests have gone, Peter Walsh comes to her and senses the excitement in her presence that he had felt long before, realizing that he is still in love with the aging but still beautiful Clarissa Dalloway.

Critical Opinion

Like Joyce's *Ulysses*, *Mrs. Dalloway* takes place in a single day and is narrated by means of the so-called "stream of consciousness" of several individual characters. The principal interior monologues are those of Clarissa Dalloway herself, sensitive, questioning, in love with life but aware of failure; and the haunted Septimus Warren Smith whom Clarissa doesn't know and never meets, except in the callous description given by Sir William Bradshaw at her party.

Of all the people in London, it is, nevertheless, to the young veteran that Mrs. Dalloway feels herself closest in spirit. In a sense both are searching for some clue to the meaning of life, something to carry them from moment to moment. Both fail in this quest. Septimus cannot communicate his feeling of guilt and emptiness to his sympathetic but foreign wife; Mrs. Dalloway cannot convey her intense, lonely perceptions of the world around her to her good-natured, practical husband.

Aligned against these two lonely people who never meet are the crass, deformed spirits of Sir William Bradshaw and

Doris Kilman. Although they, too, never meet, they are soul-destroyers for Septimus and Mrs. Dalloway. Both are egoists who seek to impose their wills on others: Sir William on his unfortunate patients and Miss Kilman on the naïve, adolescent Elizabeth Dalloway.

Various technical devices of great brilliance and ingenuity tie together the monologues and destinies of the different characters. The chimes of Big Ben tolling each hour of the day, for instance, are heard by all—each in his isolation. (Virginia Woolf's original title for the book was *The Hours.*) The various characters stop to look at the royal limousine and at the skywriting plane, and these symbolic events also help tie them together. At one point Peter Walsh sees a little girl run crying to Lucrezia Smith; he doesn't know who Lucrezia is, but he can sense her suffering. These devices are not merely mechanical. They serve to stress a major theme of the novel: the paradox that, although we seem utterly alone, a common destiny binds us together. The best people are those who are most keenly aware of their links with the rest of humanity, however much suffering this awareness may entail. The only "villains" in life are the egoists who, like Sir William Bradshaw, are oblivious and think themselves superior to their fellow men.

The Author

Virginia Woolf was born in London in 1882, the daughter of the celebrated Sir Leslie Stephen, a scholar and critic who edited the *Cornhill Magazine* and the vast *Dictionary of National Biography*. The American poet James Russell Lowell was her godfather. In her father's home she knew Hardy, Ruskin, Stevenson, and Meredith.

A frail, shy girl, Virginia educated herself in her father's massive library. In 1912 she married Leonard Woolf, a brilliant journalist who had just returned from Ceylon after seven years in the civil service. Five years later, the Woolfs, who were part of the artistic coterie of Bloomsbury, set up their own hand printing press dedicated to publishing in beautiful format the works of promising, unknown writers. This later became one of the most important of English publishing companies, introducing Freud, among other luminaries, to the English reader.

Mrs. Woolf's own career began in 1915 with *The Voyage Out,* a novel considerably influenced by her friend E. M. Forster. This was followed in 1919 by *Night and Day* and in 1922 by *Jacob's Room,* her first really characteristic novel.

The 1920's were her most productive years. *Mrs. Dalloway* (1925), *To the Lighthouse* (1927), and the strange, esoteric fantasy *Orlando* (1928) brought her fame and prestige among sophisticated readers. Her later novel *The Waves* (1931), her most experimental work, was followed by the more traditional *The Years* (1937), a novel about an English middle-class family somewhat in the tradition of Galsworthy.

Mrs. Woolf was also an ardent feminist, as *A Room of One's Own* (1929) and *Three Guineas* (1938) demonstrate. A prolific and sensitive critic, she contributed frequently to the *Times Literary Supplement.* Some of her best literary criticism appeared in *The Common Reader* (1925). She conceived of herself as a spokesman for her generation and was outspoken in her derision of such Edwardian forebears as Bennett, Galsworthy, and Wells.

Always sensitive and high-strung, Mrs. Woolf suffered a severe nervous breakdown in her youth. When World War II came, her nerves snapped again. Fearing a second breakdown and unable to accept the carnage of another war, Virginia Woolf drowned herself in a river near her country home in Sussex on March 28, 1941.

By the Same Author

To the Lighthouse: One of Mrs. Woolf's most psychologically and technically complex novels, *To the Lighthouse* tells of the Ramsay family, who spend their summers on a remote island in the Hebrides. The novel is divided into three parts. The first and longest is a detailed account of the happenings of a single summer; the second is a highly impressionistic rendering of the passage of time, during which Mrs. Ramsay dies; and the third is the story of a meeting years later of the principal characters. The lighthouse is the symbolic point about which the novel revolves. At the beginning, young James Ramsay longs to go there on an expedition but is frustrated by his egocentric father, who (like Sir Leslie Stephen) is a famous scholar. By the end of the book young James, now more compassionate and understanding of his father, finally makes the passage across the choppy water to the lighthouse, and symbolically achieves maturity through his understanding of his oedipal relationship with his parents.

Orlando: Orlando is at once one of the most baffling and one of the most delightful of Mrs. Woolf's novels. Based on the family heritage of her friend, Vita Sackville-West, *Orlando* is the fantastic tale of a sixteen-year-old Elizabethan boy who lives through the centuries, is transformed into a girl during the Victorian period, and finally, as a woman of thirty-six, glimpses a plane in the sky in 1928. Essentially, the tale of *Orlando* is an imaginative chronicle of English literary and social history filtered through the sensibilities of a poetic youth. The change in sex, for instance, symbolically represents the effeminate character of Victorian literature as opposed to the rugged masculinity of the seventeenth and eighteenth centuries. *Orlando* is a unique work—part novel, part poetic fantasy, part astute literary criticism.

Point Counter Point

by

ALDOUS HUXLEY (1894–1963)

Main Characters

Philip Quarles—A coldly intellectual "novelist of ideas."

Elinor Quarles—Philip's dissatisfied wife.

Little Phil—The Quarles' artistically precocious son.

John Bidlake—Elinor's father, a great but selfish painter, a cantankerous and lascivious man.

Walter Bidlake—Elinor's brother, the weakly romantic staff member of a pretentious magazine, *The Literary World*.

Marjorie Carling—Walter's self-pitying mistress.

Lucy Tantamount—Walter Bidlake's beautiful and amoral mistress.

Mark Rampion—Artist and writer, he sees himself as the natural man unfettered by convention.

Denis Burlap—The sanctimonious, lecherous editor of *The Literary World*.

Beatrice Gilray—A rich, repressed woman in love with Burlap.

Maurice Spandrell—A melodramatic cynic and wastrel who has never forgiven his mother for her second marriage.

Illidge—An ugly Communist biologist who aids Lucy's father in his research.

Everard Webley—The leader of a neo-fascist movement, the Brotherhood of British Freemen.

The Story

Walter Bidlake, son of the great old painter John Bidlake by his third marriage, is bored and unhappy with his pregnant mistress, Marjorie Carling. Walter stole Marjorie from her religious fanatic husband, but now, disillusioned with her self-pitying pseudo-culture, he has fallen madly in love with Lucy Tantamount, a rich, beautiful nymphomaniac. Despite Marjorie's pleadings, Walter leaves her to go to a party at Tantamount House.

There he meets his father, who despises him as a weakling, and his pious, penny-pinching employer, Denis Burlap, editor of *The Literary World*. Lucy's father, an absent-minded scientist, makes a brief and ludicrous appearance with his assistant, Illidge, while the guests are listening to Bach's *B Minor Suite for Flute and Strings*.

Bored by the pretentious party conversation, Walter pries Lucy away from the other guests and spirits her off to Sbisa's, a fashionable Soho restaurant where the intellectuals and bohemians congregate nightly. Walter wants desperately to have Lucy for himself, but she flirtatiously insists on staying at Sbisa's with the group which includes the unhappy cynic Spandrell and some worthless hangers-on in the world of art. Miserable, Walter goes home to Marjorie who nags him about giving up Lucy and trying to get a raise in salary from Burlap.

Meanwhile Walter's sister, Elinor, is in India with her husband, Philip Quarles. Their little son, Phil, is staying in England with his grandmother and a nurse, Miss Fulkes. The Quarleses are preparing to leave India. Elinor once again tries to get her husband to pay her some attention, but he is engrossed with a notebook he is keeping in preparation for writing a novel very much like *Point Counter Point*.

Although Walter fails to get a raise from Burlap who is more interested in seducing the rich Beatrice Gilray than in being honest with his employees, he does make Lucy his mistress. Their affair is short-lived. Lucy goes off to Paris in search of more piquant amorous adventures, leaving Walter with the ever-whining Marjorie.

Philip and Elinor Quarles return to England to find their son a precocious, artistically gifted young boy. He evidently takes after his maternal grandfather, John Bidlake. The return home is marred, however, because Philip's father, Sidney Quarles (a pompous, stuffy failure who has been pretending to work on a giant history of democracy), has really been using his visits to the British Museum as a cover for an affair with a cheap little cockney girl named Gladys. One day Gladys appears at the Quarles estate and announces that she is pregnant. Philip is given the unpleasant task of placating her since his father has retreated from his responsibility into a morass of self-pity. Philip, who cannot bear any emotional contact with other people, least of all his social inferiors, delegates the problem to his lawyer.

On her return to England, Elinor's life is complicated, too. Despairing of ever getting her husband interested in her, she begins to see Everard Webley, the magnetic, egocentric leader of the Brotherhood of British Freemen, a neo-fascistic organization devoted to suppressing the working class. In the past, Elinor has always rejected Webley's advances. Now she finds herself more and more fascinated by this dynamic, aggressive man of power and action, the complete opposite of her abstracted, intellectual husband.

The only people in the London literary and social set who seem happy are Mark and Mary Rampion. Mark was a talented lower-class boy when he fell in love with the aristocratic Mary. Their marriage has been a success, despite all predictions, and Mark has become a well-known painter and writer. Contemptuous of the superficiality of London life, Rampion believes in going back to nature. He believes real civilization will come when the instincts are given equal rein with the mind. He continually baits Burlap who conceals his lechery behind high spiritual talk. Burlap, indeed, is writing a popular book on St. Francis while endeavoring to seduce the skittish, repressed Beatrice.

A friend of Mark Rampion's, Maurice Spandrell, is perhaps the most desperately unhappy frequenter of Sbisa's restaurant. Plunged into melodramatic adolescent despair when his doting mother married a gruff, insensitive military man, Spandrell is totally cynical and nihilistic. Sponging off his mother, he lives in squalor, does nothing, and delights only in puncturing his friends' illusions and in subjecting innocent working girls to obscene rites.

One evening Elinor is preparing for a tryst with Everard Webley at her London flat. She receives a telegram telling her that little Phil is sick, and rushes back to the country, asking Spandrell to phone Webley that their appointment is off. Spandrell instead calls Illidge, a poor, unprepossessing biologist, a Communist who has been a bitter foe of Webley ever since he was roughed up by some of Webley's green-uniformed followers.

When Webley arrives at Elinor's flat, he is bludgeoned to death by Spandrell and Illidge, who then hide the body in the trunk of Webley's car and park it in a busy section of London. Elinor, meanwhile, on returning home, is shocked to find that little Phil is suffering horribly from meningitis. Eventually she is joined in her bedside vigil by her husband who resents having been called away from his intellectual society in London. Also staying with the Quarleses is old John Bidlake. Suffering from cancer, the painter has come home to die, though he has seen his wife, Elinor's mother, only intermittently through the years. Old Bidlake superstitiously pins his hopes for his own health on his grandson's recovery.

After days and nights of agony, little Phil dies. His guilt-ridden parents decide to travel abroad again. The news that Webley had been killed on his way to meet her, fills Elinor with more guilt and remorse. Her brother Walter is also unhappy. After inviting him to meet her in Madrid, Lucy has written a cruel letter from Paris informing him that she will stay there with her muscular Italian lover. She vividly describes their lovemaking to the wretched Walter who finally goes with Marjorie to Philip's mother's house where the elder Mrs. Quarles preaches religious resignation to Marjorie.

The police have been unable to solve Webley's murder. But one day Spandrell, disgusted with life, writes an anonymous letter to Webley's organization, informing them that the murderer of their leader can be found the following afternoon at his address. Then he buys a phonograph and a recording of Beethoven's *A Minor String Quartet*, which he insists on playing for the Rampions as a proof of the existence

of God. Mark Rampion is unimpressed by the spiritual music.
While they are listening, there is a knock on the door. Span-
drell answers it and is mowed down by the guns of the
British Freemen.

Spandrell's death is ironically counterbalanced by Burlap's
ultimate success in seducing Beatrice. The editor's joy reaches
its apex as he and his rich mistress take their bath together
like little children.

Critical Opinion

"Novel of ideas," Philip Quarles writes in his notebook. "The
character of each personage must be implied, as far as possible, in the ideas of which he is the mouthpiece. . . . The
great defect of the novel of ideas is that it's a made-up affair. . . . Living with monsters becomes rather tiresome in the
long run."

Like Gide's *The Counterfeiters, Point Counter Point* is a
kaleidoscopic novel much like the one Philip is thinking of
writing. And like *The Counterfeiters,* Huxley's work is constructed as a novel within a novel. In fact, it is a novel about
a novelist writing a novel about a novelist—as involuted as
a series of Chinese boxes. Huxley moves rapidly from one set
of characters to another, all of whose lives at some point
impinge on each other. And in the process, he applies the
contrapuntal techniques of music, especially the theme and
variations form, to fiction. The theme is sexual desire and
unfulfillment. The variations are played by the different characters.

Thus Walter loves Lucy hopelessly, just as Marjorie loves
him hopelessly. Elinor loves her husband but is willing to be
seduced by Webley who really loves only his own power.
Spandrell's love for his mother has soured into general hatred
of women, political nihilism, and self-destructiveness. Burlap
tries to conceal his lust with piety; Lucy's father has sub-
limated sex into science; and old John Bidlake is openly
promiscuous but cannot face death. Only Mark Rampion,
whose character and ideas are based on those of Huxley's
friend D. H. Lawrence, gives sex its proper place in life.

Speaking through the characters as they interact with each

other, Huxley gives the reader a panoramic view of the ideas and mores of the London sophisticates in the years just following World War I. Rootless and overcivilized, their lives consist of a series of usually sordid or ludicrous erotic adventures which generally end unhappily.

For all its nihilistic wit, erudition, and satiric puncturing of society's hypocrisies and superficialities, *Point Counter Point* attains a genuine emotional power rare in satire. Although most of the characters are indeed the "monsters" Philip Quarles predicted they would have to be, they are fascinating monsters. The play of wit and ideas in this immensely learned novel is constantly beguiling to the alert, sophisticated reader.

Brave New World

by

ALDOUS HUXLEY

Main Characters

Bernard Marx—A highly intelligent misfit in the Brave New World, shy with girls and bullied by his fellow workers.

Lenina Crowne—Promiscuous and "pneumatic" worker in the London Hatchery and Conditioning Center.

Fanny Crowne—Not related to Lenina, but a friend and confidante.

Henry Foster—An enthusiastic scientist working in the Hatchery.

The Director—A pompous man of power in the Brave New World.

Mustapha Mond—Urbane and sophisticated, a former physicist who is now one of the ten World Controllers.

John—A Shakespeare-quoting "savage" discovered on a New Mexico reservation.

Linda—John's vulgar mother.

Popé—Linda's Indian lover.

Helmholtz Watson—A poet friend of Bernard's and John's.

The Story

Proudly the pompous Director of the Central London Hatchery and Conditioning Center is showing the plant to a group of avid young students. The year is 632 After Ford, for time in the Brave New World is measured from the epoch-making discovery of the Model T Ford and mass-production assembly methods. In the hatchery, people are being mass-produced by artificial insemination and chemically conditioned to fit into the rigidly ordered hierarchy that society has become.

The Director explains that if society is to achieve its goals—Community, Identity, and Stability—there is no room for individual differences. From the fetal stage on, people are to take their predestined places in a society that ranges from Alpha Plus, the highly intelligent leaders, to Epsilon Minus Morons, the ill-shaped, ape-like goons who do the dirty work.

One of the great inventions that has made this ultra-scientific planning possible, the Director points out, is the Bokanovsky Process by means of which up to ninety-six identical twins can be produced from a single fertilized egg, thus ensuring maximum conformity. As the students assiduously take notes, the Director, now joined by his eager protegé, Henry Foster, and by one of the ten all-powerful World Controllers, the brilliant Mustapha Mond, takes them on a tour of the Conditioning Center. Here, from earliest infancy, babies are taught to keep their places in society and to repress their individualistic instincts.

Mustapha Mond lectures the students on the advantages of a totally controlled society in which such individual passions as love have given way to communal spirit and casual promiscuity. The dirtiest words in the Brave New World are "mother" and "father" because, Mond explains, in the bad old days before artificial insemination and conditioned, communal childhood, there was actually intense, private love between individuals, which kept society in a chaotic state. Now that everything is planned and ordered, he boasts, people are much happier.

One person who is not happier is Bernard Marx, a brilliant but intensely shy and misanthropic scientist. The popular theory is that too much alcohol was accidentally put into Bernard's blood-surrogate when he was a fetus. So instead of being as handsome, outgoing, and casually sensual as all the other Alphas, Bernard is morose, introverted, and dwarf-like. Because he is so peculiar, he attracts the attention of Lenina Crowne, a superficial, "pneumatically" fleshy girl who has been having an affair with Mr. Foster, one of the scientists working in the hatchery. Lenina's chum, Fanny, cautions her that remaining faithful to one man is frowned upon. Promiscuity is the order of the day in the Brave New World.

Since he occupies a high position in the intellectual ranks, Bernard has access to one of the few reservations left in the world where people are allowed to live as savages, untouched by the hypercivilization of Europe. His offer to take Lenina to New Mexico on a weekend visit to such a reservation intrigues her. Off they go to Malpais, a forbidding mesa in the desert where the Indians live in the squalid chaos they have always known.

At first, Lenina is horrified by the absence of creature comforts. There are no feelies (an especially titillating kind of movie), no cleanliness, and no great consumption of products, as in England. When a garment develops holes, it is mended instead of thrown away. Worst of all, she has forgotten her supply of soma, the universally popular tranquilizer that has taken the place of alcohol and drugs.

Watching the Indians do a wild and exotic rain dance, Bernard and Lenina meet a young man named John who speaks beautiful but rather stilted English and is always quoting Shakespeare. John is the son of Linda, a blowzy, middle-aged woman, brought to New Mexico years before by the Director of Hatcheries. As a result of a momentary lapse in contraception she bore his son. Deserted by the Director, Linda was adopted by the reservation where she took a succession of lovers, including Popé, a wild-eyed, passionate Indian keenly resented by her son.

John's position on the reservation is ambiguous. Born to white, highly civilized parents, he has been brought up part a savage, part an intelligent, if self-taught, being. He immediately falls in love with Lenina, but because of his puritanical, "savage" morality, he fails to do anything about it. Bernard, whose job is always in jeopardy because the Director dislikes him, sees in John a perfect opportunity to get even with his boss and at the same time to conduct a fascinat-

ing experiment. He gets permission from Mustapha Mond
to bring John and Linda back to England with him.

There the Director is jeered at by his students when they
learn that he was actually at one time a father. About to
exile Bernard to Iceland, the Director himself is exiled instead.

The Savage, as John is called, becomes a great social success. All the jaded sophisticates of London want to meet him
and are even willing to put up with Bernard in order to do so.
Lenina, too, finds herself greatly attracted to this natural
young man and does her best to seduce him. But although he
lusts after her, John sternly rejects her because she is representative of the loose morality of civilization. Linda, hardly
a social asset in London, is kept happy in seclusion on over-
doses of soma.

John is appalled by the hedonism of civilized society and
yearns to return to the stricter, more meaningful morality of
the primitive life. One day, as Bernard is about to show him
off to some dignitaries, including the Arch-Community-Song-
ster of Canterbury (a great religious leader in this materialistic world), John refuses point-blank. Bernard is again in disgrace.

A sudden phone call summons John to the hospital where
his mother is dying of an overdose of soma. There he is
disgusted to see a group of children cavorting about the beds
of the dying in order to be conditioned against the fear of
death. Guilt-ridden because of his mother's death, John goes
berserk and tries to destroy the soma rations that are being
doled out to the hospital workers. He harangues the incensed
Deltas, trying to get them to see how reliance on soma is
making them less than human. They mob him and nearly kill
him before a police squad arrives and quells the riot with
water pistols that shoot tranquilizers.

Bernard, John, and a frustrated poet friend, Helmholtz
Watson, are all arrested after the melee and brought before
Mustapha Mond. The urbane World Controller exiles Bernard
and Helmholtz to the Falkland Islands and then settles down
to a long philosophical argument with John. Mond explains
that the Brave New World has no room for art (it prefers
feelies to Shakespeare), science (it fosters gadgetry, not
abstract speculative science), or religion because these are
disruptive forces that require social instability and occasional

misery in order to thrive. No one who was completely happy or well-adjusted could have written *Othello*, Mond contends, or could undergo religious martyrdom. Since happiness is equated with sensual pleasure, and since every desire must be requited at the moment of its inception, the Brave New World has no room for the visionaries, cranks, and egoists who were the great culture heroes of the past.

Eloquent as Mond is, the Savage remains unconvinced. He still feels that Shakespeare, suffering, motherhood, and God are important values, and he decides to become a hermit in a lighthouse on the coast of Surrey. There he goes, determined to be self-sufficient and independent of the gadgets and creature comforts for which everyone else exists.

He fashions his own bows and arrows for hunting, plants a garden, and occasionally whips himself when he thinks of his lust for Lenina. But soon word of John's eccentric behavior gets around, and a sensation-seeking mob descends on him in helicopters. Reporters come to interview him. John kicks them out. But eventually the mob (which now includes Lenina) becomes too much for him. They want to make his whippings a mere spectacle. Enraged, John applies the whip to Lenina instead, killing her in his furious passion.

When the mob comes looking for him the next day, they find he has hanged himself in the lighthouse, unable to bear the burden of human emotions in the Brave New World.

Critical Opinion

"O brave new world that has such people in it!" exclaims Miranda on the enchanted island that is the world of Shakespeare's *The Tempest*. With characteristic cynicism, Aldous Huxley takes her words for the title of a novel that describes a future that is anything but brave. Unable to face realistically such facts of life as pain, grief, and death, protected against anything disagreeable by the ever-present soma, living for the sensation of the moment, the people of Huxley's brave new world are a grotesque projection of "civilized" life in the 1920's.

Like all utopian books from Plato's *Republic* to Orwell's *1984*, *Brave New World* merely projects into the future the tendencies of the present. Those which fascinated and repelled Huxley most were scientific gadgetry (hence Henry Ford is the God of his society); promiscuous sensuality divorced from any concept of love, sacrifice, or honor; and an increasing antiseptic sterility (exemplified by the proudly displayed motto of one famous contemporary chain of snack bars, "Human hands never touch our food").

While utopias from Plato to Sir Thomas More tended to project an idealized vision of what society could be like if human reason were employed to its utmost, more recent utopias, of which *Brave New World* has been the most influential, are a nightmare vision of the future. In Huxley's projection, civilization has been drained of love, vitality, and irrational excess. Everything is machine-made, mass-produced, and sterile. But where people should be seeking happiness through stability, they find themselves hedonistically searching for one superficial pleasure after another, immersing themselves in Community Sings (which have replaced religious services), feelies (hypersensual movies), and heavy doses of soma.

Into this twilight world Huxley injects two malcontents: Bernard Marx, who is unable to get along with his somatized fellow human beings, and the Savage, victim of a civilized heredity at war with a primitive environment. By exiling Bernard and driving the Savage to murder and suicide, Huxley seems to be saying, as H. G. Wells did in *The Time Machine*, that the world will someday be divided sharply between the ultra-civilized and the ultra-primitive. It will be impossible for an individual caught between these extremes to find a sane, satisfactory life. In *Brave New World*, neither the sterile, loveless world of Europe nor the squalid, bestial life of the Indians in New Mexico offers a satisfactory alternative for man.

The Author

Aldous Huxley was born in Surrey on July 26, 1894, into one of the most distinguished families in English intellectual life. His grandfather was Thomas Henry Huxley, an important disciple of Darwin and popularizer of science in Victorian England. His great-uncle was Matthew Arnold, one of the finest Victorian poets and essayists, and his brother, Sir Julian

Huxley, is a distinguished biologist and writer on scientific subjects.

It seemed destined that the lanky, avidly curious youth should make a name for himself in science or letters or both. That he did so was a triumph, however, over at least one great obstacle. When Huxley was seventeen and embarking on a study of medicine, he fell victim to an inflammation of the cornea that nearly blinded him. After two years of treatment, Huxley was able to read again, using a magnifying glass. After his education at Oxford, in 1919, he joined the staff of the *Athenaeum*, a London literary magazine. Although he regretted not having a scientific training (it was impossible for him to look through a microscope), he once ironically said that the affliction had fortunately prevented him "from becoming a complete public-school English gentleman."

Huxley's extraordinarily prolific career as a novelist, essayist, and philosopher began with the novels *Crome Yellow* (1921) and *Antic Hay* (1923). Both were literary sensations. The reading public was immediately caught by their irreverent wit, wild inventiveness, and scorching satire on the mores of the "Bright Young Things" who flitted about Mayfair society in the 1920's. *Point Counter Point*, published in 1928, reveals Huxley at his best as a mordant observer of the social scene and as a novelist of ideas. With *Brave New World* (1932) and *Eyeless in Gaza* (1936) Huxley's writing began to lose its satiric flash and became more serious, verging on mysticism. When he moved to California in 1937, his interests turned to philosophy, history, and mystical experiences. His later novels suffered as a result.

A friend once described Huxley as looking "like a willow that swayed and bent, not ungracefully, in the middle." Over six feet tall and very thin, Huxley's gentleness surprised people who expected only bitter sarcasm from the author of *Point Counter Point*. Later in his life, as a result of rigorous exercises described in *The Art of Seeing* (1942), Huxley regained some measure of his eyesight. He became interested in such Indian hallucinogens as peyote and mescalin which he had earlier described in *Brave New World*. He wrote a controversial book on his visionary experiences with these drugs, *The Doors of Perception*.

Married twice (his first wife died in 1955), Huxley died of cancer in Hollywood on the day of President Kennedy's assassination, November 22, 1963. Although he had often been mentioned for the Nobel prize, he never received it, perhaps because of the vitriolic nihilism of his early novels.

By the Same Author

Crome Yellow: For his first novel Huxley resorted to the technique (used by Thomas Love Peacock and Norman Douglas) of gathering a group of eccentrics in a country house and letting them act and react upon one another. A shy young poet named Denis (who resembles his namesake in *South Wind* and Bernard Marx in *Brave New World*) comes to Crome, the country house of the Wimbushes. There Denis meets Mr. Scrogan, a diabolical rationalist who tries to rid him of his romantic preconceptions; Ivor Lombard, who paints ghosts; and Anne Wimbush, with whom he falls in love. In a series of brilliantly witty conversational scenes Huxley shows how Denis tortures himself over his inability to conquer Anne, makes a complete ass of himself, and finally leaves Crome a sadder but wiser poet.

Antic Hay: Fuller and more original than his first novel, *Antic Hay* is a corrosive satire of literary, artistic, and social poseurs in London in the 1920's. The hero is a young dilettante named Theodore Gumbril who makes his unsure-footed way through London's bohemia, meeting such odd figures as Shearwater, an absent-minded scientist, and Casimir Lypiatt, a self-styled genius. A less richly developed novel than *Point Counter Point, Antic Hay* is nevertheless uproariously funny; it set the style for such later social satirists as Evelyn Waugh and Anthony Powell. Huxley expresses his urbanely nihilistic point of view as he dissects and caustically discards the intellectual frauds around him.

Decline and Fall

by

EVELYN WAUGH (1903–)

Main Characters

Paul Pennyfeather—A serious-minded, unassuming young Oxford divinity student with a talent for getting into trouble.

Sir Alastair Digby-Vane-Trumpington—A pleasure-loving young aristocrat at Oxford, member in good standing of the exclusive Bollinger Club.

Arthur Potts—Paul's high-minded friend doing confidential work for the League of Nations.

Dr. Augustus Fagan—The harried headmaster of the dreadful Llanabba School in Wales.

Peter Beste-Chetwynde—The one civilized boy at Llanabba, who soon becomes Paul's friend.

Margot Beste-Chetwynde—Peter's beautiful, unconventional mother, a luminary in Mayfair society.

Captain Grimes—A teacher at Llanabba who depends on his being a public-school man to get him out of his frequent scrapes with society and the law.

Mr. Prendergast—Another member of the Llanabba staff, a clergyman until he began to doubt.

Solomon Philbrick—A confidence man and swindler temporarily employed as butler at Llanabba Castle.

Sir Wilfred Lucas-Dockery—Governor of Blackstone Gaol and a crackpot about prison reform.

Sir Humphrey Maltravers—A political bigwig who later becomes the influential Lord Metroland.

Otto Silenus—The mad, insomniac architect responsible for Margot Beste-Chetwynde's hideous mansion, King's Thursday.

The Story

Paul Pennyfeather, a shy young divinity student at Scone College, Oxford, is minding his own business one evening when he is attacked by members of the Bollinger Club, a group of aristocratic students celebrating their annual dinner by getting roaring drunk and going berserk. Before he knows what has happened, Paul has been stripped of his trousers and has to make his way across campus in his shorts. The next day the Bollinger Club is fined £230 (which hardly puts a dent in their limitless funds), but Paul is dismissed for unseemly conduct.

Paul's guardian informs him that under the provisions of his father's will the legacy can be withheld from him if he behaves badly. Not caring to hear Paul's side of the story, his guardian cuts off his allowance, using the money to provide a husband for his daughter.

Paul must look for a job, and so he consults with Mr. Levy of Church and Gargoyle, a sleazy teacher employment agency, to help him to find a teaching post. The only school low enough to accept someone sent down from Oxford for indecent behavior, Mr. Levy tells Paul, is Llanabba School in the depths of Wales. Dr. Fagan, its headmaster, hires Paul at slave wages, telling him he should feel honored to teach at an institution boasting such aristocratic students as little Lord Tangent, son of the Earl of Circumference. Dr. Fagan is a consummate snob and hypocrite who refuses to acknowledge that the school he is running is tenth-rate at best and that his daughters, Flossie and Diana, are vulgar, penny-pinching young shrews out to catch any husband they can.

At Llanabba, Paul meets the other masters—a sorry lot. One of them, Mr. Prendergast, is terrified of the tough, semi-literate students. Mr. Prendergast had been a clergyman until he realized that he had serious doubts about his religion. Instead of concealing his doubts, he gave up his post and came to Llanabba where he now lives a penurious, miserable existence. Paul's other colleague, Captain Grimes, is a raffish man who is constantly getting into trouble but always manages to escape his just punishment because he went to a good public school. Grimes has become engaged to Flossie Fagan as insurance against losing his job at the Llanabba School. He loathes his job.

Assigned to the fifth form, Paul finds his students a noisy, squabbling group of little monsters. The first day he teaches, they try to unnerve him by all claiming to be named Tangent. Paul outwits them, however. He offers a half crown prize to whichever student can write the longest essay, regardless of merit. This keeps them all busy writing and leaves Paul in peace. He becomes the envy of Mr. Prendergast who is constantly being taunted by his students for wearing a wig.

The only decent pupil Paul has is Peter Beste-Chetwynde, a precociously alcoholic young aristocrat. Paul finds himself assigned to teach young Peter the organ, which Paul doesn't know how to play and which Peter doesn't want to learn. Instead they spend the practice hour gossiping about the school and its peculiar inhabitants.

One day Paul gets a letter from his old school friend Arthur Potts, telling him that Sir Alastair Digby-Vane-Trumpington, a member of the Bollinger Club, has offered to send Paul £20 as remuneration for his being thrown out of Scone College. Paul debates with himself whether it would be right to accept this money, but the problem is settled for him by Captain Grimes who telegraphs an acceptance in Paul's name. The hard-pressed masters use the money for a rare festive treat.

Dr. Fagan decides to hold a lawn party and sports competition in order to get some more money out of the few aristocratic parents who have sent their children to his school. The party, like everything else at Llanabba, is a ghastly failure. First, Philbrick, the butler, strenuously objects to the extra duties involved. In confidence he tells Paul that actually he is a well-known underworld figure who came to Llanabba to kidnap little Lord Tangent but under the benign influence of Diana Fagan he has reformed. He tells totally different and conflicting stories to Mr. Prendergast and Captain Grimes. Lady Circumference, Lord Tangent's mother, manages to insult everybody to whom she hands out prizes. The sports meets are either rigged or mismanaged. Mr. Prendergast, who is supposed to signal the start of races by firing a pistol, accidentally shoots Lord Tangent in the heel. Lady Circumference is beside herself with rage. The boy subsequently dies of his wound.

But the biggest sensation is caused by the arrival of Peter's mother, Margot Beste-Chetwynde, accompanied by a Negro gigolo whom she has adopted. Despite her bizarre antics, Margot fascinates Paul who promptly falls in love with her. He is hired by her to tutor Peter during vacation, and he goes to her country house, King's Thursday.

This extraordinary mansion was once one of the stately homes of England, but Margot had hired Otto Silenus, an eccentric architect, to rebuild it into a hideously modernistic affair of glass, concrete, and aluminum. Silenus cannot stand people. He lies awake nights thinking up designs for factories to house his real love—machinery.

Paul learns that he has a rival for Margot's hand in Sir Humphrey Maltravers, Minister of Transport and a political power. But Margot, seeing that her son genuinely likes Paul, tells him she will marry him, impoverished though he is. She insists that he not return to Llanabba after vacation. Instead, Paul becomes involved in Margot's mysterious business activities, which seem to be concerned with supplying show girls to South American night clubs. Paul's friend, Arthur Potts, now working for the League of Nations, also shows an interest in Margot's affairs.

Shortly before he is to be married to Margot, Paul is sent by his fiancée to Marseilles to expedite the emigration of some girls to South America. He unwittingly bribes some officials and returns to England successful. On the morning he is to marry Margot, he is drinking champagne with Alastair Trumpington when a Scotland Yard inspector breaks in on the party and arrests him. Paul learns that in all innocence he has been helping Margot Beste-Chetwynde conduct a thriving white-slave trade.

Abandoned by Margot at his trial, Paul finds the chief witness against him is Potts who has been investigating the operation for the League of Nations. Paul is convicted and sentenced to seven years in prison. He is taken to Blackstone Gaol, where he is reunited with Philbrick, a fellow prisoner, and Mr. Prendergast, the prison chaplain. Prendergast is murdered by a religious fanatic prisoner because the governor of the prison, Sir Wilfred Lucas-Dockery, is too interested in abstract, nonsensical prison reform to notice what is actually going on in his own prison.

After the murder, Paul is transferred to Egdon Heath Penal Settlement where he finds Captain Grimes a fellow prisoner. Grimes had married Flossie Fagan and, not being able to stand it, had escaped; he had presumably drowned. Once again he disappears—slipping away from a work gang into the fog—and is never seen or heard from thereafter.

Paul is visited by Margot who informs him that she is about to marry his former rival, Sir Humphrey Maltravers, now advanced to the rank of Home Secretary and to the position of Lord Metroland. However, taking pity on Paul, Margot arranges for his escape from prison. With Lord Metroland's connivance, Paul is removed to a nursing home for a fake appendicitis operation. The home is run by Dr. Fagan who has given up his career in education for one in medicine. A drunken doctor is persuaded to sign a death warrant stating that Paul died under the knife, and Paul is spirited off in a yacht to Margot's home in Corfu where he takes a much-needed rest.

After a few months, Paul unobtrusively slips back into England, and, sporting a moustache, re-enters Scone College as a sadder and wiser divinity student.

Critical Opinion

Although Waugh has claimed that he is not a genuine satirist because satire implies a fixed set of social values which he has not found in his world, his novels are most frequently discussed as satires of particularly mordant and vitriolic wit. They are not, indeed, about a stable society but about one which is crumbling before Waugh's amused, if horrified, eyes.

Decline and Fall is not merely a comedy about the decline and fall of Paul Pennyfeather's fortunes. It chronicles, by strong implication, the destruction of traditional English values in the chaotic postwar world. Thus Margot's stately Tudor home, King's Thursday, has been "modernized" into a dwelling more suitable for machines than for civilized human beings. Captain Grimes has deliberately exploited the

English tradition of the "old school tie" for criminal ends. The young aristocrats in the novel are either callous dilettantes like Alastair Trumpington or nice boys like Peter Beste-Chetwynde given to drink too early in life. The social mobility that Waugh abhors is symbolized by Margot's appearance at the Llanabba *fête* accompanied by a Negro gigolo.

Decline and Fall is not a traditional satire. Such satire implies the author's belief in the possibility of some kind of improvement in conditions as he sees them. No such implication can be found in Waugh's early novels. Life is unfair to Paul Pennyfeather; the world is grotesque and chaotic, but nothing can be done about it. For all its wit, *Decline and Fall* is essentially pessimistic—a black comedy of a kind rare in English fiction. Waugh simply laughs hollowly at the curious doings of the world about him. His ingenious and outrageous incidents and examples of human depravity force us to laugh with him. In a way, *Decline and Fall* is the counterpart in fiction of T. S. Eliot's *The Waste Land*. Both are precisely observed pictures of a world bereft of traditional values, searching—not very hard or successfully—for something to replace them.

The Author

Evelyn Waugh, the man Edmund Wilson called "the only first-rate comic genius that has appeared in England since Bernard Shaw," was born in October, 1903, into a literary family. His father, Arthur Waugh, was a famous critic and publisher; his younger brother, Alec, is a popular novelist and author of travel books. Evelyn Waugh studied modern history at Hertford College, Oxford, and art at Heatherly's Art School in London.

Like Paul Pennyfeather, he was briefly a master at a private school. He then worked as a society reporter for the *Daily Express* where he acquired valuable training as an observer of the brittle Mayfair society which later furnished the material for many of his novels.

In 1929 Waugh launched his writing career in fiction with the successful *Decline and Fall*. This was followed by a brilliant series of satiric novels including *Vile Bodies* (1930), *Black Mischief* (1932), *Scoop* (1938), and *Put Out More*

Flags (1942). In 1930 Waugh was received into the Roman Catholic Church. Since then he has enthusiastically propagated its doctrines in such diverse works as *Edmund Campion* (1935), a biography of the Elizabethan Jesuit martyr; *Brideshead Revisited* (1945), a nostalgic study of English Catholic life, and *Helena* (1950), a fictionalized biography of the mother of Constantine the Great.

In World War II Waugh joined the Royal Marines, became a commando in the Middle East, parachuted into Yugoslavia on a British military mission to Marshal Tito in 1944, and was nearly killed in the crash of a transport plane. His war experiences provided the background for his most recent major work, the trilogy, *Men at Arms*.

A postwar visit to the United States produced one of Waugh's most savage satires, *The Loved One* (1948), about the gaudy funeral practices of Southern California. It anticipated by several years the recent attacks on the funeral industry. With the exception of *The Loved One*, however, Waugh's recent books have tended to be less extravagantly comic than his earlier novels. The trend toward more serious novels started with *A Handful of Dust* (1934) and reached a culmination in *Brideshead Revisited* (1945).

Married in 1937 and the father of a large family, Waugh has an almost cherubic personal manner that belies the ferocious wit of his novels. An arch-conservative in most matters from politics to dress, he is a collector of books on early English architecture and art and lives as best he can the life of an English country gentleman in an age in which that special breed is fast becoming an anomaly.

By the Same Author

Vile Bodies: In a sense a sequel to *Decline and Fall* (Lady Margot Metroland appears in both novels), *Vile Bodies* chronicles the further doings of the "bright young things" of Mayfair in the postwar world. Waugh's hapless hero in this novel is Adam Fenwick-Symes, an innocent young writer whose autobiography in manuscript is seized by customs when he returns to England, and destroyed as pornography. This loss forces Adam to all sorts of bizarre expedients to earn enough money to marry Nina Blount, the daughter of an eccentric country squire. In his adventures Adam meets Mrs. Melrose Ape, a sordid female evangelist, and such "bright young people" as Miles Malpractice and Agatha Runcible (who cracks up in a racing car and dies). Very brief episodes are juxtaposed for an even more surrealistic comic effect than any achieved in *Decline and Fall*. The mixture, as before, is one of hilarity and despair. Waugh fiddles a jazz tune as English civilization burns.

A Handful of Dust: More somber in tone than Waugh's earlier novels, *A Handful of Dust* deals with the unhappy marriage of Tony and Brenda Last. Bored with life in magnificent Hetton Abbey and unable to see why her husband Tony delights in this relic of the past, Brenda establishes herself as an enlightened modern woman by having an adulterous fling with John Beaver, a young social climber. The accidental death of her son, John, instead of bringing the parents together, merely widens the breach. Brenda sues for divorce, demanding fantastic alimony. To escape his sick world, Tony joins an expedition to the jungles of South America, but finds jungle life no more appealing than life in England. He falls into the hands of a mad trader named Todd who keeps him prisoner in his hut, demanding that Tony read to him daily from the works of Dickens.

In this novel Waugh's conservative outrage at modern vulgarity and loose morality is at its most intense. Here, the joke of the "bright young things," with their casual, amorous escapades and hedonistic selfishness, has suddenly gone sour. A return to the old values is unlikely, Waugh seems to be saying, yet people without values are merely a handful of dust.

Lost Horizon

by

JAMES HILTON (1900–1954)

Main Characters

Hugh Conway—A British consul in the East whose daring exploits have won him the nickname "Glory" Conway, brilliant, handsome, and disillusioned with Western civilization.

Charles Mallinson—Conway's hero-worshiping subordinate, totally impervious to the charm, wisdom, and mystery of the East.

Rutherford—A novelist friend to whom Conway first tells the story of Shangri-La.

Henry Barnard—Alias Chalmers Bryant, an American embezzler escaping from the law.

Roberta Brinklow—An English missionary who wants to convert everyone to Christianity.

Chang—The mysterious, highly civilized Chinese lama at Shangri-La, who tries to help Westerners adapt to the ways of the lamasery.

Father Perrault—A French Capuchin missionary who has become the High Lama of Shangri-La.

Lo-Tsen—A beautiful, musically gifted Chinese girl living at Shangri-La.

The Story

Hugh Conway had been one of the most promising and charming young men at Oxford when Rutherford, the novelist, knew him there. During the ten years in which Conway wandered from post to post as a British consul in the East, Rutherford lost track of him.

One day in a Catholic mission hospital in Chung-Kiang, Rutherford sees his old friend again. The exhausted Conway, weak and somewhat disoriented, tells him an extraordinary story:

At thirty-seven, Conway is consul in Baskul, which, in May 1931, is torn by revolution. With heroic effort, Conway manages to evacuate the white population and to destroy secret documents. Then he boards a special plane lent by an Indian maharajah and piloted by a capable English aviator named Fenner. With Conway on the plane are Charles Mallinson, his high-strung young subordinate, Henry Barnard, a talkative but suspicious American, and Miss Brinklow, an English missionary.

After about an hour in the air, Mallinson senses that the plane is not keeping on course and that the pilot is not Fenner. Conway soon realizes, too, that they are flying over peculiar terrain—the rugged mountain ranges of Tibet. They catch a glimpse of the pilot. He is Chinese!

Gradually the pilot, making an almost impossible landing, noses the plane down into a mountain valley. Natives carrying guns hurry to meet the plane and replenish its dwindling supply of fuel. The passengers assume they have been kidnapped and will be held for ransom. But as soon as the plane is refueled, it takes off again without a word of explanation from the Chinese pilot.

Hours later, the pilot makes a forced landing high on a plateau west of the Himalaya mountains. When the dazed passengers emerge from the plane into the freezing air, they discover that the pilot is seriously injured. He tells them that they can find refuge in a nearby lamasery called Shangri-La, and then he dies. The travelers are debating whether to head for the lamasery or try to get back to civilization on their own when a group of men from the lamasery approaches.

One of them, a Chinese named Chang, introduces himself in flawless English to the bewildered travelers and insists that they accompany his men to the lamasery. Despite Mallinson's misgivings about trusting any non-European, the group have no choice but to make the tortuous journey to Shangri-La. When they arrive, they find in the midst of a forbidding mountain range a pleasant and fertile tract of land, unexplored and unmapped by any Westerner. The lamasery building is centrally heated and luxuriously furnished in a style the travelers are accustomed to associate only with Western progress.

Although they are given comfortable rooms and fine food, the travelers—especially Mallinson—immediately ask Chang when they can return to India. Chang evasively replies that since Shangri-La is so isolated they will have to wait until a band of porters arrives over the mountains. This will not be for another few weeks, and so they may as well make themselves comfortable. He tells them that the lamasery is run by a High Lama whom they will not be allowed to meet. Conway suspects from Chang's manner that they have been brought deliberately to Shangri-La and will never be allowed to leave.

After some time Chang informs Conway that he will be permitted to meet the High Lama. Mallinson sees this as an opportunity for Conway to insist on their immediate passage home. Among other things, Mallinson wants the High Lama's help in turning over to the authorities the American, Henry Barnard, who has been unmasked as Chalmers Bryant, an embezzler and confidence man traveling incognito.

When Conway is ushered into his presence, the High Lama tells him the extraordinary tale of the founding of Shangri-La. In 1734 Father Perrault, a traveling French Capuchin friar in his early fifties, found sanctuary in a Buddhist lamasery. Gradually he was won over by the serene life there and stopped trying to convert the people to Christianity. His ties with his own church severed by time and distance, Father Perrault stayed on, gradually achieving a merger of the best elements of Christianity and Buddhism.

In 1789 Father Perrault thought he was dying. However, the pure air of the place combined with some miraculous drugs known to the local inhabitants preserved his life. Workmen built the present lamasery of Shangri-La where Father

Perrault lived a life of serene contemplation and scholarship with the other lamas. Occasionally a wanderer would accidentally find his way to Shangri-La, where men lived and worked in harmony, free from the conflicts and problems of the world outside. From this utopia, however, no one was ever allowed to depart. The few who tried to escape were never heard from again.

Conway learns that he and his party have been brought to Shangri-La in order to restock the lamasery. Since the High Lama feels that a new war is about to engulf civilization, he is eager to gather enough people in Shangri-La to preserve culture and to begin civilization anew. The High Lama also tells the astounded Conway that he himself is Father Perrault, now 250 years old and nearing the end of his days.

Conway is now faced with the problem of breaking the news to his fellow travelers. Weary of the conflicts of Western civilization, he is quite content to remain in Shangri-La for the rest of his life. But he knows that Mallinson wants to return to England and is counting on the porters to lead him back through the mountain passes. Conway learns, however, that Miss Brinklow is willing to remain in Shangri-La because she still hopes to convert everyone there to Christianity. Barnard, of course, does not want to return home to certain capture and imprisonment.

Conway spends his time pleasantly and profitably in the lamasery. He makes good use of the amazingly well-stocked library and he becomes friends with two musicians—Briac, who was a pupil of Chopin and can play works never published by the master, and Lo-Tsen, an exquisite Chinese girl with whom Conway falls in love. He is shocked when he learns that Lo-Tsen is actually sixty-five years old. The serene life at Shangri-La has kept her from aging. Conway withholds this information from Mallinson when he finds that Mallinson, too, has fallen in love with her.

After several more meetings, the High Lama tells Conway that death will soon overtake him and that he wants Conway to lead the lamasery when that time comes. He has faith that Conway will preserve the great culture of Shangri-La after war has destroyed the rest of the world.

One evening, after a long discussion with Father Perrault, Conway sees him slump in his chair and realizes the end has finally come. Profoundly moved, Conway goes out into the garden. Mallinson breaks in on his reflections about the future to tell him that the porters have arrived. Mallinson has lost no time in paying the porters to take Conway, Lo-Tsen, and himself away from Shangri-La, leaving Miss Brinklow and Barnard behind. Conway tries to tell Mallinson that Lo-Tsen is really an old woman, miraculously preserved by the climate of Shangri-La, who will suddenly age and die in the outside world. Conway doesn't want to leave but succumbs to Mallinson's pleas that he help them on the long, arduous journey. He realizes that he is leaving the only place on earth untouched by human fears and anxieties.

This is the last that Rutherford hears of Conway's story until he meets him in the mission hospital. A doctor tells him that Conway was brought to the hospital by an ancient Chinese woman who must have been Lo-Tsen. When last heard from, Conway has recovered and is headed once again for the high Himalayas, hoping to find the peace and serenity of Shangri-La.

Critical Opinion

It is easy to understand the appeal *Lost Horizon* had for its readers when it first appeared in the grim year of 1933. Sick of war and fearing a new one, searching for enduring values in the chaotic world of the 1920's and finding instead the bleak depression, people saw in the easy philosophy of *Lost Horizon* a fantasy fulfillment of their deepest hopes and dreams. The peaceful, tolerant, wise world of Shangri-La—alluring, if unattainable—seemed an answer to the troubled thirties.

Essentially, *Lost Horizon* is one in a long line of utopian romances. Like most utopias, Shangri-La is physically difficult to reach and therefore has escaped contamination by the self-destructive world outside. Like most utopias, too, it is a better if a duller world than the real one. But Shangri-La can make its appeal only to those who are willing to give themselves to it. Young Mallinson, for instance, can never be happy anywhere but in the struggle of the real world and is totally unready for the timeless wisdom of the lamasery. His failure is the result of his assumption that only the values of Western "civilization" count. In her Christian ardor,

Miss Brinklow, too, cannot accept the serene, humanistic religion of the lamasery. But Conway has seen enough of the "real" world to understand its limitations and to appreciate a life of peaceful contemplation of the eternal.

The Author

James Hilton, one of the most prolific producers of best sellers in the 1930's, was the quiet, reserved son of a London schoolmaster, the model for Mr. Chips. He was born on September 9, 1900, in Lancashire.

Like Hugh Conway, Hilton was a brilliant student, winning his Cambridge degree with honors in 1921. His first article was accepted by the *Manchester Guardian* when he was seventeen, and his first novel, *Catherine Herself,* was published in 1920 when he was still an undergraduate. Leaving college during the postwar slump, he struggled for ten years as a free-lance journalist and book reviewer. His big chance came when the *British Weekly* asked him to write a Christmas story in two weeks. Hilton found himself unable to think of one until one day, taking a bicycle ride, he got the idea for *Goodbye, Mr. Chips.* Always a rapid writer, he set the story down in four days. It was published in the United States in the *Atlantic Monthly* and became a best seller in 1934 when Alexander Woollcott, the American critic, praised it on his radio program.

The success of *Goodbye, Mr. Chips* led to the republication of *Lost Horizon* which had won the highly coveted Hawthornden Prize in 1933 but had not attracted much general attention. Now, however, it, too, became immensely successful, and the name Shangri-La became a household word. President Roosevelt even named his summer retreat after the utopia in the Tibetan fastness.

From 1935 on Hilton spent much of his time in Hollywood, adapting for the screen many of his own novels, including *We Are Not Alone* (1937), *Random Harvest* (1941), and *So Well Remembered* (1945), in addition to *Goodbye, Mr. Chips.*

Unlike many other authors, Hilton felt at ease in Hollywood and never chafed at the difficulties of writing for the movies. His quiet, unassuming manner endeared him to many who heard him talk on the radio. Although he never again achieved the success of *Lost Horizon* or *Goodbye, Mr. Chips,* Hilton continued to write highly popular novels. He died in Hollywood on December 20, 1954.

By the Same Author

Goodbye, Mr. Chips: This novel is a delicate tribute to Hilton's schoolmaster father. It dwells gently on the past of Mr. Chipping, beloved by generations of schoolboys at Brookfield, a minor English public school. Sitting before his fire at the age of eighty-five, Mr. Chips, as the boys have dubbed him, realizes that his outwardly uneventful life has not been wasted. Never very brilliant, he has taught Latin in an undistinguished school. But he loved and married the beautiful Katherine Bridges, who died tragically in childbirth only a few years later. He survived the war years, giving boys the courage to face a world wholly unlike Brookfield. Grown crusty and eccentric in his late years, he has nevertheless maintained a tradition of gentle humanism and decency in the old school, and this has given value to his life. Written as a Christmas story, *Goodbye, Mr. Chips* is a nostalgic, sentimental evocation of all that is good and enduring in the English tradition.

The Power and the Glory

by

GRAHAM GREENE (1904–)

Main Characters

The priest—Guilt-ridden and tormented by his weaknesses
and sinfulness, he finally comes upon the true meaning of
grace and salvation. He sometimes assumes the name of
Montez.

The lieutenant—Single-minded and determined on principle
to rid Mexico of all priests.

The chief of police—The lieutenant's boss, more concerned
with his toothache than with pursuing priests.

María—Mother of the priest's child.

Brigida—The priest's young daughter, already wise in the
ways of sin and corruption.

Father José—A priest who has knuckled under to the anti-
clerical regime and renounced his religion.

The mestizo—A crafty, half-caste police informer.

Coral Fellows—A brave, lonely young English girl living on
her father's remote banana plantation.

Mr. Lehr—A Protestant plantation owner who gives the
priest temporary sanctuary.

The Story

Under an anti-clerical, communistic government in Mexico
in the 1930's, all priests in certain provinces have been killed,

banished, or forced to abandon their vocation. One of them is Father José who has become a laughing stock by marrying a shrewish wife. The government even gives him a pension because he brings ridicule on the Catholic Church.

But news comes from the governor's office that another priest has remained in the province and is secretly administering the sacraments, hearing confessions, and saying masses. The police lieutenant, an ardent revolutionary, is determined to rid the province of its last functioning priest.

The priest, knowing he is in mortal danger, and afraid of death, tries to slip aboard a boat headed for the safe city of Vera Cruz. At the last minute, however, a little boy pleads with him to administer last rites to his dying mother. The priest goes by mule to the boy's house.

Meanwhile the lieutenant has tacked two pictures to his wall in the police station: one of the priest in earlier, happier days, and another of an American murderer who is in hiding somewhere in Mexico. Of the two, the lieutenant is more concerned with catching the priest because he believes that only when Mexico is rid of the clergy will the poor people have a chance to improve their lot. He gets permission from the corrupt chief of police to take hostages from any town in which the priest has found shelter, and, if necessary, to shoot them.

The priest, who is an alcoholic, finds temporary refuge in a remote banana warehouse run by Captain Fellows, an unhappy English exile. The captain's daughter, Coral, who tells the priest she lost her faith when she was ten, hides him against her parents' wishes and brings him beer to drink. Determined not to make trouble for the girl, the priest painfully makes his way by mule into the interior, always on guard against the Red Shirts who will kill any priest on sight.

He eventually comes back to the tiny village where his former mistress, María, lives with their daughter, Brigida. The priest had known María in only one moment of sin and desperate loneliness. Though she is completely estranged, María gives him shelter for the night. Brigida, who does not know her own father, shocks him by her savagery. Comparing her with Coral, he realizes it will not be long before she is old in the ways of sin. Before dawn he conducts a secret mass for the villagers. In the midst of the ceremony the police arrive. María pretends the priest is her husband, and Brigida identifies him as her father. Furthermore, he has changed so much from the plump, complacent young seminarian of the police photograph that he is unrecognizable, even to the lieutenant. Although the police take a hostage from the village, no one informs on the priest. He learns to his horror, however, that another hostage from his former parish of Concepcion has been shot, and he volunteers unsuccessfully to take this hostage's place. The villagers refuse and beg him to leave.

Once again he wearily mounts his mule and plods off in search of a safe province. But soon he is accosted by a wheedling, wretched mestizo (half-caste) who travels with him to the nearby village of Carmen. Although the mestizo swears he is a good Catholic, the priest knows that eventually he will betray him to the police for the seven-hundred-peso reward. The priest does not judge him, for his poverty is extreme.

Temporarily eluding the mestizo, the priest comes to a fairly large town where he desperately goes looking for wine. He buys some contraband brandy from a corrupt official, but is soon caught by the Red Shirts with the bottle in his pocket and is arrested. Alcohol, like religion, has been officially banned in the puritanically communistic state.

Thrown into a vile jail, the priest is forced to clean up the cells in order to pay his fine. Although his fellow captives know he is a priest, they will not betray him. He sees the mestizo who as an informer is a "guest" of the police. But the mestizo refuses to betray him, for fear of not collecting his full seven-hundred-peso reward since the priest is already a captive.

Brought before the lieutenant, who does not recognize him, the priest is released, and the lieutenant gives him five pesos to ease his journey.

On the road again, the priest comes across a poverty-stricken Indian woman whose child is dying of bullet wounds. The priest learns that the child was shot while being held as a hostage by the American gangster in a gun duel with the police.

He buries the child and proceeds painfully through forbidding, uninhabited country. At last a German-American Lutheran, Mr. Lehr, gives the priest sanctuary on his plantation but clearly shows his disapproval of Catholicism and of its whiskey-sodden representative. In a few days the priest has recovered and hopes to make his way to the safe territory of Las Casas.

Just as he is about to resume his journey, the mestizo finds him, bringing news that the American gangster, a Catholic, has been mortally wounded and desires last rites. Knowing it is a trap, the priest nevertheless changes his plans and goes back with the mestizo on the dangerous journey.

When they arrive at the hut where the killer is dying, the priest offers to hear his confession; but the bandit, still seething with hate, insists only that the priest take his revolver, for he knows the police are waiting just outside. When the bandit dies, the lieutenant enters the hut and places the priest under arrest. Together they make their way to the capital of the state where the priest is placed in jail to await execution.

During the tortuous journey, the lieutenant is impressed with the priest's humility and sincerity, and grants him his illicit request to receive communion from Father José before being shot. When the lieutenant goes to fetch Father José, the old man refuses to come, fearful of losing his government pension.

The priest is tried *in absentia* for treason against the state and condemned to be shot the next morning. On his last night, terrified of death and damnation, he tries to reconcile himself to his fate. He goes to his execution convinced he has been a total failure as priest and man.

However, the evening after the priest is shot, another priest slips secretly into the town and is welcomed by a boy, once cynical about the clergy, who was impressed with the stoicism of the whiskey priest. The priest's whole wretched life has not been in vain. From his sin and corruption the power and the glory of God have been mysteriously vindicated.

Critical Opinion

François Mauriac has accurately described Graham Greene's novels as being about "the utilization of sin by Grace." Like Dostoyevski, Greene sees God's grace being bestowed on the insulted and the injured, on the wretched of the world who are close to despair but who somehow keep the faith.

Thus the hero of *The Power and the Glory* is a miserable, sodden, whiskey priest, haunted by his sins of commission and omission (he fathered a child, then abandoned her to sin), and barely believing in the possibility of his redemption. As the priest makes his painful way on mule-back, accompanied by the Judas-like mestizo, the identification with Christ on his way to Calvary, which on the suface may seem blasphemous, becomes increasingly apparent.

The priest, once a callow young man, the pudgy-cheeked innocent of the photograph in the police station, becomes ennobled through suffering. The more wretched people are, the more saint-like, Greene seems to be saying; even if they are guilty of adultery, fornication, drunkenness, and blasphemy. Those who will never achieve grace are the complacently pious, like the woman the priest meets in prison who clings to her conventional, snobbish faith, unable to recognize true holiness in the suffering wretches around her.

The priest is significantly pitted against the lieutenant who in some ways is the true tragic hero of the novel. (In Greene's own words, the film version failed because the director "gave the integrity to the priest and the corruption to the lieutenant," the reverse of what Greene had intended.) The lieutenant is a kindly man and an incorruptible idealist. He truly believes that the village children, whom he loves so much, will lead a better life than he did if the clergy are destroyed. Like the priest, the lieutenant is isolated; his chief of police is corrupt and self-centered, carrying out orders that he does not understand or believe in.

The lieutenant's tragedy, then, is that he must hound to death a man as worthy as himself. Though he executes the priest, he fails to prevail over him.

Throughout the novel a boy, Luis, is seen listening cynically to his mother's reading of a sanctimonious tale. The boy is far more impressed with the lieutenant's shining revolver and holster, and it would seem that the future belongs to the secular state. However, when the priest is executed, Luis changes sides and welcomes with a reverent kiss on the hand the new fugitive priest who comes to town. The hunted whiskey priest who, for his venial weaknesses, considered himself a failure, has triumphed in death.

The Author

Graham Greene, England's foremost Catholic novelist, is (like Evelyn Waugh) a convert to the faith. He was born on October 2, 1904, in Hertfordshire where his father was headmaster of the Berkhampstead School. Educated there and at Balliol College, Oxford, Greene became a sub-editor for *The Times* of London and later film critic for the *Spectator*.

Greene was married in 1927 to Vivien Dayrell-Browning. Before the war he traveled a good deal in the United States and Mexico (where he gathered the material for *The Power and the Glory*), and when war broke out he worked with the Foreign Office on special duty in West Africa, the scene of *The Heart of the Matter*. In 1954 he covered the Indo-Chinese War for *The New Republic*, and his experiences in the East supplied the background for one of his most controversial novels, *The Quiet American* (1955).

Always a tormented man, Greene had toyed with the idea of suicide in his youth. Later he became a Communist for a brief period. A convert to Catholicism, he is one of the most distinguished Catholic laymen in the English-speaking world. In 1952 he applied for a visa to the United States to receive the Catholic Literary Award, but ran into trouble with the McCarran Act because of his early Communist affiliation. In 1954, granted a visa, he scornfully rejected it and has been a sharp critic of American policy ever since.

Admitting to two great influences on his writing, the Scottish suspense writer John Buchan (author of *The Thirty-Nine Steps*) and the French Catholic novelist François Mauriac, Greene has himself divided his prolific literary production into "entertainments" and serious novels. The entertainments, fast-moving psychological spy and suspense yarns, include *The Man Within* (1929), *The Orient Express* (1932), *This Gun for Hire* (1936), and *The Third Man* (1950), all of which have been made into successful films.

The serious novels began with *Brighton Rock* (1938). *The Power and the Glory* (first published, unsuccessfully, in the United States as *The Labyrinthine Way*), *The Heart of the Matter* (1948), and *The End of the Affair* (1951) are the finest of these.

The interesting point about this arbitrary distinction between "entertainments" and novels is that the technique and point of view are pretty much the same in both the thrillers and in the novels which seriously explore Catholic dogma. As in Francis Thompson's famous poem, "The Hound of Heaven," God pursues man relentlessly through all of Greene's fiction. Greene's fictional forte has always been a mastery of swift pacing and a depth of psychological penetration and religious meaning recalling the novels of Dostoyevski. These gifts have been lavished equally on the pure suspense stories and the richer, more serious novels.

By the Same Author

The Heart of the Matter: Like *The Power and the Glory,* this novel, set in a steaming colony in British West Africa, deals with sin and salvation, grace and damnation. The hero is Major Scobie, for fifteen years a police chief famed for his scrupulous honesty but isolated from his fellow Europeans by his alcoholism and his difficult temperament. Scobie commits adultery with a refugee girl and shares complicity in a murder. Ultimately he commits the supreme sin of suicide by faking a heart attack so that his wife can inherit his insurance. Like the priest in *The Power and the Glory,* Scobie is guilty of every sin that would traditionally lead him to damnation, but because of the intensity of his suffering (the book implies) God's mercy will be extended to him.

1984

by

GEORGE ORWELL (1903–1950)

Main Characters

Winston Smith—An average, intelligent man, a minor employee in the Ministry of Truth, Oceania's propaganda mill.

Julia—A beautiful, rebellious young mechanic in the Fiction Department of the Ministry of Truth.

O'Brien—Ugly, highly intelligent, and a member of the Inner Party.

Mr. Charrington—The old proprietor of a London junk shop filled with charming relics of the past.

Big Brother—The all-seeing, all-powerful ruler of Oceania whose magnetic eyes stare out from every billboard.

Emmanuel Goldstein—The semi-mythical arch-enemy of Oceania.

The Story

At lunchtime on April 4, 1984, Winston Smith takes time off from his job at the Ministry of Truth to go home and begin a secret journal. He has a lovely old notebook bought at Mr. Charrington's junk shop a few days before, a dangerous act in 1984, when secret thoughts and relics from the past are forbidden.

Winston Smith lives in London, now the principal city of

Airstrip One, part of Oceania which comprises Britain and North and South America. Like the two other massive power blocs of the world, Eurasia and Eastasia, Oceania is a completely totalitarian police state, rigidly adhering to the principles of Ingsoc, or English Socialism.

The majority of the population are called Proles; they are considered too stupid to matter. To ensure the complete loyalty of its members, the Party has placed a two-way telescreen in every room. Winston, a minor white-collar worker in the Outer Party, has a room so peculiarly shaped that he can hide in a corner from the ever-watchful telescreen. And he hides as he opens his journal and several times writes the highly treasonous statement, "Down with Big Brother." Big Brother, whose heavy, moustachioed face glares down from every billboard, is the mysterious leader of Oceania in its endless wars with Eastasia and Eurasia. No one has ever seen him, but in the torture rooms and dungeons of the Ministry of Love, his power is made clear to anyone defying the State.

Returning to the Ministry of Truth, Winston settles down to his job, which consists of falsifying back numbers of the *Times* in order to keep them in line with present policy in Oceania. History is a plaything of the Party. Objective truth no longer exists. Winston is an expert at his job, but he loathes it and most of his zealous fellow workers who are compiling a new edition of the Dictionary of Newspeak, the official language of Oceania.

Winston's dreary, soul-destroying work is briefly interrupted by the Two Minutes Hate session which all workers must attend. In a large hall they watch movies of Eurasian war atrocities. The climax is reached with the picture of Emmanuel Goldstein, the almost legendary enemy of the Party, an alleged counter-revolutionary and scapegoat for all the military, social, and economic failings of the Party. As the pictures appear on the screen, the audience works itself up into a frenzy. Anyone who fails to scream curses at the screen is immediately reported to the Thought Police and is afterward "vaporized."

At the Two Minutes Hate session, Winston sees Julia, a lovely, cool, dark-haired girl who he thinks has been following him, probably because she is a member of the dreaded Thought Police. Dressed in regulation overalls (she repairs the machines that churn out cheap fiction for the Proles), with the banner of the Anti-Sex League draped around her,

Julia secretly slips Winston a note reading "I love you." Winston and Julia arrange a rendezvous in a secluded nook in the country, far from any telescreen.

Winston was married once; his wife was an ardent Party worker and member of the Anti-Sex League who looked on sex in the orthodox Party way, as a disagreeable duty to perform for the good of the State. When Winston failed to give her any children, she left him. The only love Winston ever knew was his mother's and she had disappeared many years ago—probably to be vaporized.

In the country, Julia and Winston become lovers and spend an idyllic afternoon exchanging confidences. Julia tells him that she is a member of the Anti-Sex League and a seemingly loyal Party worker only for security reasons. Actually she is promiscuous, loves life, and despises the Party. Like Winston, she is fond of exploring the black markets run by the Proles, where Party members are never supposed to venture. There she can sometimes get real coffee and chocolate instead of the synthetic "Victory" substitutes that Outer Party members are supposed to consume.

Winston is fascinated by Mr. Charrington's junk shop. He returns there again and again, searching for clues to the past which he feels must have been a happier time than the present and which could not have been as dreadful as the Party history books would have it. On one of these furtive visits, Mr. Charrington shows Winston a secret upstairs bedroom, preserved just as it was before the Ingsoc revolution.

The room is seedy but comfortable, and, best of all, has not been equipped with a telescreen. In a moment of folly, Winston rents it from Mr. Charrington, and it becomes an occasional haven for the lovers.

Bolstered by their love for each other, Winston and Julia feel there must be other secret rebels against the stifling State of 1984. If only they could make contact! Winston remembers in particular a man named O'Brien, a member of the Inner Party on whose ugly, intelligent face he thinks he has seen an ironical gleam of contempt for the Party. Winston and Julia go to O'Brien's plush apartment and ask him if there is really a counter-revolutionary conspiracy. O'Brien answers *yes* and enlists the lovers in its ranks, but warns them they will probably be killed long before their ideals are realized. He tells them that Emmanuel Goldstein exists and is the author of a heretical book which O'Brien lends Winston.

Before Winston can read Goldstein's book, however, he is engulfed in preparations for Hate Week. Oceania has suddenly and unaccountably switched sides in the war. Now Eurasia is the ally and Eastasia the enemy. All documents to the contrary must be immediately altered.

Relaxing with Julia after Hate Week, Winston is reading Goldstein's book which points out the infinite cruelties, lies, and deceptions of the State, when a voice seeming to come from nowhere orders Winston's and Julia's arrest. To his horror, Winston realizes that a telescreen has been in his secret room all along and that Mr. Charrington is a member of the Thought Police. Guards invade the sanctuary. One of them kicks Julia in the stomach. Winston is hustled off to a stinking dungeon in the Ministry of Love.

There he is kicked, clubbed, and bludgeoned for days until he no longer knows what or where he is. Then he is subjected to weeks of "conferences" with O'Brien, during which he is given electric shocks and kept barely alive so he can confess the error of his rebellion. O'Brien, however, wants more than a confession. He insists that Winston realize in the depths of his soul that Big Brother is all-powerful and all-good, that individuals have no right to private ideas, and that if the Party says two plus two equals five, that is correct. He tells Winston that he himself wrote Goldstein's book as a trap for rebels.

Through his tortures and O'Brien's inquisition, Winston clings to one small reason for pride: his love for Julia. Nothing, he thinks, can conquer that, even though he no longer knows whether she is alive or dead. But one of the techniques of the Thought Police is to find out what its victims are most terrified of. O'Brien knows that Winston cannot bear the thought of rodents. A large cage of ravenous rats is placed right next to him, and O'Brien threatens to open the door. In a moment of unreasoning panic, Winston begs him to set the rats on Julia instead; then he knows that he has nothing left worth living for.

After this great betrayal, Winston is set free. He is a shambles, physically, mentally, and spiritually. His teeth have been knocked out, his hair is gone. He is not considered worth vaporizing and is given a very minor job that leaves him plenty of time to sit in a café, alone and despised, drinking

Victory gin. One day he sees Julia who is equally beaten and dulled by her ordeal. The two have nothing to say to one another after they confess that both had betrayed their love.

One day Winston hears over the telescreen that Oceania has won a great victory in Africa. Formerly Winston would have been skeptical but now he believes it. The brainwashing and shock treatments have succeeded. In the depths of his soul, Winston knows he truly loves Big Brother.

Critical Opinion

Like Huxley's *Brave New World, 1984* is a reverse utopia—a vision of the future as nightmare rather than paradise. Significantly, when Huxley wrote his book he cast his utopia six hundred years into the future. Orwell, writing seventeen years after Huxley, saw the dangers of brainwashing, rigid social control, and political bestiality as far more imminent, and placed his nightmare state only thirty-five years into the future.

Another difference between these superficially similar books is that while Huxley concentrates on scientific "advances," Orwell is preoccupied with politics. The ideals of Huxley's state are "Community, Identity, Stability." These are taken for granted in *1984* but are made far more sinister by political absolutism. The slogans of Orwell's state are "War is Peace," "Freedom is Slavery" and "Ignorance is Strength." Huxley's world of the future is unconcerned with war; the dreariness of social predestination and of scientific gadgetry and materialism are the greatest plagues of his Brave New World. His tone, too, is wittily satiric. Orwell's is grim and bitter.

Much of the difference between these two twentieth-century visions of the future can be explained by the events between 1932, the date of Huxley's book, and 1949, the date of Orwell's. These seventeen years saw the Moscow purge trials, the Spanish Civil War, the rise of the dictators, the universal holocaust of World War II with its genocide, its promiscuous slaughter of soldiers and civilians alike, and the beginning of the cold war. Thus, life in Oceania is not merely drab and joyless; it is truly terrifying.

Primarily an essayist and polemicist, Orwell succeeds best

in *1984* when he is describing the mechanisms and techniques of the police state. His coinages "thoughtcrime," "newspeak," "Big Brother" and "doublethink" have become part of the English language. They are based on his keen perception and analysis of tendencies existing in his own time, not merely in Nazi Germany and Soviet Russia but, in a milder if no less insidious form, in the nations of the "free world." This book is both a prophecy and a warning of what life might be if individuals allow themselves to be coerced into conformity by the state.

The Author

George Orwell's real name was Eric Blair. Born in India in 1903, he became a poor "scholarship boy" in a snobbish, ill-run English prep school. The horrors of his schooldays live in a bitter essay, "Such, Such Were the Joys." He did, however, win a scholarship to Eton.

Unwilling to face university life and further snobbery, Orwell went to Burma in 1921, where he spent five years as a policeman and wrote his first novel, *Burmese Days*. Disgusted by his first-hand glimpse of imperialism, Orwell quit and lived in Paris and London, subsisting on infrequent, squalid jobs in restaurant kitchens. His experiences led him to the writing of his first great book, *Down and Out in Paris and London* (1933).

From then on Orwell struggled to earn a living as a journalist and author. He became involved in various left-wing causes during the depression but always remained suspicious of any political doctrine when it violated the basic human rights of the individual. Political idealism led him to fight on the Loyalist side in the Spanish Civil War, in which he was wounded. Returning to England, he wrote *Homage to Catalonia*, an impassioned attack on the betrayal of the Spanish Loyalists by the Communists. Orwell's blistering contempt for the police states he saw growing in Spain, Italy, Germany, and Russia, combined with his warnings to England of the coming conflict between democracy and totalitarianism, appeared in his many masterful essays, which were disregarded or attacked by Left and Right alike.

Although he had always suffered from weak lungs, Orwell

exposed himself during World War II to exhaustion and privation, serving as an air-raid warden when he was rejected by the army. A mortally ill man by the end of the war, he wrote his two masterpieces, *Animal Farm* (1945) and *1984*, before his death on January 23, 1950. Ironically, his only real popular success came after his death with *1984* which has remained his most widely read book.

By the Same Author

Animal Farm: *Animal Farm* is a brilliant fable of the success, betrayal, and ultimate failure of the Russian Revolution. Under the brutal regime of Farmer Jones, the animals are miserable. They revolt, rout Jones from his farm, and try to run things themselves. Soon, however, a new hierarchy emerges, with the cunning, selfish pigs lording it over the more docile and less assertive animals. The high ideals of animal equality and sovereignty proclaimed at the beginning of the revolution are quietly dropped. Under the oppressive rule of the scheming, power-hungry pig Napoleon, the lot of the other animals becomes as wretched as it had been under Farmer Jones. Although it is less exhaustive a treatment of totalitarianism than *1984*, *Animal Farm* is a brief, pungent tour de force in the very difficult, rarely explored genre of the political fable.

Lord of the Flies

by

WILLIAM GOLDING (1911–)

Main Characters

Ralph—The sensible, good-natured leader of the stranded
   boys.
Piggy—Ralph's fat, intelligent, asthmatic, and bespectacled
   sidekick.
Jack Merridew—Leader of the choir boys, carrot-haired and
   given to violent emotion.
Simon—A short boy, quiet and imaginative.
"Samneric"—The inseparable twins, Sam and Eric.

The Story

While being evacuated from an atomic war, a group of schoolboys aged six through twelve are ejected from their doomed
plane and land on an uninhabited island somewhere in the
Pacific. The first two to make contact are Ralph, a handsome,
good-natured lad, and Piggy, fat and lower class, who has
always been the butt of schoolboy jokes. Piggy can barely see
without his glasses, and he suffers from asthmatic attacks
brought on by any exertion.

Together the boys find a large, beautiful conch shell in
a lagoon, and Ralph learns to blow on it. He is sure that
eventually his father, a commander in the Royal Navy, will

rescue them, but first he will call a meeting of all the other boys stranded on the island, using the blast of the conch to summon them. Piggy begs Ralph not to let the other boys know his humiliating name.

The trumpeting of the conch brings the scattered boys together at a central meeting place. Among them is a group of choir boys led by Jack Merridew. They are still perspiring fiercely under their heavy black cassocks. The meeting is called to order, while the frightened younger boys, called "littluns," whimper for their parents. Ralph tells the group that apparently there are no grownups on the island, but if they organize their little society well they will surely be rescued soon. To Jack's dismay, Ralph is elected chief. Jack, as choir leader, fancies that position for himself. But Ralph has the conch shell, symbol of authority and leadership.

The boys' first action is to send a scouting party, including Ralph, Jack, and a small but intelligent boy, Simon, to explore the island. Piggy wants to go along, but he is rudely rejected by Jack after Ralph inadvertently gives away his name. Once again the unhappy Piggy is made the butt of all jokes; even the littluns laugh at him.

As Ralph, Jack, and Simon explore the island that first day, their spirits are high. Fruit grows in abundance, there are many glorious swimming places, and, above all, there are no adults to tell the boys what to do. They skip exuberantly around the island, locating a huge mountain at one end and a fortress-like rock formation which they call Castle Rock at the other. Returning to report their findings, the three youths are pleased with themselves and with their adventure.

Ralph calls another meeting to decide what to do until they are rescued. The boys agree that whoever holds the conch may speak while the others must listen. All is very democratic and parliamentary. Ralph decides that the most important thing to do is keep a smoky fire going on the mountain top so that any ship passing can spot and rescue them. Before he can outline his other plans, the boys chase off to light their fire. Their only difficulty is that they have no matches. Ralph has an idea: use Piggy's glasses to concentrate the sun's rays and thus get the fire started. This works well. But soon the whole top of the mountain is ablaze, and one of the littluns disappears, presumably burned to death.

This disaster convinces Ralph that, if the boys are to survive until they are rescued, law and order must prevail. He finds it difficult, however, to keep the boys' attention concentrated on any one project. They wander off to swim or eat fruit. Only Simon and the twins, Sam and Eric, called Samneric because they are always together, help Ralph build necessary shelters. Piggy, because of his asthma, which the boys cruelly call "ass-mar," cannot do manual work, but as he is the most intelligent boy on the island, he makes invaluable suggestions.

The boys suffer at night from bad dreams because some of the littluns claim they have spotted what they call a "beastie," a hideous, snake-like monster, somewhere on the island. At first the older boys laugh at this story, but at night everyone is rather frightened, and the littluns cling together for protection.

Soon Jack, chafing at his subordinate position under the elected leader, Ralph, decides to organize his choir boys as hunters. He is tired of the steady fruit diet and of the unglamorous labors of building shelters and tending the fire. Jack has noticed there are wild pigs on the island, and determines to kill some for food. Camouflaging his face with black and red streaks of clay until he looks like a savage, he becomes an adept and ruthless hunter.

During his first successful hunt, however, Jack allows his choir boys to neglect the fire they were supposed to tend. Ralph sees a ship on the horizon, but looking up to the mountain, sees no smoke to signal it. Furious, he confronts Jack with his negligence, but Jack laughs it off, saying that if the boys want to eat meat he needs all the hunters he can get. He hints that Ralph is concerned with such mundane things as shelters and fires because he is useless as a hunter.

Ralph calls a special evening meeting to lecture the boys about their various lapses from discipline. It is obvious, he tells them, that the most important thing they can do is to keep the smoky fire lit or else they will never be rescued. They must also build sturdy shelters against the rainy season. But by now Jack is obsessed with his hunting—he has tasted blood and wants more of it. He despises the peaceable, practical Ralph and his hopelessly fat and inactive friend, Piggy. He tries to wrest the leadership from Ralph, but the other boys are too cowed and apathetic to change. Furious and frustrated, Jack leaves the meeting with his loyal band of hunters in tow.

Meanwhile the boys are still terrified of the "beastie" on the island. During a temporary truce, Jack and Ralph join forces to investigate. First they go to Castle Rock, the only unexplored part of the island, where Jack wants to remain and build a fortress. Eventually they get back to the mountain, however, where they see a hideous, ape-like creature suspended, as if asleep, in the trees. Terrified, they return to the other boys, who decide that they can no longer use the mountain for their fire but will have to be content with a less visible fire on the shore.

Jack and his hunters, who are now staying at Castle Rock, kill a huge sow while it is nursing its piglets and cut off its head to place on a pole as an offering to the monster. But Simon, by now terrified by the proceedings on the island, investigates and sees what the monster really is. A flier whose plane was apparently downed off the island had parachuted to his death. His parachute was caught in the treetops. The monster is his decayed, hideous body, still caught in the parachute and waving back and forth in the wind.

When Simon runs to tell the other boys what he has discovered, they are celebrating their latest kill with a wild, savage dance. By now their hair has grown long, they are filthy with war paint, and they are no longer interested in listening to Ralph. When they see Simon, they all leap on him as if he were a sacrificial pig and kill him.

Morose and disillusioned at what has happened to his little civilization, Ralph is left with only the twins and Piggy whose glasses have meanwhile been broken. They are too few to keep the fire lit. One night a band of marauders from Castle Rock descends on them and, in the melee, makes off with Piggy's broken glasses to light their own fire.

Ralph goes to plead with Jack to return the glasses to Piggy, promising him that he can borrow flame for his hunters to cook pig with any time he wants. But Jack answers him contemptuously from the fortress he has built. Roger, one of the boys who has gone over to Jack's side, catapults a huge boulder at Piggy, sending the unfortunate boy careening to his death in the sea below. Sam and Eric, the twins, are forcibly brought over to Jack's side. Now Ralph is all alone. He is told by the twins that Jack intends to kill him, and he flees for safety. He is pursued all over the island by the hunters who even set fire to the island in order to smoke him out.

Ironically, this smoke attracts a passing vessel, and, just as Ralph thinks he is going to be murdered by the other boys, the whole group is rescued by an English cruiser. When the sailors land, they are appalled to find that good English schoolboys have become the savages now infesting the island. The boys are rescued, however, and "in the middle of them, with filthy body, matted hair, and unwiped nose, Ralph wept for the end of innocence, the darkness of man's heart, and the fall through the air of the true, wise friend called Piggy."

Critical Opinion

The theme of *Lord of the Flies*, according to Golding, "is an attempt to trace the defects of society back to the defects of human nature. The moral is that the shape of a society must depend on the ethical nature of the individual and not on any political system however apparently logical or respectable."

Rejecting as unreal and sentimental the myth of the "noble savage," Golding shows how the removal of civilized restraints results not in the creation of a more innocent, healthier society, but in a complete regression to savagery and brutality, the seeds of which are lodged deep in every human heart.

In a sense, then, *Lord of the Flies* is a parable much like *Heart of Darkness* (the last lines of the novel even paraphrase Conrad's title), in which the boys who, somewhat like Kurtz, start off with high hopes of creating their own utopian society free from all adult restrictions, gradually become murderous brutes, rescued from themselves just in the nick of time.

But the rescue is ambivalent and ironic. The men who take the boys off the island are sailors whose own cruiser is committed to murder and destruction during an unnamed atomic war, and, as Golding notes, "Who will rescue the adult and his cruiser?" This pessimism about the adult world is foreshadowed when Ralph cries, earlier in the book, "If only they could get a message to us. If only they could send us something grown-up . . . a sign or something." What "they," the adults, send is the hideous, decaying corpse of a parachutist. The adult world, then, is no better, only more sophisticated in its savagery, than the world the boys have built on the island.

"Lord of the Flies" is a translation of the Hebrew word,

Ba'alzevuv (Beelzebub in Greek), a name for the devil, who is ultimately the central figure in the novel. When Jack's hunters slay the harmless sow and cut her head off as propitiation to the "beastie," the head, decaying on a stake in the hot sun, seems to tell Simon that "everything was a bad business." But when Simon tries to communicate this idea, he is murdered in a savage ritual dance.

Lord of the Flies is thus a parable, like one of the first English novels, *The Pilgrim's Progress*. The intervening centuries, however, have changed the religious message from hope for salvation to fear of damnation and knowledge of original sin.

The Author

William Golding, one of the most challenging British novelists to emerge since World War II, was born in Cornwall in 1911, descended from a long line of schoolmasters. Destined to be a scientist, he changed his course after two years at Oxford and studied English literature instead, specializing in Anglo-Saxon poetry. He published a book of poems in 1934 and wrote three unpublished novels.

Appropriately enough for the author of a book about the savagery inherent in boys, Golding earned his living as a schoolmaster and was not very happy in that profession. The outbreak of World War II was a turning point in his career. Golding joined the Royal Navy, and, except for six months in New York on special assignment under Lord Cherwell, he saw active duty throughout the war, ending as a lieutenant in command of a rocket craft on D day. "The war produced one notable effect on me," Golding is quoted as having said. "It scared me stiff."

It did that in more ways than one. "It was the turning point for me," Golding has commented. "I began to see what people were capable of doing. Where did the Second World War come from? Was it made by something inhuman and alien—or was it made by chaps with eyes and legs and hearts?"

The vision of evil inherent in the human heart that Golding found in the war was the basis of his first published novel, *Lord of the Flies*. Its publication in 1954 was hailed by dis-

cerning critics on both sides of the Atlantic, but its first
American edition sold only 2500 copies. It was not until
1959, when it was published in paperback, that the novel
became immensely popular, especially among high school and
college students.

In 1955 Golding published *The Inheritors*, a strange tale
about man's ancestors on earth, the peaceful "people" who
were ruthlessly supplanted by *homo sapiens*. This was followed in 1956 by *Pincher Martin* and in 1959 by *Free Fall*.
Golding's most recent novel, *The Spire* (1964), is again about
guilt and redemption, a story of the building of a mighty but
flawed English cathedral during the Middle Ages.

Scraggly-bearded and shy, Golding is married and has two
children. In view of his bleak vision of children in *Lord of the
Flies*, he has said, "I try to treat my family with affection and
I suppose if that added up all around, we might have a better
society." Recently Golding taught for a year at Hollins College in Virginia. He lists his favorite occupations as music,
sailing, chess, archaeology—and thinking.

By the Same Author

Pincher Martin: When Christopher Martin is blown off his
ship by a submarine attack in mid-Atlantic, he manages to
make his way to a jutting rock where he tries by all rational
means to survive. But he is constantly plagued by guilt for
his past sins. He has always been a "pincher," a stealer of
everything, including love. He loses his battle for physical and
spiritual salvation. Eventually his body is washed ashore where
a naval officer notices from the condition of the corpse that
Martin could not have suffered for long. We are given to
understand that the self-questionings and desperate struggle
for survival in the novel occurred in only a split second in
Martin's mind.

Free Fall: Less of a parable than Golding's other novels,
Free Fall describes in realistic terms the rise from the slums
of Sammy Mountjoy, an egocentric artist obsessed with desire
for Beatrice, the model for his only successful picture. In
his relentless pursuit of Beatrice, he loses his own freedom of
action, ultimately deserts her, and sends her to an insane

asylum, where the doctor tells him he may or may not have been immediately responsible for plunging her into incurable madness. The degree of his guilt is something he will have to decide in his own Faustian soul.

Appendix

50 British Novels, arranged by date of publication

The Pilgrim's Progress   1678
Robinson Crusoe   1719
Gulliver's Travels   1726
Tom Jones   1749
The Vicar of Wakefield   1766
Tristram Shandy   1767
Humphry Clinker   1771
Pride and Prejudice   1813
Ivanhoe   1819
The Last Days of Pompeii   1834
The Pickwick Papers   1836
David Copperfield   1850
A Tale of Two Cities   1859
Great Expectations   1861
Jane Eyre   1847
Wuthering Heights   1848
Vanity Fair   1848
Barchester Towers   1857
Adam Bede   1859
The Ordeal of Richard Feverel   1859
Alice in Wonderland   1865
Erewhon   1872
The Way of All Flesh   1903
The Return of the Native   1878
The Mayor of Casterbridge   1886
Jude the Obscure   1896
Treasure Island   1883
The Picture of Dorian Gray   1891
The Time Machine   1895
Tono-Bungay   1909
Lord Jim   1900
Kim   1901
Heart of Darkness   1902
Green Mansions   1904

The Man of Property   1906
The Old Wives' Tale   1908
The Crock of Gold   1912
Sons and Lovers   1913
Of Human Bondage   1915
A Portrait of the Artist as a Young Man   1916
South Wind   1916
A Passage to India   1924
Mrs. Dalloway   1925
Point Counter Point   1928
Brave New World   1932
Decline and Fall   1928
Lost Horizon   1933
The Power and the Glory   1940
1984   1949
Lord of the Flies   1954

Bibliography

1. Allen, Walter. *The English Novel: A Short Critical History.* New York: E.P. Dutton & Co., 1955.
2. Church, Richard. *The Growth of the English Novel.* New York: Barnes & Noble, 1961.
3. Drew, Elizabeth. *The Novel: A Modern Guide to Fifteen English Masterpieces.* New York: Dell Publishing Co., 1963.
4. Forster, E.M. *Aspects of the Novel.* New York: Harvest Books, Harcourt, Brace & World, 1956.
5. Kettle, Arnold. *An Introduction to the English Novel.* 2 vols. New York: Torchbooks, Harper & Row, 1961.
6. Lubbock, Percy. *The Craft of Fiction.* New York: Compass Books, The Viking Press, 1957.
7. Neill, S.D. *A Short History of the English Novel.* New York: The Macmillan Company, 1952.
8. Pritchett, V.S. *The Living Novel and Later Appreciations.* New York: Random House, 1964.
9. Schorer, Mark (ed.). *Modern British Fiction: Essays in Criticism.* New York: Oxford University Press, 1961.
10. Trilling, Lionel. *The Liberal Imagination.* New York: Anchor Books, Doubleday & Co., 1953.
11. Van Ghent, Dorothy. *The English Novel: Form and Function.* New York: Torchbooks, Harper & Row, 1961.
12. Wagenknecht, Edward. *Cavalcade of the English Novel.* New York: Holt, Rinehart and Winston, 1954.

Index